Additions and Corrections

to the
W.P.A.

Inventory
of
Geauga County, Ohio:
CHARDON

Jana Sloan Broglin

HERITAGE BOOKS
2025

HERITAGE BOOKS

AN IMPRINT OF HERITAGE BOOKS, INC.

Books, CDs, and more—Worldwide

For our listing of thousands of titles see our website
at
www.HeritageBooks.com

Published 2025 by
HERITAGE BOOKS, INC.
Publishing Division
5810 Ruatan Street
Berwyn Heights, MD 20740

(Originally Titled)
INVENTORY OF THE COUNTY ARCHIVES OF OHIO

Prepared by
The Ohio Historical Records Survey Project
Service Division
Works Projects Administration

No. 28. GEAUGA COUNTY (CHARDON)

Columbus, Ohio
The Ohio Historical Records Survey Project
August 1942

International Standard Book Number
Paperbound: 978-0-7884-4710-5

County Offices and Their Records

Proceedings. Public improvements. Institutions and relief. Financial records. Miscellaneous. Aid for the blind. Relief administration: CCC records; miscellaneous.
Real property transfers: deeds: leases; mortgages; liens; registered lands; plats and surveys. Personal property transfers. Incorporations and Partnerships. Grants of authority and licenses. Financial records. Miscellaneous.
Court proceedings. Original documents. Judgments and executions. Jury and witness records. Motor vehicles. Commissions. Licenses. Partnerships. Elections. Coroner's inquest. Financial records. Miscellaneous.
Civil cases. Naturalization. Criminal cases. General court proceedings.
District Court. Circuit Court. Court of Appeals.
Civil cases. Criminal cases. General court proceedings. Original documents. Estates and guardianships: wills; determination of heirship; applications, appointments, bonds, and letters; inventories and appraisements; schedule of debts; transfers and sale bills; cost bills; accounts and settlements; inheritance tax. Assignments. Dependents.

The Historical Records Survey Program

Sargent B. Child, National Director
Willard N. Hogan, Regional Supervisor
Francis M. Foott, State Supervisor
Lillian Kessler, District supervisor

Service Division

Florence Kerr, Assistant Commissioner
Mary Gillette Moon, Chief Regional Supervisor
Ruth Neighbors, State Director
Beatrice Burr, District Director

WORK PROJECTS ADMINISTRATION

F. H. Dryden, Acting Commissioner
George Field, Regional Director
Carl Watson, State Administrator
Frank T. Miskell, Director Manager

Sponsors

The Ohio State University

The Board of County Commissioners of Geauga County

Frank N. Griffin
A. C. Stone
B. E. Hotchkiss

The *Inventory of the County Archives of Ohio* is one of a number of bibliographies of historical materials prepared throughout the United States by workers on the Historical Records Survey Program of the Work Projects Administration. The publication herewith presented, an inventory of the archives of Geauga County, is number 28 of the Ohio series.

The Historical Records Survey Program was undertaken in the winter of 1935-1936 for the purpose of providing useful employment to needy unemployed historians, lawyers, teachers, and research and clerical workers. In carrying out this objective, the project was organized to compile inventories of historical materials, particularly the unpublished government documents and records which are basic in the administration of local government, and which provide invaluable data for students of political, economic, and social history. Up to the present time more than 1,700 guides, inventories and indexes have been issued by the Survey throughout the Nation. The archival guide herewith presented is intended to meet the requirements of the day-to-day administration by the officials of the county, and also the needs of lawyers, businessmen, and other citizens who require facts from the public records for the proper conduct of their affairs. The volume is so designed that it can be used by the historian in his research in unprinted sources in the same way he uses the library card catalog or printed sources.

The inventories produced by the Historical Records Survey Program attempt to do more than give merely a list of records – they attempt further to sketch in the historical background of the county or other unit of government, and to describe precisely and in detail the organization and functions of the government agencies whose records they list. The county, town, and other local inventories for the entire county will, when completed, constitute an encyclopedia of local government as well as a bibliography of local archives.

FOREWORD

The successful conclusion of the work of the Historical Records Survey Program, even in a single county, would not be possible without the support of public officials, historical and legal specialists, and many other groups in the community. Their cooperation is greatly acknowledged.

The Survey Program was organized by Luther H. Evans, who served as Director until March 1, 1940, when he was succeeded by Sargent B. Child, who had been Field Supervisor since the inauguration of the Survey. The Survey Program operates as a nationwide series of locally sponsored projects in the Service Division, of which Mrs. Florence Kerr, Assistant Commissioner, is in charge.

F. H. Dryden
Acting Commissioner

2nd Edition

In 1929 after the stock market crash along with the Great Depression, drought and crop failures which followed, President Herbert Hoover and his successor Franklin D. Roosevelt formulated relief projects, the most successful was the establishment of the Works Progress Administration (WPA).

Established as the Works Projects Administration in 1935, the WPA was the largest of the many programs developed during Roosevelt's "New Deal." In 1939, the agency's name was changed to Works Progress Administration, and continued as such until its demise in 1943.

The Federal Writers' Project, a division of the WPA (known as Federal Project Number One), created jobs for many unemployed librarians, clerks, researchers, editors, and historians. The workers went to courthouses, town halls, offices in large cities, vital statistics offices and inventoried records. Besides indexing works, many records were transcribed. One of these many projects was the *Inventory of the County Archives* which has benefitted genealogists and historians. The inventories listed the records, either by volumes or file boxes and years per record type, within the office. Although the WPA oversaw this project, the information for each volume of records may differ significantly by the information submitted.

The information herein is verbatim except for obvious spelling errors. Records listed may have met the requirement for retention and have been destroyed as per the records retention act, while other records are considered permanent records. (*See:* **https://codes.ohio.gov/ohio-revised-code**) Ohio Revised Code, sections 149.31 and 149.34). Records once considered "open" to the public, such as lunacy, idiotic, and juvenile cases, may be "closed" due to a revision of state laws. However, the records may be opened to family members with adequate proof of lineage.

The addresses and website section of this edition list an up-to-date location guide to each office mentioned.

This project was to encompass all of Ohio's eighty-eight counties although approximately thirty of these inventories have been located while others may not have been done.

Jana Sloan Broglin
Fellow, Ohio Genealogical Society
Swanton, Ohio
2025

The Historical Records Survey of the Work Projects Administration began operation in Ohio in February 1936. The Project was organized and operated by the district supervisors of the Writers' Project until November 1936, when it became an independent part of the Federal Project No. I. With termination of the Federal Projects in September 1939, the Ohio unit became the Ohio Historical Records Survey Project, sponsored by the Ohio Archaeological and Historical Society. On August 3, 1941, the Ohio Historical Records Survey Project became a unit of the Consolidated Records Assistance Project in Ohio, sponsored by the Ohio State University.

One of the purposes of the Survey in Ohio has been the preparation of complete inventories of state, county, and municipal records. The *Inventory of the County Archives of Ohio* will, when completed, consist of a set of 88 volumes numbered according to the position of the county name in an alphabetical list of Ohio counties. Thus, the inventory herein presented for Geauga County is number 28. The inventory of State Archives and of municipal and other local records will constitute separate publications.

The principle followed in the inventory of the county records has been to place a record in the office of origin rather than in the office of deposit. The records are arranged with those of the executive branch of government first, followed by law enforcement, fiscal, welfare, and miscellaneous agencies. Minor agencies are placed in the general arrangement according to function rather than according to constitutional or statutory responsibility to a minor subdivision. The legal development of each office or agency has been treated in a prefatory section preceding the inventory of the records of the office. Although a condensed form of entry is used, information is given as to the limiting dates of all extant records, the contents of individual series, and the location of records in courthouse, statehouse, or other depository.

The Ohio Historical Records Survey was inaugurated in Summit County in May 1936. From July 1940 to February 1942 the project was under the administrative and technical supervision of Ruth Sloan. Since February 1942 the project has been under the supervision of Lillian Kessler. The wholehearted cooperation of the county officials helped to assure the thoroughness and completeness of the inventory. The Board of County Commissioners, serving as a contributing co-sponsor, provided the materials for the publication of this volume.

PREFACE
1st Edition

For the accuracy of the inventory the project personnel in Geauga County, working under the direction of Melville E. Strock, is entirely responsible. The Summit County office staff, under the immediate supervision of Florence Carnahan, arranged and edited the volume. The state office personnel, under the immediate supervision of Winifred Smith, Assistant State Supervisor, prepared the index, and criticized and edited the volume. The duplicating and binding of the volumes were done in Cuyahoga County under the immediate supervision of Grace Clift.

 The various units of the *Inventory of the County Archives of Ohio* are issued in mimeographed or printed form for free distribution to state and other public officials and to public libraries in Ohio, and to a limited number of libraries outside the state. Requests for information concerning particular units of the *Inventory* Should be addressed to the Ohio Historical Records Survey Project, Room 216, Clinton Building, Columbus, Ohio.

Frances M. Foott
State Supervisor
Consolidated Records Assistant Project

Columbus, Ohio
August 1942

adm. . . . . administration
am.. . . . . amended
Arch. . . . . Archaeological
Art. . . . . Article
bull. . . . . bulletin
c. . . . . copyright
capias . . . . a warrant or order for arrest of a person,
typically issued by the judge or magistrate in a case.
CCC. . . . . Civilian Conservation Corps
centiorari . . . . to be more fully informed
chap (s). . . . . chapter(s)
comp. . . . . compiler
Const. . . . . Constitution
De bonis non . . . . goods of the deceased have not all been administered
ed(s). . . . . editor(s)
et al. . . . . (et alii), and others
(et) passim . . . . and here and there
ex officio . . . . as a result of one's status or position
et seq. . . . . and following
fee simple . . . . full and irrevocable ownership
G. C. . . . . General Code
habeas corpus . . . . protection against illegal imprisonment
ibid. . . . . the same reference
LL.D. . . . . Doctor of Laws
loc. cit. . . . . *(loco citato)* in the place cited
mittimus. . . . . a court order or warrant that directs a jailer to
keep a person in custody until they are released by another order
N. P. . . . . The Ohio NISI PRIUS REPORTS
n. p. . . . . no place of publication shown
n. s. . . . . new series
nolle prosequi . . . . notice of abandonment by a
plaintiff or prosecutor of all or part of a suit or action
O.L. . . . . *Laws of Ohio*
op. cit. . . . . *(opere citato)* in the work cited
posse comitatus . . . . a group of citizens called upon to assist the sheriff
praecipes . . . . a written request for action

LISTS OF ABBREVIATIONS, SYMBOLS AND
EXPLANATORY NOTES

prima facie . . . . on the first impression
pro rata . . . . in proportion
procedendo . . . . sends case from appellate court to a lower court
pt. . . . . part
quo warranto. . . . . by what authority or warrant
replevins . . . . return of personal property
wrongfully taken or held by a defendant
R. . . . . River
rep. . . . . reporter
R.S. . . . . Revised Statutes
sec(s) . . . . section(s)
sic . . . . thus, following copy
supersedeas . . . . a stay of enforcement of a judgment pending appeal
v. . . . . versus
venires . . . . a group of people summoned for jury duty
vol(s). . . . . volume(s)
WPA . . . . Works Progress/Projects Administration
writ . . . . a formal, legal document, a decree
x . . . . by
— . . . . current, to date
4-H . . . . (Four - H)

Each chapter or section of Part B of the volume consists of an essay describing the legal status and functions of one department of county government and an inventory of the records of that department.

Each record constitutes a separate entry. Entries are arranged under topical headings and subheadings.

Each entry sets forth, insofar as applicable, the following:

1. Entry number. Entries are numbered consecutively throughout the inventory.
2. The exact title as it appears on the record or if the record has no title a supplied title in brackets. If the title of the record is non-descriptive, misleading, or incorrect an additional title (in capitals and lowercase letters), also enclosed in brackets, has been supplied.
3. Dates show inclusive years or parts of years covered by the record. Breaks in dates indicate that the record is missing or was not kept between dates shown. A dash in place of the final date indicates an open record. If no current entries have been made the date of the last entry is noted. Where no statement is made that the record was discontinued at the last date shown, it could not be definitely established that such was the case. Where no comment is made on the absence of prior and subsequent records, no definite information could be obtained.
4. Quantity, given in chronological order wherever possible.
5. Labeling. Numbers and letters within parentheses indicate labeling on volumes, file boxes, or other containers.
6. Variations in title. The current or most recent title is used but significant variations are shown with dates for which each was used.
7. Change of agency. Occasionally a record is discontinued as a county record and kept by some other agency.
8. Description. A statement of the nature and purpose of the record and of what the record shows. As the contents of a record may vary over time, the description may differ somewhat from the record at any one period. Wherever feasible, changes in content are shown with dates. In map and plat entries the names of author and publisher and the scales are omitted only when not available.

9. Arrangement. Records said to be alphabetically arranged are frequently alphabetized only as to the initial letter of the surname. This is true especially where there is a secondary arrangement.

10. Indexing. Self-contained indexes are described in the entry. Separate indexes constitute separate entries with cross references to and from the record entry.

11. Nature of recording. Changes are indicated with dates.

12. Condition. No statement is made if good or excellent.

13. Number of pages. Averaged for the series.

14. Dimensions show the size of volumes, maps, file boxes, or other containers and are expressed in inches in every instance. The dimensions of volumes are given in order of height, width, and thickness; of file boxes in order of height, width, and depth.

15. Location. Rooms referred to are in the county courthouse unless some other building is specified.

Title line cross references are used to complete series where a record is kept separately for a period of time or in other records for different periods of time. They are also used in all artificial entries which are made to show, under their proper office, records kept in the same volume or file with records of another office. In both instances, the description of the master entry shows the title and entry number of the record from which the cross reference is made. Dates shown in the description of the master entry are for the part or parts of the record contained therein, and are shown only when they vary from those of the master entry. Artificial entries show only title, dates, and description.

Separate third paragraph cross references from entry to entry, are used to show prior, subsequent, or related records which are not a part of the same series. If, however, both entries are under the same subject headings, no third paragraph references are made. "See also" references from subject headings refers to entries in the same department which contain records logically belonging under that heading but which have been classified under an equally appropriate heading.

Geauga County is situated in northeastern Ohio between Cleveland and Youngstown. Neighboring counties are Lake on the north, Ashtabula and Trumbull on the east, Portage on the south, and Cuyahoga on the west. Geauga has 16 townships, each five miles square. The county is four townships wide on the north, five on the east, four on the south, and three on the west. It has an area of 407 square miles and a population of 19,430. Both in area and population it is one of the smaller counties in Ohio.[1]

Geauga County is a rolling plateau surrounded by deep valleys. The close proximity to Lake Erie, which is 500 feet lower, gives an impressive high altitude, although the range above sea level is only 1100 to 1200 feet.[2] Little Mountain, a cone-shaped sandstone butte in the northwestern corner of the county, is 750 ft above Lake Erie. The summit is seamed with layers of white pebbles and pierced with deep fissures and caverns. It had a sacred importance to the Indians, and as early as 1846 became a popular summer resort.[3]

The Grand, Cuyahoga, and Chagrin are the three main rivers of the county. They empty into Lake Erie. Only Silver Creek, a small stream, flows south and into a tributary of the Mahoning, its waters eventually reaching the Gulf of Mexico. The Grand River drains about one third of the northern and eastern part of the county, the Cuyahoga, the central part, and the Chagrin the western area. The Cuyahoga has such a slight fall that in former years the bottom lands were frequently swampy. Drainage methods were employed and the swamps eliminated. Originally, the river bottom lands were covered with water, even in summer. The soil is a heavy muck many feet deep. There are several small lakes in the county. Better known among them is Geauga, Crystal, and Bass.[4]

---

1. U.S. Bureau of the Census, *16ᵗʰ Census of the United States, 1940, Population, First Series, Number of Inhabitants, Ohio; 4.*
2. W. A. Lloyd, J. I. Falconer, and C. E. Thorne, *The Agriculture of Ohio,* 306.
3. Ohio Geological Survey, *Reports,* I, pt. i, 523.
4. *Ibid.,* 520, Lloyd, Falconer, and Thorne, *op. cit.,* 306. At the mouth of Grand River is Fairport Harbor, one of the best protected natural shelters along Lake Erie. Extensive use of the cove caused the United States in 1825 to authorize the building of a lighthouse there. Lighthouse and port became a part of Lake County in 1840. *United States Statutes at Large,* IV, 179.

Geauga County was covered with ice sheets during the glacial era. Rock layers under the surface consist of shale, sandstone, and limestone,[5] known geologically as Huron, Devonian and Waverly.[6] About half of the area of the county consist of rocks formed during the carboniferous or coal-bearing age, but this stratum lies so deep it has never been mined.[7] The underlying rocks have chiefly determined the content of the soil, which is mostly sandstone and clay loam from the shales.

Geauga has a higher terrain than its neighboring counties. At Auburn the elevation is 1200 feet above sea level, 1260 feet at Little Mountain, and 1277 feet at Welshfield. The county has a moderate climate. For the 14-year period from 1867 to 1881 the mean annual temperature was 47.6 degrees, with an average for July of 69.7 degrees, and 27.4 degrees for December.[8] Hardships were endured because of the great drought during the summer of 1845. No rain fell from the last of March to June 10 when a slight shower occurred. Relief from the arid condition did not come until July 2 when enough rain fell to make the roads muddy. From then on there was no more rain until early in September.[9] The county now has an ample supply of moisture. The mean annual precipitation is 42 inches, 4.5 inches above the mean for the state. Although the winters are not rigorous, the snowfall is heavy, the mean annual snowfall being 50 inches.[10]

Only a few of the prehistoric races known as mound-building Indians inhabited the region now known as Geauga County. Its rough surface did not attract them. As a result there are few ancient relics. In the southern part of the county are two mounds, one cemetery, and four burial places.[11]

Successors of the mound-builders were the American Indians. In this section the first tribe was the elusive Erie, called the Cats because of their peculiar walk or glide, and mewing manner of speech. They were vanquished by the Iroquois in 1656.[12]

---

5. Geological Survey of Ohio, *Report* I, pt. i, 524-525.

6. Charles Smith Prosser, "The Nomenclature of the Ohio Geological Formations," *Ohio State University Bulletin,* Series Eight, No. 3, 520-521.

7. Geographical Survey of Ohio, *Report,* I, pt. i, 521-522.

8. William H. Alexander, *A Climatological History of Ohio,* 293-295.

9. Henry Howe, *Historical Collections of Ohio,* I, 682-683.

10. Alexander, *op. cit.,* 294.

11. William C. Wills, *Archaeological Atlas of Ohio,* 28.

12. Reuben Gold Thwaites, ed., *The Jesuit Relations and Allied Documents,* VIII, 302; XLI, 83.

Northeastern Ohio became the home of the Seneca, Wyandot, Ottawa, Chippewa, Tonawanda, Iroquois, Delaware, Massasaquas, and Shawnee tribes. In the area that later became Geauga County the Tonawandas and Massasaquas were the most numerous. After the conclusion of several treaties, including those at Fort McIntosh in 1785, Fort Harmar, 1789,[13] Greenville, 1795,[14] and at Fort Industry in 1805 the Indians had sold or ceded all their lands in the Western Reserve.[15] At no time were the Indians a serious menace. They were friendly with the whites and even worshiped with them. During the War of 1812 most of the Indians moved west. Except for rumors of impending raids, the settlers of the county were unmolested.[16]

The land now comprising Geauga County was claimed by Connecticut under a charter of 1662. It was first known as the Connecticut Reserve and later, the Western Reserve.[17] Connecticut owners of lands in Ohio territory in October 1796, were incorporated under the name of "The Proprietors of the Half Million Acres of Land, lying South of Lake Erie."[18] The Governor of Connecticut, on May 30, 1800, was authorized by Congress to cede the state's claims to the United States.[19]

The Reserve comprised 14 counties, and in the eastern part the four best townships were divided into 100 lots. As there were 400 shares of stock in the company, the four townships yielded one lot for each share. Certain acres set aside and cut into strips of different size, we called equalization townships. They were attached to various other townships to make them average in size. Auburn, Newbury, Munson, Chardon, Bainbridge, Russell, and Chester were equalization townships. Parkman was of average, standard size; Thompson, Troy, Huntsburg, Middlefield, Clairdon, Burton, Montville, and Hambden where below average and had equalization parcels attached.[20]

---

13. Eugene Holloway Roseboom and Francis Phelps Weisenburger, *A History of Ohio,* 69-99.
14. *United States Statutes at Large,* VII, 49.
15. Roseboom and Weisenburger, *op. cit.,* 99.
16. Lester Taylor and others, *Pioneer and General History of Geauga County,* 265-266.
17. Benjamin Perley Poore, *Federal and State Constitutions and other Organic Laws of the United States,* I, 252-253.
18. *Laws of Ohio,* X, 163-165.
19. *United States Statutes at Large,* I, 485.
20. Williams Brothers comps., *History of Geauga and Lake Counties, Ohio,* 12-13.

Most of the pioneers were from Connecticut.[21] The first were Thomas Unberfield, Isaac Fowler, Amariah Beard, and their families who established the initial settlement in Geauga County in 1798 at Burton. Community centers were formed in Middlefield Township in 1799, Thompson in 1800, Chester in 1801, and Parkman in 1804.[22] Because of the peculiar system of land ownership the Western Reserve was not occupied from east to west in the usual manner. Settlements were widely scattered. For many years pioneer life was isolated and insecure.[23]

The population grew steadily and soon a demand arose for the creation of a new county, and on December 31, 1805, Geauga was set off but not made an organized division.[24] The name was taken from the Indian language. The red men named Grand River, Sheauga, meaning raccoon. Organizers of the county pronounced it Geauga.[25] On March 1, 1806 the general assembly passed laws erecting the county. The original area contained practically all of the present counties of Ashtabula, Lake, and Cuyahoga.[26] The following years the general assembly set aside certain parts of Geauga to form sections of Ashtabula and Cuyahoga Counties. These counties were set aside but were not to be organized as separate units until the population increased.[27] Numerous changes have been made in Geauga County boundaries, notably by the creation of Cuyahoga County in 1810, Ashtabula in 1811, and Lake in 1840.[28]

The first courts of the new county were held at New Market, between the present towns of Painesville and Fairport. The general assembly in 1808, appointed Robert Simison, Reason Beadle, and Samuel Hunter as commissioners to select a permanent county seat for Ashtabula, Geauga, and Portage Counties.[29]

---

21. Taylor, *op. cit.*, I, 26.
22. Williams Brothers, *op. cit.*, 20.
23. Howe, *op. cit.*, I, 682.
24. Western Reserve and Northern Ohio Historical Society, *Tract 29*, 11.
25. Maria Ewing Martin, "Origin of Ohio Place Names," *Ohio State Archaeological and Historical Quarterly*, XIV, (1905), 278. The Indian name was in use prior to white settlement. The map of John Fitch in 1785 and of Manasseh Cutler in 1787 show the river to be named Grand. Frederick C. Waite, "Sources of the Names of the Counties of the Western Reserve," *Ohio State Archaeological and Historical Quarterly*, XLVIII (1939), 61.
26. *Laws of Ohio*, IV, 65-66.
27. *Ibid.*, VI, 3-5.
28. Randolph C. Downes, "Evolution of Ohio County Boundaries," *Ohio State Archaeological and Historical Quarterly*, XXXVI (1927), 458-459.
29. *Laws of Ohio*, VI, 179-180.

Three years later they bought a site in the unbroken wilderness and named it Chardon for the owner, Peter Chardon Brooks, of Boston, who had platted the village in 1808. Because of its isolated position Chardon grew slowly, and in 1816 it contained only 40 families.[30] The first courthouse was built at Chardon in 1813 at the cost of $750, but it soon proved too small. It is said that during one trial case the jury retired to the near-by woods and used a log as a voting table.[31] In 1840 the general assembly created Lake County but left it unorganized. Officials of Geauga County were given jurisdiction in the section of Lake that was taken from Geauga until such time as Lake became an organized county.[32]

With the erection of Geauga County population increased and other settlements were soon established. Huntsburg Township was settled in 1807, Claridon and Chardon in 1808, Newbury, 1810, Troy and Bainbridge, 1811, Auburn and Montville, 1815, Munson, 1816, and Russell, 1817.[33]

From 1860 to 1900 the population of the county has been almost stationary. Geauga had 2917 inhabitants in 1810; in 1820, 7791; 1840, 16,297; 1850, 17,827; 1880, 14,251; and in 1900, 14,744.[34] The total in 1930 was 15,414, of which 87.1 percent were native born-whites, 12.3 percent foreign-born whites, and 6 percent Negroes. Majority of foreign-born whites came from Czechoslovakia, Poland Germany, and England.[35] Several Russians came to Huntsburg during the 1920s. Finns began migrating to the Western Reserve and by 1930 Geauga County had 133 Finnish inhabitants. Most of them settled in Burton and Chardon townships.[36] Middlefield had a considerable colony of Amish.[37] Population of the county reached its peak in 1940 with a total of 19,430.

30. John Kilbourne, *The Ohio Gazetteer and Traveler's Guide*, 104.

31. Taylor, *op. cit.*, 34.

32. *Laws of Ohio*, XXXVIII, 171-172.

33. Williams, *op. cit.*, 20.

34. United States Bureau of the Census. *Twelfth Census of the United States, 1940, Population*, I, pt. i, 34.

35. *Ibid., Fifteenth Census of the United States, 1930, Population*, III, pt. i, 480, 500.

36. John I. Kolehmainen, "Founding of the Finnish Settlements in Ohio," *Ohio State Archaeological and Historical Quarterly*, XLIX, (1940), 156-157.

37. Ohio Study of Local School Units, *A Study of the Public Schools of Geauga County with Recommendations for Their Future Organization*, 16, 24. Hereinafter cited, *Geauga Schools Survey*.

Geauga County has no cities. Of the incorporated villages Chardon contained 2001 people, Middlefield, 932, and Burton 761.[38]

Agriculture, the primary industry of the pioneers in Geauga County, retains its importance. The soils being predominantly of a sandstone and shale content are better adapted to raising grass than food crops.[39] A hilly topography also deters extensive crop raising. The pioneers, cognizant of the difficulties of general farming, early began the raising of livestock. Sheep were introduced at an early period and wool production became large.[40] Geauga County is said to have had the first agricultural society in the Western Reserve. It was organized in 1823 as the "Geauga County Agricultural and Manufacturing Society."[41] The first fair, held on the village green at Chardon, October 23, 1823, was a success.[42]

Agriculture began to expand and in 1836 there were 339,241 acres in farmlands. The land value plus that of the buildings was $1,335,988. The value of town lots and buildings was $162,000, and 14,144 cattle valued at $113,152.[43]

As an aid to crop cultivation, the general assembly in 1837, appointed Eleazer Hickcox, James Peffers, and Simion Rose of Burton, and John Fox and John Nash of Troy as commissioners to hire surveyors and supervise the draining of marsh lands near the Cuyahoga River.[44] The following year the county was under a good state of cultivation, and in addition to grains, large numbers of cattle, sheep, hogs, and horses were raised.[45]

Members of the old Agricultural and Manufacturing Society had lost interest in the organization. Mr. S. Rosa, in 1845, wrote to the State Board of Agriculture and reported that "a society for the promotion of agriculture was organized in Geauga County some 18 or 20 years since." He explained that this society was practically abandoned and emphasized the need for its reorganization.[46]

---

38. U.S. Bureau of the Census, *16th Census of the United States, 1940, Population, First Series, Number of Inhabitants, Ohio*, 16.
39. W. A. Lloyd, J. I. Falconer, and C. E. Thorne, *The Agriculture of Ohio*, 306.
40. Taylor, *op. cit.*, 32-33.
41. Cleveland *Plain Dealer*, August 26, 1935.
42. Williams Brothers, *op. cit.*, 41.
43. Auditor of State. *Report to 35th General Assembly, 1836*, p. XXIX
44. *Laws of Ohio*, XXXV, 435-436.
45. Warren Jenkins, *Ohio Gazetteer and Traveler's Guide*, 199.
46. Ohio Dept. of Agriculture, *Report of the Ohio Department of Agriculture and the County and Independent Fairs held in Ohio in 1936*, 31.

At a meeting held in the courthouse at Chardon, July 30, 1846, the Geauga County Agricultural Society was formed.[47] Interest in farming and proper care of the land revived as the society began functioning. The following year the county had a total of 254,670 acres of farmlands with a value of $2,424,260.[48]

Horticulturally, Geauga County ranked high in 1879, when its 3856 acres of orchards yielded 106,650 bushels apples, 1614 of peaches, and 876 of pears. Only one county and northern Ohio had a larger average - Lucas, with 3913 acres of orchards raised 127,123 bushels of apples, 3353 of peaches, and 2405 of pears.[49] Oats had become a principal crop by 1918. It had been steadily increasing in acreage and yield for 60 years. By the end of that period it was a larger crop than wheat and corn combined.[50]

Geauga County's rugged terrain and its loamy soil, better adapted to grass than crop cultivation, have caused dairy farming to become the principal industry. Slightly better soil on the narrow bottom lands and the proximity to Cleveland has, however, enabled vegetable raising to obtain much importance. Geauga, in 1930, ranked second among the counties of Ohio in vegetable and milk production.[51] A census taken in 1940 for the preceding year showed that 8,717,947 gallons of milk were produced. A census report from 2183 of the county's farm showed the total value of the vegetables grown, excluding Irish and sweet potatoes, were $132,240. Only seven counties in the state had vegetable crops with higher values, and each of those had more farms reporting.[52] Geauga had 2497 farms on April 1, 1940. They were of an average size of 84 acres, and represented 80.5 percent of the total land area of the county.[53]

47. Ohio Dept. of Agriculture, *Agriculture Report of 1846*, 31.
48. Auditor of State, *Special Report*, XII, pt. i, 1848.
49. Ohio Dept. of Agriculture, *35th Annual Report, 1880*, p. 275
50. Lloyd, Falconer, and Thorne, *op. cit.*, 306.
51. U.S. Bureau of the Census, *Fifteenth Census of the United States, 1930, Agriculture, Ohio*, III, pt. i, p. 281.
52. *Ibid.*, *16th Census of the United States, 1940, Agriculture, Ohio, First Series*, 36; *Second Series*, 47-53.
53. *Ibid., First Series*, 8.

Geauga is the one county in the Western Reserve which has never had any great industrial enterprise or growths of urban population. The topography is unfavorable to either. The soil content is such that farmers early became interested in dairying instead of crop cultivation. Geauga's rolling hills and maple forests make it a scenic section, and are factors which contribute to making the county the home of large herds of dairy cows and of maple sugar camps instead of numerous manufacturing plants.[54]

Butter and cheese making, started early by the pioneer women of the county in their homes, soon developed into an important business.[55] Export trade began in 1820 when Harry Baldwin transported a load of cheese by river barges to New Orleans markets. Plants were built to manufacture the product,[56] and by 1861 cheese making was the prominent industry. Then, Geauga, with a total of 5,299,144 pounds had nearly a million more pounds than the next highest production county in the Western Reserve. With 723,681 pounds of butter, Geauga was eighth among the counties of the Western Reserve in annual production.[57]

The Maple Hill Cheese Factory in Munson Township, erected in 1862, was the first plant of its kind in the state. The buildings were destroyed by fire in 1896.[58] The Sand Hill Cheese Factory was built in 1869 and a curing house erected in 1872. Using 1,275,000 pounds of milk a year, it produced eleven forty-pound cheeses per day. Butter and cheese production lagged at the beginning of the 20th century and has never regained its volume. Farmers have found it more profitable to sell milk directly to metropolitan centers.[59]

The extensive maple forests of the county have been a valuable reservoir for maple sugar and syrup. In 1870 Geauga was the largest producer of maple sugar of any county in the state.[60] Ten years later Geauga maintains its lead, being almost 300,000 pounds ahead of its nearest competitor, Ashtabula County.[61]

54. John Struthers Stewart, *History of Northeastern Ohio*, I, 279.
55. Taylor, *op. cit.*, 29.
56. Stewart, *op. cit.*, I, 284-287.
57. "Fifth Annual Report of the Commissioners of Statistics to the Governor of Ohio for the year 1861," *Ohio Executive Documents, 1861-1862.*
58. *Geauga Republican Record*, January 10, 1940.
59. Stewart, *op. cit.*, 287.
60. Secretary of State, *Annual Report*, 1871, 91.
61. Ohio Dept. of Agriculture, *Thirty-fifth Annual Report, 1880*, pp. 309-310.

Production was not so great in 1891, when Geauga made 448,583 pounds of maple sugar. Ashtabula made 228,522 pounds. In the 11-year period from 1880 Geauga went from sixth to second place and maple syrup making.[62] In 1900 production dropped to 134,657 pounds of sugar in Geauga County. It was, however, the leader in both sugar and syrup.[63]

In order to protect the maple forest from ravages, and create a demand for the products, the Geauga Maple Festival was founded in 1926 with A. B. Carlson as chairman. A varied supply of maple products was served and the first festival was a success.[64] The festival has continued to increase in popularity. In spite of the ban on tire buying an estimated crowd of 60,000 attended the last day of the festival, April 13, 1942.[65]

An early industrial organization was the Bondstown Logging Society, founded in 1810 as a cooperative enterprise. Constitution and bylaws authorized each member to hire chopping done. The society was bound to do all the logging any member had to do for four years. This was accomplished by logging bees. In order to maintain sobriety, it was a rule that no one could supply more than a gallon of whiskey to each 10 men. Any member failing to have his place properly cleared when asking for a "bee" was fined a gallon of whiskey. After the lapse of about a year the society was abandoned because the wealthier members of the organization were able to have large lots cleared but the poorer men received nothing except their board and an abundance of whiskey.[66]

Gristmills, first of the manufacturing industries in Geauga County, were erected in Munson Township in 1818 by Chester Langdon and Joseph Post, who also built a sawmill. About 1820 a large stone quarry was started on the farm of John Gloin. Grindstones were made and stone for building the courthouse at Chardon was quarried here. By 1830 Daniel Hager and Joseph Haskell had erected saw- and gristmills. Eight years later William and Sylvester Rider began the manufacturing of iron at Chardon. They built a furnace and secured the iron from bog ore found mostly in the vicinity of Munson Pond, and by skimming the tops of the stagnant pools.[67]

---

62. *Ibid., Forty-fifth Annual Report, 1890.*
63. *Ibid., Forty-fifth Annual Report, 1900*, p. 44.
64. *Program 6th Annual Maple Festival, 1931*, p. 4.
65. *Columbus Dispatch*, April 13, 1942.
66. Taylor, *op. cit.*, 362.
67. *Geauga Republican Record*, January 3, 1940.

State records for 1941 show that Geauga County had 13 manufacturing plants, employing 585 men and 314 women. Although situated near the Great Lakes, the county had few manufactories because of the high terrain which makes railroad building too costly. The Johnson Rubber Company of Middlefield is the largest user of labor, having 319 men and 187 women on their pay roll. The Snap Out Forms Company of Chardon employees 111 men and 47 women to produce printed office forms. Products manufactured are rubber goods, printing, cider, flour, baked goods, dairy products, packed meats, tools, and sawmill work. There are 38 business establishments which employ 237 men and 70 women, the largest being the Geauga County Agricultural Society at Burton. Forty-two men and 22 women work there.[68]

As cheese making and other pioneer manufacturing began to develop, a need for a financial institution became apparent. The general assembly, on February 10, 1829, granted incorporation privileges until 1844 to the Bank of Geauga at Painesville, then in Geauga County.[69] By 1834 the Geauga Insurance Company was incorporated in this village. A capital of $100,000 was sold in $50 shares.[70]

The charter of the bank of Geauga expired as provided in 1844,[71] and the following year the general assembly authorized the trustees of the institution to distribute among the stockholders, the judgments, promissory notes, and other cases in action belonging to the corporation.[72] In the spring of 1857 L. J. Randall, O. A. and T. M. Burton established a private banking house at the Chardon. They did a large business until 1861 when they closed.[73] The Chardon Savings Bank Company was established as a private enterprise in 1891 by Smith Fowler and Company. It is now a state bank, and the oldest financial institution in the county.[74] In 1911 there were three banks, the First National at Burton, the Chardon Savings Bank, and the Middlefield Banking Company, of Middlefield.[75]

---

68. State Dept. Industrial Relations, Division Labor Statistics, Files for 1941 (unpublished).
69. *Laws of Ohio*, XXVII, 27-32.
70. *Ibid.*, XXXII, 310-314.
71. Carl Wittke, ed., *The History of the State of Ohio*, III, 277.
72. *Laws of Ohio*, XLIII, 343.
73. Williams Brothers, *op. cit.*, 118.
74. *Geauga Republican Record*, January 17, 1940.
75. "First Annual Report of the Tax Commission of Ohio," *Ohio Executive Documents, 1910*, Part i, 163.

The depression years which caused the closing of many banks, and the President's bank holiday of 1933, a measure that consolidated others, did not change the Geauga County banks. They remain the same as in 1911.[76]

Because of the high terrain transportation development has been retarded in Geauga County. Only a few miles of railroad lines transverse the county. Water courses accommodated many settlers. Some pioneers entered the region over one of the oldest routes in Ohio, the "Girdled Road," first throughfare in the Western Reserve. Beginning at the western bounty of Pennsylvania, it entered the Reserve in southeast Trumbull County and passed through the northern part of Middlefield, slightly east of Chardon. Its name was derived from the girdled trees which marked its route.[77] The next highway through the county passed through the western tier of townships. It was the old "Chillicothe Road," laid out by territorial government. Captain Edward Paine, of Chardon, was one of the committee which planned the route.[78] A post road, established by the Federal government in 1825, ran from Parkman, in Geauga County to the towns of Windsor and Mesopotamia in Trumbull County.[79] A state road from Ravenna, in Portage County, to Painesville, in Geauga, was laid out in 1833.[80] Six years later, mail stages were running from Pittsburgh and Zanesville to meet at Chardon. A daily stage from Fairport to Wellsville, on the Ohio River, in Columbiana County, also ran through Chardon.[81]

Indicative of the impracticability of extensive road building in Geauga County are highways figures for 1910. Then there were 13 miles of improved road, six miles of stone, and several of gravel.[82]

Railroad transportation in Geauga County began in 1856 when the Painesville and Hudson Company completed its line. The company soon failed because of excessive construction cost, and many local stockholders lost money.[83]

---

76. U.S. Comptroller of the Currency, *Individual Statements of National Banks, December 31, 1940,* p. 116-125. State of Ohio, Division of Banks, *Thirty-third Annual Report of the Division of Banks, December 31, 1940,* 36-40.

77. Cleveland *Plain Dealer,* November 8, 1940.

78. Taylor, *op. cit.,* 27.

79. *United States Statutes at Large,* IV, 95-100.

80. *Laws of Ohio,* XXXII, 130; 9-10.

81. Warren Jenkins, *The Ohio Gazetteer and Traveler's Guide,* 105.

82. "Sixth Annual Report of the State Highway Department of Ohio," *Executive Documents, 1910,* Part i, 57.

83. *Geauga Republican Record,* January 10, 1940; Taylor, *op. cit.,* 28.

On July 3, 1872, the Painesville and Youngstown Railroad was finished through Geauga County. It used much of the old Hudson roadbed. The Geauga, Cleveland, and Mahoning Valley Railway Company's main line was completed in 1874. A total of 1.99 miles was within Geauga County.[84] At the present, three railroads, the Baltimore and Ohio, Erie, and Wheeling and Lake Erie operate in the county with a total of 36.66 miles of tracks.[85]

Three United States Routes transverse the county, U.S. 422 connecting Pittsburgh and Cleveland, and U.S. 322 running through central Pennsylvania to Cleveland, and U.S. 6, a main transcontinental route running east and west. State Routes 608, 43, 306, 44, 80, 528, and 168 follow through Geauga County from north to south, and 88, 166, and 87 run east and west. There are approximately 800 miles of highway within the county.

Social contacts among Geauga County pioneers were afforded by religious gatherings. Services were first held in Hambden Township in 1804, by a Reverend Mr. Robbins, a Presbyterian minister from Connecticut. He had established a congregation by 1809. Methodists met in 1806 at Burton, and in Chester Township in 1812. Pioneer preachers were the Reverends Charles, Ewens, Sheffield, and Riley. Congregationalists first met at Burton in 1808.[86]

The Methodists worshiped at Chardon in 1818, and the Congregationalists in 1834. Alexander Campbell came to the village in 1824. Although his preaching drew large crowds, it was 12 years before a Disciple church was built.[87] Ely Odell, Fredoniad Whiteman, Tibbeus Norton, Isaac Hingman, and Daniel Huntington were recognized by the general assembly on March 3, 1834 as incorporators of the First Baptist Church at Chester.[88]

Religious activity increased in the county and by 1859 the Methodists, Baptists, Presbyterians, Roman Catholics, Disciples, and the Union or Free Church denominations were well represented. The Methodists had church property valued at $10,275, the Baptist, $5230, Presbyterians $11,987, Roman Catholics, $315. Disciples, $5200, and the Union or Free church, $400.[89]

---

84. "Eighth Annual Report of the Commissioners of Railroads and Telegraphs," *Old Executive Documents,* 1874, Part i, 768.
85. *Geauga Schools Survey,* 9.
86. Williams Brothers, *op. cit.,* 128; 111-210 *passim.*
87. Stewart, *op. cit.,* I, 294-295.
88. *Laws of Ohio,* XXXII, 386.
89. Ohio Commissioner of Statistics, *Third Annual Report, 1859,* p. 83.

There were 3509 church members in the county in 1926. The Baptists had 125 members, Congregational, 902, Disciples of Christ, 340, Eastern Orthodox, 60, Friends, 19, Methodist, 766, and Roman Catholics, 534. All other denominations had a combined total of 763 members.[90]

An increase of 4016 in Geauga County population from 1930 to 1940, proportionally increased the church membership. In 1936 the Disciples of Christ had 377 members, Baptists, 118, Congregational, 816, Mennonites, 515, Methodists, 723, Roman Catholics,1215, and all other denominations, 320. This made a total church membership of 4084 for the county.[91]

Geauga County pioneers, imbued with the New England appreciation of learning, immediately established schools. These were maintained by the parents paying a small fee for three months schooling of their children during the winter. Schools were open at Burton in 1802, Parkman in 1807, Hambden and Thompson in 1809, Chester and Huntsburg in 1810, and in other settlements soon thereafter. Sallie Miner, Joseph Royce, Anna Pomeroy, Lurena Hurbert, Susannah Babcock, and Paul Crisp were among the early teachers.[92]

The first Academy in Geauga County was the Erie Literary Society, chartered by the general assembly in 1803.[93] Three years later William Law, of Connecticut, gave the society 1130 acres of land. Soon thereafter, an academy was opened at Burton. Among the teachers was Peter Hitchcock,[94] one of the framers of the Ohio Constitution of 1851.[95] Burton Academy possessed a good reputation and families of northeastern Ohio sent their sons here to receive schooling preparatorily for Yale. The academy was moved to Hudson in 1826. It eventually became Western Reserve University.[96] Several other academies were then soon founded, the "Brick Academy" at Chardon in 1826, Parkman Academy in 1839, Geauga Academy at Chester in 1841, and another at Burton in 1845.[97]

---

90. U.S. Bureau of the Census, *Religious Bodies, 1926*, I, 656-660.
91. *Ibid., 1936*, I, 799-802.
92. Williams, *op. cit.*, 111-210, *passim*.
93. *Laws of Ohio*, I, 117.
94. *Geauga Schools Survey*, 4.
95. J. V. Smith rep. *Official Reports of the Debates and Proceedings of the Ohio State Convention. . . held at Columbus Commencing May 6, 1850, and at Cincinnati, Commencing December 2, 1850.*
96. Edward A. Miller, "The History of Educational Legislation in Ohio,' *Ohio State Archaeological and Historical Quarterly*, XXVII, (1919), 97-102.
97. W. W. Boyd, "Secondary Education in Ohio Previous to the Year 1840," *Ohio State Archaeological and Historical Quarterly*, XXV, (1916), 118-134.

Geauga County, in1837, had 131 schoolhouses with a value of $18,301. One hundred and seven teachers were employed in the grade schools and 190 in the academics.[98] Fourteen years later there were 233 common schools with 73 men and 157 women teachers. The average daily attendance was 2977 boys and 2671 girls.[99] By 1859 Geauga had one seminary and two teachers and 60 students.[100] The general assembly, on March 26, 1884, authorized the school board of Burton Township to create a $13,000 building which would be "free to all youths of school age in the township." This was among the first of the larger high-school buildings in the county.[101]

In 1930 the percentage of illiteracy was only 2.4 percent.[102] There are now 35 elementary and 12 high-school buildings within the county. Eighty-four grade school teachers give instruction to 2675 pupils and 64 teachers direct the studies of 1140 high school students.[103]

Geauga County's courthouse, though too small for efficient use, continued to be occupied until July 25, 1868, when about two o'clock in the morning a fire broke out. At this time the business district of Chardon was comprised of flimsy wooden buildings which were an easy mark for flames. The town possessed no engine, bucket or ladder, or reservoir of water. Half-clad men battled the flames unsuccessfully, and by daylight the business section and part of the residence district was leveled to the ground. One of the buildings destroyed was the courthouse.[104] The present substantial courthouse was built the year following the fire.[105]

98. Ohio Supt. of Common Schools, *Report,* 1837, 42.
99. Ohio Secretary of State, *Annual Report,* 1851, 33, 73.
100. Ohio Commissioner of Statistics, *Third Annual Report,* 1859, 131-139.
101. *Laws of Ohio,* LXXXI, 285.
102. U.S. Bureau of the Census, *Fifteenth Census of the United States, 1930, Population,* III, pt. ii, 480.
103. Ohio Department of Education, Division of Statistics, Files for 1942.
104. William Brothers, *op. cit.,* 118-119.
105. Taylor, *op. cit.,* 34.106.

Cultural and humanitarian interests were early manifest. On March 1, 1834, Sherman Dayton, David Underwood, Henry Wells, Spencer Garrett, Seth Stevens, Thomas Smith, James Holly, Ephraim Stephens, Elijah Nye, Charles Moore, Henry Pratt, Josiah G. Moore, Noyes Baldwin, Samuel Nye, Amos Dewey, William Dewey, Josiah Miller, Randall Hart, Absalom Wells, Samuel Loudon, and their associates were named incorporators of the Montville Social Library Company.[106.]

The board of commissioners met March 15, 1859, and for $2400 bought the farm of Nathaniel Stone in Chardon Township as a home for the aged and indigent.[107] On October 28, 1933, Lewis L. Pope presented to the people of the county, his large brick mansion and 120-acre estate at Pope's Corners in Troy. This has been the Pope family homestead since 1818. It is now known as Lewis L. Pope - Dorcas Home for the Aged.[108]

Like other Ohio counties, Geauga has had its share of noted people. Among them have been Calvin Pease, state senator from 1806-1807, and a noted jurist. Samuel Huntington, the third governor of Ohio, came from Connecticut in 1800. He was presiding judge of the first court in the territory. Huntington was a member of the Constitutional Convention of 1802, and by that body was appointed State Senator. For sometime he was Speaker of the senate, and later a judge of the supreme court. He was elected governor of Ohio in 1808. He died in 1817 at 52 years of age.[109] A second Geauga County citizen to become the governor was Seabury Ford of Burton. A staunch Whig, he was elected to the general assembly in 1840, and became speaker of the house. As a leader of his party he prevented the antislavery Whigs from deserting the state ticket, and was elected the 15th governor of Ohio and 1848. He died at Burton in 1855.[110] Charles Martin Hall, a former resident of the county attained fame as a chemist. He graduated from Oberlin in 1885 and the following year discovered the only commercially successful process of making aluminum.

---

106. *Laws of Ohio,* XXXII, 265.

107. Taylor, *op. cit.,* 70.

108. Cleveland *Plain Dealer,* October 29, 1933.

109. Western Biographical Publishing Company, *The Biographical Cyclopedia* and Portrait Gallery, with an historical sketch of the State of Ohio, vol. I, 141.

110. Wittke, *op. cit.,* III, 405, 460-467.

Hall secured the financial support of the Mellons and other inventors, and under the name of Pittsburgh Reduction Company began to produce aluminum at New Kensington, Pennsylvania. His system brought the price down to 18 cents a pound, making it available for commercial use. He died in 1914. He left one-third of his estate to Oberlin College. This bequest was valued at $15,000,000.[111]

  Journalism began in Geauga County in 1833 when Alfred Phelps founded the *Chardon Spectator and Geauga Gazette*. Phelps was an ardent Whig and the paper strongly advocated the principles of that party, as did its successor, the *Freeman,* which appeared in 1840. Other Whig papers were the *Republican and Whig* and the *Republic*. They thrived from 1842 to 1849, when the *Free Democrat,* a Free Soil publication was introduced. This paper was bought in 1859 by J. O. Converse, who published it for more than 30 years. In 1872 he changed the name to the *Geauga Republican*. The *Record* was started in 1880, and nine years later was published by Denton Brothers and King as the *Democrat Record*. In 1922 the *Republican* and the *Record* were combined as the *Republican Record*.[112] With Richard L.Denton as editor, it is the weekly Republican paper of Chardon. The other paper of the village is the *Geauga County News,* published each week by the Geauga Publishing Company. At Burton is the *Geauga Leader,* a weekly Republican paper. The *Cryptogram,* a bimonthly publication of the American Cryptogram Association, is also published there. The *Times,* a weekly Republican paper of Middlefield, was established in 1915 by F. L. Olds, its present editor.[113]

---

111. *The New York Times* August 28, 1914, p. 9.
112. Osman Castle Hooper, *History of Ohio Journalism,* 1793-1933, 130.
113. N. W. Ayer and Sons, *Ayer's Directory of Newspapers and Periodicals,* 1941 edition, pp. 714-715, 734.

Politically, Geauga County has been a rock-ribbed Republican stronghold for many years. Sentiment in the county was for the new Free Soil Party in 1848. Geauga County gave the majority of its vote to Martin Van Buren.[114] In the election of 1860, the county went overwhelmingly for Abraham Lincoln. Four years later, the vote for Lincoln was even larger. Geauga voters have since then consistently voted for Republican candidates - for national, state, and local offices. The electorate staunchly remained loyal to their party even in 1932, 1936, and 1940.[115] The only exception was in 1905 when a Democrat was elected for prosecuting attorney. W. G. King was the lone successful Democrat. At that time the political campaign was bitter between Myron T. Herrick and John M. Pattison for governor. Factions from both sides accused the other of conniving with the liquor interests. To offset Republican charges of being allied to the saloon element, Geauga County Democrats placed King, the local antisaloon league chairman as the candidate for prosecuting attorney.[116] He refused to accept the nomination at first, but later became imbued with the campaign and labored hard for election. He was elected by the narrow margin of 39 votes.[117]

---

114. Wittke, op. cit., III, 468.
115. "Annual Report of the Secretary of State," Ohio Executive Documents, 1867, pt. i, 330-332; Ohio Secretary of State, Ohio Election Statistics, 1932, 103; 1936, 131-138; 1940, 128, 185, 277.
116. Geauga County Record, November 10, 1905.
117. Geauga Republican, November 10, 1905.

The county as a political institution and as a subdivision of the state for purposes of political and judicial administration is of ancient origin.[1] In a form substantially similar in all general features and functions it has existed in England since early times, and in America since its settlement. As the tide of migration moved westward, following the American Revolution, the institutions of seaboard states were transferred to the newer west, undergoing such alteration as best suited frontier conditions.[2]

The earliest provision for the organization of counties in what is now the state of Ohio was contained in the Ordinance of 1787, by which the governor of the Northwest Territory was directed to "lay out the parts of the district in which the indian [sic] titles shall have been extinguished into the counties and townships subject, however to such alterations as may thereafter be made by the legislature."[3] The organization of county government, therefore, began before the organization of the state and before the adoption of a state constitution. Prior to statehood nine counties were organized. The first county lines were drawn in 1788.[4] The last county lines were altered in 1888, exactly 100 years later.[5]

The establishment of local government in the Northwest Territory was one of the first concerns of Governor St. Clair. The Ordinance of 1787 furnished the framework, but details of institutions had to be constructed.

---

1. Thomas Hodgkin, *From the Earliest Times to the Norman Conquest* (New York and London, 1906), 432

2. Beverley W. Bond, Jr., *The Civilization of the Old Northwest: A Study of Political, Social, and Economic Development, 1739-1812* (New York, 1934), 58-59.

3. Clarence Edwin Carter, ed. and comp., *The Territorial Papers of the United States* (Washington, 1934), II, 44.

4. *Ibid.*, III, 279.

5. *Laws of Ohio*, LXXXV, 418: Randolph Chandler Downes, "Evolution of Ohio County Boundaries," *Ohio State Archeological and Historical Quarterly*, XXXVI (1927), 449.

All county officials, under the provisions of the ordinance, were made appointed by the governor. St. Clair, a former resident of Pennsylvania, in providing for local administration depended in a large part upon the Pennsylvania code, which in some instances, was altered to meet the needs of the pioneer communities.[6]

The provisions for local administration were, for the most part, simple and effective. In each county the court of general quarter sessions of the peace, composed of three or more justices of the peace, served as a fiscal and administrative board of the county, estimating county expenditures, appointing tax commissioners, and providing for highway and bridge construction.[7] By the end of the decade the court was authorized to enter into contracts for building or repairing the county jail and the courthouse.[8] Other county officials appointed during the territorial period included a sheriff, coroner, recorder, treasurer, license commission, and justices and clerks of the various courts.[9]

Officers having been appointed, the next step in the organization of government was the establishment of a system of local courts. Evidence seems to indicate that the judicial system for the county had been carefully planned. The court of common pleas, composed of not less than three nor more than five appointive judges, was an inferior court having limited civil jurisdiction.[10] The court of general quarter sessions of the peace, besides serving as a fiscal and administrative board of the county, had jurisdiction in lesser criminal cases.[11]

---

6. The governor and judges were given power to "adopt and publish in the district such laws of the original states" as they thought necessary and these laws were to remain in force unless disapproved by Congress. In many cases the governor and judges had not adopted laws of the original states, as the Ordinance stipulated, but had passed measures that conformed in spirit. Since there were some question of the legality of these laws, St. Clair, in 1795, after the lower house of Congress disapproved of the laws passed at the legislative session of 1792, called a legislative session to revise the territorial code. The commission, after sitting for three months, completed Maxwell's Code named in honor of the printer, W. Maxwell. Few changes were made in the Maxwell Code by the territorial assembly which was elected in 1798. Carter, *op. cit.* II, 43. Minutes of the legislative assembly were reproduced in the *Ohio State Archeological and Historical Quarterly*, XXX (1921), 13-53.

7. Theodore Calvin Pease, comp., *The Laws of the Northwest Territory, 1788-1880* (Illinois State Bar Association Law Series, Springfield, 1925, I), 4, 36, 337; 69, 467, 74, 77, 453, 456, 485.

8. *Ibid.* 485

9. *Ibid.* 8, 24, 61, 68, 197.

10. *Ibid.,* 7.

11. *Ibid.,* 4-7.

A probate court, compose of a single judge, was given jurisdiction in probate and testamentary matters.[12] In 1795, following St. Clair's revision of the territorial code, circuit courts were established and orphans' courts were instituted.[13]

In the meantime the local government was further developed by the organization of civil townships. The governor and judges adopted a law from the Pennsylvania Code requiring the justices of the court of quarter sessions to divide each county into townships and appoint in each township a constable to serve specifically in his township and in the county, a clerk, and one or more overseers of the poor.[14]

The territory entered the second stage of administration when, in 1798, the population having reached the requisite 5,000 the governor ordered the election of a representative assembly.[15] The system of local government continued as established by the governor and judges, and the transition was achieved without a disturbance of local administration.

The admission of Ohio as a state did not, in the main, materially affect county organization and administration. The system of local government having been organized by the governor and judges and the legislature of the Northwest Territory, the basic offices were continued. Except for the provision for the election of a county sheriff and a county coroner in each county, two officials of utmost importance in pioneer communities, the constitution was silent on such matters as titles, number, and duties of officials.[16]

It devolved, therefore, upon the legislature to confer powers upon the county. In 1804 the legislature made provision for a board of county commissioners, composed the three members elected for a three-year term.[17]

12. *Ibid.,* 9.

13. *Ibid.,* 157, 181-188.

14. *Ibid.,* 37-41, 338. The system of local governmental administration was the result of sectional compromise, since it combined the county system of the southern and middle states with the elements of the New England town. Dwight G. McCarty, *The Territorial Governors of the Old Northwest: A Study in Territorial Administration* (Iowa City, 1910), 53-54.

15. Carter, *op. cit.,* III, 514-515.

16. *Ohio Const. 1802,* Art. VI, sec. 1.

17. *Laws of Ohio,* II, 150.

The board of county commissioners, supplanting the court of general quarter sessions, became the administrative and fiscal board of the county. In 1803 the legislature, recognizing the need for a more adequate system of land records, provided for a recorder to be appointed by the court of common pleas for a seven-year term and for a surveyor to be appointed by the court of common pleas.[18] Another act authorized the appointment of a county treasurer by the associate judges, a later one provided for his appointment by the county commissioners.[19]

The legislature also provided during its first session for a prosecuting attorney to be appointed by the supreme court to prosecute cases on behalf of the state.[20] In 1805 the appointing power was transferred to the court of common pleas.[21]

A new office was created in 1820, that accounting auditor. The auditor, first appointed by the legislature, had as his duty the preparation of the tax duplicate.[22] The county board of revision, the purpose of which was to correct some of the inequalities of assessments, was established in 1825. The first board of revision or equalization, as it was sometimes called, was composed of the county commissioners, the auditor, and the assessors.[23]

The judicial power of the state in matters of law and equity was vested in the supreme court, the court of common pleas, and the justices' courts. The articles of the constitution provided for a court of common pleas to be composed of a president and associate justices. The members of the court, appointed by a joint ballot of both houses of the general assembly, were to hold court in three judicial circuits into which the state was to be divided by the legislature.[24] The court was assigned common law and chancery jurisdiction in all cases as provided by law.[25]

---

18. *Ibid.,* I, 136, 90-93.
19. *Ibid.,* I, 97-98; II, 154.
20. *Ibid.,* I, 50.
21. *Ibid.,* III, 47.
22. *Ibid.,* XVIII, 70.
23. *Ibid.,* XXIII, 68-69.
24. *Ohio Const. 1802,* Art. III, secs. 3, 8.
25. *Ibid.,* Art. III, sec. 3.

To the court was assigned jurisdiction in probate and testamentary matters and in the appointment of guardians, functions performed during the territorial period by the probate court.[26] Finally, the court was authorized to appoint a clerk.[27]

The county offices created by the legislature were designed to transact the business of a state as yet unaffected by transformations wrought by industrialism and problems presented by large urban areas. Aside from the maintenance of the county poorhouse, the county had no functions in the administration of public welfare.

As a wave a democratic philosophy swept across the county in the eighteen twenties and thirties there arose a demand not only for an extension of the franchise but also for the election of public officials. Accordingly the auditor became an elective official in 1821, the treasurer in 1827, the recorder in 1829, and the prosecuting attorney in 1833.[28]

While the legislature responded to the general demand for the election of county officials, there arose a further demand for a revision of the constitution which failed to meet the needs of an expanding state. This movement came as a result of the dissatisfaction with the judicial system which placed the burden of judicial administration upon four judges who had the task of holding court each year in all the counties.[29] Then, too, there arose a demand for the election of all public officials, for the prohibition of charters that granted special privileges, and for a limitation on the power of the legislature to create a state debt. In February 1850 the legislature, following a favorable popular vote on the proposition, called for the election of delegates, to meet in convention in May. The constitution drafted by the delegates, was approved by special election on June 17, 1851. The constitution of 1851, like the constitution of 1802, failed to provide a definite form of county government and administration.

---

26. *Ibid.,* Art. III, sec. 5; Pease, *op. cit.,* 9.
27. *Ohio Const. 1802,* Art. III, sec. 9.
28. *Laws of Ohio,* XIX, 116; XXV, 25-32; XXVII, 65; XXXI, 13-14.
29. J. V. Smith, rep., *Official Reports of the Debates and Proceedings of the Ohio State Convention . . . held at Columbus, Commencing May 6, 1850, and at Cincinnati, Commencing December 2, 1850* (Columbus, 1851), 597 *et seq.* [Jacob] Burnet, Notes on the Early Settlement of the North-Western Territory (Cincinnati, 1847), 356. *See also* the *Ohio State Journal,* Dec. 11, 1840.

Aside from the constitutional provision for the election of a county treasurer, sheriff, and clerk of courts, and recreating the probate court which had existed during the territorial period, the organic instrument was silent on the administrative duties of the county.[30] Again all matters pertaining to county government were entrusted to the legislature. While the legislature conferred certain powers upon the county, it was limited by constitutional provision which required all laws of a general nature to be uniform throughout the state.[31]

The present administrative organization of Ohio county government presents a picture of extraordinary complexity. Each county quadrennially elects, besides the board of county commissioners, nine administrative officials: recorder, clerk of courts, probate judge, prosecuting attorney, coroner, sheriff, treasurer, auditor, and county engineer. While these officials conduct a major portion of the county's business, there is a variety of appointive officers and boards, as well as *ex-officio* commissioners. For convenience the work of county government may be classified under the following heads: Administration, judicial system, law enforcement, finance and taxation, elections, health, public welfare, and public works.

Administration

The board of county commissioners is the central feature of the present structure of county government. The functions of this board touch either directly or indirectly every other branch and department. The board is the agency in whose name actions for and against the county are brought. This board is empowered to determine certain matters of policy for the conduct of county affairs such as adoption of the budget, establishment of services left optional by law, and the authorization of improvements.[32] Thus, in a limited sense it constitutes the legislative branch of the county. The commissioners, however, have no ordinance-making powers.

---

30. *Ohio Const. 1851*, Art. X, sec. 3; Art. IV, sec. 16; Art. IV, sec. 7.
31. *Ibid.*, Art. II, sec. 26.
32. General Code sec. 2421.

The board also functions as the central administrative body although much of the administration, centered in the other elective offices, is beyond its immediate control. The county auditor was originally made secretary of the board and still functions as such in a majority of the counties. Later provisions of the law permitted the board to appoint its own clerk, thus removing this duty from the auditor.[33]

Judicial System

The constitution of 1851 made significant changes in the composition of the court of common pleas. The judges, heretofore appointed by the legislature, were made elective for a term not to exceed five years. For the purpose of electing judges the state was divided into nine districts. Each district was divided into three parts, in each of which one common pleas judge was to be elected. Court was to be held in every district or county with such jurisdiction as should be provided by law.[34] The legislature provided for the district but left the jurisdiction of the court much as it had been in the earlier years of its existence.[35] The constitutional amendment of 1912 abolished the divisions and subdivisions provided by the constitution of 1851, and authorized the election of one or more common pleas judges in each county.[36]

The judicial system was extended in 1851 by the creation of district courts composed of one supreme court justice and several common pleas judges in each district.[37] For administrative purposes the nine common pleas districts were apportioned into five judicial circuits.[38] The courts were assigned original jurisdiction in the same matters as the supreme court and such appellate jurisdiction as might be provided by law.[39]

---

33. *Laws of Ohio*, XIX, 147; G. C. sec. 2566.
34. *Ohio Const, 1851*, Art. IV, secs. 3, 4, 10.
35. Willis A. Estrich, *et al*, eds., *Ohio Jurisprudence*, XI, 827-839.
36. *Ohio Const. 1851* (Amendment), Art. IV, sec. 3.
37. *Ohio Const. 1851*, Art. IV, sec. 5.
38. *Laws of Ohio*, L, 69.
39. *Ohio Const. 1851*, Art. IV, sec. 6.

The district courts, abolished by the constitutional amendment of 1883, were superseded by the circuit courts which were given the same jurisdiction as their predecessors. The state was divided into seven circuits. In each circuit three judges were to be elected.[40] The judicial system was again altered in 1912 when, by constitutional amendment, the circuit courts were renamed courts of appeals.[41] The state is divided into nine appellate districts. There are three judges in each district elected by the people of the district for a six-year term.[42]

The constitution of 1851 re-created the probate court, which, existing during the territorial period, was abolished by the first constitution, its authority and jurisdiction being then vested in the courts of common pleas. Each county has one probate judge elected by the people for a four-year term.[43] By constitutional provision, the probate judge has original jurisdiction in probate and testamentary matters, the appointment of guardians, the settlement of the account of executors, administrators, and guardians,[44] and the issuance of marriage licenses. An amendment to the constitution of 1912 authorized the common pleas judge, when petitioned by 10 percent of the voters in the counties having a population less than 60,000 to submit to the voters at any general election the question of combining the probate and common pleas courts.[45] This combination exists in Adams, Henry, and Wyandot Counties.

Due to an increased amount of juvenile delinquency, the legislature in 1904 authorized the judges of the court of common pleas, the probate court, and the superior and insolvency courts, where established, to appoint one of their members as juvenile judge to hear cases involving neglected, dependent, and delinquent children. In counties which have a court of domestic relations the judge of that court serves in this capacity.[46]

---

40. *Ibid.,* Art. IV, sec. 6; *Laws of Ohio,* LXXXI, 168.
41. *Ohio Const. 1851,* Art. IV, sec. 6 (Amendment, 1912).
42. G. C. sec. 1514.
43. *Laws of Ohio,* CXIV, 320; *Ohio Const. 1851,* Art. IV, sec. 7.
44. *Ohio Const. 1851,* Art. IV, sec. 8.
45. *Ibid.,* Art. IV, sec. 7 (Amendment, 1912).
46. *Laws of Ohio,* XCVII, 561, 562; G. C. sec. 1532.

Law Enforcement

Closely related to the courts are the agencies of law enforcement in the county. Law enforcement is conducted by four officials: the sheriff, prosecuting attorney, coroner, and dog warden. These officials are concerned primarily with the enforcement of state laws, and leave the enforcement of municipal ordinances, and, in some instances, of state statutes in urban centers to municipal law enforcement agencies.

The county sheriff, whose duties have been materially curbed by municipal law enforcement agencies and the state highway patrol, has as his duty the enforcement of state laws.[47] He serves as custodian of the county jail,[48] and as an executive agent of the courts.[49] It has been estimated that approximately one-half of the sheriff's time is devoted to duties connected with the courts. The sheriff is restricted by lack of scientific equipment which has become essential to law enforcement.[50]

The county prosecuting attorney, the most important agent in the enforcement of criminal law, is directed by a law to "inquire into the commission" of crime within his county, and to prosecute on behalf of the state all complaints, suits, and controversies to which the state is a party.[51] In conjunction with the state attorney general, he prosecutes in the supreme court cases arising in his county.[52] He acts also in a civil capacity as legal counsel for the commissioners and other county officials.[53]

---

47. G. C. sec. 2833. The sheriff's authority extends to all parts of the county, although for obvious practical reasons he rarely makes an arrest in incorporated areas.
48. G. C. sec. 3157.
49. G. C. sec. 2834.
50. *The Reorganization of County Government in Ohio: Report of Governor's Commission on County Government* (n. p. December 1934), 102 *et seq.* The sheriff system worked admirable in rural communities. From the standpoint of police administration, it is unsatisfactory in areas of dense population. In such areas there is a need for a force of officers whose duty it is not merely to apprehend law violators but to prevent the infraction of the law by patrolling the territory. For an interesting discussion of some of the newer problems confronting law enforcement agencies see Donald C. Stone, "The Police Attack Crime," *Nat. Mun. Review,* XXIV, 91935, 39-41.
51. G. C. sec. 2916.
52. G. C. sec. 2916.
53. G. C. sec. 2917.

The prosecuting attorney may institute proceedings against an individual, but as a rule charges must be filed against the offender before action is taken. The prosecuting attorney has certain administrative duties such as serving as a member of the county budget commission and of the board of sinking fund trustees.[54]

The county coroner has the ancient duty of determining the cause of death where death occurs under suspicious circumstances or by unlawful means,[55] the proper distribution of property found on or about the deceased,[56] and the management of the county morgue.[57] It has been suggested by authorities on county administration that the office be abolished and the duties transferred to a medical examiner appointed by the prosecuting attorney.[58]

Another law-enforcement agent existing within the county is the dog warden. This official is appointed by and is responsible to the county commissioners. No special qualifications are required for the office. The dog warden has as his duty the enforcement of the section of the General Code "relative to the licensing of dogs, the impounding and destruction of unlicensed dogs, and the payment of compensation for damage to livestock inflicted by dogs." The dog warden and his deputies, in the performance of his legal duties, have the same "police powers" as those conferred by statute upon the sheriff and police.[59] Prior to 1927 the duties now performed by the dog warden were performed by the county sheriff.[60]

Law enforcement in the county is defective in two respects: first, there is little or no coordination between the four agencies of law enforcement, and second, there is little or no responsibility for neglect of duty. Evidence seems to indicate that the present inefficient and antiquated system could be corrected by consolidating all law-enforcement agencies into a county department of law enforcement under the immediate supervision of the county prosecuting attorney.[61]

---

54. *Laws of Ohio,* CXII, 399-400; CVIII, pt. i, 700-702.

55. G. C. sec. 2856.

56. G. C. secs. 2863, 2864.

57. G. C. sec. 2856-1.

58. W. F. Willoughby, *Principles of Judicial Administration* (Washington, 1929), 165-173. According to a recent act, effective June 8, 1937, only a licensed physician or a person who shall have previously served as coroner is eligible to fill the office. G. C. sec. 2856-3.

59. *Laws of Ohio,* CVIII, pt. i, 535; CXII, 348; G. C. sec. 5652-7.

60. *Laws of Ohio,* CVIII, pt. i, 535.

61. *The Reorganization of County Government,* 117-122.

The administration of criminal justice in the county has grown up in more or less hit or miss fashion and is for the most part unsatisfactory and extremely cumbersome. Arrests are made by the sheriff, or other police officer, who is theoretically an officer of the state, but who is under little or no supervision. The accused person is brought before a local magistrate for a preliminary hearing. In the event the accused is committed, it is necessary, in most cases, to receive an indictment before a grand jury.[62]

Finance and Taxation

There are three types of financial functions performed by county officers: tax administration, handling of the fiscal affairs of the county, and the trusteeship of funds held for individuals in court procedure. The principal financial authorities are the board of county commissioners, the auditor, and the treasurer. The commissioners levy taxes, appropriate funds, and authorize payments.[63] The auditor's primary duties are keeping accounts, issuance of warrants, valuation of real estate, and preparation of the tax list.[64] The treasurer collects taxes, receives and has custody of county money, and disburses it upon warrant from the auditor.[65] Other functions relating to county finance are performed by the board of revision, budget commissioners, and the board of sinking fund trustees.

During the early years of Ohio history, the principal sources of state and county revenue were the general property tax, poll tax, and fees received from licenses and permits to engage in certain kinds of business.[66]

---

62. For a criticism of the administration of criminal justice, see Edwin H. Sutherland, *Principles of Criminology* (Chicago, 1934), chap. xiv; Willoughby, *op. cit.,* chaps. xi, xxxvi.

63. G. C. secs. 5630, 5637, 7419.

64. G. C. secs. 2568-2570, 2573, 2583-2589.

65. G. C. secs. 2649, 2649-1, 2656, 2674.

66. An act of 1825 levied a tax on the income of attorneys, physicians, and surgeons for state purposes. Amount of tax was determined by the court of common pleas. Salmon P. Chase, ed., *The Statutes of Ohio and of the Northwestern Territory, 1788-1833* (Cincinnati, 1833), II, 1471. This act was repealed in 1852. Maskell E. Curwen, comp., *Public Statutes at Large of the State of Ohio* (Cincinnati, 1853), 1755. The poll tax was perpetually abolished by the constitutional authority in 1802. *Ohio Const. 1802,* Art. VIII, sec. 23.

A tax law enacted by the first territorial legislature (1799) designated certain types of property as taxable for county purposes. All houses in towns, town lots, and out-lots, water and windmills, ferries, cattle, and horses, were put on the county tax duplicate. A tax on land, subsequently used also for county purposes, was originally devoted exclusively to the needs of the territorial government. County officials were to assist in the administration of this tax as well as that of the county levy.[67]

In the course of time many additions were made to the original list of taxables. Taxable property came to include capital employed and merchandising (1826), and by exchange brokers (1825), pleasure carriages (1825), money loaned at interest (1831), and stock in steamboats.[68] In the latter year dividends of bank, insurance, and bridge companies were also made taxable.[69] The first act of a general nature directing the taxation of railroads was passed in 1851.[70] In 1862 a tax on the gross receipts of express and telegraph companies was enacted.[71] A levy of the capital stock of freight lines was authorized in 1896.[72] Subsequent enactments brought into the category of "general property" the possessions of public utilities in general. By such accumulations "property," by the end of the 19th century, had become a much more inclusive term than it had been one hundred years earlier.

County agencies became even more useful with the discovery of new tax sources. When, at the turn into the 20th century the general property tax lost its importance as a revenue source for the state, taxes on inheritance and cigarettes, then later, on gasoline, liquid fuel, liquor, retail sales, malt, and the like, took its place.[73] County officials continued to administer the general property tax, which was devoted henceforth to the uses of local governments, but they assisted in the administration of a number of those newer taxes as well.

---

67. Chase, *op. cit.*, 267-269. Previous acts of 1792 and 1795 were temporary in nature.
68. Chase, *op. cit.*, III, 1517; II, 1476; *Laws of Ohio*, XXIX, 272-280.
69. *Laws of Ohio*, XXIX, 302-303.
70. Curwen, *op. cit.*, 1647.
71. J. R. Sayler, comp., *The Statutes of the State of Ohio* (Cincinnati, 1876), 301.
72. *Laws of Ohio*, XCII, 89-93.
73. Ohio Tax Commission, *Financing State and Local Government in Ohio, 1900-1932*, (mimeographed, Columbus, 1934), 2.

The assistance rendered by county officials has been equally extensive and the system of issuing licenses and permits. The issuance of marriage licenses began during the territorial period (1788).[74] An act to license merchants, traders, and tavern keepers was passed in 1792.[75] Ferry licenses were authorized in 1799.[76] With the passage of time, one license after another has been required until unlicensed businesses have become something of an exception rather than the rule. Even with the increasing assumption of licensing authority by the state, county officials have continued to issue certain licenses assigned to the jurisdiction long ago.[77]

Under the early laws (1792) tax commissioners, appointed to annual terms by the courts of common pleas, were to list the male inhabitants above the age of 18, stocks of cattle, yearly value of improved land, and other property. Valuation of this property was made by township and village assessors, appointed annually by the court of common pleas.[78] These local assessors, who became elective in 1795, were again appointed in 1799.[79] In 1825 property valuation was assigned to a new official, the county assessor, also appointed by the court of common pleas.[80] This official became elective in 1827 and was succeeded in turn, in 1841, by township assessors to be elected annually.[81]

In conjunction with these administrators a system of real estate reappraisal was initiated. In 1846 county commissioners were directed to divide their counties into suitable districts and to appoint an assessor for each whose chief function should be to revise the valuation of real property.[82] An act of 1863 made these officers elective and provided for reappraisal every tenth year.[83] This was subsequently changed (1868) to every fifth year and in 1878 returned to the ten-year interval.[84]

---

74. Chase, *op. cit.*, I, 101.
75. Chase, *op. cit.*, I, 114-115.
76. Chase, *op. cit.*, I, 219.
77. *See* p. 35.
78. *Laws of the Territory of the United States Northwest of the River Ohio* (Philadelphia and Cincinnati, 1792-1796), II, 17-18.
79. Chase, *op. cit.*, I, 169, 273.
80. Chase, *op. cit.*, II, 1477.
81. Curwen, *op. cit.*, 775-779.
82. Curwen, *op. cit.*, 1269.
83. Sayler, *op. cit.*, 413.
84. Sayler, *op. cit.*, 1641; *Laws of Ohio*, LXXV, 459.

In 1913 the assistance of county officers in tax administration was temporarily dispensed with and their duties were given to state officials. The county was again made an entire assessment district but district (or county) assessors were now to be appointed by the governor. The tax commission (established in 1910) was directed to supervise and direct the assessment of real and personal property.[85] This attempt at unification of authority in the state was partially abandoned, however, in 1915, when assessment was returned to the county auditor and to elected township, village, and ward assessors.[86] In 1925 the latter officers were discontinued and the duties of assessment developed upon the county auditor alone.[87]

The advent of the state tax commission brought no great alteration in the process of assessment. The county remains the basic unit and the county auditor continues to serve as an agent of the state. Though the state commission now assesses certain forms of property, certification is made to the county auditor. For example, public utilities are now assessed by the commission and proportional shares of the revenue are apportioned to the counties which contain such property.[88] Financial institutions report directly to the commission which certifies to each county auditor the assessment of each taxable deposit.[89] Intangible property (defined in 1931) owned by individuals and corporations, not otherwise excepted, is listed and valued by the county auditor. Returns showing more than $500 of taxable income are forwarded to the commission for appraisal and certified by it back to the county auditor.[90] From these certifications of the commission, the personal property list returned to him by individuals, and the real estate assessment for which he is personally responsible, the auditor makes up the grand duplicate of real and personal property taxes.

---

85. *Laws of Ohio*, CIII, 786-787.
86. *Ibid.*, CVI, 246 et seq.
87. *Ibid.*, CXI, 486-487. Revaluation of real estate was required in 1925 and every sixth year thereafter.
88. G. C. sec. 5430.
89. G. C. secs. 5411, 5412, 5412-1.
90. Report of the Governor's Commission, 75; G. C. secs. 5372-3, 5376, 5377.

The county continues to be the basic unit also in the matter of budgeting and levying of taxes on property. In 1792 the courts of general quarter sessions were directed to estimate the sums needed to defray the cost of county government, specifying as nearly as possible the purpose for which such sums were necessary. This earliest of budgets was to be laid before the governor and judges and approved by the legislature. Special commissions were to apportion or levy the tax.[91] In 1799 it became the duty of these commissioners to ascertain the probable expenses of the county as well as levy the tax–a duty which continued until refinements in administration were made necessary because of the increasing number of taxing authorities.[92]

In order to achieve some systematic arrangement in the county fiscal system, the function of estimating expenses, or budgeting, was consolidated in recent years in the hands of a county budget commission. Since the Ohio legislature, in 1911, established a tax rate limitation, it was necessary to establish a commission vested with the authority to reduce the amounts set up in the annual tax budgets when the overlapping districts required more than the aggregate maximum tax rate permits.[93] The county budget commission organized in 1911 was composed, for a time, of the auditor, the mayor of the largest municipality, and the prosecuting attorney. Taxing authorities in the county were directed to submit their budgets to this body through the agency of the auditor.[94] The board was authorized to make adjustments in the budgets, alterations which the taxing authority might appeal to the tax commission. The budget commission, directed in 1911 to certify its actions to the auditor, was subsequently instructed by law to make such certification to the various taxing units which should themselves authorize the necessary tax levies and certify them to the auditor.[95] In 1927 the composition of this board was altered when the county treasurer replaced the mayor.[96]

---

91. Chase, *op. cit.,* I, 118-119.
92. Chase, *op. cit.,* I, 276-277.
93. G. C. sec. 5625-3. Since 1934 there has been a limitation of 10 mills on the dollar. G. C. sec. 56252-2.
94. *Laws of Ohio,* CII, 270-272.
95. G. C. sec. 5625-25.
96. *Laws of Ohio,* CXII, 399.

Early appeals against unjust assessments (1792) were heard by judges of the general territorial court, judges of the common pleas court, or justices of the general quarter sessions court.[97] After 1795 petitions for redress were directed to the county commissioners.[98] This appeal agency was superseded in 1825 by the board of equalization, composed of the commissioners, assessors, and the auditor.[99] This agency continued to function through the following years though occasional changes in personnel were made.[100]

With the reorganization of property administration in 1913 the function of tax revision was taken away from county officers. In each district (county) the tax commission was directed to appoint three persons with the term of three years to form a district board of complaints.[101] An act of 1915 abolished this plan, however, and returned the function of revision to the care of county officials. A board composed of the treasurer, the prosecuting attorney, the probate judge, and the president of the board of county commissioners, was directed to appoint a county board of equalization.[102] This plan, also, was soon dispensed with. An act of 1917 constituted the treasurer, auditor, and president of the board of commissioners as a county board of revision.[103]

---

97. *Laws of the Territory of the United States Northwest of the River Ohio,* II, 20-21.
98. Chase, *op. cit.,* I, 171.
99. Chase, *op. cit.,* II, 1476-1492.
100. The county surveyor became a member at times, in 1868, for example. Sayler, *op. cit.,* 1642.
101. *Laws of Ohio,* CIII, 790-791.
102. *Ibid.,* CVI, 254-255.
103. *Ibid.,* CVII, 40; G. C. secs. 5580, 5596. *See also* p. 231. Highest appellate jurisdiction, held originally by the general court and later (1805) by the associate judges of common pleas, was given, in 1825, to a state board of equalization composed of the state auditor and one member from each congressional district. Later these boards were composed of the state auditor and a member from each state senatorial district. With the establishment of the state tax commission that agency was made the body of final appeal. *Laws of Ohio,* III, iii; Chase, *op. cit.,* II, 1481; Curwen, *op. cit.,* 1784; G. C. sec. 5625-28.

The history of tax collection is equally intricate. The fiscal duties of the county treasurer, who now collects the property tax, comprised, in the very early period, only the receipt and custody of revenue funds. The actual collection was performed by other agencies. Due to the fact that in earlier years there were two district tax levies – one on land for the territory and later the state, and one on other property for county purposes – tax collections involved a double operation and duplicate officials.

The collectors of the county levy assessed in 1792 were appointed by the judges of the court of common pleas who were empowered to designate the sheriff, constable, or any other suitable person to perform this function.[104] By an act of 1795 township collectors were appointed by the commissioners and assessors.[105] From 1799 to 1805 taxes for county purposes were collected by county collectors.[106] An act of 1805 designated the township listers as collectors of the county levy, but in 1806, the commissioners were permitted to appoint a county collector instead if they believed such a course to be expedient. This arrangement remained in force until 1825.[107]

The first statute of a general nature providing for a tax on land for territorial purposes was enacted in 1799. From 1799 to 1803 the collectors of the county tax were to collect the territorial tax also.[108] In 1804, however, the county sheriff was specifically designated as a collector of the state tax.[109] From 1806 to 1816 the county commissioners were again permitted to use their own discretion as to whether a county or township collector should be appointed.[110] The county collector of the land tax mentioned in the statutes from 1816 to 1825 was, in all probability, the same official who collected the county tax, though due to a lack of definite terminology it is impossible to be certain.[111]

---

104. Chase, *op. cit.*, I, 119.
105. Chase, *op. cit.*, I, 171.
106. Chase, *op. cit.*, I, 277.
107. Chase, *op. cit.*, I, 471, 527; II, 771, 1384-1385.
108. Chase, *op. cit.*, I, 270.
109. Chase, *op. cit.*, I, 415.
110. Chase, *op. cit.*, I, 537, 727; II, 973.
111. Chase, *op. cit.*, II, 973, 1370-1371.

In 1825 the arrangement for a separate tax duplicate for state and county purposes was abolished and levies for both were made on the same property. In 1827 the office of county collector, who had performed that function in the intervening two years, was abolished and the treasurer, henceforth to be an elective officer, was given the duty of tax collection.[112]

The collection of certain taxes other than that on general property is performed by county agencies. Thus, for example, inheritance taxes, authorized by the legislature in 1894, are computed by the county auditor, adjusted by the probate court, collected by the county treasurer, and distributed to the proper agencies by the county auditor.[113] County auditors certified to the tax commission lists of persons licensed to engage in the business of selling cigarettes. County treasurers are the agents of the state treasurer for the sale of cigarette tax stamps.[114] The tax on wines, cordials, and beer is collected by means of the sale of stamps by county treasurers in a matter similar to that employed in collecting the cigarette tax.[115] The tax on brewers' wort and malt is collected in an identical manner.[116]

The dispersal of administrative functions among county agencies is demonstrated more effectively, perhaps, in the issuance of licenses and permits which furnish a source of revenue for both the state and the county. The county auditor has issued, collected, and accounted for dog licenses from 1917 to the present;[117] he has issued and the treasurer has collected the fees from cigarette (1893—),[118] malt (1933—),[119] peddlers' (1862—),[120] and show licenses (1827—).[121] Hunting and fishing licenses have been issued by the clerk of courts since 1904 and 1919 respectively.[122]

---

112. *Laws of Ohio*, XXV, 25.
113. G. C. secs. 5338, 5341, 5345, 5348-11.
114. G. C. sec. 5894-1 *et seq.*
115. G. C. sec. 6064-42.
116. G. C. sec. 5545 *et seq.*
117. *Laws of Ohio*, CVII, 534.
118. Jay F. Laning, comp., *Revised Statutes of the State of Ohio* (Norwalk, 1905), 1513.
119. G. C. sec. 5545-5 *et seq.*
120. Sayler, *op. cit.,* 273; *Laws of Ohio,* LIX, 67-68; G. C. sec. 6347.
121. Chase, *op. cit.,* III, 1582; G. C. secs. 6374, 6375.
122. *Laws of Ohio,* XCVII, 474; G. C. (Page and Adams) sec. 1430.

In addition, the clerk has issued for the court of common pleas, ferry licenses (1805—),[123] auctioneers' licenses (1818—),[124] and peddlers' licenses (1810-1862).[125] Marriage licenses, were issued by the clerk of courts from 1803 to 1851 since the latter date, have been in the jurisdiction of the probate court.[126]

The establishment of the board of trustees of the sinking fund (1919) was a logical development in county fiscal administration. This board, composed of the auditor, treasurer, and prosecuting attorney, has as its principal function the payment of bonds issued by the county and the investment in bonds of moneys credited to the sinking fund. Bonds issued in the process of county borrowing must be recorded in the office of the sinking fund trustees and signed by the auditor, as secretary of the board. The trustees certify to the board of commissioners the rate of tax necessary to provide a sinking fund for the payment of the principal and interest of the bonded indebtedness. The trustees are required to keep a full and complete record of transactions and a complete record of the funded debt of the county.[127]

Elections

During the first nine decades of Ohio history the county sheriff was charged with the duty of announcing the time and place of holding elections, providing ballot boxes, ballots, and other supplies, and the township trustees were directed by law to serve as judges of the election.[128] This system continued, with slight alterations designed to facilitate the conduct of elections in municipal centers until 1892. At that time there were created the offices of state supervisor of elections and deputy state supervisors of elections with duties prescribed for the conduct and supervision of all elections in the state.[129]

---

123. *Laws of Ohio,* III, 96; VIII, 107; XXIX, 447. Ferry licenses were issued by the associate judges 1803-1805. *Ibid.,* I, 94.
124. Chase, *op. cit.,* II, 1040; G. C. secs. 5868, 5869.
125. Chase, *op. cit.,* I, 670.
126. Chase, *op. cit.,* I, 354; *Ohio Const. 1851,* Art. IV, sec. 8.
127. G. C. sec. 2976-18 *et seq.*
128. *Laws of Ohio,* I, 76-77; III, 331-332; VII, 113; XXIX, 44; L, 312.
129. *Laws of Ohio,* LXXXIX, 455. This act, however, did not apply to the election of school directors.

The secretary of state, designated as state supervisor of elections, was authorized and instructed to appoint four deputy supervisors for each county, who, in turn, appointed in all precincts four judges and two clerks of elections.[130]

Under the present election laws, provision is made for a chief election officer, a board of elections in each county, and judges and clerks in each precinct. The board of elections in each county consists of four qualified electors in the county, the members of which are appointed by the secretary of state, two of such members being appointed on the first day of March and the even-numbered years to serve a four-year term.[131] In making appointments to the membership of the board, equal representation is given to the political party polling the highest and next highest number of votes for the office of governor in the last proceeding state election. In this connection provision is made for party recommendations of persons for such appointments.[132]

Under the early election laws the canvassing board was composed of the clerk of court of common pleas and two justices of the peace called by him to his assistance.[133] This practice continued until 1892 when the board of state supervisors of elections succeeded to the duties formally performed by both the clerk of the court of common pleas and the county sheriff. The sheriff, however, continued to announce the time and place of holding elections in the county until January 1, 1930 when the board of elections assumed this historic duty.[134] The duty of canvassing the returns, under the present statutes, is performed by the board of elections. The board in each county is required, within five days after each general or special election, to canvas the returns, and to prepare abstracts of the votes cast.[135]

---

130. *Laws of Ohio*, LXXXIX, 455. In 1870, each township, exclusive of the territory embraced within the limits of a municipal corporation which was divided into wards, composed an election precinct. *See Ibid.*, LXVII, 47. An act of 1891 provided for the division of precincts in which 500 or more votes had been polled. *Ibid.*, LXXVIII, 464.
131. G. C. secs. 4785-6, 4785-8, *See also* p. 204.
132. G. C. sec. 4785-9. Under the Ohio election law, it is the duty of the secretary of state to appoint persons so recommended, unless he has reason to believe that such a person would not be a competent member of the board.
133. *Laws of Ohio*, I, 83; III, 336-337; VII, 119-120; XXIX, 49; L, 316; LXI, 68; LXXXII, 30.
134. G. C. sec. 4785-5; *Laws of Ohio*, LXXXIX, 455; CXIII, 307. The election laws of Ohio were revised and recodified by an act of the general assembly, passed April 5, 1929. *Laws of Ohio*, CXIII, 307-413.
135. G. C. secs. 4785-152, 4785-153.

A certified copy of the abstract is to be transmitted to the secretary of state, and another copy filed in the office of the board.[136] The board is required also to prepare and transmit to the president of the senate a separate abstract of the returns of election of governor, lieutenant governor, secretary of state, auditor of state, and attorney general.[137]

Health

Prior to 1919 the county had few responsibilities regarding health administration. With the development of urban centers with congested areas the problem of health administration was brought to the attention of the legislature. Prior to the enactment of the present health code in 1919, jurisdiction in matters of health was vested in the cities, villages, and townships. Under the act of 1919, all villages and townships in the county were combined into a general health district under the supervision of a county board appointed by the advisory council composed of the mayors of villages and chairmen of township trustees. Each city in the district is organized as a separate health district. Two general health districts or a general health district and a city health district located within such a district may be combined.[138] All physicians are required to report communicable diseases to the district health commissioners who impose quarantines.[139]

The legislature has placed on the county the burden of responsibility in the treatment of tuberculosis. Any county, regardless of its size, may employ nurses, operate clinics, and care for patients in private, municipal, or county sanatoriums. Any county having a population of 50,000 or more inhabitants may, with the consent of the state department of health, erect and operate sanatoriums, and two or more counties may form districts for the same purpose. The sanatoriums are operated by the county commissioners or special boards appointed by the county commissioners.[140]

---

136. G. C. sec. 4785-153.
137. *Ohio Const. 1851*, Art. III, sec. 3; G. C. sec. 4785-154.
138. *Laws of Ohio*, CVIII, pt. i, 238; CVIII, pt. ii, 1085-86.
139. *Ibid.*, CVIII, pt. ii, 1088-89.
140. G. C. secs. 3148-1 - 3148-3. *See* p. 1.

Besides establishing sanatoriums for the treatment of tubercular patients, counties are authorized to operate general hospitals. Evidence seems to indicate that the county is the proper unit for hospital administration.

Public Welfare

The administration of public welfare is one of the most complex and one of the most expensive functions of county government. The administration of institutional and outdoor relief is delegated to eight boards and commissions operating independently with little regard for efficiency.

The administration of the county home is vested in the county commissioners and a superintendent appointed from a list of names of persons eligible under civil service regulations. Employees are appointed by the superintendent.[141]

Although provision was made for the institutional care of the county's indigent as early as 1816, it was not until after the conclusion of the War between the States when hundreds of Ohio children were left homeless, that the legislature enacted measures for the care of dependent children.[142] Prior to the act of 1865, the trustees of the poorhouses were authorized to apprentice dependent children.

The board of county visitors, an agency for the examination of county institutions, was created by the general assembly in 1882. Until 1906 the board was appointed by the court of common pleas and after that date by the probate judge.[143] The board consists of six persons appointed for terms of three years.

In 1886 counties were required by law to provide relief for indigent soldiers and sailors and their indigent wives, children, and parents.[144] Soldiers' relief is administered by a commission consisting of three persons appointed by the court of common pleas for terms of three years. This commission, in turn, selects township and ward committees.[145]

---

141. G. C. secs. 2522, 2523.
142. *Laws of Ohio,* III, 276; VIII, 223-224.
143. *Ibid.,* LXXIX, 107; XCVIII, 28; G. C. sec. 2971.
144. *Laws of Ohio,* LXXXIII, 232-234.
145. G. C. secs. 2930, 2933.

In 1884 the legislature made provision for a soldiers' burial committee in each county.[146] The administration of soldiers' burials is vested in a committee consisting of two persons in each township and ward appointed by the county commissioners.[147]

Counties maintain a system of pensions for the needy blind. Prior to 1936, blind relief was administered in the county by the probate judge (1904-1908), by a blind relief commission appointed by the probate judge (1908-1913), and by the county commissioners (1913-1936).[148] The present system originated in 1936 when the legislature accepted the provisions of the Federal Social Security Act. Blind relief is financed by federal, state, and local funds and is administered in the state by the Ohio Commission for the Blind and in the county by the county commissioners, whose decisions are subject to review by the Ohio Commission for the Blind.[149]

Prior to 1932 the county confined its relief activities to the institutional care of the indigent. Outdoor relief, except for those persons lacking a legal settlement, was provided and administered by the townships and cities. With the coming of the economic depression the resources of the municipalities and townships proved inadequate for financing relief activities. Accordingly, in 1932, the legislature conferred on all counties the authority to care for the poor in their own homes. Funds for such purposes were provided by the issuance of bonds and by a diversion of gasoline taxes for financing such services. While the State Relief Commission, created for administering state relief, is required to pass upon local relief budgets, the county relief offices, administered by the county commissioners, provided relief services in the county.

Today old age pensions are relieving the counties of the increased burdens of institutional relief. This system, originating in 1933, provides for persons 65 or more years of age. No persons may be granted a pension if the net value of his property is in excess of $3000 or his annual income is in excess of $480.[150]

---

146. *Laws of Ohio*, LXXXI, 146-147.
147. G. C. sec. 2850.
148. *Laws of Ohio*, XCVII, 392-394; XCIX, 56-58; CIII, 60.
149. *Ibid.*, CXVI, pt. ii, 195-200.
150. *Ibid.*, CXV, pt. ii, 431-439; CXVI, pt. ii, 86-88, 216-221; G. C. sec. 1359-2.

The old age pension system is financed by state and federal funds and is administered by a division of the department of public welfare through county boards of aid for the aged.[151] Under the provision of the initial act the county commissioner served as *ex-officio* members of the board of aid for the aged in the county. Since May 1, 1937 the chief of the division has been required by law to appoint an advisory board in each county consisting of five members. This board, appointed for a two-year term, succeeded to the duties formerly performed by the county commissioners.[152]

Aid to dependent children, although provided by the legislature in 1913 in the form of mothers' pensions, assumed a new significance, when, in 1936, the legislature accepted the provisions of the Federal Social Security Act. Aid to dependent children is financed by federal, state, and local funds. The administration of the act in the state is delegated to the department of public welfare and in Geauga County to the probate judge serving as juvenile judge.[153]

Public Works

The responsibility for the administration of public works in the county rests with the board of county commissioners, the county engineer, and the sanitary engineer. The county commissioners, since the inauguration of county government, have had the responsibility for the authorization and financing of public works. With the immense development of highway improvement, occasioned by the introduction of automobiles and trucks as means of transportation, public works became one of the most important functions of the county commissioners and consequently the county engineer, who, during the first 120 years of this office, had as his principal duty the surveying of lands, received new duties and responsibilities with respect to the construction of roads, culverts, ditches, and in most cases bridges.[154]

---

151. *Laws of Ohio,* CXV, pt. ii, 431-439.
152. G. C. sec. 1359-12. *See also* p. 233.
153. *Laws of Ohio,* CXVI, pt. ii, 188-196.
154. *Ibid.,* XCVIII, 245-247; CVIII, pt. i, 497.

Within the last two decades the township roads, under the joint authority of the county and township trustees, have been gradually absorbed by the county-state system of highways.[155]

The Ohio counties were formed to meet the needs of rural pioneer communities with a population spread relatively uniformly over the entire state. Recent decades have brought remarkable changes. Many sections of the state have become thoroughly industrialized, and, as a result of the change, have been forced to deal with such problems as housing, health, sanitation, police administration, scientific transportation, and sewage disposal. These problems with which the county organization has been unable to cope are rapidly taking the form of city problems.

When it is considered that in 1930, of the 1,217,250 persons in Cuyahoga County 878,336 were in Cleveland, of the 388,712 people in Franklin County 306,087 were in Columbus, of the 621,987 people in Hamilton County 455,610 were in Cincinnati, and of the 344,333 people in Lucas County 282,349 were in Toledo, it is not strange that demands were made for a reorganization of county government to eliminate the waste and confusion occasioned by overlapping jurisdiction of county and municipal functions.[156]

In view of the growth of large cities and the confusion occasioned by the conflict of county and municipal powers, there has been an attempt to work out a more satisfactory relationship between the two organs of local government. This took the form of a constitutional amendment, which, defeated in 1919, was placed on the ballot in 1933 by initiative petition and adopted by the electorate. The amendment provides:

---

155. The centralization of highway construction was guaranteed under the road law of 1915. The township trustees, at one time one of the most important agencies in local highway construction, have become a local improvement board with powers to authorize but not to supervise road construction. *Laws of Ohio*, CVI, 589-594.

156. U.S. Bureau of the Census, *16th Census of the United States, 1940, Population, First Series, Number of Inhabitants, Ohio*, 8-10. C. A. Dykstra, "Cleveland's Effort for City-County consolidation," *Nat. Mun, Review*, VIII, (1919), 551-556.

"The General Assembly shall provide by general law for the organization and government of counties, and may provide by general law alternative forms of government. No alternative form shall become operative in any county until submitted to the electors thereof and approved by a majority of those voting thereon under regulations provided by law. Municipalities and townships shall have authority, with the consent of the county, to transfer to the county any of their powers or to revoke the transfer of any such power, under regulations provided by general law, but the rights of initiative and referendum shall be secured to . . . every major . . . giving or withdrawing such consent."[157]

The arguments advanced in favor of the system fall under three heads:
1.   It makes possible a different form of government for urban centers where political, social, and economic conditions differ from those of rural counties.
2.   It promotes efficiency and economy by the elimination of duplicate officers and employees.
3.   It promotes efficiency by the centralization of power and responsibility.[158]

A commission on county government was appointed by Governor White in 1933 to formulate optional plans of county government for submission to the legislature.[159] Accordingly, in 1935, the commission submitted to the legislature 10 bills embodying its recommendations as to matters of county reorganization. The major bills authorized three optional forms of county government, subject to the adoption by local electorate (1) a county manager plan, (2) the elective plan, (3) the appointive executive plan.[160]

---

157. *Ohio Const. 1851,* (Amendment, adopted November 7, 1933), Art. X, sec. 1.
158. *Ohio State Journal,* October 9, 1933; Dykstra, *loc, cit.*
159. R. C. Atkinson, "County Home Rural Developments in Ohio," *Nat. Mun. Review,* XXIII, (1934), 235.
160. R. C. Atkinson, "Ohio– Optional County Legislation," *Nat. Mun. Review,* XXIV, (1935), 228.

Of the 10 bills presented, two became laws. One of these authorized the transfer to the county of any local governmental activity by voluntary agreement between the county and a local subdivision within the county. This measure, of course, opened the way for the consolidation of such activities as welfare, police, and sewer construction which need unification in counties having a large urban population.[161] The other act authorized the charter county to take over health administration, noninstitutional relief, and park construction.[162]

While the amendment offers an opportunity for the improvement of local government in counties in which large municipalities have developed, no use has been made of the provision.[163] At present Franklin County with a population of 388,712 has essentially the same type of county government as Vinton County with a population of 11,573.[164]

While unsuccessful attempts have been made to correct some of the defects of county administration in areas containing large urban populations, little consideration has been given to rural counties where, due to a constant decline in population, the old governmental organization has become unduly expensive and ill-suited to the needs of the population. This is particularly true in the counties located in the southeastern and northwestern portions of the state where the population has steadily declined since 1880. There is a question whether the services of modern government in such counties can continue to be maintained without the consolidation of contiguous territory for purposes of administration. The state constitution, from its beginning in 1802, has contained a restriction upon the legislature regarding the minimum area of counties. None could be formed with less than 400 square miles – or reduced below that size.[165]

---

161. *Laws of Ohio,* CXVI, 102-104.

162. *Ibid.,* CXVI, 132-135.

163. Home rule charters were submitted to the voters in Hamilton, Cuyahoga, Lucas, and Franklin Counties. Advocates of home rule attributed the defeat of these measures to politicians who saw in the scheme the destruction of the spoils system. *See* R. C. Atkinson, "Ohio– County Charter Elections," *Nat. Mun. Review,* XXIV, (1935), 702-703.

164. U.S. Bureau of the Census, *16th Census of the United States, 1940, Population, First Series, Number of Inhabitants, Ohio,* 4-5.

165. *Ohio Const. 1802,* Art. VII, sec. 3; *Ohio Const. 1851,* Art. II, sec. 30.

The minimum size now should be much larger. For with the development of modern means of transportation and communication this area of 400 square miles has become ridiculously small. The combination for administrative purposes of sparsely populated counties, having social and economic interests would eliminate waste, overhead, and duplication of personnel.

Governmental service is constantly requiring the employment of better trained officials. Evidence seems to indicate that only by enlarging the size of the administrative area to make possible the specialization and work can the requisite degree of training and skill be secured in the performance of public service.[166]

The relation of the county to the state is also a matter of importance. As a result of radical changes in economic life, matters which were at one time a purely local interest and concern had become of statewide importance. During recent years the old type of county organization has proved inadequate to meet the needs of modern civilization. Recognition of this fact is found in the steady growth of state control of such matters as public accounting, health and welfare administration, and law enforcement.

At the same time the county has definitely supplanted the township as the administrative unit. This is particularly noticeable in the substitution of the general health district for which the township district, and the transfer of tax assessment from the township assessors to the county auditor. The county-state administration of highway maintenance and public welfare has been affected. Although many deplore the passing of the little red schoolhouse, the substitution of the county school district for the township area has resulted in better educational advantages for children residing in rural areas.

It is significant that modern invention has removed the necessity for the rural administrative units of such small proportions. The transfer of power from the smaller to the larger unit has arisen out of the desire for better service and economy. Little remains to justify the retention of the township.

---

166. Cf. H. Eliot Kaplan, "A Personal Program for County Service," *Nat. Mun. Review*, XXV, (1936), 596-600.

Records System

It has been the duty of most officials since the beginning of county government to keep a record of the business of their offices. Differences in population between counties however, forced a wide variance in the recording as evidenced by the fact that several types of records were kept in the same book in some counties, and in others were kept in separate books. As indicated in detail in the office essays, preceding the record of each office, the legislature eventually prescribed not only what records were to be kept but also the content. In this field there was a remarkable advance following the adoption of the constitution of 1851. Such legislation assured some uniformity in the county records system.

There are three clerical officers whose work consists mainly in the preparation and custody of records: the recorder, clerk of courts, and judge of probate court. All three have some part in the recording documents and instruments affecting the title of property and of other documents presented for record. The last two have as a principal duty the keeping of court records; the clerk of courts serves as clerk of both the court of common pleas and the court of appeals, and the probate court keeps its own records.

It is the duty of the county recorder to copy, index, and file documents authorized to be recorded in his office. The system of recording is prescribed in detail by law. In most counties recording is done by typewriter with considerable use of printed forms. The photographic method of copying is in use in Clark, Cuyahoga, Hamilton, Lucas, Montgomery, and Summit Counties. Deeds, mortgages, plats, and leases must be copied into separate books, and indexed by direct and reverse indexes.[167] The recorder is required, also, to prepare daily an alphabetical index to such instruments.[168]

The principal records of the clerk of courts are prescribed by statute. They include an appearance docket, a trial docket, an execution docket, a journal, and a complete record of proceedings, a system of indexes, and a file of original papers.[169]

---

167. G. C. secs. 2757, 2764.
168. G. C. secs. 2764, 2766.
169. G. C. secs. 2878, 2884, 2885.

The clerk is responsible for a variety of non-judicial records work of which the filing and indexing of automobile bills of sale was the major item. The bill of sale law was repealed by an act effective January 1, 1938, requiring the clerk to issue certificates of title to motor vehicles in triplicate and to file a duplicate of the certificate.[170] At present the clerk of courts may act as the agent of the state for the sale of hunting, trapping, and fishing licenses.[171] He also issues auctioneer's and ferry licenses.[172]

The office of the probate court performs the following clerical services: the recording of miscellaneous instruments, including marriage licenses[173] and certificates of physicians, surgeons, and nurses which authorize them to practice their professions in the state.[174] The court record system of the office originating in 1853 and continued by the probate code of 1931, is prescribed by statute and involves the proper keeping of papers in each case and copying materials in appropriate record books.[175]

Few records are prescribed for the law-enforcement agencies. The county sheriff is required by law to keep at least three books: a foreign execution docket,[176] a cashbook,[177] and a jail register.[178] Indexes, direct and reverse, to the foreign execution docket were prescribed in 1925.[179] The system of recording is prescribed by statute. The county coroner's records consist of two: a report of findings in cases of unlawful death,[180] and inventory of articles found on or about the body of the deceased.[181] Such records are required by law and the contents of the records minutely prescribed.

---

170. G. C. sec. 6290-6.
171. G. C. secs. 1430, 1432.
172. G. C. secs. 5868-5869, 5947-5950.
173. *Ohio Const. 1851,* Art. Iv, sec. 8.
174. *Laws of Ohio,* XCII, 45-47; XCIX, 499; CVI, 192.
175. *Laws of Ohio,* CXIV, 321-322.
176. G. C. sec. 2837.
177. G. C. sec. 2839.
178. *Laws of Ohio,* XLI, 74; G. C. sec. 3158.
179. *Laws of Ohio,* CXI, 31.
180. G. C. sec. 2857.
181. G. C. sec. 2859.

The number and type of records kept by the prosecuting attorney in the different counties of the state vary widely. In some counties the records of the prosecuting attorney are kept on standard forms and include such records as a grand jury docket, grand jury testimony record, and a criminal court docket. In Geauga County the grand jury records are kept by the county clerk of courts. The prosecuting attorney, however, as in many counties of the state, keeps no records or files and individual memoranda are disposed of by the incumbent. Since the prosecuting attorney is vested with large discretionary powers, there is need of a special records and files. Such records according to authorities on judicial administration should include, among others, a permanent record of the names and addresses of witnesses, the deputy or division handling the case, and the reason for failure to prosecute, and the reason for which a *nolle prosequi* was asked and granted.

The records of the financial agencies of the county government are prescribed by statute. Although records were kept in the earlier years, it was not until 1902 that the manner of keeping and the content of such records attracted the attention of the legislature. It was evident that accounts had not only been poorly kept but there had been little uniformity among the counties of the state. Accordingly, in 1902, the legislature enacted the most important and far-reaching laws on the subject. This act provided for a uniform system of accounting, auditing, and reporting, under the supervision of a newly created bureau of inspection located in the office of the auditor of state. The act further provided for the annual examination of the finances of all public offices.[182]

The governor's commission on the reorganization of county government, after studying the county records system and noting the illogical combination of administrative, judicial, and financial functions, made the following recommendations:[183]

    1.   County charters and optional forms of government should provide for a department of records and court service to take over the functions of the recorder and clerk of courts, the nonjudicial record work of the probate court, and the functions of the sheriff as a court officer.

---

182. *Laws of Ohio*, XCV, 511-515.
183. *Report of Governor's Commission*, 186-187. *See also* R. E. Heiges, *The Office of Sheriff in the Rural Counties of Ohio* (Findlay, 1933), 55-56, 60-61.

2.   The issuance of licenses should be transferred from the clerk of courts to the department of finance.

3.   Wider use should be made of the photographic process of recording in large counties.

4.   Legislation should be adopted permitting the destruction of chattel mortgages and automobile bills of sale after they have ceased to have effect.

5.   The requirement of three systems of indexes of cases in the clerk's office should be eliminated from the code and only the index of pending suits and living judgments should be required.

6.   Provisions should be made in the rules of the common pleas court for service of process by mail and that method should be brought into general use.

Concurrently with the development of a record system, steps were taken to assure the proper restoration of damaged or dilapidated records treating of lands and surveys. The county engineer, when directed by the county commissioners, is required by law to transcribe any and all dilapidated maps and the records of plats and field notes of surveys from the records of the court of common pleas, auditor, recorder, or other officers in the state where they may be procured.[184] Similarly the county recorder when authorized by the county commissioners, is required to transcribe from the records of the counties all deeds, mortgages, powers of attorneys, and other instruments of writing, for the sale, conveyance, or encumbrance of lands, tenements, or hereditaments situated within his county.[185]

The large accumulation of county records occasioned by increasing governmental service, presents a serious problem. It is important, on the one hand, that valuable space in county courthouses and other county depositories be not cluttered up with vast quantities of useless materials. On the other hand, it is more important that every precaution be taken to prevent public officials from destroying valuable public records in order to make space for current business.

---

184. G. C. sec. 2804.
185. G. C. sec. 2763.

Within recent years photography has become an increasingly important aid in archival administration. The Ohio legislature, following the modern trends in recording, has enacted measures looking forward to the conservation of space in the county courthouses by permitting county officials to destroy records which have been reproduced photographically. Under this act, passed in 1937, any county official charged with keeping public records may, when the space requires it, have such records copied or reproduced by any photographic process and destroy the original papers. The original records, however, must be preserved until the time for filing legal proceedings based upon the documents shall have elapsed.[186]

While the legislature has attempted to enact legislation looking forward to the conservation of much needed space in county courthouses a significant trend is to be observed in the increasing interest which is being displayed for a department of county archives where all noncurrent records may be properly housed, classified, listed, and made more readily accessible to those interested in consulting them. The arguments advanced in favor of such a system are: (1) that the preservation of county records should be viewed as a distinct function of county government, (2) that the administration of county archives should be under the direction of those qualified to serve efficiently and effectively both the needs of the administration and historians, (3) that the construction of county archives buildings for noncurrent records would make available more space for current business, which, at present, is seriously curtailed.

In the field of archival administration the state, rather than the county, has been the experimental laboratory and the results have been eminently successful.[187]

---

186. G. C. sec. 32-1.
187. For an interesting and informative article on the administration of state archives, *see* Charles M. Gates, "The Administration of State Archives," *The Pacific Northwest Quarterly,* XXIX, (January 1938), No. 1; also in *The American Archivist,* I (July 1938), 130-141.

The first county building in Geauga County was a combination courthouse and jail built of logs, in the village of Chardon, by contract between the county commissioners and Abraham Skinner. Construction was begun in March 1806 and completed in June 1807.[1]

By 1813, this building proved to be inadequate, so the county commissioners entered into a contract with Samuel King to build a jail and courthouse "on the town plat of Chardon on lots Nos. 27 and 28," for the sum of $600.[2] Completed in March 1814, the building was two stories high and of wooden frame construction. It was destroyed by fire on July 25, 1868.

On May 18, 1869, plans were approved for the present courthouse, which stands on the village square in Chardon. This building was constructed of brick and concrete at the cost of $70,000 and was completed August 20, 1870.[3] The architect was Joseph Ireland, while the construction was under the supervision of L. J. Randall.

The present jail in Geauga County was built in 1869 and is located at 221 Main Street, Chardon, Ohio. Due to a well-managed maintenance policy, the jail is kept in a relatively good condition. It contains six cells and the sheriff's office, the latter serving as a depository for some of the county jail records.

County Commissioners. The commissioner's office is located along the south wall of the second floor, and consists of one room. Bound records are kept on steel shelves, unbound records are kept in steel file drawers, located along the north and east walls of the auditor's office and current records of aid for the blind are located in the probate judge's office. Aid for the aged records are housed in the commissioners' office. Ventilation and both natural and electric lighting facilities are good. The office is crowded, with no room for expansion. The records number 30 volumes, 5 file drawers, 2 file boxes, and 3 file folders.

Relief Administration. The relief welfare office is located in the northwest corner of the third floor, and consists of three rooms, numbered one, two, three. It contains no bound volumes. Unbound records are kept in room numbered 1, in steel file drawers located along the east wall. These offices have good ventilation and lighting, are not crowded, and have room for expansion. Records number 6 file drawers, and 1 file box.

---

1. Commissioners' journal, I (1806-1864), 10, *See* entry 1.
2. *Ibid.,* 88.
3. Record of Proceedings of Commissioners, I (1865-1879), 39, *See* entry 1.

Recorder. The recorder's office is located in the southwest corner of the first floor. Bound records are kept on steel shelves, located along the south and east walls. Unbound records are kept in steel file drawers, located along the north wall. The recorder's private office is located north of the main office. Bound records are kept on steel shelves, located along the east wall. Unbound records are kept on steel shelves, located along the north wall. Lighting and ventilation facilities for both rooms are good, but they are crowded, and there is no room for expansion. The records number 325 volumes, 82 file drawers, and 1 file box.

Clerk of Courts. The department of the clerk of courts is located on the second and third floor of the courthouse. His office is located in the southeast corner of the second floor. Bound records are kept on steel shelves, located along the north and east walls, while the unbound records are kept in steel file drawers, located along the south and west walls. The clerk of courts also has records housed in the third floor storeroom, and in the attic. The certificate of title office is located in the southwest corner of the third floor. Bound records are kept on steel shelves, located along the north wall, while unbound records are kept in steel file drawers, located along the east wall. Ventilation and lighting for each office are good, but the rooms are crowded, with no room for expansion. The records number 339 volumes, 194 file drawers, 263 file boxes, 1 bundle, 1 file folder, 1 wooden box, and 2 pads.

Court of Common Pleas. Records for this court are housed in the clerk of courts' office, in the third floor storeroom, and in the attic. The records number 363 volumes, 3 shelves, 4 wooden boxes, and 38 booklets.

Supreme Court. The records for this court are housed and a clerk of courts' office, and number 9 volumes.

Court of Appeals. This includes district court and circuit court, the records of which are housed in the clerk of courts' office. The records number 20 volumes.

Probate Court. The probate court is located on the northwest side of the first floor, and consists of three rooms. The probate office is located north of the recorder's private office. Bound records are kept on steel shelves, located along the south and east walls, while unbound records are kept in steel filed drawers, located along the north wall. The office and court room of the probate judge is located north of the probate office. The juvenile probation officer who is also investigator for aid to dependent children and aid for the blind is located in the east end of the office and court room and records are housed in steel file cases on south wall. The probate storeroom is located north of the probate judge's office and court room. Bound records are kept on steel shelves, located along the north and west walls, while unbound records are kept on steel shelves and in steel file drawers, located along the east wall. Ventilation and lighting for these rooms are good, while ventilation and lighting in the storage room are unsatisfactory. All rooms are overcrowded at present. The records number 335 volumes, 392 file boxes, and 2 shelves.

Juvenile Court. The records for this court are housed in the probate office. The records number 7 volumes and 2 loose leaf folders.

Aid to Dependent Children. These records are housed in the probate judge's office and courtroom. Records number 3 file drawers.

Jury Commissioners. These records are housed in the court of common pleas witness room. The records number 2 volumes and 1 file drawer.

Grand Jury. The grand jury keeps no separate records.

Petit Jury. The petit jury keeps no separate records.

Prosecuting Attorney. The prosecutor has no separate office, so no separate records are kept.

Coroner. Permanent records of the coroner are filed in the clerk of courts' office and the sheriff's office, 221 Main Street, Chardon, Ohio. The records number 2 volumes.

Sheriff. The sheriff's office is located at 221 Main Street, Chardon, Ohio, and consists of one room. Bound records are kept on steel shelves, located along the east wall. There are no unbound records kept by the sheriff. Some of the sheriff's records are also housed in the clerk of courts office. Ventilation and lighting are good, but the office is crowded, with no room for expansion. The records number 36 volumes.

Dog Warden. Since the dog warden has no separate office, no separate records are kept.

Auditor. The auditor's office is located in the southeast corner of the first floor of the courthouse, and contains two rooms. Bound records are kept on steel shelves, located along the north and west walls. Unbound records are kept in steel file drawers located along the east wall. The auditor's office also houses records of the commissioners. The auditor also has records stored in the basement storeroom, the third floor storeroom, and the attic. The auditor's private office is located north of the main office. Current records are housed here. Ventilation and lighting for the two offices are good, but they are crowded, with no room for expansion. The records number 1,411 volumes, 72 file drawers, 24 file boxes, 86 bundles, 8 cardboard boxes, 35 abstracts, 118 envelopes, 9 folders, 3 cartons, and 2,000 warrants.

Treasurer. The county treasurer's office is located on the east side of the first floor and consists of one room and a vault. The treasurer's office is located south of the engineer's office. Bound records are kept on steel shelves, located along the north and east walls. Unbound records are kept in steel file drawers, located along south wall. The treasurer also has records housed in the basement storeroom, in the third floor storeroom and in the attic. The vault is located south of the treasurer's office. Bound records are kept on steel shelves, located along the south and east walls, while unbound records are kept in steel file drawers located along the west wall. It is constructed of fireproof steel. Ventilation and lighting for the offices are good, but the office and vault are crowded, with no room for expansion. The records number 286 volumes, 1 file drawer, 1 file box, 179 bundles, 10 cardboard boxes, 53 folders, 1 box, and 2 pigeon holes.

Budget Commissioners. Records are housed in the auditor's office and number 1 volume.

Board of Revision. Records are housed and the auditor's office, and basement storeroom and number 3 volumes.

Board of Trustees of the Sinking Fund. The records are housed in the auditor's office and number 1 volume.

Board of Election. The board of elections office is located in the southeast corner of the third floor and consist of one room. Bound records are kept on steel shelves, located along the east wall, while unbound records are kept in steel file drawers located along the west wall. Ventilation and lighting are good, but the office is crowded, with no room for expansion. The records number 274 volumes, 1 file drawer, 1 bundle, 2 folders, and 48 pigeon holes.

Board of Education. The offices are located in the southwest corner of the second floor and consists of two rooms and a storeroom. The superintendent's office is located in the southwest corner of the second floor, and all records are housed here. Bound records are kept on steel shelves, located along the south wall, while unbound records are kept in steel file drawers, located along the west wall. The board of education office is located north of the superintendent's office. Ventilation and lighting for the two offices are good, but they are crowded, with no room for expansion. The records number 9 volumes and 21 pamphlets.

Board of Health. This office is located at 124 Huntington Street, Chardon, Ohio, and consists of one room. Bound records are housed on top of a steel file cabinet. Unbound records are kept in steel file drawers located along the west wall. Ventilation and lighting are good. The records number 3 volumes, 3 file drawers, and 3 file boxes.

Superintendent of the County Home. The county home office is located 2 ½ miles south of Route 322, in Chardon Township, and consists of one room. Bound records are kept in a steel file cabinet, located along the east wall, while unbound records are kept in steel file cabinet drawers located along the east wall. Ventilation and lighting are good, but the office is crowded, with no room for expansion. The records number 4volumes and 3 file drawers.

Board of County Visitors. No records are kept by the board of county visitors.

Soldiers' Relief Commission. Records are housed at the home of the secretary, Dr. J. W. Moats, 139 North Street, Chardon, Ohio. Records number 2 volumes.

Soldiers' Burial Committee. No records are kept by the soldiers' burial committee.

Blind Relief Commission. No records of blind relief commission located in inventory.

Board of Aid for the Aged. This office is located in the north end of the commissioner's office. All records are housed in steel file drawers on the north wall, and number 4 volumes and 6 file drawers.

County Engineer. The engineer's office is located in the northeast corner of the first floor. Bound records are kept on steel shelves, located along the south and west walls, the unbound records are kept in steel file drawers located along the north wall. Some of the engineer's records are also housed in the auditor's office. The engineer's storeroom is located on the south side of the basement floor. The supplies for the engineer's office are housed here. Lighting and ventilation for the storeroom are inadequate. Lighting and ventilation for the engineer's office are good. Both office and storeroom are crowded, with no room for expansion. Records number 203 volumes, 6 file drawers, 55 file boxes, and 27 sheets.

Agricultural Society. This office is located on the fairgrounds, Burton, Ohio. Bound records are on the office desk. Other records are kept at the home of the secretary, Charles Riley, R. F. D., Burton, Ohio. The office as well lighted and well ventilated. It is not overcrowded at present. Records number 3 volumes and 6 pamphlets.

Agricultural Extension Agent. This office is located in the old Burton High School, Burton, Ohio. Records are kept in steel file drawers, located along the west wall. Ventilation and lighting are good. The office is not overcrowded at present. Records number 7 volumes and 48 file drawers, 26 pamphlets, 7 reports, 1 map, and 4 shelves.

Basement Storeroom. This fireproof storeroom is located on the east side of the basement floor. The records are kept in good condition, although the housing space is very inadequate. Records of the board of revision, the auditor, and the treasurer are housed here. Ventilation and lighting are inadequate. The room is crowded, with no space for expansion. Records number 1122 volumes, 21 file boxes, 39 bundles, 26 abstracts, 13 cardboard boxes, 83 sheets, and 13 booklets.

Third Floor Storerooms. This storage space is located on the east side of the third floor, and consists of three rooms. Records which are stored here are in good condition. Records of the commissioners, clerk of courts, court of common pleas, auditor, and the treasurer are housed here. Ventilation and lighting are inadequate. The rooms are crowded, with no room for expansion. Records number 84 volumes, 1 file drawer, 1 file box, 44 bundles, 63 folders, 1 wooden shelf, 2 cardboard boxes, 9 abstracts, 62 envelopes, 2000 warrants, and 116 pads.

Attic. The attic is on the fourth floor of the courthouse. There is no systematic arrangement for the housing of records, and they are exposed to damage from dust and dampness. Records of the clerk of courts, court of common pleas, auditor, and the treasurer are housed here. Ventilation and lighting are inadequate. The attic is crowded, with no room for expansion. Records number 65 volumes, 8 bundles, 3 boxes, 8 booklets, 4 wooden boxes, 4 cartons, 15 envelopes, 1 folder, 3 cardboard boxes, and 1 sheet.

TANK ROOM

MEN'S TOILET

WOMEN'S TOILET

FURNACE ROOM

COAL ROOM

CORRIDOR

CUSTODIAN'S STOREROOM

STAIRWAY SPACE

BASEMENT STOREROOM

MEN'S TOILET

ENGINEER'S STOREROOM

CUSTODIAN'S STOREROOM

N

SCALE

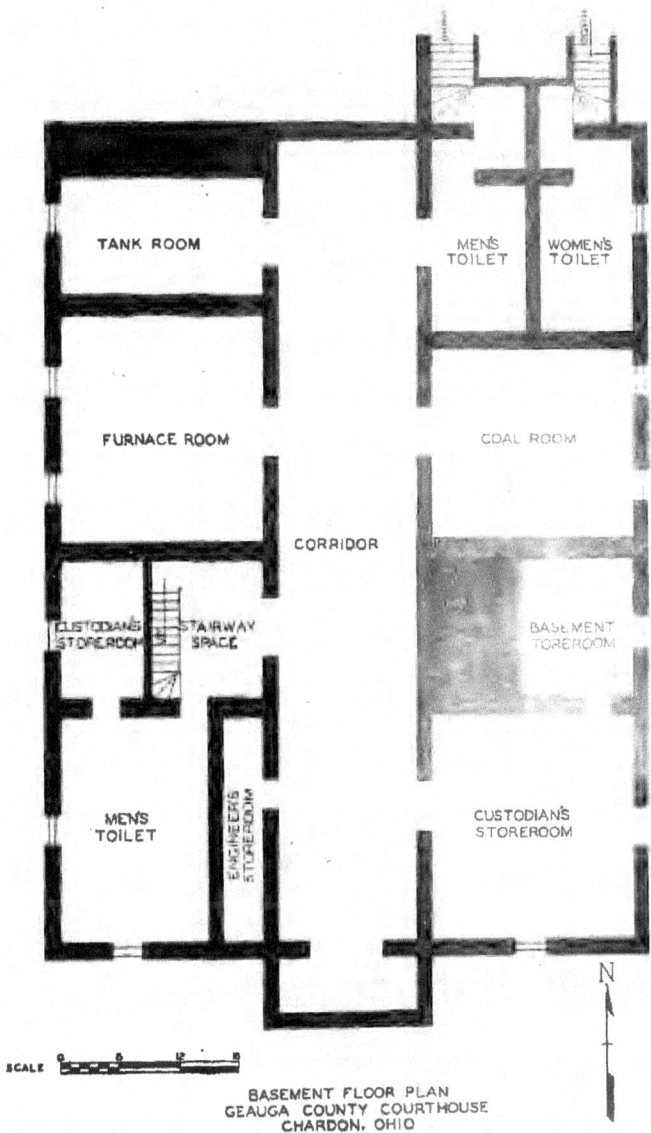

BASEMENT FLOOR PLAN
GEAUGA COUNTY COURTHOUSE
CHARDON, OHIO

WOMEN'S
TOILET

PROBATE
STORE-
ROOM

HALL VESTIBULE

PROBATE JUDGE'S
OFFICE
AND
PROBATE COURT
ROOM

ENGINEER'S
OFFICE

PROBATE
OFFICE

TREASURER'S
OFFICE

RECORDER'S
PRIVATE
OFFICE

CORRIDOR

S
LT

AUDITOR'S
PRIVATE
OFFICE

RECORDER'S
OFFICE

AUDITOR'S
OFFICE

N

SCALE 0 6 12 18

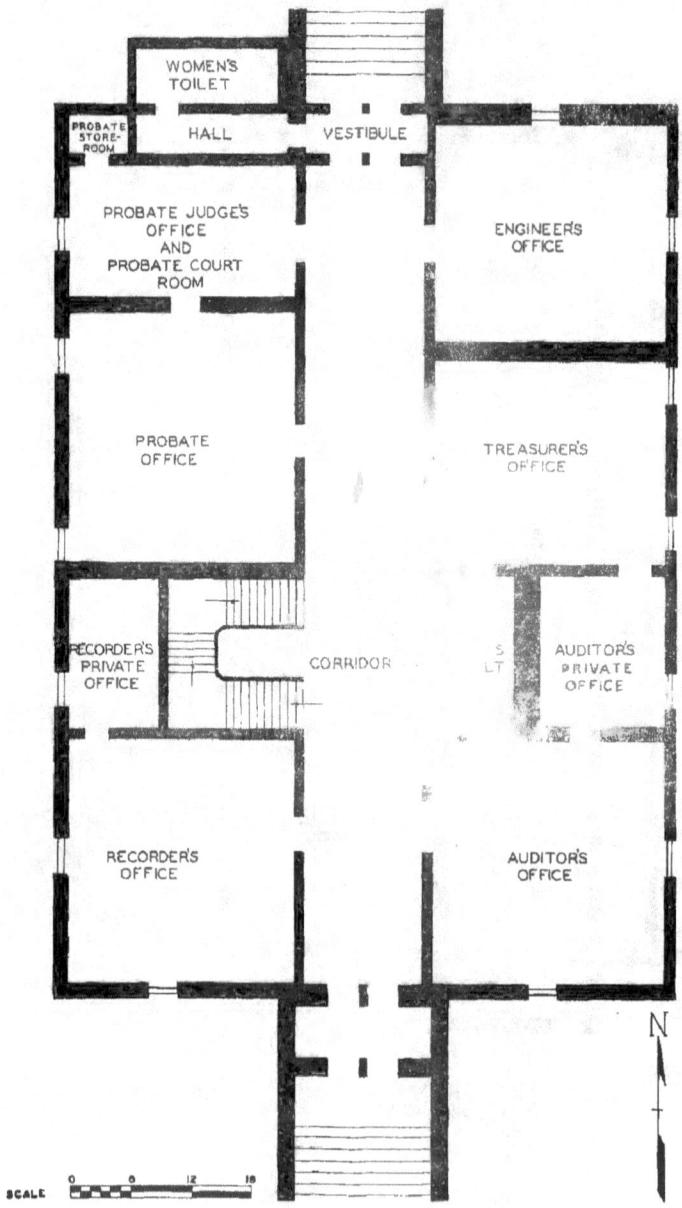

FIRST FLOOR PLAN
GEAUGA COUNTY COURTHOUSE
CHARDON, OHIO

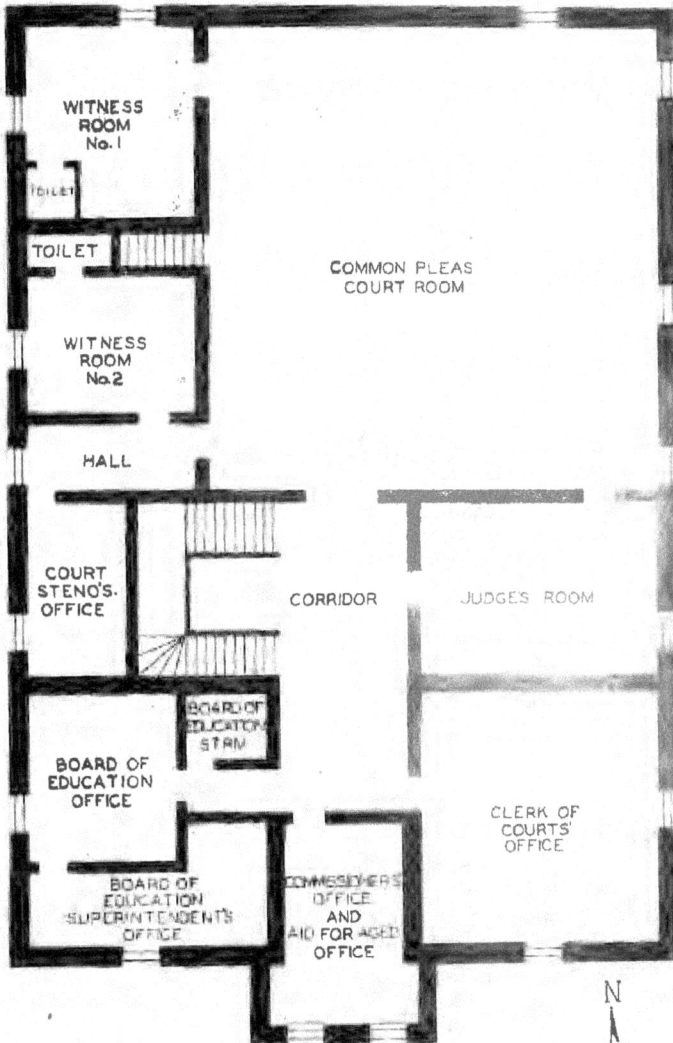

WITNESS ROOM No. 1

TOILET

TOILET

WITNESS ROOM No. 2

HALL

COURT STENO'S. OFFICE

BOARD OF EDUCATION OFFICE

BOARD OF EDUCATION SUPERINTENDENT'S OFFICE

BOARD OF EDUCATION STRM

COMMON PLEAS COURT ROOM

CORRIDOR

JUDGES ROOM

COMMISSIONERS OFFICE AND AID FOR AGED OFFICE

CLERK OF COURTS' OFFICE

N

SCALE 0 6 12 18

SECOND FLOOR PLAN
GEAUGA COUNTY COURTHOUSE
CHARDON, OHIO

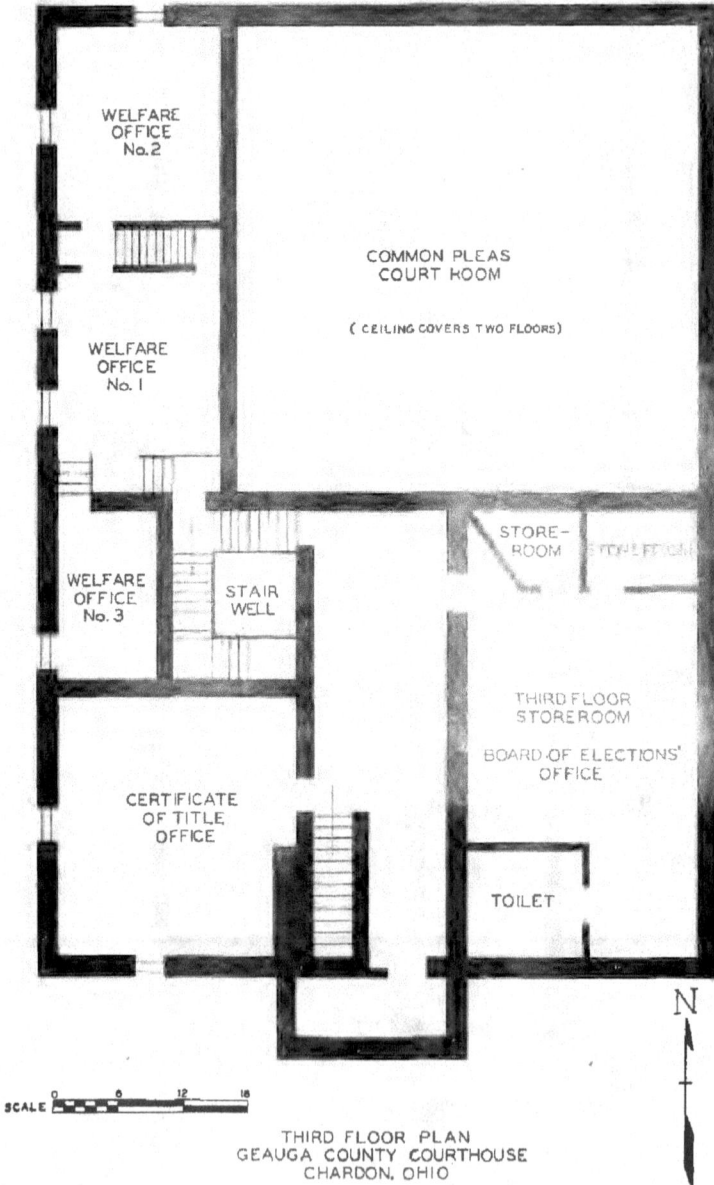

SCALE

THIRD FLOOR PLAN
GEAUGA COUNTY COURTHOUSE
CHARDON, OHIO

ATTIC

STORE ROOM

ROOF SLOPES TO MEET FLOOR ON
EAST AND WEST SIDES

CLOCK
WORKS

N

SCALE

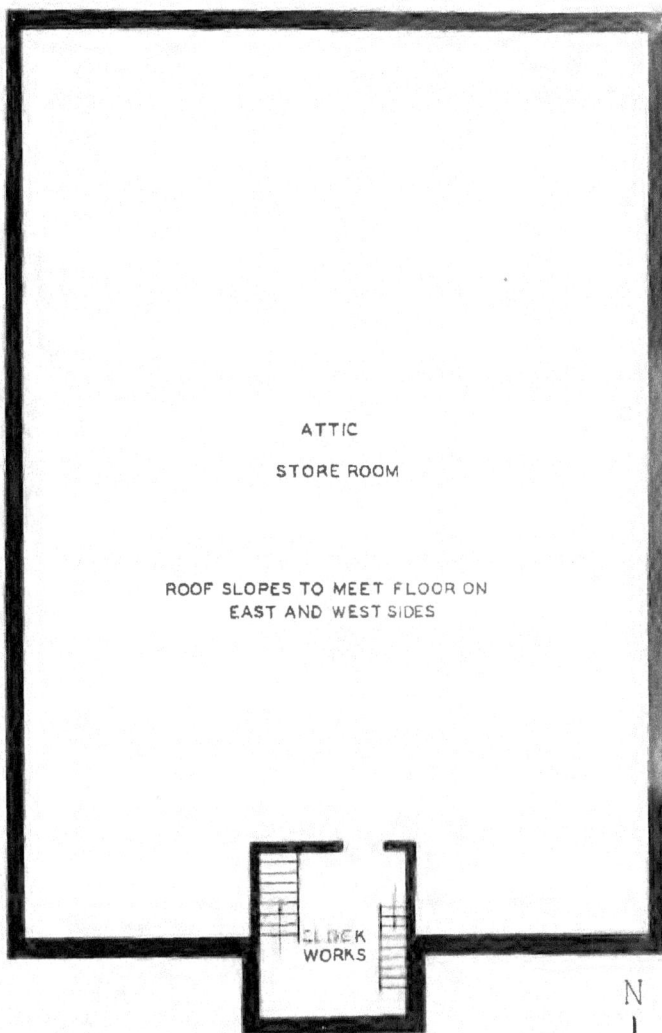

ATTIC FLOOR PLAN
GEAUGA COUNTY COURTHOUSE
CHARDON, OHIO

The governmental system established in 1802, under the first constitution of Ohio, made no provision for the office of county commissioners and its existence is due entirely to statutory enactment. The board, created in 1804, was the successor of the courts of general quarter sessions of the peace, which, during the territorial period, served as the representative agent of the county. The board of county commissioners consisted of three members elected for a three-year term.[1] In 1807 the commissioners were made a corporate body vested with a power to sue and be sued.[2] They were required to keep a record of their proceedings, to levy taxes for the support of the county, appoint a county treasurer, and to supervise the construction of bridges.[3] They were paid on a per diem basis. Moreover, during the early period they were given the task of constructing courthouses, jails, and offices for the clerk of courts, court of common pleas, sheriff, auditor, and treasurer.[4] From 1805 to 1820 the commissioners were required to fix the amounts of tavern and ferry licenses and the rates for transportation by ferry.[5] Of these earlier duties the commissioners retain all but those of fixing the amounts of tavern and ferry licenses and ferriage rates and that of appointing a county treasurer. However, since 1831 they have been authorized to examine and compare the accounts of the county treasurer and to examine the condition of county finances.[6]

Besides the duties regarding county building construction and finance, the commissioners were given the task of constructing local highways when so authorized by the legislature. During the first 30 years of Ohio history the duties of the commissioners in this respect were local in nature, but as the system of road construction expanded they were given the additional duty of converting free turnpikes into state roads.[7] Although many turnpikes were constructed by private companies during the 1840s it was not until 1850 that the legislature authorized incorporation for the purpose.[8] When those companies were caught in the stringency of a financial depression in 1857, the commissioners were authorized to purchase their holdings.

---

1. *Laws of Ohio*, II, 150.
2. *Ibid.*, V, 97.
3. *Ibid.*, VIII, 45.
4. *Ibid.*, II, 154-157; XXIX, 315.
5. *Ibid.*, III, 96; VIII, 107; XVIII, 170.
6. *Ibid.*, XXIX, 291. *See also* G. C. sec. 2644.
7. *Laws of Ohio*, XLVI, 74.
8. *Ibid.*, XLVIII, 49; L, 282.

If such transaction was made, the transfer signed by the president of the company was to be deposited with the county auditor.[9] In 1871 the commissioners, although earlier subjected to regulatory measures by the legislature, were prohibited from levying taxes for roads to exceed three and a half mills on the dollar on the taxable property in the county.[10] Later, in 1885, they were authorized to levy taxes not to exceed five mills on the dollar on all taxable property in the county for the maintenance of roads which had been damaged by excessive wear or were damaged from other causes.[11]

With the development of modern means of transportation, scientific principles were applied to road construction and maintenance. Although the county surveyor, now the county engineer, had in earlier years furnished the commissioners will estimates for bridge construction, it was not until the latter part of the 19th century that they were authorized to utilize his scientific knowledge in road construction.[12] At the beginning of the present century the surveyor was directed to appoint a maintenance engineer, with the consent of the commissioners, to supervise the repairing of improved roads in the county.[13]

Although the county commissioners have never been closely associated with the administration of criminal justice, their duties regarding the construction of county jails qualified them in the earlier period, for additional duties in this respect. During the middle of the 19th century the commissioners of Cuyahoga County were authorized to employ persons on construction work who were confined in the county jails.[14] While this provision was repealed by the criminal code, adopted in 1853, other earlier functions applicable to all counties were continued. Since 1843 the commissioners have provided equipment and fixtures for places of incarceration, food and clothing for prisoners, and have appointed a jail physician.[15] Since 1869 they have been authorized to offer a reward for the detection or apprehension of any person charged with a felony and a county.[16]

---

9. *Ibid.,* LIV, 198
10. *Laws of Ohio,* LXVIII, 117.
11. G. C. sec. 7419.
12. *Laws of Ohio,* LXXXIX, 172; XCVIII, 245-247. *See also* P. 238.
13. *Ibid.,* CVIII, pt. i, 497.
14. *Ibid.,* XXXVII, 54
15. *Ibid.,* XLI, 74; LXXXVII, 186.
16. *Ibid.,* LXVI, 321.

Since 1893 the commissioners in any county where there is no workhouse may, under certain conditions, release or parole an indigent person confined in the jail.[17] With the extension of modern crime into rural areas in the form of small town bank robbing, the commissioners were given the duty of furnishing motorcycles to the sheriff and his deputies in an attempt to compete with a high powered equipment used by modern gangs. One of the latest functions in this respect is the contracting with radio stations for the broadcasting of descriptions of fleeing criminals.[18]

Besides providing for those who have violated the laws, the commissioners were given the duty of caring for persons who, because of poverty or physical or mental defects, became public charges. Thus, county relief for the indigent, one of the most pressing problems of the 20th century, was met in frontier Ohio. As early as 1805 an act, modeled from the territorial law, was passed which was similar in all respects to the poor laws of the 17th century England.[19] Under the early enactments the township trustees were authorized to appoint overseers of the poor. In 1816 the county commissioners were authorized to construct " poor houses" for the care of the county's indigent. As the system developed in succeeding decades the county was made responsible for those who have become permanently disabled, and for paupers who could not be satisfactorily cared for except at the county infirmary, now called the county home. Since 1913 they have been authorized, in any county containing a city which has an infirmary, to contract with the director of public safety for the care of the county's indigent.[20]

The township trustees and officials of municipal corporations were made responsible for providing temporary relief to needy residents of the state, or the county, township, or city. In the event any person became chargeable to a township in which he had not gained legal residence, it was the duty of the overseers, later the township trustees, to remove him to the township where he was legally settled. With slight alterations, the principles of this system continued until the 20th century.[21]

---

17. *Ibid.,* LXXXIX, 408; CXIII, 203.
18. G. C. sec. 2412-1.
19. *Laws of Ohio,* III, 272.
20. G. C. sec. 2419-1.
21. For an excellent study, but biting criticism, of the administration of relief in Ohio prior to 1934 *See* Aileen Elizabeth Kennedy, *The Ohio Poor Law and its Administration* (Sophonsba P. Breckinridge, ed. *Social Service Monographs* No. 22, University of Chicago Press, Chicago, 1934).

Since 1908 the commissioners have been authorized to issue warrants for the relief of the blind in sums varying from $100 to $400 per year.[22] When the blind relief commission was abolished in 1913 its powers and duties were transferred to the county commissioners who were authorized, on evidence furnished by a registered physician or surgeon that the applicant or blind relief might have such disability benefited or removed by medical or surgical treatment, and with the written consent of the patient, to expend all or part of a year's relief allowance for this purpose.[23]

Six years later, in 1919, this allowance for blind relief was raised to $200 a person annually, and the county commissioners were authorized to appoint such clerks as they might deem necessary to investigate applications and to serve at the pleasure of the county commissioners.[24]

In 1927 the maximum benefit for blind relief was increased to $400 a person annually, but in the event both husband and wife being blind and both receiving relief, the total maximum amount for the two was fixed at $600 annually.[25]

In April 1936 the state accepted the provision of the federal social security act approved August 14, 1935, providing federal grants for state aid to the blind, and the legislature designated the Ohio Commission for the Blind the administration agency in the state, and the county commissioners were made the administration agency in the county. The county commissioners were directed to appropriate from the general fund of the county a sum sufficient when supplemented by federal and state grants to provide for the blind a substance "compatible with decency and health," and if they failed to make such appropriations the attorney general was directed to bring *mandamus* proceedings against them.

The act of 1936 as amended in 1941, provides that those entitled to blind relief are persons not less than 18 nor more than 65 years of old, who have lost their site while residents of the state, and who have resided in the state for a period of five years in the nine years immediately preceding application, the last year of which period shall have been continuous. Applications for blind relief are filed with the county commissioners who are required by statute to list such claims in their order of application in books kept for that purpose.

---

22. *See* p. 232.
23. *Laws of Ohio,* CIII, 60.
24. *Ibid.,* CVIII, pt. i, 421, 422.
25. *Laws of Ohio,* CXII, 109.

At least 10 days prior to action on a claim the applicant files a duly certified statement, including a certificate from a registered physician "skilled in diseases of the eye" Stating to what extent the applicant's vision is impaired, and written evidence from two reputable citizens that they know the applicant to be blind and that "he has the qualifications to entitle him to the relief ask." The county commissioners may allow the examining physician a fee not to exceed $3, and may employ an additional physician to examine the applicant. If after such inquiry the county commissioners are satisfied that the applicant is entitled to relieve, they are directed by statute to issue an order for such sum as a board finds necessary, not to exceed forty dollars a month, such sum to be paid monthly from the fund created for that purpose. The ruling of 1913 concerning medical and surgical treatment for applicants remain in effect. Persons whose applications are denied by the county commissioners may appeal to the state department of public welfare which on its own motion may revise any decision of the county commissioners. Both the department of public welfare and the county commissioners have power to issue subpoenas, compel presentation of papers, and examine witnesses.

At least once a year, oftener if directed by the department of public welfare, the county commissioners must examine the qualifications, disabilities, and needs of all persons on the list of the blind, and may increase or decrease the amount of relief according to the budgetary requirements within the limits fixed by law. If the county commissioners remove a name from the list of the blind they are required to notify the county auditor and the department of public welfare as to their action.[26]

The commissioners of Geauga County allowed $1000 in the year 1940 for the relief of the needy blind.[27] Benefits were granted to four clients who received from $10 to $24.50 monthly, according to the needs, which were determined by an investigator appointed by the commissioners.[28]

In addition to furnishing financial aid to the civilian population the commissioners were authorized, in 1886, to levy a tax for the relief of Union soldiers, sailors, or marines of the Civil War, or if such veterans were deceased, for their dependents.[29] In 1919 the provisions of the original act were amended to include all indigent veterans of the World War.[30]

---

26. G. C. secs, 2965-1; 2967; 2967-1; 2967-2; 2968.
27. Commissioners' Journal, General, XI, (1936-1941). 330.
28. *Ibid.,* 386.
29. *Laws of Ohio,* LXXXIII, 232. *See also* p. 2530.
30. *Ibid.,* CVIII, pt. i, 633.

The commissioners were authorized also, in 1884, to defray the funeral expenses of any honorably discharged soldier, sailor, or marine who died indigent. Ten years later the provisions of the act were extended to include the mother, wife, or widow of any soldier, sailor, or marine; and war nurses.[31]

The humanitarian duty of caring for the county's dependent and neglected children was delegated to the county commissioners. Since 1866 they have been authorized to establish and maintain children's homes. At the beginning of the present century, when the treatment of children was undergoing a remarkable change, they were authorized to place dependent and neglected children in private homes or institutions where they would receive food, clothing, and medical and dental treatment.[32] The development of the juvenile court system added new responsibilities. In order to segregate completely juvenile offenders from adults being tried in the regular criminal courts, the commissioners were authorized to provide a separate building, to be known as the "juvenile court."[33]

During the early months of 1932 the governor, aware of the widespread suffering in the state, called the legislature into special session.[35] At this session the legislature authorized him to appoint a state relief commission composed of five members to study the relief situation. This commission was permitted to cooperate with the national, state, or local relief commission, which, in many counties, had been established and was already functioning. Since the county and township treasuries were depleted, on account of the excessive drain caused by the mounting relief load and the steady decline of tax collections, the legislature authorized an excise tax on utilities, for the years 1932-1937, to be used for relief purposes. This state tax was to be allocated to the counties on the basis of population, the tax duplicate, and the value of the utilities property in the county as of 1930. The funds allocated to each county under this act were to be credited to the "county poor relief excise fund."[36]

31. *Ibid.,* XC, 177. *See also* p. 230.
32. *Ibid.,* CIX, 533.
33. *Ibid.,* CXIII, 470.
34. *Ibid.,* CXIV, 11, 12.
35. *See* message of the governor to the eighty-ninth general assembly in *Laws of Ohio,* XCXIV, pt. ii, 6-8.
36. *Laws of Ohio,* CXIV, pt. ii, 19-20.

The county commissioners were authorized to borrow money for emergency relief and evidence such indebtedness by the issuance of negotiable bonds and notes. Upon submission of such resolution to the state tax commission, the commission was directed to estimate the amount which would probably be allocated to the county from the public utility excise taxes and was directed to calculate the total amount of bonds, the principal and interest on which might be paid out of such estimated allocation. The date of maximum maturity of such bonds was to be on or before March 15, 1938. If, in the year 1932, additional funds were needed for poor relief, the county commissioners were authorized, after the state tax commission found that no other funds were available, to issue additional bonds in the amount not exceeding one-tenth of one percent of the general tax list and duplicate of the county. The maturity date of such additional bonds was to be on or before September 15, 1940.[37]

The proceeds of the sale of such bonds were to be placed in a special fund, denominated the "emergency relief fund." No expenditures were to be made from this fund except in accordance with the method and under the uniform regulations prescribed by the state relief commission, and in no case after December 31, 1933. The county commissioners were authorized to distribute, prior to the first of March 1933, portions of the fund to the political subdivisions of the county, according to the needs for poor relief determined by the county and set forth and such an approved budget. The money distributed to the subdivisions was to be expanded in them for poor relief, including the renting of lands and the purchase of seeds for gardening by the unemployed.[38] County poor relief included mothers' pensions, soldiers' relief, temporary assistance to nonresidents, maintenance of a county and a children's home, and work and direct relief. In the townships and municipalities relief was interpreted to be the support of the poor and the burial of persons who died indigent. Each subdivision administering funds under the act was expected to require labor in exchange for relief given to any family in which resided an able-bodied wage earner.[39]

In the same year the county commissioners were designated as a board to administer the state law providing aid for the aged.[40]

---

37. *Ibid.,* CXIV, pt. ii, 18-21.
38. *Ibid.,* CXIV, pt. ii, 21, 22.
39. *Laws of Ohio,* CXIV, pt. ii, 17.
40. *Ibid.,* CXV, pt. ii, 431-439.

In February1933, the tenure of the state relief commission was extended to March 1, 1935.[41] In the same year the legislature levied an additional stamp tax on the sale of bottled and bulk beer, malt, cosmetics, and toilet preparations to furnished additional funds for emergency relief.[42] The state treasurer was authorized to appoint the county treasurer as deputy for the purpose of selling tax stamps to be fixed to such articles.[43]

The commissioners' duties regarding poor relief were further extended in 1935. They were authorized to provide noninstitutional support, care, assistance, or relief for the indigent in the county.[44] In 1935 the state relief commission ceased to exist by reason of the terms of the act creating it. The legislature, however, passed a measure designed to co-ordinate and correlate all emergency poor relief work, activities, and administration with the Federal Emergency Relief Administration which was authorized to administer and direct the distribution and expenditures of federal funds for relief in the state. Accordingly, all powers previously vested in the state relief commission were transferred to the county commissioners. Whenever, in their discretion such action was necessary in order to continue the co-ordination and correlation of the state, local, and federal funds they were authorized to appoint, with the approval of the director of finance of the state of Ohio, a representative or representatives of such emergency poor relief.[45] If such an officer were appointed, the representative succeeded to all powers and functions, which, under the act, were delegated to the county commissioners. This represented, however, was subjected to such terms and conditions in respect to auditing, examinations, and reports as were directed by the county commissioners and such federal agency. The county commissioners were directed to conduct relief activities outside limits of municipal corporations through the township trustees, insofar as practicable, and were to be guided by the recommendations of the township trustees with respect to relief need and such political subdivisions. Again, as in 1932, the commissioners were authorized, if the state commission found that no other means existed to provide funds, to borrow money and issue bonds in the year 1935-1936.

---

41. *Ibid.,* CXV, 22.
42. *Ibid.,* CXV, 642, 649; CXV, pt. ii, 5, 33, 83, 177, 200 247, 256.
43. *Ibid.,* CXV, 642.
44. *Ibid.,* CXVI, 571.
45. *Ibid.,* The county commissioners recommended to the state relief commission on January 6, 1936, the appointment of De Forrest Allyn as first director of emergency relief for Geauga County. *See* p. 10.

The maximum maturity date of such bonds was to be on or before March 1, 1944.[46] Other bonds, in addition to those secured by the county's share of the excise tax, might be issued not to exceed one-fifth of one percent of the general text list of the county.[47] If the county was unable to issue bonds by reason of limitations imposed by the constitution,[48] the taxing authority of each subdivision was authorized to submit the question of issuing bonds to the electorate either at a general or special election.[49]

The year 1936 saw the re-creation of the state relief commission. Consisting of four members appointed by the governor, this body was authorized to serve until January 31, 1937. Again, as a 1932, the commission was directed to study problems of relief, to receive advice from federal, state, and local governmental departments, to co-operate with agencies of the national and local governments and private agencies engaged in the administration or financial support of direct or indirect relief, to administer moneys appropriated to the commission for poor relief, to examine the conduct of local governmental agencies in administering relief, and to order the distribution and payment of moneys from state treasury.

The county commissioners were authorized to administer all advances by the state to the relief commission and were directed to operate through duly authorized agencies of townships, municipalities, and school districts. Within the appropriations made by the commissioners and subject to the rules and regulations of the state relief commission, the commissioners were instructed to appoint assistants and such other employees as were necessary.[50]

The county commissioners, like the state relief commission, were directed to co-operate with all agencies of the federal, state, and county governments, and with private agencies which were engaged in administering relief or financial support to the needy. It was made the duty of all county, township, and municipal governments administering relief or assistance to dependents to report to the county commissioners, at their request, the names and addresses of all persons to whom they were providing aid and the amount and character of aid given.[51]

---

46. *Laws of Ohio,* CXVI, 571.
47. *Ibid.,* CXVI, 575.
48. *Ohio Const. 1851,* Art. XII, sec. 2.
49. *Laws of Ohio,* CXVI, 578.
50. *Ibid.,* CXVI, pt. ii, 133-145.
51. *Ibid.,* CXVI, pt. ii, 133-148, 240.

The principle of issuing bonds and securing them by the county's share of the utility taxes was continued. Moreover, there was appropriated to the state relief commission from the general revenue fund the sum of $3,000,000 which was designated as the "state relief rotary fund." The various counties of the state which had not issued bonds and were not authorized to do so without the consent of the people, were empowered to obtain an advance from the state relief rotary fund in an amount equal to that of bonds which were permitted to be issued under the provision of this act. If the county failed to repay the total of all advances and interest at two percent before June 1936, the state relief commission was directed to refuse to make further allocations or distributions to the county.[52]

In the early months of 1937 the legislature authorized the staff relief commission to serve until April 1937. Under this act the county commissioners are authorized to give temporary support and medical relief to nonresidents and to all needy persons possessing legal residence in the county. Funds may be expended for both direct and work relief. However, all persons on relief able and competent to perform labor who refuse to accept private employment under prevailing conditions and prevailing wages, maybe dropped from the relief rolls. This ruling does not apply, however, to areas where strikes are prevalent. On the other hand, any person receiving relief in the county is permitted to engage in any business without losing his relief status. During the period of such employment, he is required to forfeit the *pro rata* amount of relief received by him, and is eligible to his former relief status upon the conclusion of such employment.

The county commissioners are required to file with the state relief commission a budget and a detailed statement and plan, showing how the funds received are to be expended, the purpose for which they are to be used, the nature and kind of works to be carried on, and the number of persons to be aided by such relief. Besides this, the county commissioners must file a complete analysis of their proposed expenditures, together with an estimate of all available resources, including the unencumbered proceeds of any bonds heretofore issued and the amount of bonds which the county commissioners have a right to issue without a vote of the people on the approval of the state tax commission of Ohio as authorized in 1935.

---

52. *Laws of Ohio,* CXVI, 133-148.

Of the funds allocated to the county by the state relief commission for direct relief, the commissioners may, when they believe that the cost of administration may be reduced, reallocate the funds on a percentage basis of relief requirements of the various subdivisions.[53]

The emergency relief measures passed during the period 1932-1937 gave the counties for the first time a centralized relief administration. All records of this work are located in the relief administration office.

The first relief director of Geauga County was appointed by the commissioners on January 6, 1936,[54] when the state relief commission ceased to exist,[55] and the powers previously vested in the state relief commission were transferred to the commissioners. During the years of the depression five bond issues totaling $73, 060 were issued against the excise tax expectancy,[56] the county not being able to handle its relief load without resorting to the other extraordinary expedience permitted by depression legislation. In the year 1940 the commissioners expended $20,924.68 for direct relief,[57] maintaining an average monthly roll of 67 families.[58]

In addition to other forms of relief the county commissioners provided funds for aid to dependent children.[59] They are required to include in the annual tax budget an amount not less than that computed to yield a levy of fifteen hundredths of a mill on each dollar of the general tax list of the county. Funds are also provided by the federal and state governments. If the commissioners fail to comply with the provisions of the act relative to appropriations, the state department of welfare is directed to institute *mandamus* proceedings against them.[60]

While control over relief work has become one of the most important phases of the commissioners' work, particularly in recent years, many other responsibilities have been assigned to them. The commissioners, by the authority conferred upon them to construct public buildings, were given duties regarding educational advancement.

---

53. *Ibid.,* CXVII, 133-148.
54. Commissioners Journal, General, X [1933-1936], 418.
55. *Laws of Ohio,* CXVI, 571.
56. Record of Bonds – County Commissioners, *see* entry 300.
57. Case Records and Case Histories, 1935—, entry 18.
58. *Ibid.*
59. *See* p. 108.
60. G. C. secs. 1359-31 - 1359-45 ; *Laws of Ohio,* CXVI, pt. ii, 188-195.

Since 1871 they have been authorized to accept bequests for the construction of county libraries, and since 1923 to issue bonds, after receiving the approval of the voters, for the construction of libraries, or to contract with existing libraries for the use of people in the county.[61] Moreover, during the same period, they were authorized to provide and maintain civic centers in the county and to employ an expert director to supervise and administer them.[62]

Other duties not closely related to the original ones have been added from decade to decade. For example, in 1850 the commissioners were authorized to subscribe for one leading newspaper of each political party in the county and cause them to be bound and deposited with the county auditor as public archives.[63] An amendment to the original act, passed in 1923, provided for the preservation of such newspapers for a period of 10 years, after which they may be removed to the Ohio State Archaeological and Historical Society library.[64] They have been authorized also to promote historical research by appropriating annually a sum not to exceed $100 to defray the expense of compiling and publishing historical data for historical societies not incorporated for profit.[65]

During the early years of the 20th century the commissioners were given the duty of providing facilities for county sanitation, which, in previous years had been sadly neglected. In 1917 they were authorized to layout, establish, and maintain one or more sewer districts within the county. Since 1917 no sewer or sewage treatment works may be constructed outside of any incorporated municipality by any person, persons, firms, or corporations until the plans have been approved by the commissioners.[66]

Then, too, during the same period the commissioners were authorized to provide facilities for the treatment of tuberculosis. In 1908 they were authorized to establish a county tuberculosis hospital and in 1909 to co-operate with the commissioners of other counties for the establishment of a district tuberculosis hospital.[67]

---

61. C. G. secs. 2454, 2455; *Laws of Ohio,* CX, 242.
62. G. C. sec. 2457-4.
63. *Laws of Ohio,* XLVIII, 65.
64. *Laws of Ohio,* CX, 4.
65. G. C. sec. 2457-1.
66. G. C. sec. 6602-1; *Laws of Ohio,* CVII, 440.
67. *Laws of Ohio,* XCIX, 62; C, 87.

Geauga County maintains no tuberculosis hospital. Patients are sent to Pope Convalescent Home only by the authority of Dr. W. A. Reed, who specializes in lung diseases. No patients are discharged without his authority.[68] Severe cases are sent to state or city hospitals, sanatoriums and institutions adopted for expert medical care of tuberculosis.[69] Since 1917 the commissioners have been authorized to establish tuberculosis dispensaries and provide by tax levies necessary funds for their establishment and maintenance.[70]

Finally, the county commissioners have acted in a supervisory capacity over other county officials. Since 1850 they have been authorized to compare the annual reports and statements made to them by the prosecuting attorney, clerk of courts, sheriff, and treasurer; take measures to rectify errors, correct discrepancies, and record in their journal results of such examinations. This county does not have a full time commissioners' clerk, the auditor having served in this capacity, and all signatures required of commissioners' clerk have been done by the auditor.[71] In 1896 the commissioners were given their present duty of visiting hospitals, detention homes, private asylums, and other institutions exercising a reformatory or correctional influence over individuals, and reporting on the sanitary conditions and the treatment of inmates.[72] Although these reports are required to be filed with the county prosecuting attorney and kept open to the inspection and examination of the public, they were not located in the inventory of Geauga County records.

The board of county commissioners offers a typical example of an office, which, designed primarily for an agricultural society, has expanded to meet the needs and requirements of modern society. At present the commissioners are elected for a four-year term.[73]

---

68. Commissioners' Journal, General, XI (1932-1941), 489.
69. *Ibid.,* 24.
70. G. C. Secs. 3148-1, 3153-4, 3153-5.
71. Commissioners' Journal I [1806-1864], 25.
72. *Laws of Ohio,* XCII, 212.
73. *Ibid.,* CVIII, pt. ii, 1300

Geauga County, being primarily agricultural, has always been extremely conservative in its management. All bonds having so far been paid when due, no refunding of issues have ever been necessary. The county has exceeded the 10 mill limit once, in 1919, when it issued bonds to raise funds for road purposes. This issue was liquidated in 1935.[74]

By the nature of its people and their needs, Geauga County tends toward a less complex county government than most. It has no county water supply or sewer system, no metropolitan park system, no county law library, no planning commission, and no tuberculosis sanatorium. The county has never built a workhouse, but boards such prisoners in Cleveland.[75]

Much of the work of road maintenance and repair is now delegated to the engineer, though responsibility for its performance still rests with the commissioners, who have in their charge the average of 223.6 miles of highway and all the bridges and culverts of Geauga County.[76] Here, as everywhere, upkeep rather than new construction constitutes by far the greater part of the work.

---

74. Commissioners' Journal, VIII [1919-1923], 5.
75. *Ibid.,* General, X [1932-1936], 48.
76. Road Records, 1941, *See* entry 408.

Proceedings

1. COMMISSIONER'S JOURNAL
1806—. 12 vols. (1, 2, 2-11). Subtitled General, 1924—. 3 vols.
Record of all proceedings at commissioners' meetings, showing date of meeting and record of all business transacted, including copies of petitions and authorization for establishing, constructing or vacating roads, bridges, and ditches, showing dates of petitions and authorization, name and location of improvement, and date and name of road vacated; reports of road viewers and surveyors with estimates of cost by surveyors, showing date of survey, name and location of road, and estimate of the amount of cost; record of all resolutions, contracts, bids, estimates, specifications, and other proceedings taken by commissioners in conducting county business, showing date of report, estimated amount of bids and contracts, the name and address of contractor; lists of bills and claims filed monthly, showing name of creditor, amount of bill, purpose of bill, and amount approved for payment; record of procedure on claims for damage to livestock caused by dogs, 1879—, showing name of owners, amount approved, amount claimed, amount paid, name of

witnesses and witness fees; record of approval of paroles from county jail, 1915—, showing names of prisoners, type of crime, term of sentence, and date of parole; records of allowance for sheriff's fees and board of prisoners in county jail, 1845—, showing date of report, number of prisoners and meals served, amount of sheriff's fees and total amount paid; copies of infirmary director's reports, 1874-1888, showing statement of all receipts and disbursements with totals and balances, number of inmates at beginning of period, number received, discharged, deceased, and number remaining at the end of period; from 1888—, the journal contains merely a notation of receipt and acceptance of infirmary reports (1874-1913 were semiannual reports and 1913—, annual reports); record of appointments of deputies, clerks, and officers for all offices, 1806—, showing name of appointee, amount of remuneration and date of appointment; record of appointment of real estate assessors, 1850—, showing name and address of assessor, and date appointment begins and expires; record of construction of county jail, 1807, showing name of contractor, date completed and total cost of construction; record of approval or rejection of county officer's bonds, 1806—, showing name and address of bonded officer, name of office, and reason for rejection; record of receipts and approval or rejection of bids for depository of county funds, 1894—, showing name and address of depository, date of report and reason for rejection; records of approval of reports of all county offices, 1904—, showing subject matter and date approved; record of comparison of auditor's and treasurer's monthly statements, 1866-1904, showing date of statements, amount of deficiency and reason; record of appropriation and distribution of funds for soldiers' relief and soldiers' burial funds, 1865—, showing name and address of soldier or sailor, amount of aid granted, date of death and amount of burial expenses; record of applications and grants for blind relief, 1908-1936, showing name and address of applicant, number rejected or approved, amount of aid approved and granted; approval of monthly accounts of auditor and treasurer, 1904—, showing date of approval, name of fund, amount certified by the auditor to the treasurer for payment, and balance on hand in each fund; record of moneys paid to private families for the board and care of dependent children, 1860—, showing names of persons caring for children, address, amount allowed, date, and signatures of commissioners; record of Geauga County hospital patients, 1925—, showing number of patients cared for, date received, date discharge, and amount allowed; record of emergency relief appropriations, 1806-1935, showing date and amount of appropriation. Also contains: Commissioners' Journal [Roads], 1806-1920 entry 2; Road Records, 1823-1872, 1885—, entry 5, Infirmary Record [Journal], 1839-1871, 1913—, entry 7, Annual Report of County Home, 1874—, entry 8. Arranged chronologically by dates of reports. No index, 1806-1864; 1 volume 1936—, indexed alphabetically by names of procedures; for separate index, 1865—, see entry 3. 1806-1923 handwritten; 1924—, typed. Average 450 pages. 16 x 12 x 2. Auditor's office.

For original documents on paroles see entry 14.

2. COMMISSIONERS' JOURNAL [ROADS]
1921—. 3 vols. (8-10). Initiated in 1921. 1806-1920 in Commissioners' Journal, entry 1.

Record of commissioners' proceedings relative to roads, ditches, bridges, county buildings, and improvements on miscellaneous county property, containing record of petitions, bids, contracts, estimates, specifications, and all other procedure of commissioners in respect to the above items, showing name of petitioner, location of roads, ditches, and bridges, total estimated cost of improvements, names of contractors, and amount of material. Arranged alphabetically by names of townships and alphabetically thereunder by names of improvements. Indexed alphabetically by names of roads, bridges, ditches, or other improvements; for separate index, see entry 3. Typed. Average 475 pages. 16 x 11.5 x 2.5. Auditor's office.

3. GENERAL INDEX TO COMMISSIONERS' JOURNAL
1865—. 7 vols. (One unlabeled; 1-3, 5-7).

General index to Commissioners Journal, entry 1, and Commissioners' Journal [Roads], entry 2, under column headings of road, bridge, and ditch, showing name of road, bridge, ditch or name of person concerned with same, location of improvement, date and kind of proceedings, volume and page numbers in journals; under column heading, bills, showing date of bill, amount, purpose, volume and page numbers in journal; under column heading, purchases, name of vendor, items purchased, date of purchase, amount paid, and volume and page number in journal; under column heading, levies, name and purpose of levy, date of levy, amount, volume and page numbers in journal; under miscellaneous, showing name of person or procedure, date, volume and page numbers in journal, and kind of proceedings. Arranged alphabetically by subjects and chronologically thereunder by dates of proceedings. Handwritten on printed forms. Average 400 pages. 18 x 12 x 2.25. Auditor's office.

4. CONTRACTS, UNDER LITIGATION
1922. 1 file box.
Copies of contracts and agreements entered into by county commissioners with firms or individuals to furnish material or labor, or both, in construction or repairs of county roads, bridges, and buildings, showing date of contract, name of contractor, condition of contract, date contract to be completed, amount of bond filed by contractor, and amount of contract. Arranged chronologically by dates of contracts. No index. Handwritten on printed forms. 10 x 5 x 14. Auditor's office.

Public Improvements

5. ROAD RECORD
1873-1874. 1 vol. (1). 1823-1872, 1885—, in Commissioners' Journal, entry 1.
Record of petitions for damages incidental to road building, showing date of entry, name of petitioner, location of alleged damage, date petition filed, names of viewers appointed and dates of appointment, name of surety, amount of damages allowed, by whom paid, and other action taken. Arranged chronologically by dates entered. No index. Handwritten on printed forms. 160 pages. 18 x 12.5 x 1.5. Auditor's office.

6. RECORD OF MISCELLANEOUS DITCH AND RIVER IMPROVEMENTS
1869-1887. 4 vols.
Miscellaneous record of improvements on river ditches along the Cuyahoga and other small rivers, including records of commissioners' proceedings on improvements, copies of estimates, specifications, bids, and contracts between commissioners and contractors, tax duplicates for special river ditch assessments, showing date of recording, names of owners, description and location of land, number of acres and amount of assessment; hand drawn maps of rivers and ditches, showing rivers, location of ditches, townships, and village boundary lines, names of lot owners and size of land. Maps were prepared by county surveyor and are sketched in ink on the pages of these volumes. Arranged chronologically by dates recorded. No index. Handwritten. Average 100 pages. 10 x 7 x .5. Auditor's office.

Institutions and Relief

7. INFIRMARY RECORD [Journal]

1872-1912. 1 vol. 1839-1871, 1913—, in Commissioners' Journal, entry 1. Record of procedure of board of directors of infirmary including resolutions of board, and list of infirmary bills filed monthly, showing date of bill, name and address of creditor, amount of bill, for services rendered or goods supplied, and amount approved for payment. Arranged chronologically by dates of bills. No index. Handwritten. 475 pages. 14 x 9 x 1.5. Auditor's office.

8. ANNUAL REPORT OF COUNTY HOME

1934—. 1 file box. 1874—, in Commissioners' Journal, entry 1.
Copies of annual reports of county home, showing date of report, itemized accounts of all county home receipts, expenditures and costs of new buildings and equipment, general statistics and detailed analyses of inmates of home, and inventory of county home property. Arranged chronologically by dates of reports. No index. Handwritten on printed forms. 10 x 5 x 15. Auditor's office.

9. [REPORT OF SOLDIERS' RELIEF COMMISSION]

1916-1923, 1936—, in Soldiers' Relief and Mothers' Pensions, entry 301. Reports of soldiers' relief commission including a complete list of persons awarded relief, showing name of recipient, service record or relation to ex-service man, amount to be paid to recipient each month and remarks; also includes separate typed orders to place individuals on soldiers' relief list, showing name of recipient, date of order, and amount of award.

Financial Records

10. COMMISSIONERS' REPORT BLOTTER

n. d. 1 vol.
Record of accounts with all county offices and funds, showing account number, name of account, amount paid and received, purpose of payments, source of receipts, and balance in accounts. Arranged numerically by account numbers. Indexed alphabetically by names of accounts. Handwritten on printed forms. 600 pages. 14 x 17.5 x 3.5. Auditor's office.

Miscellaneous

11. RESOLUTIONS RECORDED AND COMMISSIONERS' JOURNAL
1920-1927. 1 file drawer.
Records of resolutions adopted by board of county commissioners for the purchase of road building materials, road graders for certain townships, and building of roads which have been petitioned and made, showing date of resolution, name and location of road, cost of road material, expense of construction, and proposed amount of bonds to be sold. Arranged chronologically by dates of resolutions. No index. Typed on printed forms. 10 x 5 x 14. Auditor's office.

12. TOWNSHIP ROAD RESOLUTIONS – LINE FENCE
1936—. 1 file drawer.
Duplicate copies of petitions to township trustees by landowners as submitted to the recorder, asking for a division or petition of line fences separating adjoining lands, and landowners' assigned portion of the fence to be maintained, showing date of petition, names of litigants, township, description of adjoining lands and dividing line, date filed for record, and date recorded. Arranged alphabetically by names of townships and chronologically thereunder by dates of petitions. No index. Typed on printed forms. 10 x 5 x 14. Auditor's office.
For record of line fence agreements, 1906—, see entry 60.

13. ANNUAL INVENTORY COUNTY PROPERTY, BOARD OF COMMISSIONERS
1935. 1 vol.
Inventory of county property in county offices, showing name and location of office, description of articles, quantity, price unit, and total estimated value; disposition of property, showing amount received, disposition, and date of disposition. Arranged alphabetically by names of offices. No index. Typed on printed forms. 200 pages (50 pages used). 16 x 15 x 1.5. Auditor's office.

14. WORKHOUSE CONTRACTS AND PAROLE OF PRISONERS
1923—. 1 file box.
Record of parole of prisoners from county jail, including original applications for parole of prisoners, recommendation of parole by justice of the peace and sheriff, and approval of parole by county commissioners, showing name of parolee, conditions of parole, custodian of parolee, date of approval, and signatures of

commissioners and prosecuting attorney in approval; also contains four workhouse contracts, 1925—, entered into by the Geauga County commissioners and Stark County commissioners for board and work of prisoners from Geauga County in the Stark County workhouse, showing daily rate to be paid by Geauga County for prisoners, and other conditions pertaining to the contract. Arranged chronologically by dates of approval of paroles. No index. Typed. 10 x 5 x 15. Auditor's office.

15. DOG WARDEN [Reports]
1928—. 3 file folders, 1 file drawer.
Dog warden's weekly reports to commissioners of animal claims investigated, showing name and address of claimant, date of claim, description of animals killed or injured, and amount of claim; also includes correspondence and record of impounded dogs, showing date of report, description of dog, and tag number. Arranged chronologically by dates of reports. No index. Handwritten on printed forms. File folders, 14 x 9.5 x 1.5; file drawer, 10 x 5 x 15. 3 file folders, 1928-1936, 3rd floor storeroom; 1 file drawer, 1937—, Auditor's office.

Aid for the Blind

16. BLIND RELIEF CERTIFICATES [And Applications]
1904-1936. 1 file drawer.
Original blind relief applications and certificates of award; applications, showing application number, name of applicant, date of filing, and amount allowed; certificates of award, showing date, name of applicant, amount of award, address of applicant, date approved, date effective, signatures of commissioners, and executive secretary of Ohio Commission for the Blind. Also includes certificates of examining physician, showing condition of applicant's eyesight, and evidence of applicant's eligibility for relief. Arranged chronologically by dates of applications. No index. Handwritten and typed, some on printed forms. 10 x 5 x 15. Auditor's office.

17. RECORD OF AID FOR THE BLIND
1936—. 1 file drawer.
Record of aid for the blind including certification of award, showing name of applicant, date approved, amount awarded a year, post-office address of applicant, date award effective, and signatures of county commissioners; includes physician's report on eye examinations, showing application number, name, address, sex, race,

and date of birth of applicant, diagnosis of eye condition, central visual acuity, peripheral vision, prognosis, recommendations, remarks, date of examination, date of report, signatures and address the physician, and record of re-examination; applications for blind relief, showing name, address, citizenship, age, previous address, date of loss of eyesight, marital status, and employment information as sworn to by applicant. Arranged alphabetically by names of applicants. No index. Handwritten and typed, some on printed forms. 8.5 x 6 x 17.5. Probate court judges' office.

Relief Administration

18. CASE RECORDS AND CASE HISTORIES
1935—. 2 file drawers.
Case records and case histories of relief recipients, including applications, showing case number, name of applicant, record of past and present addresses, name and addresses of landlords, number of rooms and rent a month, name, age, and occupations of members of family and others in household, naturalization record, marital status, record of military service, names and addresses, and other information regarding children and other relatives away from home, work record of each working member of family, reports from social service agencies, and names and addresses of churches, unions, lodges and other societies to which members of family belong; also includes financial sheets, showing case number, name, address, estimated weekly needs for food, clothing, and other items of direct relief, estimated weekly income, property information and record of life insurance, debts, savings, and automobile. Arranged alphabetically by names of applicants. No index. Handwritten and typed, some on printed forms. 13.5 x 12 x 26.5. Welfare office, room 1.

19. W[ork] P[rojects] A[dministration] CERTIFICATIONS – ACTIVE CASES
1935—. 1 file drawer.
Records of active Work Projects Administration cases, including copies of certifications of eligibility, showing social security number, name and address of worker, relief district, case number, date of certification, primary and secondary classification, military and marital status, age of worker, naturalization information, and identification number; copies of notices to report for work on projects, assignment slips, reassignment slips, and notices of change in work status, showing

name, address, age, sex, color, wage class, identification and case number of worker, hour, date and location of work project, and signature of placement officer. Half of this file drawer contains certifications of applications waiting assignment. Arranged alphabetically by names of workers. No index. Typed on printed forms. 8.5 x 6 x 17.5. Welfare office, room 1.

20. W[ork] P[rojects] A[dministration] CERTIFICATIONS – CLOSED CASES

1935—. 1 file drawer.

Records of closed Work Projects Administration cases including copy of certifications of eligibility, showing social security number, name and address of worker, relief district, case number, date of certification, primary and secondary work classification, naturalization information, and identification number; copies of cancellations of certificates of eligibility, showing name and address of worker, case number, reason for cancellation, copies of notices to report for work on projects, assignment slips, reassignment slips, and notices of change in work status. Arranged alphabetically by names of workers. No index. Typed on printed forms. 8.5 x 6 x 17.5. Welfare office, room 1.

21. W[ork] P[rojects] A[dministration] CERTIFICATIONS

1938—. 1 file drawer.

Copies of certifications of eligibility, the originals of which were sent to the Akron Work Projects Administration office, includes individual occupational classification cards, revised Work Projects Administration form 144-A, and handwritten records of past employment, showing name and address of client, age, date of birth, height, weight, personal record of finances, statement regarding health of applicant, number of dependents, case number, identification number, classification, family background, and educational record. Arranged alphabetically by names of clients. No index. Handwritten and typed, some on printed forms. 8.5 x 6 x 17.5. Welfare office, room 1.

CCC Records

22. C[ivilian] C[onservation] C[orps] RECORDS
1933—. 1 file box.
Civilian Conservation Corps records including accepted applications, showing applicant's name and address, date application received, where received, age and physical description of applicant, education, information concerning previous employment, designation of allottee, and authorization for disposition of applicant's earnings as sworn to by applicant; also includes bulletins, notices of acceptance, reports, advanced reports, and correspondence. Arranged chronologically by dates of enrollments and alphabetically thereunder by names of applicants. No index. Typed, some on printed forms. 8.5 x 6 x 17.5. Welfare office, room 1.

Miscellaneous

23. COUNTY MINOR SERVICE
1935—. 1 FILE DRAWER.
Miscellaneous correspondence concerning applications for direct relief that have not been accepted and record of investigations, showing names of applicants, dates of applications, and reasons rejected; correspondence with other counties pertaining to relief clients, showing date of letter, name of correspondent, to whom sent, subject matter, and signature of correspondence. Arranged alphabetically by names of applicants and subjects. No index. Typed. 13.5 x 12 x 26.5. Welfare office, room 1.

The office county recorder, although not unknown as an early English institution for the registration of land titles, developed in colonial America, where, because of the mobility of the restless pioneers, changes in land titles were frequent and some system was needed to protect purchasers against previous encumbrances. Public land registers, established in most of the colonies during the colonial period and continued by the states following independence, served as a model of land registration for the territory of which the present state of Ohio was then a part. Thus the office of county recorder was established by an act of the Northwest Territory, effective August 1, 1795. This act, adopted from the Pennsylvania Code, provided for the appointment by the governor of a recorder in each county whose principal duty was the recording of deeds.[1]

When Ohio entered the Union in 1803 no constitutional provision was made for the continuance of the office, but the legislature during its first session passed an act providing for a recorder in each county to be appointed by the judges of the court of common pleas for a seven-year term.[2] The recorder continued to be an appointive officer until 1829, when, by an act of the legislature, the office became elective for a three-year term.[3] The tenure of the office remained at three years until the constitutional amendment on November 7, 1905, which provided for the election of all county officers in the even numbered years.[4] The term of office was fixed at two years, and so continued until the amendment of 1933, which extended the tenure of the incumbent until January 1937, at which time the recorder elected at the regular election in November 1936 began to serve a four-year term.[5]

The first county recorder was directed by statute to record "all deeds, mortgages and conveyances of lands and tenements," lying within his county, and also all instruments and writings required by law to be recorded.[6] In 1805 he was directed to record all plats and maps of newly laid out villages.[7]

---

1. Theodore Calvin Pease, comp., *The Laws of the Northwest Territory, 1788-1800 (Illinois State Bar Association Law Series,* Springfield, 1925), I, 197-199.
2. *Laws of Ohio,* I, 136.
3. *Ibid.,* XXVII, 65.
4. *Ohio Const. 1851,* (Amendment, 1905), Art. XVII, secs, 1, 2; *Laws of Ohio,* XCVIII, 271.
5. *Laws of Ohio,* CXV, 191.
6. *Ibid.,* I, 137.
7. *Ibid.,* III, 213-215.

In 1835 he was permitted, when authorized by the county commissioners, to transcribe from the records of other counties all deeds, mortgages, and other instruments of writing for the sale or conveyance of lands, tenements, or hereditaments, affecting land titles in his county.[8]

Since the establishment of the office many duties besides those of recording land titles have been added. The present practice of recording powers of attorney had its beginning in 1818.[9] Although the mechanics of Cincinnati were authorized to file mechanics' liens with the recorder as early as 1823, it was not until 1843 that the privilege was extended to the laborers of all counties.[10] Successive acts in 1865, 1872, 1881, 1884, 1888, 1904, and 1923 added new duties to the office in the recording of soldiers' discharges,[11] copies of certificates of compliance authorizing insurance companies not incorporated under the laws of Ohio to transact business in the state, and certified copies of renewal as granted by such companies to their agents,[12] limited partnership agreements,[13] stallion keepers' liens,[14] oil and gas leases,[15] partition fence records,[16] and federal tax liens.[17] The recording of chattel mortgages and conditional sales began in 1846. Such instruments were to be deposited with the township clerk where the mortgagor was a resident. In all townships, however, in which the recorder maintained his office such instruments were to be deposited with him.[18] Since 1906 chattel mortgages have been filed with the county recorder exclusively.[19] It is provided that in order to be valid against subsequent mortgages, the chattel mortgage must be deposited with the county recorder of the county where the mortgagor resides at the time of its execution, and to retain its validity the mortgage must be renewed every three years.[20]

---

8. *Laws of Ohio,* XXXIII, 8; XXXV, 10-11.
9. *Ibid.,* XVI, 155-156.
10. *Ibid.,* XXI, 8-10; XLI, 66.
11. *Ibid.,* LXII, 59.
12. *Ibid.,* LXIX, 32, 148; XCVII, 405.
13. *Ibid.,* LXXVIII, 248.
14. *Ibid.,* LXXXI, 43.
15. *Ibid.,* LXXXV, 179.
16. *Ibid.,* XCVII, 140.
17. *Ibid.,* CX, 252.
18. *Ibid.,* XLIV, 61.
19. G. C. sec. 8561.
20. G. C. sec. 8565.

An important extension of the method of recording land titles known as the "Torrens System," was provided by an act of the general assembly in 1896.[22] In 1897 this act was declared unconstitutional by the supreme court of Ohio as being contrary to section 16 of the bill of rights of the state constitution.[23] The act of 1913, amended in 1913 and 1915, provided for the examination of land titles by the recorder and the issuance, if the title proved to be held in free simple, of a certificate of title by the court of common pleas or probate court. The official certificate becomes the title of ownership and is indefeasible. However, in the event an interest is found in the land, after the issuance of the certificate, a claim is allowed to the legal claimant from a fund created for that purpose at the time of registration.[24] The system was adopted in Geauga in 1914, and is still in use, although no records were kept until 1915.[25]

The recorder, like other county officials, had been required in earlier years to keep records of the business of his office, but it was not until the middle of the 19th century that the legislature, looking forward to some uniformity in land registration, enacted measures prescribing the form and content of such records. Since 1850 the recorder has been required to keep a record of deeds in which is recorded all deeds, powers of attorney, and other instruments of writing for the unconditional sale of land, tenements, or hereditaments.[26] The same year saw the beginning of a record of mortgages in which was recorded all mortgages, powers of attorney, and other instruments of writing by which land, tenements, or hereditaments "shall or maybe mortgaged" or otherwise conditionally sold; and a record of plats in which was to be recorded all plats and maps of town lots and of the subdivisions thereof, and of other divisions of surveyed lands, in like regular succession according to the priority of the presentation.[27] Since 1851 the recorder has been required to keep a separate record of deeds and mortgages denominated respectfully as "Record of Deeds" and "Record of Mortgages."[28] Since 1865 the recorder has been required to keep a separate record of leases.[29]

---

21. *Laws of Ohio,* CXVI, 324.
22. *Ibid.,* XCII, 220.
23. *Ohio State Reports* (Cincinnati, 1853—), LVI, 575.
24. G. C. secs. 8572-34 - 8572-56; *Laws of Ohio,* CIII, 814-960; CVI, 24; CXV, 443.
25. *See* entries 42 - 46.
26. *Laws of Ohio,* XLVIII, 64.
27. *Ibid.,* XLVIII, 64.
28. *Ibid.,* XLIX, 103.
29. *Ibid.,* LXII, 170.

The present practice of keeping a daily register of deeds and a daily register of mortgages has been required by statute since 1896.[30] In Geauga County the register was duly instituted in that year and has been continued to date.[31]

Although indexes have been prepared in earlier years, the present system of indexing had its beginning in 1851 and took practically its present form in 1896.[32] At present the recorder, at the beginning of each day's business, is required to make and maintain a general alphabetical index, direct and reverse, of all names of both parties of all instruments recorded by him. The indexes show the kind of instruments, the date, the range, the township and section, the survey number, and the number of acres or the lot and sublot numbers and the part thereof, of such tract or lot of land described in any such instrument of writing; The name of each grantor is entered in the direct index under the appropriate letter and followed on the same line by the name of the grantee; the name of each grantee is entered in a reverse index under the appropriate letter and followed on the same line by the name of the grantor.[33]

Since 1859 the county commissioners have been authorized to provide sectional indexes to the records of all real estate in the county, beginning with some designated year and continuing through a period of years as may be specified.[34]

The present duties of the recorder do not differ, in the main, from those prescribed in the middle of the 19th century. His bound records are open to the inspection of the public and are transferred to his successor.

The recorder in Geauga County recorded in 1940 approximately 1001 deeds and conveyances, 40 mechanics' liens, 840 leases, 5 powers of attorney, 1555 chattel mortgages, and 405 real estate mortgages.[35] The office is self supporting, the total fees running over $4400 annually, while expenses average only $3729 in 1940.[36] All fees are paid into the county treasury and salaries and expenses are appropriated by the commissioners annually. The recorder is under a $2000 bond[37] and his salary is $92.22 monthly.[38]

---

30. *Ibid.,* XCII, 268.
31. *See* entries 27, 34.
32. *Laws of Ohio,* XLIX, 103; XCII, 268; CII, 288.
33. G. C. Sec. 2764.
34. G. C. Sec. 2766; *Laws of Ohio,* LXIV, 256; LXXVI, 49; CII, 289.
35. *See* entries 24, 36, 30, 52, 53, 32.
36. Financial Report, 1940, entry 306.
37. Treasurer's Record of Bonds of Officials, 1940, entry 352.
38. Commissioners' Journal, General, XI [1936-1941], 423-428.

Real Property Transfers

Deeds (See also entries 46, 62)

24. DEED RECORD
1795—. 145 vols. (1-43, 45-47, 49-52, 54, 55, 57, 58, 60, 61, 63-65,67, 68, 70, 71, 73, 74, 76, 77, 79, 81, 83, 85, 87, 88, 89, 91, 92, 94, 96, 98, 99, 101, 103-105, 108, 109, 111, 112, 114, 116, 117, 119, 120, 122-124, 126-128, 130, 131, 134, 135, 138, 140, 142, 143, 145, 147, 151, 152, 154, 156, 157, 159, 162, 163, 165, 167, 169, 170, 173, 174, 177-180, 182, 184, 186-189, 192, 193, 195, 196, 199, 200, 201, 203, 205, 206, 208, 210).

Record of deeds, showing names of grantor and grantee, description of land deeded, kind and date of instrument, amount of consideration, condition of instrument, and signatures of parties concerned; 1795-1810 transcribed from entry 26; includes powers of attorney, 1800—, showing names of principal and agent, date of entry, and terms of agreement. Also contains; Record of Leases, 1829-1849, entry 30; Mortgage Record, 1800-1849, entry 32; Mortgage Releases [Certificate of Release of Mortgages], 1800-1849, entry 35; Record of Plats and Surveys, 1795-1848, entry 48; Plats, 1795-1814 entry 407. Arranged chronologically by dates of instruments. Indexed alphabetically by names of grantors and grantees; for separate index, see entry 25. 1795-1917 handwritten; 1918—, typed. Average 600 pages. 18.5 x 12 x 3. Recorder's office.

25. GENERAL INDEX TO DEEDS
1795—. 12 vols. (1-12).

Index to Deed Record, entry 24, showing names of grantor and grantee, date of transaction, volume and page numbers of record, range, tract, town, section, lot, sublot, number of acres and remarks. Arranged alphabetically by names of grantors and grantees. Handwritten on printed forms. Average 600 pages. 18 x 13 x 3. Recorder's office.

26. DEED RECORD
1795-1810. 2 vols.

Original record from which deed record, entry 24, was transcribed. First half of volume 1795-1810, record of deeds granted by the Connecticut Land Company (these are really mortgages - purchase of land by grantee on time payment plan). Last half of volume contains a record of deeds showing information as in entry 24.

One volume, 1806-1808, contains copies of deeds, showing names of grantor and grantee, description of land, conditions of instruments, and signatures of parties concerned. Arranged chronologically by dates of instruments. Indexed alphabetically by names of grantors and grantees. 1 volume 500 pages. 17 x 11 x 2; 1 volume 275 pages. 12.5 x 8 x 1.5. Recorder's office.

27. DAILY REGISTER OF DEEDS
1896——. 4 vols. (1-4).

Daily registered deeds filed for recording, showing names of grantor and grantee, consecutive number of instrument, date of filing, and remarks. Arranged alphabetically under tabs by names of grantors. No index. Handwritten on printed forms. Average 375 pages. 17.5 x 13.5 x 2. Recorder's office.

28. RECORD OF REAL ESTATE DEVISED BY WILL
1906——. 1 vol. (123).

Copies of certificates of real estate, devised by will, made by probate judge for recorder, showing dates and terms of will, volume letter and page number of Record of Wills, entry 159, description of property willed, date certificate received, date recorded, and filing fees. Arranged chronologically by dates recorded. Indexed alphabetically by names of grantors. Handwritten on printed forms. 586 pages. 18 x 13 x 3. Recorder's office.

29. GENERAL REAL ESTATE INDEX OF PROBATE AND COMMON PLEAS RECORDS
1810-1904. 1 vol. (1).

Index record of probate court and common pleas court records of transfers of real estate for various reasons (devised by will, sales, and deeds), to be found in probate and common pleas records, showing date of transfer, names of grantors and grantees, volume number or letter, and page number of probate and common pleas records where original transaction is recorded, description of property transferred, and remarks. Arranged alphabetically by names of grantees. Handwritten on printed forms. 584 pages. 20 x 15 x 3. Recorder's office.

Leases (See also entries 35, 45, 62)

30. RECORD OF LEASES
1865—. 18 vols. (1-18). 1829-1849 in Deed Record, entry 24, 1850-1864 in Mortgage Record, entry 32.

Copies of leases and agreements, showing names of lessors and lessees, description of property leased, dates and condition of lease, signatures of lessor and lessee witnessed by notary public and recorder, date received, date recorded, and recording fee; also includes copies of releases of leases and notations concerning the same and Oil and Gas leases, 1884—. Arranged chronologically by dates leased. Indexed alphabetically by names of lessors; for separate index, see entry 31. 1865-1916 handwritten; 1916-1919, handwritten on printed forms. Average 525 pages. 16 x 12 x 3. Recorder's office.

31. GENERAL INDEX TO LEASES
1865—. 2 vols. (1, 2).

Index to Record of Leases, entry 30, showing name of lessor and lessee, date of lease, volume and page numbers of record, range, tract, town, section, lot, sublot, number of acres, duration of lease, and remarks. Arranged alphabetically by names of lessors. Handwritten on printed forms. Average 600 pages. 17.75 x 12 x 3. Recorder's office.

Mortgages (See also entries 46, 62).

32. MORTGAGES RECORD
1850—. 65 vols. (44, 48, 52, 56, 59, 62, 66, 69, 72, 75, 78, 80, 82, 84, 86, 90, 93, 95, 97, 100, 102, 106, 107, 110, 113, 115, 118, 121, 125, 129, 132, 133, 136, 137, 139, 141, 144, 146, 148-150, 153, 155, 158, 160, 161, 164, 166, 168, 171, 172, 175, 176, 181, 183, 185, 190, 191, 194, 197, 198, 202, 204, 207, 209). 1800-1849 in Deed Record, entry 24.

Copies of mortgages, showing names of grantors and grantees, description of property mortgaged, conditions of instrument, and signatures of parties concerned. Also contains: Record of Leases, 1850-1864, entry 30; Mortgage Releases [Certificate of Release of Mortgages], 1850-1890, entry 35. Arranged chronologically by dates of instruments. Indexed alphabetically by names of grantors; for separate index, see entry 33. 1850-1918, handwritten; 1918—, typed. Average 650 pages. 18.5 x 12 x 3. Recorder's office.

33. GENERAL INDEX TO MORTGAGES
1795—. 10 vols. (1-10).

Index to Mortgage Record, entry 32, showing date of mortgage, names of grantors and grantees, volume and page numbers of record, tract, town, section, lot, sublot, number of acres, amount of mortgages, and remarks. Index 1795-1805 was transcribed from Jefferson and Trumbull County records. Arranged alphabetically by names at grantors. Handwritten on printed forms. Average 600 pages. 18 x 13 x 3. Recorder's office.

34. DAILY REGISTER OF MORTGAGES
1896—. 4 vols. (1-4).

Daily register of mortgages filed for recording, showing names of mortgagors and mortgagees, consecutive numbers of instruments, date of filing, and remarks. Arranged alphabetically under tabs by names of mortgagors. No index. Handwritten on printed forms. Average 375 pages. 17.5 x 13.5 x 2. Recorder's office.

35. MORTGAGE RELEASES [Certificate of Release of Mortgages],
1891—. 3 vols. (1-4). 1800-1849 in Deed Record, entry 24; 1850-1890 in Mortgage Record, entry 32.

Copies of mortgage releases, showing names of grantor and grantee, description of property mortgaged, certificate of satisfaction and discharge, and signatures of witnesses, notary public, and recorder. Two volumes, 1925—, also contains record copies of releases from leases, assignments of mortgages and leases, partial releases of mortgages, leases and notes, waivers, special assignments, certificates of release of mechanics' liens, and other releases. Arranged chronologically by dates released. Indexed alphabetically by names of grantors and grantees. 1891-1917, handwritten; 1917-1925, handwritten on printed forms; 1925—. typed. Average 475 pages. 16 x 11.5 x 2. Recorder's office.

Liens (See also entries 35, 42,-47, 62)

36. MECHANICS' LIENS
1848—. 5 vols. (A; 1-4). Title varies: Record of Mechanics' Liens Book, 1848-1880, 1 vol.; Laborers' Liens, 1883-1897, 1 vol.

Record of mechanics liens charged against property for labor and material, showing names of debtor and creditor, amount of claim, date filed, and signatures of creditor, notary public, and recorder; also includes laborers; liens, 1883-1897, 1882—, indexed alphabetically by names of creditors; 1873-1881, no index. Handwritten. 3 volumes average 475 pages. 16 x 11.5 x 2; 1 volume 150 pages 12 x 7.5 x 1; 1 volume 136 pages 8 x 6.5 x 1. Recorder's office.

37. PERSONAL TAX LIEN RECORD
1932—. 1 vol.

Record of liens against personal and classified personal property for non-payment of taxes, showing year entered, name of taxing district, name and address of property owner, page number of Auditor's Classified Duplicate, entry 230, tax, penalty, total amount due, and date lien discharged. Arranged alphabetically under tabs by names of property owners. No index. Typed on printed forms. 100 pages. 12 x 9.5 x 1. Recorder's office.

38. EXCISE AND FRANCHISE TAX LIEN INDEX
1931—. 2 vols. (Last entry 1935). (1 vol. transcribed from the other).

Index record of excise and franchise tax liens certified by the state tax commission, showing filing number of original papers, name of firm, date filed, amount of tax, penalty, total cost, and date released. Also includes tax liens, showing names of property owner and occupant, date filed, filing number of [Original Instruments], entry 62, amount of tax, cost, and date released. Both volumes are identical except the typed volume was copied from the handwritten one. They cover the same dates and show the same information. Each contains one page of federal tax liens 1932—. Arranged alphabetically by names of taxpayers. No index. 1 volume handwritten. Transcribed volume typed on printed forms. Average 135 pages. 12 x 8 x 1. Recorder's office.

39. NOTICE OF DISCHARGE OF LIEN IN RECOGNIZANCE
1931—. 1 file drawer.

Original notices of discharge of lien in recognizance, showing names of sureties and defendant, file number, description of real estate, amount of bond, and date of discharge; also includes notices of pledge of real property from common pleas court to the recorder, showing date, recorder's file number, names of sureties and defendants, description of real estate, and amount of recognize; notices of lien in recognizance, showing recorder's file number, date and hour of filing, names of sureties and defendant, amount of recognizance, description of real estate, notice of discharge of recognizance, and date and hour of filing notice of discharge of recognizance, federal notices of tax liens, showing recorder's file number, name of taxpayer, residence, collector's notice number, date and hour of filing, amount of tax assessed, penalty, collector's serial number, certificate of discharge, amount of tax assessed and paid, and date and hour of filing certificates of discharge. No obvious arrangement. For index, see entry 40. Handwritten and typed, some on printed forms. 10 x 4 x 13.5. Recorder's office.

40. INDEX TO LIEN AND NOTICE OF DISCHARGE OF RECOGNIZANCE
1929—. 1 vol.

Index record to Notice of Discharge of Lien in Recognizance, entry 39, showing recorder's file number, name of court, names of surety and defendant, date of issue, date of filing, amount of surety, description of property, and date of cancellation. Arranged alphabetically by names of sureties. Handwritten on printed forms. 150 pages. 16 x 11.5 x 1. Recorder's office.

41. INDEX TO LIENS – STALLION SERVICE.
1885-1902. 1 vol.

Index record of liens for stallion service, showing names of lienors and lienees, number of original instrument, date of service, date of filing lien, amount of lien, and date of cancellation. Arranged alphabetically under tabs directed by names of lienors and lienees. Handwritten on printed forms. 150 pages. 14 x 9.5 x 1. Recorder's office.

Registered Lands

42. REGISTERED LANDS
1916—. 2 vols. (1, 2). Initiated in 1916.

Record of registered Torrens land, containing original certificates of title and transfer certificates of title; original certificates of title issued by common pleas court, showing date of certificate, case number, document number, names of owners, description of land, volume and page numbers of Deed Record, entry 24, and signatures of clerk of court and recorder; transfer certificate of title, showing from whom transferred, certificate number, document number, date originally registered, volume and page numbers of Deed Record, entry 24, names of owners, and signature of recorder; both contain memorials of lessor estates and liens in and against the land described in the certificate of title, showing number and kind of document, terms of instruments, date registered, signature of recorder, notations of assignment, and continuation or cancellation; also contains reference to volume and page numbers of Records of Plats and Surveys, entry 48, and sketches of property in question. Arranged chronologically by dates of instruments. For index, see entry 43. Handwritten and typed some on printed forms. Average 300 pages. 18 x 15 x 1.5. Recorder's private office.

43. INDEX TO REGISTERED LANDS
1916—. 1 vol.

Index to Registered Lands, entry 42, showing names of grantor and grantee, document number, certificate number, date of entry, volume and page numbers of record, lot number, and date transferred or cancelled. Arranged alphabetically by names of grantors and grantees Handwritten on printed forms. 500 pages. 20 x 18 x 2.5. Recorder's private office.

44. DAILY RECEIPT OF DOCUMENTS AFFECTING REGISTERED LANDS
1916—. 1 vol.

Daily register of documents affecting registered lands, showing date filed, document number, kind of document, from whom or against whom, in favor of whom, date of document, terms, description of lands involved, and certificate numbers. Arranged chronologically by dates filed. No index. Handwritten on printed forms. 500 pages. 20 x 19 x 2.5. Recorder's private office.

45. REGISTERED LANDS – RECORD OF LIENS, LEASES, TRUSTS, AND EXCEPTIONAL ESTATES
1919—. 1 vol. (1). Initiated in 1919.

Copies of liens, leases, trusts, and exceptional estates on registered lands, showing names of grantor and grantee, description of registered land, conditions of document, signatures of notary public and recorder, date received, date recorded, recording fee, and notes of releases. Arranged chronologically by dates received. Indexed alphabetically by names of grantors and grantees. Handwritten on printed forms. 720 pages. 20 x 19 x 2.5. Recorder's private office.

46. [LAND TITLE REGISTRATION DOCUMENTS]
1915—. 4 file drawers.
Original documents and instruments filed with the recorder pertaining to registered
lands, including mortgages, liens, powers of attorney, administrator's or executor's
deeds, orders to vacate roads, and certificates of partial discharge or release of
mortgages and deeds, showing date of filing, document number, names of grantor
and grantee, description of land, and type of instrument. No obvious arrangement.
No index. Handwritten and typed, some on printed forms. 11.5 x 16.5 x 25.5.
Recorder's private office.

47. [SIGNATURE CARDS OF HOLDERS OF LESSER ESTATES]
1931—. 1 file box.
Signature cards of holders of lesser estates and liens on registered lands, showing
signature and address of holder of estate, date, kind of instrument delivered to
holder, and date delivered. Arranged alphabetically by names of holders of lesser
estates. No index. Handwritten on printed forms. 5 x 6 x 17. Recorder's private
office.

Plats and Surveys

48. RECORD OF PLATS AND SURVEYS
1849—. 4 vols. (One unlabeled; 2, 3, 4). 1795-1848 in Deed Record, entry
24.
Record of surveys and resurveys made by county engineer containing sketches of
surveys, showing name of survey, boundary lines, allotments, villages, roads,
railroads, names of owners of lots, and date of entry. These records contain the
survey of registered lands; also perpetuation of testimony to establish boundary
lines, including copies of dispositions of interested parties, records of resurveys,
and other testimonies. Arranged chronologically by dates entered. Indexed
alphabetically by names of surveys. Table of contents in front of each volume
showing page numbers. Hand drawn, black on white. Average 36 pages. 20.5 x 16
x 1.5. Recorder's office.

49. PLATS OF GEAUGA COUNTY BY TOWNSHIPS AND VILLAGES

1927—. 6 vols. Last entry 1937. Subtitled by names of townships and villages.

Physical maps of Geauga County by townships and villages, three volumes are village lots and three volumes are township lots. Plats showing boundary lines, names of owners, roads, rivers, railroads, townships, and villages, lot, sublot, and tract numbers, and notations of resurveys. One volume, 1937, prepared by Samuel Gould, 413 ½ West Madison Avenue, Youngstown, Ohio, others prepared by county engineer. Arranged alphabetically by names of townships and villages. No index. Maps blue on white and hand drawn. Scale, 1 inch equals 10 chains. Average 50 plats, 24 x 31 x 1. Recorder's office.

50. PLATS OF GEAUGA COUNTY

1820-1870. 4 vols.

Physical map of Geauga County by townships, showing boundary lines, names of owners, tract, range, and lot numbers, and size of lots and sublots. Prepared by county engineer. No obvious arrangement. No index. Maps are hand drawn, black on white. Scales vary. 1 volume. 20 pages. 16 x 16 x 1; 3 volumes average 28 pages. 21 x 20 x 1. Recorder's office.

51. GEAUGA COUNTY ATLAS

1927, 1 vol.

Physical plats of incorporated and unincorporated villages, recording county townships, showing names of property owner, village, and township, boundary lines, section, lot, and sublot numbers. Prepared by county engineer. Publisher, Frank Zethmayer, 211 South Street, Chardon, Ohio. Arranged alphabetically by names of townships and villages. Indexed alphabetically by names of townships and villages. Plats are blue on white. Scale, 1 inch equals 100 feet. Average 32 pages. 24 x 28.5 x 1. Recorder's office.

Personal Property Transfers
(See also entries 55, 62)

52. [ORIGINAL CHATTEL MORTGAGES]

1908—. 18 file drawers. (Labeled by contained instrument numbers).

Original chattel mortgages, showing name of mortgagor and mortgagee, mortgage number, date of filing, amount, consideration, and list of chattels. Arranged numerically by consecutive instrument numbers. For index, see entry 53. Handwritten and typed, some on printed forms. 14 file drawers, 10 x 5 x 13.5; 4 file drawers, 12 x 13.5 x 25.5. 4 file drawers, 1916-1936, Recorder's private office; 14 file drawers, 1908—, Recorder's office.

53. CHATTEL MORTGAGE INDEX
1878—. 9 vols. (two unlabeled; 2-8).
Index record of chattel mortgages and conditional bills of sale, showing name of grantor, grantee, or assignee, consecutive instrument numbers, date of original instrument, date of filing, consideration, date of refiling, date cancelled, and remarks. Serves as index to (Original Chattel Mortgage), entry 52 by showing instrument number. Arranged alphabetically by names of grantors, grantees, and assignees. Handwritten on printed forms. Average 265 pages. 18 x 12 x 1.5. Recorder's office.

Incorporations and Partnerships

54. RECORD OF INCORPORATION
1845-1906. 1 vol. (1).
Record of incorporation and election of officers of churches, societies, schools, banks, and other businesses, showing date of incorporation, procedure of incorporation, or election of officers, date received, and date filed; also includes resolutions granting franchises to railroads. This record, 1845-1855 is transcribed from an old record which has been destroyed. Arranged chronologically by dates filed. No index. Handwritten. 500 pages. 15 x 10 x 2. Recorder's office.
For record 1817-1824, 1831-1840, see entry 128.

55. CERTIFICATES OF PARTNERSHIP AND RECORD OF CHATTEL MORTGAGES
1876-1884. 1 vol. (1). 1884-1886 in Partnership and Trader's Record entry 56.
Copies of certificates of partnership and chattel mortgages, showing date of entry, names of parties concerned, conditions of partnership or mortgage, signatures of witnesses and principals, date received, and date recorded. Arranged chronologically by dates entered. Indexed alphabetically by names of partnerships or grantors. Handwritten. 191 pages. 13 x 8 x 1. Recorder's office.

56. PARTNERSHIP AND TRADER'S RECORD
1884-1886. 1 vol. (1).

Partnership and trader's record, showing date of partnership entered into, names and addresses of partners or traders, type of business, name and location of firm. Also contains certificates of partnerships and Record of Chattel Mortgages, 1884-1886, entry 55. Arranged chronologically by dates of partnerships. Indexed alphabetically by names of firms. Handwritten on printed forms. 300 pages. 12 x 18.25 x 1.5. Recorder's office.

For other records, see entry 94.

Grants of Authority and Licenses
(See also entries 24, 46)

57. CERTIFICATES OF COMPLIANCE OF INSURANCE COMPANIES
1919—. 4 file drawers.

Original certificates of compliance of insurance companies, showing date of certificate, name of company, financial statement, and signature of Ohio superintendent of insurance; also certified copies of agents' licenses, showing name and address of agent, conditions of license, and signature of superintendent of insurance. Arranged chronologically by dates of certificates. No index. Handwritten and typed, some on printed forms. 3 file drawers, 5 x 10 x 13.5; 1 file drawer, 12 x 13.5 x 25.5. 1 file drawer, 1934-1937, Recorder's private office; 3 file drawers, 1919—, Recorder's office.

Financial Records

58. RECORDER'S CASH BOOK AND RECORD OF FEES
1907—. 11 vols. (1-11).

Record of fees received by recorder and paid into treasury, showing date of entry, chattel mortgage number, consecutive number of all other instruments, by who paid, kind of instrument or service, total and itemized amounts for recording, filing papers, cancellation, searches, and sundries. Earlier volumes contained pasted-in receipts of treasurer. Later volumes contain pay-in orders of auditor and receipted by treasurer for money paid into treasury by recorder. Arranged chronologically by dates entered. No index. Handwritten on printed forms. Average 225 pages. 17 x 12 x 1.25. Recorder's office.

Miscellaneous

59. RECORD OF SOLDIERS' DISCHARGE
1862-1865, 1918—. 2 vols. (1, 2).
Record of discharge of soldiers, sailors, and marines, showing date and conditions
of discharge, name and description of soldier or sailor, date discharge received, and
date recorded. One volume, 1862-1865, contains discharge of Ohio Volunteers from
the Civil War. One volume, 1918—, contains discharges of soldiers from the World
War, and general service in army and navy. Arranged chronologically by dates
recorded. Indexed alphabetically by names of soldiers or sailors. Handwritten on
printed forms. Average 410 pages. 17 x 12 x 2. Recorder's office.

60. [PETITION FENCE RECORD]
1906—. 1 vol. Last entry 1937.
Record of applications to township trustees to assign partition fences and the repair
and maintenance of same, showing date of application, names of contracting
persons, terms of agreement, cost of assignment, signatures of trustees recording
fee, and signature of recorder. Record is contained in volume originally intended for
receipts and disbursements of the treasurer of the board of education of the various
school districts. Arranged chronologically by dates of applications. Indexed
alphabetically by names of complainants. Handwritten. 240 pages. 13.5 x 18.5 x 1.
Recorder's office.
For duplicate petitions 1936—, see entry 12.

61. [INDENTURES OF APPRENTICESHIP]
1825-1858. 1 vol.
Record of indentures of apprenticeship, showing names of master and apprentice,
date of entry, age of apprentice, conditions of indenture, signatures of parties
concerned, date received, and date recorded. Arranged chronologically by dates
entered. No index. Handwritten. 500 pages. 12.5 x 8 x 2. Recorder's office.

62. [ORIGINAL INSTRUMENTS]

1822—. 55 file drawers. (one unlabeled; A-Z; 5, 6).

Original instruments, including deeds, warranty deeds, sheriff's deeds, quit claim deeds, mortgages, affidavits of real estate transfers, records of real estate inherited, affidavits to obtain liens, mortgage release certificates, certificates of wills, copies of assignments of trustees on partition fences, certificates for transfer of real estate devised by will, leases, certified copies of court journal entries regarding real estate or personal property chattel mortgages to 1919, mechanics' liens, and assignments of leases and mortgages, showing date of instrument, document number, name of grantors and grantees, description of lands, and type of instrument. No index. Handwritten and typed, some on printed forms. 10 x 5 x 13.5. Recorder's office.

The office of clerk of courts, an ancient English institution originating before the time of Edward I[1] was transplanted to America during the colonial period. The American Revolution made no radical change in the political heritage derived from England, and the office was continued by the states. The duties of the office were modified in the newer states, however, because of a separation of administrative and judicial functions, which under the English system had been combined.

The sections of the Ohio Constitution, of 1802, creating the judicial system for the state provided for the appointment of a clerk of courts by the judges of the court of common pleas. He was to serve a seven-year term, but was subject to removal by the appointing power for a breach of good behavior.[2] The constitution of 1851 made the office of clerk elective with a three-year term.[3] A constitutional amendment in 1905 provided that the terms of all elective offices should be for an even number of years not exceeding four. In compliance with this amendment, the general assembly passed an act fixing the term of office of the clerk at two years.[4] The term remained at two years until 1936 when it was extended to four years.[5] The remuneration of the office was by fees until 1906 when the legislature prescribed a definite salary based on the population of his county.[6]

The duties of the clerk of courts, like those of other county officers, are prescribed by statute. In 1853 a code of civil procedure was adopted summarizing the earlier duties and forming the basis for the present ones which are in most respects similar to those prescribed during the earlier years of the office. The clerk of courts was directed to issue all *writs* and orders for provisional remedies; endorse the date upon all papers filed in his office; keep the journal, record books, and papers appertaining to the court of common pleas and record its proceedings, keeping the appearance docket and the trial docket, as well as a printed duplicate of the trial docket, journal, record, and the execution docket.[7]

1. Sir Frederick Pollock and Frederic William Maitland, *The History of English Law Before the Time of Edward I* (Cambridge, 1895), I, 184.
2. *Ohio Const, 1802,* Art. III sec. 9.
3. *Ohio Const. 1851,* Art, IV, sec. 16.
4. *Laws of Ohio,* XCVIII, 273.
5. *Ibid.,* CXVI, pt. ii, 184.
6. *Ibid.,* XCVIII, 94, 117.
7. *Ibid.,* LI, 107, 158-159; LXXVIII, 108; LXXIX, 115; LXXXVI, 174.

The present practice of preparing an index, direct and reverse, to judgments began in 1866.[8] In 1871, the clerk was made official custodian of the law reports and books furnished by the state for the use of the court and bar, and was made liable in the event of their destruction.[9]

Some of the duties of the clerk as defined by the civil code of 1853 are still effective, others have been added by subsequent legislation. Thus for example, in 1858 the clerk was directed to receive notary commissions for record.[10] He was required, also, to receive for record special police commissions (1867), timber trade-marks (1883), partnerships agreements (1894), copies of judgments of federal courts (1898), marks of ownership [trade-marks] (1911), motor vehicle bills of sale (1921), and certificates of judgments to operate as a lien (1935).[11] Since January 1, 1938 he has issued certificates of title to motor vehicles.[12] On the other hand, many of the earlier duties of the clerk have been transferred to other departments of local government or have been abolished. The clerk issued marriage licenses and recorded ministers' license until 1852. Since that date the former have been issued and the latter recorded by the probate court,[13] to which court the records have been transferred. Moreover, the clerk issued peddlers' licenses until the decade of the sixties, since when they have been issued by the auditor.[14] These records were not found in the inventory. The clerk has been authorized to act as an agent of the state in the sale of hunting and trapping licenses to non-residents of the state since 1904 and to residents since 1919.[15] He has been authorized also to serve as agent in the sale of fishing licenses to non-residents since 1919 and to residents since 1925.[16] The practice of recording in the office of the clerk, the name of black or mulatto persons to be used as certificates of freedom was, of course, discontinued after the close of the War between the States in 1865.

---

8. *Ibid.,* LXIII, 10; LXXV, 103; LXXVIII, 88; LXXII, 33; LXXXVI, 26.
9. *Ibid.,* LXVIII, 109.
10. *Laws of Ohio,* LV, 13; XCIII, 406.
11. *Ibid.,* LXIV, 60; LXXX, 195; XCI, 357; XCII, 25; XCIII, 285; CII, 513-514; CIX, 333; CXVI, 274.
12. G. C. sec. 6290-6.
13. *Laws of Ohio,* I, 312; XXIX, 429; L, 84; *Ohio Const. 1851,* Art. IV, sec. 8.
14. *Laws of Ohio,* LIX, 67.
15. *Ibid.,* XCVIII, 474; CVIII, pt. i, 595.
16. *Ibid.,* CVIII, 923; CXI, 276.

In 1856 the clerk was directed by the legislature to preserve a list of births, marriages, and deaths as returned to his office by the assessors, and to transmit annually, on or before the first day of June, a copy of such statistics to the secretary of state. These lists are no longer preserved. From these county lists, the secretary of state prepared tabular statements showing the vital statistics in each county. The clerk received 10 copies of the report, one of which he was required to preserve in his office.[17] The clerk was relieved of the task of collecting and preserving vital statistics, when, in 1867, such powers and duties were vested in the probate judge.[18]

The clerk of courts was giving other duties in addition to those of serving the court of common pleas and receiving documents for record. Since 1850 he has been required to report each year to the county commissioners all fines assessed by the courts in criminal cases, together with the names of the parties to each case, and the amount of money he has paid to the county treasurer.[19] Duplicate copies of these reports have not been preserved in the clerk's office. Moreover, since 1867 he has been required to report annually to the secretary of state the number of crimes committed in his county, the number of pending cases, and the amount of fines collected.[20] An act of 1927, amending the act of 1867, directed the clerk to report on any matters which the secretary of state might require, and to forward a duplicate copy of his report on crime in his county to the state board of clemency [board of pardons and paroles].[21] The state board of clemency was abolished in 1921 and its duties were assigned to a board of pardons and parole within the department of public welfare.[22]

The county clerk of courts, like the county prosecuting attorney, is one of the important persons in the judicial system. His significance and influence, however, were not recognized until recent years.

---

17. *Ibid.*, LIII, 73-75.
18. *Ibid.*, LXIV, 63-64.
19. *Laws of Ohio*, XLVIII, 66; LVIII, 69; LXXXVI, 239.
20. *Ibid.*, LXIV, 17.
21. *Ibid.*, CXII, 203.
22. *Ibid.*, CIX, 111, 124.

The clerk of courts in Geauga County is bonded for $10,000,[23] and receives a salary of $1515 annually.[24] He is assisted by two deputies, also bonded, and one clerk, who receive an annual aggregate compensation of $3897.98. The office is self-supporting. Fees received during the year 1940 for services rendered to the public totaled $6979.93, [25] far exceeding the cost of operation.

---

23. Treasurer's Record of Bonds of Officials, 1940, entry 352.
24. Appropriation Ledger, 1940, entry 248.
25. *Ibid.*

Court Proceedings

63. PRAECIPE DOCKET
1874—. 5 vols. (three unlabeled; 2; one dated).
Docket of orders to clerk of courts to issue papers, including orders of sale, executions, summonses, *writs* of partition, orders of sale or confirmation in partition, *writs* of possession, notices of motions, and all other orders pertaining to common pleas court, showing signatures of attorneys and plaintiff and defendant, title of case, names of plaintiff and defendant, date filed, orders to issue paper, and date paper issued. Arranged chronologically by dates filed. No index. Handwritten on printed forms. Average 175 pages. 14 x 9 x 1.25. Clerk of courts' office.

Original Documents

64. BILLS OF EXCEPTION
1890—. 4 wooden boxes, 3 shelves.
Original bills of exception to procedure and decision in cases heard in common pleas court, showing date of trial, title of case, names of witnesses, date exception filed, date received by judge, date corrected and allowed, date filed in court of appeals or circuit court, transcripts of all proceedings in common pleas court, copies of briefs filed by plaintiffs and defendants in court of appeals or circuit court, statements on motions for a new trial, judge's affidavits, and all exceptions. Each bill bound separately. Arranged chronologically by dates of trials. No index. Handwritten and typed. Boxes average 20 x 30 x 20; shelves average 40 x 40. 4 wooden boxes, 1890-1825, Attic storeroom; 1 wooden shelf, 1925-1929, third floor storeroom; 2 steel shelves, 1930—, Clerk of courts' office.

65. [PENDING CIVIL CASES]

1921—. 16 file drawers. (Labeled by contained letters of the alphabet). Original papers in pending civil cases, showing information as in Original Papers – Civil Cases, entry 70, except there are no decrees. Papers of each case in separate jacket, showing names of plaintiff and defendant and case number. Arranged alphabetically by names of plaintiffs. No index. Handwritten and typed, some on printed forms. 11 x 5 x 13.5. Clerk of courts' office.

66. [PENDING CRIMINAL CASES]

1935—. 1 file drawer. Original papers in pending criminal cases, showing information as in Original Papers – Criminal Cases Filed, entry 71, except there are no verdicts. Papers of each case in separate jacket, showing names of plaintiff and defendant and case numbers. Arranged numerically by case numbers. No index. Handwritten and typed, some on printed forms. 11 x 5 x 13.5. Clerk of courts' office.

67. ORIGINAL PAPERS IN CLOSED CASES PENDING FINAL DISPOSITION

1928—. 3 file boxes. (Labeled by contain letters of alphabet). Original papers in civil cases that have been closed but which lack final disposition, including foreclosure proceedings on which sheriff's sale has not been held, judgments in which payments on judgments are not complete, cases in which final order or decree of court has not been carried out, showing case number, names of plaintiff and defendant, title of case, date petition filed, proceedings, volume and page numbers of Common Pleas Journal, entry 129 and Appearance and Execution Docket, entry 118, and name of attorney. Papers filed in separate jacket, showing names of plaintiff and defendant in case numbers. Arranged alphabetically by names of plaintiffs. No index. Handwritten on printed forms. 12 x 17 x 24. Clerk of courts' office.

68. INDEX TO ORIGINAL PAPERS – CIVIL CASES

1844-1926. 4 vols. Obsolete index to filed, Original Papers – Civil Cases, entry 70 and Original Papers – Criminal Cases Filed, entry 71, showing names of plaintiff and defendant, file box number, and remarks. In January 1938, the papers in all file boxes were rearranged according to case numbers, and the labeling on the file boxes changed, showing the case numbers includes in each box; therefore this no longer serves as an index to entries 70, 71. Arranged alphabetically by names of plaintiffs. Handwritten on printed forms. Average 238 pages. 16 x 12 x 1.5. Clerk of courts' office.

69. INDEX TO FILED DEFENDANTS
1844-1926. 4 vols.

Obsolete index to filed, Original Papers – Civil Cases, entry 70 and Original Papers – Criminal Cases Filed, entry 71, showing names of defendant and plaintiff, file box numbers, and remarks. In January 1938, the papers in all file boxes were rearranged according to case numbers, and the labeling on the file boxes changed, showing the case numbers in each box; therefore this no longer serves as an index to entries 70, 71. Arranged alphabetically by names of defendants. Handwritten on printed forms. Average 238 pages. 16 x 12 x 1.5. Clerk of courts' office.

70. ORIGINAL PAPERS – CIVIL CASES
1844—. 331 file boxes. (Labeled by contained case numbers).

Original case papers from all courts of civil cases that have been completed including journal entries, certification of publication, petitions, *praecipes,* certificates of judgment, orders of attachment, affidavits, dispositions, sheriff's returns, civil cost bills, motions, application for postponement, summonses, appraisements, decrees, answers, *demurrers,* bills of exception, and all other papers pertaining to case, showing case number, title of case, names of plaintiff and defendant, date petition filed, volume and page numbers in Common Pleas Journal, entry 129; Appearance Docket, entry 117; Execution Docket, entry 128; Appearance and Execution Docket, entry 118; Common Pleas Record, entry 119, term of court in which case was closed, and names of attorneys. Papers for each case are enclosed in separate jacket, showing case number and title of case. Arranged numerically by case numbers. For index, see entry 68. Handwritten and typed, some on printed forms. 11 x 5 x 13.5. Clerk of courts' office.

71. ORIGINAL PAPERS – CRIMINAL CASES FILED
1844—. 23 file boxes. (Labeled by contained case numbers).

Original papers in all criminal cases contained in separate jackets, showing case number, name of defendant, volume and page numbers in Appearance Docket, entry 117; Criminal Appearance Docket, entry 124; Common Pleas Journal, entry 129; Criminal Record, entry 125, and term of court, including criminal cost bills, affidavits, *mittimus.* state warrants, transcripts, common pleas court criminal records, information, recognizances, sheriff's returns, warrants, executions, verdicts, indictments, subpoenas, journal entries, notices, record of bonds given in criminal case, 1929—, and all other papers pertaining to each case. Arranged numerically by case numbers. No index. Handwritten and typed, some on printed forms. 11 x 5 x 13.5. Clerk of courts' office.

72. TRANSCRIPTS FROM MAGISTRATES COURTS
1909—. 3 file boxes. (Labeled by contained letters of alphabet).
Original papers of cases filed in common pleas court which originated in the court of the mayor or justice of the peace, including *praecipes,* transcripts from the court of the mayor or justice of the peace, executions, notices, journal entries, affidavits, and all other papers pertaining to case; each case filed in separate jacket, showing case number, names of plaintiff and defendant, date transcript filed, volume and page numbers in Common Pleas Journal, entry 129; Execution Docket, entry 128; Appearance and Execution Docket, entry 118; Common Pleas Record, entry 119, term of court in which case was closed, and names of attorneys. Arranged alphabetically by names of plaintiffs. No index. Handwritten and typed, some on printed forms. Average 500 documents in file boxes, 11 x 5 x 13.5. Clerk of courts' office.

Judgments and Executions

73. [JUDGMENT DOCKET]
1935—. 1 vol. Initiated in 1935.
Certificates of judgment to operate as liens, showing name of court, case number, title of action, parties to action, names of judgment creditors and judgment debtors, amount of judgment and interest, date judgment or decree rendered, volume letter of number, and page number in Common Pleas Journal, entry 129, date of filing, and date of cancellation (if cancelled). Arranged chronologically by dates filed. Indexed alphabetically by names of judgment creditors and debtors. Handwritten on printed forms. 600 pages. 18.5 x 13 x 3.25. Clerk of courts' office.

74. JUDGMENT INDEX [DIRECT]
1878-1916. 2 vols. (1, 2).
Index to judgments, showing case number, names of judgment creditors and debtors, volume and page numbers in Appearance Docket, entry 117 and Common Pleas Journal, entry 129, amount of judgment, date of judgment, volume and page numbers in Common Pleas Record, entry 119 and Execution Docket, entry 128,

number of execution and remarks. Arranged alphabetically by names of judgment creditors. Handwritten on printed forms. Average 225 pages. 18 x 12.5 x 1.5. Clerk of courts' office.

75. JUDGMENT INDEX [REVERSE]
1878-1916. 2 vols. (1, 2).
Index to judgments, showing case number, names of judgment debtors and creditors, volume and page numbers in Appearance Docket, entry 117; Common Pleas Journal, entry 129; Common Pleas Record, entry 119; Execution Docket, entry 128, amount and date of judgment, number of execution, and remarks. Arranged alphabetically by names of judgment debtors. Handwritten on printed forms. Average 225 pages. 18 x 12.5 x 1.5. Clerk of courts' office.

76. INDEX TO PENDING SUITS, LIVING JUDGMENTS, AND LIVING EXECUTIONS
1877—. 5 vols. (two unlabeled; three labeled by contained letters of alphabet).
Index to pending suits, living judgments, and living executions, showing date of suit, names of plaintiff, defendant, administrator, executor, trustees, and all other appointees, name of court, case numbers of pending suits in Appearance Docket, entry 117 and Appearance and Execution Docket, entry 118; for living judgments, volume and page numbers in Execution Docket, entry 128 and Appearance and Execution Docket, entry 118; case number of living executions, living judgments, and judgment liens, and volume and page numbers in [Judgment Docket], entry 73, and case number of Original Papers – Civil Cases, entry 70. Arranged alphabetically by names of plaintiffs and defendants. 1877-1899, handwritten on printed forms; 1900—, typed on printed forms. Average 320 pages. 18 x 13 x 2. Clerk of courts' office.

Jury and Witness Records

77. [WITNESS RECORDS]
1834-1840, 1848-1851, 1864-1924, 1928—. 10 vols. (four unlabeled; 1, 1, 2, 2, 3, 4). Title varies: Docket, 1834-1840, 1 vol.; Witness Record, 1848-1851, 1 vol.
Record of witnesses appearing before common pleas court, showing term of court, date of trial, case number, title of case, names of plaintiff and defendant, names and

addresses of plaintiff's and defendant's witnesses, miles traveled, amount due witnesses, and date paid; 1928——, shows only mileage and amount due; includes district court records 1848-1851. Also contains: Witness Records – State Cases, 1834-1840, 1848-1851, 1864-1907, entry 78; Cashbook, 1928——, entry 98. Arranged chronologically by court terms and chronologically thereunder by dates of trials. No index. 1834-1840, 1848-1851, handwritten; 1864-1924, 1928——, handwritten on printed forms. Average 200 pages. 12 x 9 x 1.5. 8 volumes, 1834-1840, 1848-1851, 1864-1924, third floor storeroom; 2 volumes, 1928——, Clerk of courts' office.

78. WITNESS RECORDS – STATE CASES
1908——. 1 vol. (1). Initiated in 1908. 1834-1840, 1848-1851, 1864-1907, in [Witness Records], entry 77.

Record of witnesses brought before common pleas court in criminal cases, showing term of court, date of trial, case number, volume and page numbers of Criminal Appearance Docket, entry 124, names of defendants and witnesses, number of days witnesses served, miles traveled and amount of witnesses' fees; also contains record of payments of grand jury fees, showing names of grand jurors, number of days served, miles traveled, and amount of payment. Arranged chronologically by court terms and chronologically thereunder by dates of trials. Indexed alphabetically by names of defendants. Handwritten on printed forms. 208 pages. 14 x 10 x 1. Clerk of courts' office.

79. JURY DOCKET
1874——. 4 vols. (one unlabeled; 1, 2, 4). Title varies: Jury Book, 1874-1933, 3 vols.

Record of jurors' service on grand jury, petit jury, and regular juries in criminal and civil cases, showing term of court, title of case, names of plaintiff and defendant, assigned numbers, names of jurors, and number of days served 1934——, showing names and addresses of jurors, individual jurors particular dates of service, mileage, fee, total mileage and fees, date paid, whether case postponed, excused, or discharged, and reason, further date of trial, names of jurors who did not attend or serve, and amount and date of fine. 1874-1933, arranged chronologically by court terms; 1934——, arranged by chronologically by dates served. No index. Handwritten on printed forms. 3 volumes average 300 pages. 14 x 9.5 x 1.25; 1 volume 100 pages 14 x 22 x 1. 2 volumes, 1902-1933 third floor storeroom; 2 volumes, 1874-1901, 1934——, Clerk of courts' office.

80. ANNUAL JURY LIST
1935—. 1 file drawer.

Annual list of persons chosen for jury service in Geauga County, showing date filed, assigned number, name and address of juror, total number of jurors, date list filed in common pleas court, and signatures of jury commissioners. Arranged chronologically by dates filed. No index. Typed on printed forms. 11 x 5 x 13.25. Clerk of courts' office.

Motor Vehicles

81. [Index Of Motor Vehicle Bills Of Sale And Statements Of Ownership] GRANTORS DIRECT
1921-1937. 3 vols. (1-3). Discontinued, law repealed.

Direct index to Bills of Sale [Motor Vehicles], entry 84 and Sworn Statements of Ownership, entry 83, showing names of grantor and grantee, date of filing, consecutive instrument numbers, fee, make of vehicle, type, model, change of ownership, reference and date of transfer, Arranged alphabetically by names of grantors and chronologically thereunder by date filed. Handwritten on printed forms. Average 500 pages. 15 x 18 x 3. Certificate of title office.

82. [Index Of Motor Vehicle Bills Of Sale And Statements Of Ownership] GRANTEES REVERSE
1921-1937. 3 vols. (1-3). Discontinued, law repealed.

Reverse index to Bills of Sale [Motor Vehicles], entry 84 and sworn Statement of Ownership, entry 83, showing names of grantee and grantor, date of filing, fee, make of vehicle, type, model, change of ownership, date of transfer, and consecutive instrument numbers. Arranged alphabetically by named of grantees and chronologically thereunder by dates filed. Handwritten on printed forms. Average 500 pages. 15 x 18 x 3. Certificate of title office.

83. SWORN STATEMENTS OF OWNERSHIP
1921-1937. 5 file drawers. (Labeled by contained instrument numbers). Discontinued, law repealed.

Copies of sworn statements of motor vehicle ownership, showing date of filing, name and address of owner, how motor vehicle was acquired, date of acquisition, instrument number, description of motor vehicle, signature of owner, and witnessed by notary or other authorized person; also includes duplicates of bills of sale attached to statement of ownership. Arranged numerically by instrument numbers. For indexes, see entry 81, 82. Handwritten and typed, some on printed forms. 11 x 5 x 13.5. Certificate of title office.

84. BILLS OF SALE [Motor Vehicles]
1921-1937. 88 file drawers. (Labeled by contained instrument numbers). Discontinued, law repealed.
Copies of motor vehicle bills of sale, showing bill of sale number, names of grantor and grantee, date of filing, description of motor vehicle, and witnessed by notary public; sales tax stamps are affixed, 1935-1937. Arranged numerically by instrument numbers and chronologically thereunder by dates filed. For indexes, see entries 81, 82. Handwritten and typed, some on printed forms. 11 x 5 x 13.5. Certificate of title office.

85. CERTIFICATES OF TITLE
1938—. 6 file drawers. Initiated in 1938.
Carbon copies of certificate of title for motor vehicles, showing number of certificate, previous certificate number, name and address of owner, description of vehicle, itemization of mortgages or liens on motor vehicle, amount of sales, tax paid, purchase price, and date of issue of certificate; also includes assignments of certificate of title. Arranged numerically by certificate numbers. For index, see entry 86. Typed on printed forms. 12 x 13.5 x 27.5. Certificate of title office.

86. CARD INDEX TO CERTIFICATE OF TITLE
1938—. 2 file drawers. Initiated in 1938.
Card index to Certificates of Title, entry 85, showing certificate number, previous number, name and address of owner, description of motor vehicle, and name and address of previous owner. Arranged alphabetically by names of owners. Typed on printed forms. 6 x 13.5 x 27.5. Certificate of title office.

Commissions

87. RECORD OF NOTARIES' COMMISSIONS
1858—. 5 vols. (one unlabeled; 2-5).

Copies of notaries' commissions and oaths; commissions, showing name of notary, duration and date of commission, name of governor, appointment and authorization to act as notary, date of issuance of commission, and signatures of governor and secretary of state; oaths, showing declaration to support constitution and discharge duties of office, sworn to and signed by notary, date of signature, date received and recorded, and signature of clerk; appointment and oath of railroad police, 1900—, showing names of commission and person appointed, date and length of time appointed, names of governor and secretary of state, date recorded, and signature of clerk of courts; also five records of issuance optometrist's license, 1920-1932, showing name of optometrist, by what authority granted, date and place granted, and signatures of optometrist and clerk of state board. Also includes record of Justices' Oaths and Bonds, 1861-1882, entry 88. Arranged chronologically by dates of issuance of commissions. Indexed alphabetically by names of notaries, justices of peace, railroad policemen, and optometrists. Handwritten on printed forms. Average 300 pages. 14 x 9 x 1.5. 1 volume, 1901-1924, third floor storeroom; 4 volumes, 1858-1901, 1924—, Clerk of courts' office.

88. RECORD OF JUSTICES' OATHS AND BONDS
1883—. 3 vols. (2-4). 1861-1882 in Record of Notaries, Commission, entry 87.

Copies of oaths and commissions of justices of peace; commission, showing signature and address of justice of peace, name of governor of the state, township in which elected, authorization to act as justice of the peace, date of issuance, and signatures of governor and secretary of state; oaths, showing sworn statement of the justice of peace to support the constitution and discharge his duties, sworn to before a clerk or other justice of the peace, date bond filed, names of sureties, dates of beginning and expiration of term, and certified by clerk of courts. Arranged chronologically by dates bonds filed. Indexed alphabetically by names of justices. Handwritten on printed forms. Average 300 pages. 14 x 9 x 2. Clerk of courts' office.

CLERK OF COURTS 53

89. RAILROAD POLICE COMMISSIONS
1829—. 1 file drawer.

Original commissions to act as railroad police issued by state executive department, showing names of policeman and railroad, dates of commencement and duration of commission, date of issue, and oath of policeman. Arranged chronologically by dates issued. No index. Typed on printed forms. 11 x 5 x 13.5. Clerk of courts' office.

Licenses

90. REGISTER OF REAL ESTATE LICENSE
1935—. 1 vol.

Register of real estate brokers' licenses, showing name and address of licensee employing broker, classification, date of issue, date of cancellation, and revocation or suspension. Arranged chronologically by dates issued. Indexed alphabetically by names of licensees. Handwritten on printed forms. 150 pages. 14.5 x 18 x 1. Clerk of courts' office.

91. RECORD OF FISHERS' LICENSES
1924-1935. 1 vol. (1).

Record of licenses issued to fish with rod and reel, showing license number, date of issue, name of licensee, age, occupation, residence, post-office address, citizenship, physical description of licensee, and amount of fee. Arranged alphabetically by names of licensees. No index. Handwritten on printed forms. 101 pages. 16 x 12 x 1. Clerk of courts' office.

92. RECORD OF HUNTERS' AND TRAPPERS' LICENSES
1913-1935. 2 vols. (1, 2).

Record of hunters' and trappers' licenses issued, showing license number, date of issue, name of licensee, age, occupation, residence, post-office address, citizenship, physical description of licensee, and amount of fee. Arranged alphabetically by names of licensees. No index. Handwritten on printed forms. Average 121 pages. 16 x 12 x 1. Clerk of courts' office.

93. EMBALMERS' LICENSE RECORD
1902-1917. 1 vol.

Record of embalmers' licenses issued, showing license number, name of embalmer, authority to act as embalmer, date of license, date received for record, date recorded, and signatures of president and secretary of the Ohio State Board of Embalming Examiners by whom licenses were issued. Arranged chronologically by dates recorded. Indexed alphabetically by names of embalmers. Handwritten on printed forms. 275 pages. 14 x 9 x 1.25. Clerk of courts' office.

Partnerships

94. REGISTER OF PARTNERSHIPS AND PARTNERS
1894—. 1 vol. (1).

Record of partnerships, showing date of filing papers, purpose of partnership, and names and addresses of partners. Arranged alphabetically by names of partnerships and chronologically thereunder by dates filed. No index. Handwritten on printed forms. 175 pages. 16 x 11 x 1. Clerk of courts' office.

For other records, see entry 56.

Elections

95. POLL BOOKS AND TALLY SHEETS
1930—. 235 vols. (Dated and labeled by precinct numbers and ward letters).

Poll books and tally sheets of primary and general elections; poll books, showing date of the election, name and address of elector, party ballot, non-partisan ballot, and question and issues ballot; tally sheets, showing names of candidates for office, and total number of votes cast; also includes certification of number of votes received by counting officials. Arranged chronologically by dates of elections. No index. Handwritten on printed forms. Average 28 pages. 17.5 x 10.25 x .25. 98 volumes, 1930-1934, third floor storeroom; 137 volumes, 1934—, Clerk of courts' office.

Coroner's Inquest

96. CORONER'S INQUEST
1900-1924, 1932—. 1 wooden box, 1 file drawer.
Coroner's reports of inquest held in cases of death under suspicious or doubtful
circumstances, showing date of report, name of decedent, last address, date and
cause of death, names of witnesses or jurors, date itemized cost bill filed with
commissioners, and date filed. 1900-1924, no obvious arrangement; 1932—,
arranged chronologically by dates reported. No index. Handwritten and typed, some
on printed forms. Wooden box 12 x 16 x 20; file drawer 11 x 5 x 13.5. 1 wooden
box, 1900-1924, attic storeroom; 1 file drawer, 1932—, Clerk of courts' office.

97. INDEX TO CORONER'S INQUEST
1910-1935. 1 vol. (dated).
Index record of coroner's inquest, showing name of decedent, name of coroner who
held inquest, and date of filing. Arranged alphabetically by names of decedents and
chronologically thereunder by dates filed. No index. Handwritten on printed forms.
100 pages. 16 x 11 x 1. Clerk of courts' office.

Financial Records

98. CASHBOOK
1907—. 20 vols. (2-21). 1928— also in the [Witness Records], entry 77.
Record of all receipts and disbursements, showing docket and case numbers, name
of plaintiff or defendant, date of receipt or payment, where court costs or fees were
made in installments at different dates; notation of installments, showing check
number and volume and page numbers of entries in cash book in which installments
on the same court costs or fees were entered. Also contains: Alimony Docket,
1907—, entry 110; Unclaimed Costs and Fees, Deposited in Treasury, 1929—,
entry 103. Arranged chronologically by dates of receipts or disbursements. 1907-
1921, 1935—, indexed alphabetically by names of plaintiffs, showing names of
defendants and case numbers; 1921-1934, no index. Handwritten on printed forms.
Average 250 pages. 17.5 x 15 x 1.5. 2 volumes, 1907-1913 attic storeroom; 4
volumes, 1913-1922, third floor storeroom; 14 volumes, 1922—, Clerk of courts'
office.

99. JURY FEES
1935——. 2 pads of stubs, 1 vol. Initiated in 1935.

Stubs of certificates of fees issued to witnesses or jurors in state cases, showing certificate number, date of issue, name of witness or juror, number of days served, number of miles traveled, and amount paid. Arranged numerically by certificate numbers and also arranged chronologically by dates issued. No index. Handwritten on printed forms. Stubs 200 pages. 6 x 2 x 1; 1 volume 150 pages. 16 x 14 x 1. Clerk of courts' office.

100. CLERK'S FEE BOOK
1907-1925. 2 vols. (1, 2).

Record of fees received, showing date of accrual, title of case, volume and page numbers in Execution Docket, entry 128, date fees received, date fee deposited in treasury, and remarks. Volume 2, 1914-1925, is an accrued fee book, showing date of filing, case number, title of case, to whom charged, total, civil and criminal cases, due from county, and date of payment. 1907-1913, arranged chronologically by dates of receipts; 1914-1925, arranged chronologically by dates filed. No index. Handwritten on printed forms. Average 160 pages. 18 x 12 x 1.25. Attic storeroom.

101. [CARD INDEX FILE – UNPAID COURT COSTS]
1907——. 1 file drawer.

Card index record of unpaid cost in civil and criminal cases, showing case number, kind of action taken, amount of unpaid cost which date back to 1907, title of case, names of plaintiff and defendant, names and addresses of payer and payee, dates of statement of cost and other correspondence sent; also contains record of payments on cost, showing dates and amounts. 1907-1934 transcribed from entry 128. Arranged alphabetically by names of persons from whom the costs are due. Typed on printed cards. 6 x 12 x 23. Clerk of courts' office.

102. COST DOCKET
1853-1957 1 vol. (A).

Record of costs in civil and criminal cases before magistrate's and county courts, showing court term, date of trial, title of case, names of plaintiff and defendant, cost itemized for all services, including filing, docketing, and clerk's witnesses', and sheriff's fees, recording, and all other costs pertaining to case, total, and volume and page numbers in Common Pleas Journal, entry 129. Arranged chronologically by court terms and chronologically thereunder by dates of trial. Indexed alphabetically by names of plaintiffs showing names of defendants. Handwritten. 350 pages. 15.5 x 11 x 2. Clerk of courts' office.

103. UNCLAIMED COST AND FEES, DEPOSITED IN TREASURY
1909-1928. 1 vol. (1). 1929— in Cashbook, entry 98.
Record of unclaimed moneys, and fees paid into county treasury, showing to whom due, on what account, volume and page numbers in Execution Docket, entry 128, amount due, date paid into treasury, date certified, and total amount. Arranged alphabetically by names of persons to whom due and chronologically thereunder by dates of payments into treasury. No index. Handwritten on printed forms. 400 pages. 16 x 12 x 2. Clerk of courts' office.

Miscellaneous

104. MORTGAGE RELEASES
1935—. 2 file drawers. Initiated in 1935.
Certificates of releases of mortgages in cases in common pleas court, showing title of case, case number, term of court, volume and page numbers in Appearance and Execution Docket, entry 118, Common Pleas Journal, entry 129, Common Pleas Record, entry 119, and Mortgage Record, entry 32, names of grantor and grantee, and date released. Arranged chronologically by dates released. No index. Typed on printed forms. 11 x 5 x 13.5. Clerk of courts' office.

105. DEPUTY SHERIFF'S APPOINTMENTS
1935—. 1 file drawer. Initiated in 1935.
Certificates, with common pleas judge's approval of appointment of sheriff's deputies by sheriff, showing date of appointment, names of deputy and sheriff, date appointment approved, signature and oath of deputy, and signature of common pleas judge. Arranged chronologically by dates of appointments. No index. Handwritten on printed forms. 11 x 5 x 13.5. Clerk of courts' office.

106. ESTRAY RECORD
1869-1906, 1938—. 1 vol.
Record of strayed livestock taken into custody, showing kind of animal, date found, description of animal, date record filed and recorded, and signatures of clerk of courts and person finding animal; also contains 36 loose notices to clerk findings of estrays, 1872-1907. Arranged chronologically by dates filed and recorded. No

index. Handwritten. 100 pages. 12 x 7.5 x .5. Clerk of courts' office.

107. [Trade-mark] RECORD
1936—. 1 vol.
Record of trade-marks, showing name of owner, location of business, date issued, pencil and hand drawn diagram of trade-mark, name used on trade-mark, amount of recording fee, and size of container on which trade-mark is used. Arranged chronologically by dates issued. No index. Handwritten. 50 pages. 10 x 12 x .5. Clerk of courts' office.

108. [REPORT TO PROSECUTING ATTORNEY ON UNPAID COSTS]
1935—. 1 file drawer.
Copies of reports of clerk to prosecuting attorney on unpaid and uncollected court costs, showing names of plaintiff and defendant, date costs due, kind of case, case number, volume and page numbers in Appearance and Execution Docket, entry 118, amount of court costs, and name and address of person from whom due. This report is made up from the Card Index File – Unpaid Court Costs, entry 101, and is closely related to it. Arranged alphabetically by names of plaintiffs. No index. Typed. 12 x 17 x 24. Clerk of courts' office.

109. REPORT ON JUDICIAL STATISTICS TO SECRETARY OF STATE
1867—. 2 wooden boxes, 1 bundle, 1 file drawer.
Copies of annual statistical reports to the secretary of state on civil and criminal cases before common pleas court, showing date of report, detailed statistics on suits for divorce, civil judgments, criminal cases, crimes against the person and property, and amount of grand jury fees and petit jury fees. Also includes copies of annual reports of clerk of courts to commissioners of all fines assessed by common pleas court and civil and criminal cases 1935—, showing name of party fined and amount assessed, name of party paying fine, and amount collected; source of funds paid into county treasury, showing total amount of fines to state and treasury, and totals for stenographic and clerk's fees and fines. Arranged chronologically by dates reported. No index. Handwritten and typed, some printed forms. Bundles, 8 x 11 x .5; boxes, 20 x 16 x 13; file drawer, 12 x 17 x 24, 2 boxes, 1867-1910, attic storeroom; 1 bundle, 1911-1931, third floor storeroom; 1 file drawer, 1931—, Clerk of courts' office.

110. ALIMONY DOCKET

1925—. 1 vol. (1). Initiated in 1925. 1907— in Cash Book, entry 98.

Docket of alimony payments made, showing case number, names of plaintiff and defendant, dates of payments, names of payer and payee, volume and page numbers in Cash Book, entry 98, amount of payment, date paid to payee, check number, and amount of check. Arranged chronologically by dates paid. Indexed alphabetically by names of plaintiffs and defendants. Handwritten on printed forms. 400 pages. 18.5 x 13 x 3. Clerk of courts' office.

111. TRANSCRIPTS FROM MAGISTRATES COURTS

1835-1939. 4 vols. (S, U, V, W). 1820-1834, 1840— in Common Pleas Record, entry 119.

Record of cases appealed from minor courts (justice and mayor), including copies of certified transcripts dockets of justice of the peace and mayor, *writs* of summonses, pleas, petitions, and sheriff's returns, showing name of plaintiff, defendant, and attorneys, date of filing, record of proceedings, and verdicts or decrees of common pleas court. Arranged chronologically by dates filed. Indexed alphabetically by names of plaintiffs, showing names of defendants. Handwritten. Average 600 pages. 16 x 10 x 3.5. Clerk of courts' office.

112. RECOGNIZANCE RECORD

1862-1929. 3 vols. (one unlabeled; 2, 3).

Record of recognizance bonds, showing case number, cause of indictment, date and amount of bond, names of principals and sureties, condition bond, signatures of sureties and principals, and date of forfeiture. Arranged chronologically by dates of bonds. Indexed alphabetically by names of principals. Handwritten on printed forms. Average 150 pages. 14 x 10 x 1. Clerk of courts' office.

113. MISCELLANEOUS

1920, 1923, 1924, 1927, 1931, 1932, 1936-1941. 1 file drawer.

Miscellaneous papers filed with clerk of courts including:

    a.   Two court of appeals cases, 1932-1937, showing case number, title of case, names of plaintiff and defendant, cause of action, date filed, and proceedings.

    b.   One contract, 1923, between the board of welfare of the city of Cleveland, Ohio, and the Geauga County commissioners, for board and care of Geauga County prisoners by the Cleveland board, showing date of filing, terms of agreement, and amounts to be paid by commissioners to board of welfare.

c.   Five certificates of authority to practice optometry, 1920, 1927, 1939, 1941, showing date of issue, name of optometrist, record of schooling of licensee, and date of filing.

d.   Two certificates registering milk bottle labels, for the same dairy, 1924, 1931, showing name of dairy, date of filing, and labeling of bottle; one certificate, 1924, contains a hand drawn sketch of milk bottle with labeling on it.

e.   One grant of authority by common pleas judge to commissioners for purchase of an automobile for county use, 1939, showing reasons for purchase, record of common pleas judge's grant, type of automobile, and cost.

f.   Five list of unclaimed fees posted, 1936-1940, showing title of case, case number, to whom money belongs, volume and page numbers and [Witness Records], entry 77 and Cashbook, entry 98, amount, and date of payment.

No obvious arrangement. No index. Handwritten and typed, some on printed forms. 11 x 5 x 13.5. Clerk of courts' office.

The court of common pleas, like many other county institutions, originated in England during the reign of Henry II.[1] Established in America during the colonial period, the office was continued by the states following the War of American Independence.

The Northwest Ordinance of 1787 established a government consisting of a governor, a secretary, and three judges all appointed by Congress. The judges were to form a court, known as the general court, which had common law jurisdiction and together with the governor was authorized to draw up a code of civil and criminal law. The territorial act of 1788, establishing the American colonial policy in the newer west in respect to the judiciary, contained sections authorizing the establishment in each county of a common pleas court to be composed of not less than three nor more than five members. These members appointed and commissioned by the territorial governor, were given jurisdiction in all civil matters.[2] The same act established in each county a primary court called the court of general quarter sessions of the peace to be composed of not more than five nor less than three justices of the peace, appointed and commissioned by the governor.[3] This court, which had limited jurisdiction in criminal matters, was not re-established by the constitution of 1802 and the jurisdiction which had been exercised by this court was conferred upon the justices of the peace and the court of common pleas.[4]

When a constitution was drafted for Ohio in 1802, preparatory to the entrance of the state into the Union, provision was made for a continuation of the territorial court of common pleas.[5] The articles of the Ohio Constitution, regarding the judiciary, provided for a court of common pleas in each county to be composed of a president and associate judges. For each county[6] not more than three nor less than two associate judges were to be appointed, with one president for each of the three judicial districts into which the counties were grouped. The associate judges were not as a rule men who had a legal education.[7]

---

1. George Burton Adams, *Constitutional History of England* (New York, 1921), 109, 134.
2. Pease, *op. cit.,* 7.
3. Pease, 4.
4. Pease, 5; *Laws of Ohio,* I, 40; II, 235.
5. *Ohio Const. 1802,* Art. iii, sec. 1.
6. At this time there were nine counties in the state.
7. Francis J. Amer, *The Development of the Judicial System and Ohio from 1787 to 1932* (Johns Hopkins University, Baltimore, 1932. *Institute of Law Bulletin No. 8*), 17.

The members of the court, appointed by joint ballot of both houses of the general assembly, were to hold court in three judicial districts into which the state was to be divided by legislative action. Their term of office was seven years "if so long they behave well."[8]

It was almost half a century before any significant changes were made in the structure of the court. The constitution of 1851 provided that judges of the common pleas court were to be elected or a five-year term. For the purposes of their election the state was divided into nine districts composed of three or more counties. Each district, and turn, was to be subdivided into three parts, in each of which one common pleas judge was to be elected. The court of common pleas was to be held by one or more of these judges in each county in the district.[9] Power was given to the general assembly to increase or diminish the number of districts of the court of common pleas, the number of judges in any district and to change the districts or the subdivision thereof, whenever two-thirds of the legislature concurred therein.[10] Provision was also made for the removal of judges by a concurrent resolution of two-thirds of the members elected to each house of the legislature.[11] An appellate court known as the district court was created, and was to be composed of one supreme court judge and the several common pleas judges of the district. This court was to be held in each county of the district at least once in each year or at least three annual sessions in not less than three places.[12] The district court was not a success, and after many attempts at revision the circuit courts, staffed by separate group of elected judges, were adopted by vote of the people in 1883, thus relieving the common pleas judges of this appellate work.[13]

The juvenile court was created in 1904 with the jurisdiction in special matters relating to minors and was to be held by a judge of the court of common pleas, court of insolvency, or probate court who should be designated by the judges to hold such court.[14]

---

8. *Ohio Const. 1802,* Art. III, sec. 8.

9. *Ibid., 1851,* Art. IV, secs. 3, 4.

10. *Ibid.,* Art. IV, sec. 15.

11. *Ibid.,* Art. IV, sec. 17.

12. *Ibid.,* Art. IV, secs. 5, 6.

13. Amer, *op. cit.,* 31-33; *Laws of Ohio,* LXXXI, 168.

14. *Laws of Ohio,* XCVII, 562.

At the opening of the 20th century sweeping changes in the organization of the courts were made. Constitutional amendments adopted in 1912 abolished the divisions and subdivisions of the court of common pleas provided by the constitution of 1851, and authorized the election of one or more common pleas judges in each county.[15] The chief justice of the supreme court was given authority to determine the disability or disqualification of any judge of the court of common pleas and also to assign any judge to hold court in any county.[16] Eleven years later the selection of a chief justice of the court of common pleas was authorized. Under an act of March 13, 1923, in counties having two or more common pleas judges, a chief justice was designated by vote of the judge. The justice so designated by his colleagues was to serve in such capacity until the expiration of his term, after which time the office was to be an elective one.[17] The elective section of the act was nullified in effect in 1924 by the supreme court on the grounds that the creation of a new elective office was unconstitutional. Accordingly in 1927 an amendment was passed eliminating the elective provision of the act.[18]

In recent years attempts have been made to improve the efficiency of the court by imposing stricter qualifications upon those who seek election to the bench. In 1917 an act was passed providing that a common pleas judge shall have been admitted to practice as an attorney at law for a period of six years preceding his election.[19] A salary of the office was also increased to $3000 per year plus an amount based on the population of the county[20] – thus making the position financially attractive, especially as a term of office is six years.[21] In addition to the regular salaries, common pleas judges maybe paid a per diem allowance and expenses when assigned to special duties by the chief justice of the supreme court in a district not their own. When dockets become overcrowded or judges are incapacitated or disqualified, such assignments may be made.[22]

---

15. *Ohio Const. 1851,* Art. IV, sec. 3.
16. *Ibid.,* Art. IV, secs. 3, 6.
17. *Laws of Ohio,* CX, 52.
18. *State ex rel.* v. *Powell, Ohio State Reports,* CIX, 383; *Laws of Ohio,* CXII, 5; G. C. sec. 1558.
19. *Laws of Ohio,* CVII, 164.
20. G. C. secs. 2251-2252.
21. G. C. sec. 1532.
22. *Ohio Const. 1851* (Amendment, 1912), Art. IV, sec. 3; G. C. secs. 1469, 1687, 2253.

In the populous counties, judicial efficiency is promoted by assigning to certain common pleas judges specialize duties such as the hearing of domestic relations and juvenile court cases.

The jurisdiction of the court of common pleas has also been the product of a long period of historical development. The territorial law of 1788 which created the court provided that "the judges so appointed and commissioned . . . shall hold pleas of *assizes, scire facias, replevins,* and hear and determine all manner of pleas, actions, suits, and causes of a civil nature, real, personnel, and mixed, according to the constitution and the laws of the territory."[23] Individually, each judge of the common pleas was given jurisdiction over contract actions not exceeding five dollars.[24] The probate court was established by an act adopted August 30, 1788, and two of the judges of the court of common pleas sat with this judge in ruling on contested points, definitive sentences, and final judgments. Under the laws of 1788 the common pleas had no criminal jurisdiction, and the court of quarter sessions of the peace had no civil jurisdiction. There was no provision for an appeal from one court to another except for the probate court to the general court of the territory.[25]

In 1795 the judicial system underwent the first general revision and this increased the duties of the court of common pleas. A single justice of the peace or judge of the common pleas was given jurisdiction to hear certain civil actions up to $12. Actions under $5 were exclusive with the judges or justices and there was no appeal on their judgment. Actions between $5 and $12 could be appealed to the court of common pleas. In 1799 this jurisdiction was raised to $20, and appeals could be taken to the common pleas if the judgment was over $2. If the judgment was for the plaintiff, he could appeal only if the original demand was $4 or more than the sum recovered.[26] Appeal from the common pleas to the general court provided for in 1795, and could not be taken unless the title to land was in question or when the amount and controversy exceeded $50.[27]

---

23. Salmon P. Chase, ed. *The Statutes of Ohio and of the Northwest Territory, 1788-1833* (Cincinnati, 1833), I, 94.
24. Pease, *op. cit.,* 8.
25. Chase, *op. cit.,* I, 96.
26. Chase, *op. cit.,* I, 143, 233, 307.
27. Chase, *op. cit.,* I, 306.

The constitution of 1802 gave the court of common pleas jurisdiction in such common law and chancery cases as should be directed by law. In addition it was given jurisdiction in all probate and testamentary matters, and the appointment and supervision of guardians.[28] Moreover, the court of common pleas and the supreme court were assigned original cognizance of criminal cases as might be provided by law.[29] By statutory provision in 1804 appeals in civil cases might be made to the court of common pleas from the county commissioners, justices of the peace, and other inferior courts.[30]

An act of the first general assembly in 1803 provided for the organization of the courts and defined their jurisdiction. The court of common pleas was given original jurisdiction in all cases, both in law and equity, when a matter in dispute exceeded the jurisdiction of the justice of peace; of all probate, testamentary, and guardianship matters; and of all criminal matters exceeding the jurisdiction of the justice of peace, except when the punishment of the crime was capital. It was allowed to review certain cases from the justice of peace and also to review the decisions of the county commissioners in highway matters. In addition, the court had the same power to issue remedial and other process, *writs* of error and *mandamus* excepted, as had the supreme court.[31] In 1804 the court's jurisdiction in chancery cases was limited to cases involving less than $500,[32] and in 1805 it was given appellate jurisdiction from the justices of peace in all cases regardless of the amount involved.[33] In 1806 crimes wherein the punishment was capital could be tried in common pleas court if the accused so elected.[34] In 1807 it was given jurisdiction in all chancery cases and concurrent jurisdiction with the supreme court in such cases involving over $500.[35] In 1810 all cases in which the common pleas had original jurisdiction were permitted to be appealed to the supreme court.[36]

28. *Ohio Const. 1802,* Art. III, secs. 3, 5.
29. *Ibid.,* Art. III, sec. 4.
30. Chase, *op. cit.,* I, 421, 425.
31. Chase, *op. cit.,* 355.
32. *Laws of Ohio,* II, 261.
33. *Laws of Ohio,* III, 14.
34. *Ibid.,* IV, 57.
35. *Ibid.,* V, 117.
36. *Ibid.,* VIII, 259.

By this act the right to appeal was established in Ohio in all civil cases. However the business of the supreme court increased so rapidly that in 1845 the right to appeal the judgment of the common pleas court to the supreme court in actions at law was abolished. Instead, new trials were allowed "when law and justice required it."[37] Even earlier, appeals to the common pleas from inferior courts had been limited.[38] The chancery act adopted in 1824, conferred general chancery powers on the court,[39] and in 1843 it was given concurrent jurisdiction with the supreme court in cases of divorce and alimony.[40]

The constitution of 1851 left the jurisdiction of the common pleas court to be fixed by law.[41] The jurisdiction conferred on this court by subsequent legislation was essentially the same as that exercised since 1810, with the exception of the jurisdiction which transferred to the probate court,[42] and the addition, in 1853, of exclusive jurisdiction in divorce and alimony cases.[43] The court of common pleas was denied jurisdiction in cases of probate, testamentary, and guardianship matters, but final orders, judgments, and decrees of the probate court could be reviewed in common pleas on appeal or by *writs* of *certiorari*.[44] In 1853 the court of common pleas was given original jurisdiction of all cases and offenses except minor criminal cases, the exclusive jurisdiction of which was vested in the justice of peace or other minor courts.[45]

The creation of criminal, mayors', and police courts also made certain changes in the powers and duties of common pleas courts.[46] The right to appeal from common pleas to the district court was restored in all civil actions in which the common pleas had original jurisdiction,[47] but by an act of 1858 appeals were allowed to the intermediate court only in nonjury cases. However, the same act provided for a second jury trial in common pleas as a matter of right in jury cases.

---

37. *Ibid.*, XLIII, 80.
38. *Ibid.*, XXXVIII, 27.
39. *Ibid.*, XXII, 75.
40. *Ibid.*, XLI, 94.
41. *Ohio Const. 1851,* Art. IV, secs. 3, 4.
42. *Laws of Ohio,* L, 87. Records pertaining to probate matters were to be transferred to the probate court wherever it was possible to separate them from common pleas records. *Laws of Ohio,* L, 88.
43. *Ibid.,* LI, 377.
44. *Ibid.,* L, 84; LI, 145.
45. G. C. sec. 13422-5; *Laws of Ohio,* LI, 474, LII, 73.
46. *Laws of Ohio,* L, 90, 240, 246, 251, 253.
47. *Laws of Ohio,* L, 93.

This was granted upon demand made by either party at the close of the first trial on condition of his giving bond.[48] The abuse of this privilege led to its abolishment in 1875.[49]

This period witnessed the re-establishment of superior courts in the state, which were given the same jurisdiction as the court of common pleas with certain exceptions.[50] At the same time as the superior court was established at Cincinnati, the legislature abolished the criminal court and transferred its jurisdiction to the common pleas court.[51] The criminal jurisdiction of the probate court was transferred to the common pleas court in 1857.[52] A limitation was placed on the right to appeal from probate court to common pleas in 1854.[53] This limitation was repealed, however, in 1856.[54]

For many years there were few changes in the powers of the court of common pleas except in the forms of appeal to higher courts,[55] and such added powers as resulted from the decline in the number of superior courts.[56] In 1906 the probate court was given concurrent jurisdiction with common pleas in all counties in the trial of misdemeanors and all proceedings to prevent crimes.[57]

Since 1906 the court of common pleas has had jurisdiction in naturalization proceedings. In that year the federal statute was amended to limit jurisdiction in the granting of naturalization to the United States district courts and state courts having a clerk, a seal and jurisdiction in matters of law and equity in which the amount of controversy is unlimited.[58]

Constitutional amendments adopted in 1912 had little effect upon the jurisdiction of the court of common pleas, this power being determined by law.[59]

---

48. *Ibid.,* LV, 81.
49. *Ibid.,* LXXII, 34.
50. *Ibid.,* LII, 34; LIII, 38; LIV, 37.
51. *Ibid.,* LII, 107.
52. *Ibid.,* LIV, 97.
53. *Ibid.,* LII, 104.
54. *Ibid.,* LIII, 8.
55. *Ibid.,* LXXIV, 359; LXXXII, 230.
56. *Ibid.,* LXII, 58; LXXII, 89, 105; LXXXII, 85.
57. *Ibid.,* XCVIII, 49.
58. *United States Statutes at Large,* XXXIV, pt. i, 596.
59. *Ohio Const. 1851,* Art. IV, sec. 6.

In 1911 the juvenile courts were given jurisdiction of all misdemeanors against minors and certain other offenses.[60] Provision was also made for error proceedings from juvenile court to the court of common pleas.[61] The jurisdiction of the common pleas court of today is essentially the same as that of 1913. The few changes that have been made in the judicial system are found in the local, special courts, particularly in the rapidly developing municipal courts.

The common pleas court has never possessed extensive appointive powers. The constitution of 1802 authorized each court to appoint a clerk,[62] and in 1805 it was directed to appoint a county prosecuting attorney.[63] During the first three decades of Ohio history, the movement for the extension of the popular election of public officers deprived the court of common pleas of the privilege of appointing the county recorder (1829), county surveyor (1831), and county prosecuting attorney (1833).[64] The court continued to appoint a clerk of courts until 1851. In recent years, however, as new functions have added to the county government, the court has again been given a limited appointive power. Successive acts in 1886, 1891, 1913, 1914, and 1925 authorized the court to appoint a soldiers' relief commission, jury commission, an assignment commissioner, conservancy district board, and probation officer.[65] In 1882 the court was empowered to appoint a board of county visitors but this power was transferred to the probate court in 1906.[66] Other appointments authorized were those of court interpreter and criminal bailiff (1911)[67] inspectors of meetings of corporation stockholders, trustees for county memorial buildings, boards of trustees for endowed libraries, and one member of the metropolitan housing authority in such counties as maintain these agencies.[68]

The court may also appoint a court reporter (or reporters),[69] and may co-operate with the county commissioners for the establishment of a county department of probation, in which case the court appoints certain probation officers and

---

60. *Laws of Ohio,* CII, 425.
61. *Ibid.,* CIII, 875.
62. *Ohio Const. 1802,* Art. III, sec. 9.
63. *Laws of Ohio,* III, 47.
64. *Ibid.,* XXVII, 65; XXIX, 399; Chase *op cit.,* III, 1935.
65. *Laws of Ohio,* LXXXIII, 232; LXXXVIII, 200; CIII, 512; CIV, 13-64; CXI, 423.
66. *Ibid.,* LXXIX, 107; XCVIII, 28.
67. G. C. sec. 1541.
68. *Laws of Ohio,* LXXXIV, 115; XCV, 41; CVI, 485; CXV, pt. ii, 56.
69. G. C. secs. 1546-1554.

supervises their work.[70] If the sheriff is absent, disabled, or disqualified from serving the court's warrant, the judge may appoint temporarily an officer for this service.[71] By and large, however, the patronage power of the court of common pleas is a negligible factor in county government. Since 1805 the court has been authorized to issue ferry licenses[72] and tavern keepers' licenses.[73] Both ferry and tavern licenses may now be issued by municipal corporations also and the latter by the state fire marshal.[74] From 1803 to 1852 this court also issued licenses to ministers to solemnize marriage ceremonies; this function has since been exercised by the probate court.[75]

The keeping of the records of the common pleas court presented no particular difficulties for many decades. However, with the increased number of issues presented to the court in recent years, the problem of judicial administration has become greater. The problem was solved in part by the creation of the office of chief justice of the court of common pleas who has been given the duties of superintending the business of the court, classifying it, and distributing it among the judges. Besides the duties enumerated, the chief justice annually makes a report to the clerk of courts, showing the work performed by the court and by each judge in the preceding calendar year. Moreover, he reports such other data as the chief justice of the supreme court may require.[76]

Judges of the common pleas court are also required to issue an annual order as to the exact time of sessions. The clerk of courts is required to make this information public and to send a copy to the secretary of state. The law sets certain requirements as to the sessions of the court and the power of the judge to call special sessions.[77] The records of the court are deposited for safekeeping with the clerk of courts. The clerk is custodian also of all law reports and books furnished by the state for the use of the court and the bar and is made liable and the event of their destruction.[78]

---

70. G. C. secs. 1554-1 - 1554-6.
71. G. C. sec. 2828.
72. *Laws of Ohio,* III, 96; G. C. secs. 5947, 5949.
73. *Laws of Ohio,* III, 96; XXIX, 310.
74. G. C. secs. 3642, 3672, 843-3.
75. *Laws of Ohio,* I, 31; L, 84.
76. G. C. sec. 1558.
77. G. C. secs. 1533-1539.
78. *Laws of Ohio,* LXVIII, 109.

This court and Geauga County is presided over by but one judge, whose salary is $3000 annually, $462 of which is paid by the county.[79] During the year 1940, this court heard 139 civil cases,[80] 9 criminal cases,[81] 60 petitions for naturalization,[82] and granted 53 divorces.[83] A clerk from the clerk of courts' office is usually in attendance, as well as a bailiff.

---

79. G. C. secs. 2251-2252, 1192.
80. Appearance Docket, 1940, entry 117.
81. Criminal Appearance Docket, 1940, entry 124.
82. *See* entries 121, 122, 123.
83. Appearance and Execution Docket, 1940, entry 118.

Civil Cases

114. COURT CALENDAR
1900, 1912, 1926—. 8 booklets, 2 file drawers.

Calendar of common pleas court, civil and criminal cases, showing names of plaintiff and defendant, date of trial, case number, title of case, attorneys initials or name, and kind of action; also includes rules of practice, names of common pleas judge, clerk, sheriff, prosecuting attorney, court stenographer, and bailiff, list of practicing attorneys in county, county officers, soldiers' relief commissioners, mayors, justice of the peace, notaries, grand jurors, and petit jurors. Arranged chronologically by dates of trial. Indexed alphabetically by names of plaintiffs. Printed. Booklets average 75 loose-leaf pages. 7 x 4.5 x .25; file drawer, 5 x 11 x 13.5. 8 booklets, 1900, 1912, attic storeroom; 2 file drawers, 1926—, Clerk of courts' office.

115. GENERAL INDEX DIRECT
1807—. 9 vols. (1-9).

General index to common pleas court records including judgment index, showing name of plaintiff or judgment creditor, name of defendant or judgment debtor, term of court in which judgment or decree issued, number of case, volume and page numbers in Appearance Docket, entry 117, Appearance and Execution Docket, entry 118, Execution Docket, entry 128, Common Pleas Journal, entry 129, and Common Pleas Record, entry 119, nature of suit, nature and amount of judgment or decree, date of execution, date of satisfaction, and remarks. Arranged alphabetically by names of plaintiffs or judgment creditors. Handwritten on printed forms.

Average 350 pages. 18 x 13 x 1.5. Clerk of courts' office.

116. GENERAL INDEX REVERSE
1807—. 9 vols. (1-9).

General index including judgment index to common pleas court records, showing name of defendant or judgment debtor, name of plaintiff or judgment creditor, term of court in which judgment or decree issued, case number, volume and page numbers in Appearance Docket, entry 117, Execution Docket, entry 128, Appearance and Execution Docket, entry 118, Common Pleas Journal, entry 129, and Common Pleas Record, entry 119, nature of suits, nature and amount of judgment or decree, date of execution, date of satisfaction, and remarks. Arranged alphabetically by names of defendants or judgment debtors. Handwritten on printed forms. Average 350 pages. 18 x 13 x 1.5. Clerk of courts' office.

117. APPEARANCE DOCKET
1845-1927. 17 vols. (A-Q).

Docket of all civil actions tried in common pleas court, showing names of plaintiff, defendant, and attorneys, kind of action, record and date of proceedings, volume and page numbers of Execution Docket, entry 128, sheriff's returns, dates of summonses, service, returns, and court entries. Also contains Criminal Appearance Docket, 1845-1901, entry 124. Arranged chronologically by dates of proceedings. Indexed alphabetically by names of plaintiffs and defendants. 1845-1866, handwritten; 1866-1927, handwritten on printed forms. Average 250 pages. 18 x 13 x 1.25. Clerk of courts' office.

118. APPEARANCE AND EXECUTION DOCKET
1927—. 11 vols. (1-11).

Appearance and execution docket, showing case number, volume and page numbers in Common Pleas Journal, entry 129, Common Pleas Record, entry 119, and Cashbook, entry 98, names of plaintiff, defendant, and attorneys, kind of action, date of proceedings, sheriff's returns, cost bill, and receipts. Arranged chronologically by dates of proceedings. Indexed alphabetically by names of plaintiffs. Handwritten on printed forms. Average 500 pages. 18 x 13 x 3. Clerk of courts' office.

119. COMMON PLEAS RECORD

1806-1835, 1839—. 111 vols. (A, A-S, U-Y, AA, BB, DD-FF; 36-116).
Complete record of all civil court proceedings in common pleas court, including
copies of petitions, answers, journal entries, affidavits, judgment entries,
executions, *praecipes,* certificates of judgment, sheriff's returns, exhibits, motions,
pleas, and appeals, showing case number, plaintiff, defendant, and names of
attorneys, title of case, title of proceedings in case, and jury verdict or court decree;
also includes divorce and alimony records 1843—. Also contains: Transcripts from
Magistrates Courts, 1820-1834, entry 111; Chancery Records, 1820-1834, 1855,
entry 120; and Criminal Record, 1806-1834, entry 125. Arranged chronologically
by dates filed. Indexed alphabetically by names of plaintiffs showing names of
defendants. 1806-1935, 1839-1912, handwritten; 1913—, typed. Average 600
pages. 18.5 x 12.5 x 3. Clerk of courts' office.

120. CHANCERY RECORDS

1835-1854. 5 vols. (R, Z, CC, EE, FF), 1820-1834, 1855— in Common
Pleas Record, entry 119.

Record of chancery cases heard before common pleas court, involving settlement
of estates and equities in property, showing title of case, date filed, names of
plaintiff, defendant, and attorneys, case number, and proceedings of court. Arranged
chronologically by dates filed. Indexed alphabetically by names of plaintiffs and
defendants. Handwritten. Average 600 pages. 16 x 10.5 x 3. Clerk of courts' office.

Naturalization

121. DECLARATIONS

1907—. 5 vols. Title varies: Record of Declaration of Intentions, 1907-
1919, 2 vols.

Record of declarations, showing name of alien, age, occupation, race, complexion,
height, weight, color of hair and eyes, and other visible distinctive marks, country
where born, date of birth, present address, name of country sailed from, name of
ship, and last foreign address, port of arrival, date of landing, and signature of alien;
includes sworn statement, of intention to become a citizen, before clerk of courts
or deputy. Arranged alphabetically by names of aliens. No index. Handwritten on
printed forms. Average 100 pages. 9 x 11 x 1.5. Clerk of courts' office.

122. PETITION AND RECORD – NATURALIZATION SERVICE

1907—. 4 vols. (two labeled Form 2204; two labeled by contained petition numbers).

Copies of petitions of aliens to become citizens of the United States, including affidavits of witnesses and petitioners, oath of allegiance, court orders, declaration of intention, and dispositions of witnesses, showing date of petition, name and address of petitioner, certificate number, nativity, date and name of port of arrival in United States, names of witnesses, date and naturalization or date refused, and reason for refusal. Arranged chronologically by dates of petitions. Indexed alphabetically by names of petitioners. 1907-1929, handwritten on printed forms; 1930—, typed on printed forms. Average 100 pages. 15 x 10.5 x 1. Clerk of courts' office.

123. ORDERS [Naturalization]

1929—. 1 vol.

Record of orders, showing date of order, list number, naturalization petitions recommended to be granted, names of court and county where sitting, name of petitioner, date submitted, and signatures of examiner or officer and judge granting the citizenship; also includes a record of cases continued for further hearing, and cases denied. Arranged chronologically by dates of orders. No index. Typed on printed forms. 25 loose-leaf pages. 8.5 x 11 x .5. Clerk of courts' office.

Criminal Cases

124. CRIMINAL APPEARANCE DOCKET

1902—. 2 vols. (1, 2). 1845-1901 in Appearance Docket, entry 117.

Docket of criminal cases filed for appearance in comment pleas court, showing name of defendant, volume and page numbers in Execution Docket, entry 128, and Common Pleas Journal, entry 129, charge, date indictment filed, name of magistrate from whom transcript of docket filed, date transcribe filed, sheriff's returns, verdict, and itemized cost of filing, serving papers and trying cases in common pleas and magistrates' courts. Arranged chronologically by dates indictments were filed. Indexed alphabetically by names of defendants. Handwritten on printed forms. Average 550 pages. 18 x 13 x 3. Clerk of courts' office.

125. CRIMINAL RECORD

1835—. 6 vols. (T: 42-46). 1806-1834 in Common Pleas Record, entry 119. Complete record of all criminal cases prosecuted in common pleas court, showing case number, date of filing, name of defendant, charge, copy of affidavit of information, and transcripts for magistrate's court, indictment by grand jury, plea of defendant, recording of hearing or trial, verdict of jury, and sentence of court. Arranged chronologically by dates filed. Indexed alphabetically by names of defendants. 1835-1928, handwritten; 1929—, types. Average 500 pages. 17 x 11 x 2.5. Clerk of courts' office.

General Court Proceedings

126. TRIAL DOCKET

1840—. 110 vols. Title varies: Trial Lists, 1840-1845, 1849-1894, 9 vols; Bar List, 1849-1853, 1857-1875, 3 vols.

Docket of civil and criminal cases tried before common pleas court, showing term of court, date of trial, case number, title of case, names of plaintiff and defendant, all *writs* issued, court orders and decrees, and disposition of case. Arranged chronologically by court terms and chronologically thereunder by dates of trials. No index. 1833-1900 handwritten; 1901-1928, handwritten on printed forms; 1929—, handwritten and typed, some on printed forms. 20 volumes average 200 pages. 15 x 10 x 1.5; 84 volumes average 75 pages. 16 x 11 x 1; 6 volumes average 700 pages. 14.5 x 9 x 3.5. 41 volumes, 1900-1915, attic storeroom; 69 volumes, 1840-1900, 1916—, Clerk of courts' office.

127. TRANSFER COMMON PLEAS COURT DOCKET [Final Entry]

1910-1918. 1 vol.

Record of final verdicts of common pleas court, showing date of trial, final decree or decision of the judges, name of plaintiff and defendant, case number, title of case, names of attorneys, and nature of action. Arranged numerically by case numbers and chronologically thereunder by dates of trials. Indexed alphabetically by names of plaintiffs and defendants. Handwritten and typed, some on printed forms. 700 loose-leaf pages. 9 x 14.5 x 3.5. Clerk of courts' office.

128. EXECUTION DOCKET

1811-1824, 1831-1936. 28 vols. (two unlabeled: B, E-Z; 27; two dated).Title varies: Letter Book [1836-1852], 1 vol.; License Record [1847-1879], 1 vol.

Docket of executions on court orders in civil and criminal cases, showing case number, date of execution, volume and page numbers in Common Pleas Journal, entry 129, and Common Pleas Record, entry 119, nature of case, names of plaintiff and defendant, sheriff's returns, cost bill including clerk's, sheriff's, and attorneys fees, expense of advertising and publishing, and all other costs in respect to civil and criminal cases, and disposition of cases 1907-1934, entry 103; also includes a record of incorporation of churches and religious societies, 1817-1824, 1831-1840 entry 54. Arranged chronologically by dates of executions. Indexed alphabetically by names of plaintiffs and defendants. 1811-1824, 1831-1858, handwritten; 1858-1936, handwritten on printed forms. Average 500 pages. 18 x 13 x 2.5. Clerk of courts' office.

For records of incorporations 1845-1906, see entry 54.

129. COMMON PLEAS JOURNAL

1806—. 41 vols. (A, D, F-Z; 27-44).

Journal entries of decisions in all civil and criminal cases filed in common pleas court, showing names of plaintiff and defendant, title of case, nature of proceedings, names of attorneys, dates of entry and pleadings, and case number after 1828; also includes reports of the grand jury on indictments and inspection of county jail 1859—, showing date of report, date of inspection and recommendations; appointments of deputy sheriff, jury commission, bailiff, and court reporter. Arranged chronologically by dates entered. 1806-1825, 1828-1866, no index; 1826-1827, indexed alphabetically by names of defendants; 1867—, indexed alphabetically by names of plaintiffs and defendants. 1806-1914, handwritten; 1915—, typed. 6 volumes average 200 pages. 9 x 8 x 1.5. 21 volumes average 500 pages. 16 x 12 x 2.25; 13 volumes average 600 pages. 18 x 12 x 3. Clerk of courts' office.

The first constitution of Ohio provided for a supreme court consisting of three judges appointed by a joint ballot of the legislature for a seven-year term. This court was required to hold sessions at least once a year in each county.[1] The number of judges, according to constitutional provisions, might be increased to four after a period of five years, in which case the judges were permitted to divide the state into two circuits. Accordingly, in 1808, the membership of the court was increased to four and the state was divided into the requisite number of circuits.[2] Two years later, in 1810, the membership of the court was reduced to three;[3] in 1824 it was again increased to four.[4]

By constitutional provision, this court was given original and appellate jurisdiction "both in common law and chancery," in such cases as should be provided by law.[5] Accordingly, by statutory provision, the court was assigned exclusive cognizance of all cases of divorce and alimony and concurrent jurisdiction of all civil cases both of law and equity where a title to land was in question, or the matter in dispute exceeded $1000; and appellate jurisdiction from the court of common pleas "in all cases respecting the title of land, or where the matter and controversy exceeds the value of $1000 and all cases where the proof or validity of wills or the right of administration should be in question."[6] During the first half century of Ohio history the legislature granted decrees of the divorce. Although the constitution of 1802 did not prohibit the legislature from exercising such jurisdiction, the supreme court prohibited the practice in 1848.[7] The constitution of 1851, Article II, section 32, contained a prohibiting clause. Moreover, the court was given original cognizance in the trial at capital offenses.[8] All cases which the title to land for freehold was in question were to be tried in the county where the land was situated. Furthermore, the court was given appellate jurisdiction from the court of common pleas in all cases in which the court of common pleas had original jurisdiction.[9]

---

1. *Ohio Const. 1802,* Art. III, secs. 2, 8, 10.

2. *Laws of Ohio,* VI, 32.

3. *Ibid.,* VIII, 259.

4. *Ibid.,* XXII, 50.

5. *Ohio Const. 1802,* Art. III, sec. 2.

6. *Laws of Ohio,* I, 36-37; XIV, 310.

7. *Bingham* v. *Miller, Ohio Reports,* XVII, 445.

8. *Laws of Ohio,* I, 36-37.

9. *Ibid.,* XIV, 310-354.

In 1831 the supreme court was directed to meet annually in the town of Columbus for the final adjudication of all such questions of all as may have been reserved in any county for decision. This session of the court, known as the court in bank, was required to have its decision in each case reduced to writing, and transmitted to the clerk of the supreme court in each county in which such question was reserved. The clerk was directed to enter such decisions "on the journal of the said court" and such proceedings were to be taken as if such decisions had been made in the county.[10] Six years later, in 1837, an act was passed providing that the final judgments in the supreme court, held within any county within the state, could be re-examined and reversed or affirmed in the court in bank upon a *writ* of error.[11]

This judicial arrangement continued until the adoption of the constitution of 1851, which provided a judicial system modeled upon the federal system existing at the time. The supreme court, as established in 1851, became for the first time in Ohio history a reviewing court of last resort in the state. At the same time the jurisdiction of the supreme court was restricted. In 1853 the court of common pleas, rather than the supreme court, was given original cognizance of all crimes and offenses, except minor criminal cases, the exclusive jurisdiction of which was vested in the justices of the peace and other minor courts.[12] The supreme court, which, between the years 1803 and 1843, had had exclusive original cognizance in divorce and alimony cases and from 1843 to 1853 had concurrent jurisdiction with the court of common pleas in such cases, was denied such jurisdiction in 1853 when the latter court was granted exclusive jurisdiction in these cases.[13]

The opinions of the supreme court on circuit and the decisions of the court in bank, as transmitted to the clerk of the supreme court in each county, are in the offices of the respective clerks of courts.

---

10. *Laws of Ohio*, XXIX, 93-94.
11. *Ibid.*, XXXV, 60-62.
12. G. C. sec. 13422-5; *Laws of Ohio*, LI, 474; LII, 72.
13. *Laws of Ohio*, XLI, 94; LI, 377.

130. SUPREME COURT JOURNAL
1810-1849. 3 vols. (two unlabeled; A). Initiated 1810. 1850-1851 in [District Court Journal] Record of Bonds entry 135.

Journal entries of all court orders and decrees filed in supreme court, showing case number, date of court term, date of entry, title of action, names of plaintiff and defendant, and record of proceedings; one volume 1844-1849 contains a Supreme Court Docket 1806-1814, showing term of court, title of case, names of plaintiff and defendant, attorneys, and record of disposition of case. Arranged chronologically by court terms and chronologically thereunder by dates entered. No index. Handwritten. Average 300 pages. 12 x 8 x 1.5. Clerk of courts' office.

131. SUPREME COURT EXECUTION DOCKET
1828-1874. 1 vol.

Record of executions ordered by supreme court on judgments, showing date of judgment, date execution ordered, title of action taken, names of plaintiff and defendant, itemized record of costs and judgment, and order for execution; record of payments on execution, showing amount and date; district court record of cost, 1852-1874, showing title of case, names of plaintiffs and defendants, record of itemized costs for filing, date of filing, and witnesses' fees; copies of receipts for payment of cost, showing date of receipt, amount paid, by whom paid, and by whom received. Arranged chronologically by dates filed. No index. Handwritten. 500 pages. 15.5 x 10.5 x 2. Clerk of courts' office.

132. SUPREME COURT [Final] RECORDS
1806-1827, 1831-1852. 5 vols. (1806, B-E).

Complete record of all cases filed in supreme court, showing date of case, term of court, date of filing, case number, title of action, names of plaintiff and defendant, and record of all proceedings; 1806 and Book D are records transcribed from the original records, which cannot be located. Also contains the District Court [Final] Record, 1852, entry 136. Arranged chronologically by dates of cases. Indexed alphabetically by names of plaintiffs and defendants. Handwritten. Average 600 pages. 17.5 x 12 x 2.5. Clerk of courts' office.

Until 1851 the judicial power of the state of Ohio in matters of both law and equity was vested in the supreme court, the court of common pleas, and the justices' courts.[1] During the first fifty years of Ohio history the supreme court served as a court of appeals, holding court in each county annually.[2] When a new constitution was adopted in 1851 the judicial system was extended by the creation of the district courts composed of one supreme court justice and several common pleas judges in the district. These courts were assigned original jurisdiction in the same matters as the supreme court, and such "appellate jurisdiction" as might be provided by law. Thus by constitutional provision the courts were assigned original cognizance in *quo warranto, mandamus, habeas corpus,* and *procedendo.*[4] In addition to this, in 1852 the legislature authorized the courts to issue *writs* of error, *certiorari, supersedeas, ne exeat,* and all other *writs* not specifically provided by statute, whenever such *writs* were necessary for the exercise of its jurisdiction. The same act gave the courts appellate jurisdiction from the court of common pleas in civil cases wherein the latter court had original jurisdiction.[5]

For the purposes of the district courts the nine common pleas districts were apportioned into five judicial districts. A judge of the supreme court was designated to preside at the sessions of the district courts; in the event that no judge of the supreme court was present, as was often the case, the judge of the court of common pleas in whose subdivision court was being held, was directed to preside.[6]

The district courts failed to function properly. Evidence seems to indicate that the increasing number of cases coming before the supreme court made it difficult for the justices to attend the meetings of the district courts. Indeed, six years before the creation of the district courts, the supreme court dockets were overcrowded. In 1845 the legislature found it necessary to afford temporary relief by prohibiting appeals from the courts of common pleas to the supreme court.[7] A similar condition of overcrowding existed in the sixties, so that, in 1865, the supreme court justices were relieved of the duty of attending the meetings of the district courts for that particular year.[8]

---

1. *Ohio Const. 1820,* Art. III, sec. 1.
2. *See* p. 76.
3. *Ohio Const. 1851,* Art. IV. Secs. 5, 6.
4. *Ibid.,* Art. IV, sec. 2.
5. *Laws of Ohio,* L, 69.
6. *Ibid.,*
7. *Ibid.,* XLIII, 80.
8. *Ibid.,* LXII, 72.

The judicial system had become slow and cumbersome. The courts declined rapidly after 1865 and were finally abolished.

Following the complete collapse of the district courts an amendment to the constitution, adopted in 1883, made provision for circuit courts. "The circuit courts," stated the amendment, "shall be the successor of the district courts, and all cases, judgments, records, and proceedings pending in said district courts, in several counties, of any district, shall be transferred to the circuit courts." The district courts, however, were to be continued in existence until the election and qualification of the judges of the circuit court.[9] The circuit courts were assigned the same "original jurisdiction with the supreme court, and such appellate jurisdiction as may be provided by law." The composition of the courts and the number of circuits were left to the discretion of the legislature. Accordingly, in 1884, an act was passed dividing the state into seven circuits, and providing for the election of three judges in each circuit.[10]

The circuit courts, in addition to the jurisdiction conferred upon them by the constitution,[11] were authorized by the legislature to issue *writs* of *supersedeas* in any case, and all other *writs* not specifically provided by statute when they were necessary for the exercise of the jurisdiction.[12] Moreover, the courts were authorized to make and publish, as they deemed expedient, rules of procedure in their respective circuits, not in conflict with the law or rules of the supreme court. The legislature directed that all cases taken to the circuit courts were to be entered on the docket in the order in which they were commenced, received, or filed, and "to be taken up and disposed of in the same order." However, cases in which persons seeking relief were imprisoned or were convicted of a felony; cases involving the validity of any tax levy or assessment; cases involving the constitutionality of a statute; and cases involving public right and proceedings in *quo warranto, mandamus, procedendo,* or *habeas corpus,* could be taken up in advance of their assignment or order on the docket.[13]

---

9. *Ohio Const. 1851,* Art. IV, sec. 6.
10. *Laws of Ohio,* LXXXI, 168.
11. *Ohio Const. 1851,* Art. IV, sec. 6.
12. *Laws of Ohio,* LXXXI, 168.
13. *Ibid.*

The judicial system of Ohio was again slightly changed in 1912 when, by constitutional amendment the circuit courts were renamed courts of appeals. "The court of appeals shall continue the work of the respective circuit courts and all pending cases and proceedings in the circuit courts shall proceed to judgment and be determined by the respective courts of appeals." The judges of the several circuit courts were designated as judges of the courts of appeals, and were directed to perform the duties thereof until the expiration of their terms of office. Vacancies cause by the expiration of terms of office of the judges were to be filled by the electors of the respective appellate districts. The term of office was fixed at six years.[14]

Jurisdiction of the court of appeals remained much the same as that of the district court in 1851. However, the court was assigned original cognizance in *writs* of prohibition and appellate jurisdiction in the trial of chancery cases.[15] Certain restrictions were imposed upon the court: "No judgment of a court of common pleas, a superior court or other court of record shall be reversed except by the concurrence of all judges of the court of appeals."[16]

At present the court consists of three judges in each of the nine districts into which the state is divided, each of whom shall have been admitted to practice as an attorney at law in the state for a period of six years immediately preceding his election. The salary of the court of appeals judge, fixed at $6000 a year in 1913, was increased to $8000 in 1920 and so continues.[17] The judges hold at least one session of court annually in each county in the district.[18]

Geauga County was assigned to the seventh circuit court district when these courts were established[19] following the constitutional amendment of 1883.[20] It has remained in the seventh district to the present time. As in all counties, a court of appeals holds at least one session in Geauga County each year. The record reveals an average of eight cases heard annually since 1910.[21]

---

14. *Ohio Const. 1851* (Amendment 1912), Art. IV, sec. 6.
15. *Ohio Const. 1851* (Amendment 1912), Art. IV, sec. 6.
16. *Ibid.*
17. *Laws of Ohio,* CIII, 418; CVIII, pt. ii, 1301.
18. G. C. sec. 1517.
19. *Laws of Ohio,* LXXXI, 168.
20. *Ohio Const. 1851,* Art. IV, secs. 1, 6.
21. Circuit Court Docket, 1910-1913, *passim* entry 137; [Court of Appeals Docket] 1913—, *passim,* entry 142.

District Court

133. [District Court] APPEARANCE DOCKET
1852-1884. 1 vol.

Docket of all cases filed for hearing in district court, showing term of court, title of case, names of plaintiff, defendant, and counsel, kind of action, case number, and disposition of case. Arranged chronologically by court terms and numerically thereunder by case numbers. No index. Handwritten. 600 pages. (100 pp. used) 13.5 x 9 x 3. Clerk of courts' office.

134. BAR LIST
1852-1882. 1 vol.

All cases filed in district court, showing term of court, title of case, names of plaintiff, defendant, and council, kind of action, and case number. Arranged chronologically by court terms and numerically thereunder by case numbers. No index. Handwritten. 125 pages. 9.5 x 8.5 x 1. Clerk of courts' office.

135. [District Court Journal] RECORD OF BONDS
1850-1884. 1 vol.

Journal entries of all court orders and decrees filed in district court, including civil, criminal, and chancery cases, showing term of court, title of action, names of plaintiff and defendant, case number, date of filing, record of proceedings, and decrees and court orders; also includes copies of mandates of supreme court, regarding cases appealed from district court 1852-1884; also contains Supreme Court Journal, 1850-1851, entry 130. Arranged chronologically by court terms and chronologically thereunder by dates filed. No index. Handwritten. 500 pages. 15 x 10 x 2. Clerk of courts' office.

136. DISTRICT COURT [Final] RECORD
1853-1884. 2 vols. (I, J). 1852 in Supreme Court [Final] Records, entry 132.

Complete record of all cases filed in district court, showing term of court, title of action, names of plaintiff and defendant, date filing, and proceedings of court. Arranged chronologically by court terms and chronologically thereunder by dates cases filed. Indexed alphabetically by names of plaintiffs and defendants. Handwritten. Average 600 pages. 16.5 x 12 x 3. Clerk of courts' office.

Circuit Court

137. CIRCUIT COURT DOCKET
1885-1913. 1 vol. (1).

Appearance docket of circuit court, showing term of court, case number, names of plaintiff, defendant, and attorneys, kind of action, notations, dates of filing of all pleadings, and copies of sheriff's returns. Arranged chronologically by court terms and numerically thereunder by case numbers. Indexed alphabetically by names of plaintiffs and defendants. Handwritten. 175 pages. 18 x 12.25 x 1. Clerk of courts' office.

138. TRAIL DOCKET – CIRCUIT COURT
1885-1913. 1 vol. (1).

Docket of circuit court orders, decrees, and verdicts, showing term of court, case number, names of attorneys, title of case, names of plaintiff and defendant, state of pleadings, and appeals; orders of the court, showing dates and page numbers in Circuit Court Journal, entry 139. Arranged chronologically by court terms and numerically thereunder by case numbers. No index. Handwritten on printed forms. 135 pages. 16 x 11 x 1. Clerk of courts' office.

139. CIRCUIT COURT JOURNAL
1885-1913. 1 vol. (1).

Journal entries of all court orders and decrees in cases filed in circuit court, showing term of court, case number, title of action, names of plaintiff and defendant, date of filing, and record of proceedings, court orders, and decrees. Arranged chronologically by court terms and chronologically thereunder by dates filed. Indexed alphabetically by names of plaintiffs and defendants. Handwritten. 512 pages. 16 x 12 x 2.25. Clerk of courts' office.

140. FINAL RECORD – CIRCUIT COURT
1885-1913. 2 vols. (1, 2).

Complete record of all cases filed for hearing in circuit court, showing term of court, name of originating court, title of case, case number, date of filing, names of plaintiff and defendant, and record of proceedings, decrees, and verdicts of court. Arranged chronologically by court terms and chronologically thereunder by dates filed. Indexed alphabetically by names of plaintiffs and defendants. Handwritten. Average 600 pages. 18 x 13 x 3. Clerk of courts' office.

Court of Appeals

141. APPEARANCE DOCKET [Court of Appeals]
1913—. 2 vols. (1, 2).

Docket of all cases filed in court of appeals, showing case number, names of plaintiff, defendant, and attorney, kind of action, date of filing sheriff's returns, and other entries, volume and page numbers of [Final] Record [Court of Appeals], entry 144, and when there are clerk's fees, volume and page numbers of Cashbook, entry 98. Arranged chronologically by dates filed. Indexed alphabetically by names of plaintiffs and defendants. Handwritten on printed forms. Average 250 pages. 18 x 13 x 1.5. Clerk of courts' office.

142. [COURT OF APPEALS DOCKET]
1913—. 3 vols. Title varies: Circuit Court Docket, 1913, 1 vol.; Transfer Court of Appeals Docket, 1914-1938, 1 vol.

Docket of judges' decisions, orders, decrees, and verdicts in court of appeals, showing names of plaintiff, defendant, and attorneys, kind of action, date of filing, court orders, decisions, decrees, verdicts, and dates of same. Arranged chronologically by dates filed. No index. 1913, handwritten on printed forms; 1914—, handwritten and typed, some on printed forms. 1 volume 40 pages. 16 x 11 x 1; 2 volumes average 225 loose leaf-pages. 9 x 15 x 1. Clerk of courts' office.

143. JOURNAL
1913—. 2 vols. (1, 2).

Journal entries of all decisions filed or made by court of appeals, showing date of hearing, names of plaintiff and defendant, title of case, date of filing, case number, and all proceedings. Arranged chronologically by dates of hearings. Index alphabetically by names of plaintiffs and defendants. Handwritten. 508 pages. 16 x 12 x 2.5. Clerk of courts' office.

144. [Final] RECORD [Court Of Appeals]

1913——. 3 vols. (1-3).

Final and complete record of all cases tried or heard by court of appeals in Geauga County, showing case number, date of filing, title of case, names of plaintiff and defendant, proceedings, verdicts, orders, and decrees of court; proceedings include docket entries, petitions, affidavits, summonses, sheriff's returns, order of attachment, journal entries, motions, notices of motions, exceptions, *praecipes,* decrees and transcripts of records of lower courts. Arranged chronologically by dates filed. Indexed alphabetically by names of plaintiffs and defendants. 1913-1935, handwritten; 1936——, typed. 600 pages. 18 x 13 x 3. Clerk of courts' office.

86	PROBATE COURT

The probate court, established by an act of the Northwest Territory on August 30, 1788, consisted of a probate judge with jurisdiction in probate, testamentary, and guardianship matters, and two judges of the court of common pleas, who set with him and ruled on contested points, definitive sentences, and final judgments[1]

The judicial system established under the first constitution of Ohio in 1802 did not provide for a probate court but vested the court of common pleas with such powers as had been exercised by the court in the territorial period. The constitution of 1851 re-created the probate court and gave it original jurisdiction in "probate and testamentary matters, the appointment of administrators and guardians, the settlement of the accounts of the executors, administrators and guardians, and such jurisdiction in *habeas corpus, . . .* and for the sale of land by executors, administrators and guardians, and such other jurisdiction, . . . as may be provided by law."[2] An amendment to the constitution, adopted in 1912, authorized the common pleas judge, when petitioned by 10 percent of the qualified voters in counties having a population less than 60,000 to submit to the voters at any general election on the question of combining the probate court and court of common pleas.[3]

One of the primary functions of the court since its inception has been the settlement of estates. The civil code adopted in 1853 gave the court original jurisdiction in taking proof of wills, in granting letters testamentary, and settling accounts of executors and administrators.[4] Until 1854 the court had jurisdiction in enforcing the payment of debts and legacies of deceased persons. While the court retains the original jurisdiction regarding estates, new duties have been added in recent years. With the development of inheritance tax laws in 1919 as a new means of taxation, the probate court has been required to determine and assess the tax after the county auditor has appraised the descendant's estate.[5]

By constitutional provision the probate court has original jurisdiction in granting marriage licenses.[6]

---

1. Pease, *op. cit., 9.*
2. *Ohio Const. 1851,* Art. IV, secs. 7, 8.
3. *Ibid.,* Art. IV, sec, 7.
4. *Laws of Ohio,* LI, 167.
5. *Ibid.,* CVIII, pt.i, 561.
6. *Ohio Const. 1851,* L, 84.

The court also issues licenses to ministers to solemize marriages.[7] The former provision was modified by an act adopted in 1931, which requires a lapse of at least five days between the time of application and that of the issuance of marriage licenses. However, power to suspend the operation of the act is vested in the probate judge.[8]

The jurisdiction of the court extends to the state's unfortunates. By the probate court code of 1853, re-enacted in 1854, exclusive jurisdiction was granted to the court to make inquest respecting lunatics, insane persons, idiots, and deaf and dumb persons, subject by law to guardianships.[9] In 1856 the court was authorized to commit mentally incompetent persons to state institutions maintained for the care of such persons.[10] Two years later the court was given power to appoint and remove guardians over minors.[11] The act of 1859 authorized the court to render adoption decrees.[12] In 1904 the court was given jurisdiction in trial cases involving neglected, dependent, and delinquent children,[13] and on December 22, 1908 Geauga County established a juvenile department under the jurisdiction of the probate court.[14]

Since the middle of the 19th century the probate judge has been required to keep a record of vital statistics. In 1867 the duty of keeping a permanent record of births and deaths, which, in 1856, had been conferred upon the clerk of courts, was transferred to the probate judge.[15] When, in 1908 a bureau of vital statistics under the direction of the secretary of state was created the probate judge was relieved temporarily of this task.[16] In 1921 the act of 1908 was amended so as to require the local registrars to transmit to the district health commissioner, who was directed to serve as a state deputy registrar of vital statistics, all certificates of births and deaths received during the proceeding month, and a copy of all such certificates to the probate court.

---

7. *Laws of Ohio*, L, 84.
8. *Laws of Ohio*, CXIV, 93.
9. *Ibid.*, LI, 167; LII, 103.
10. *Ibid.*, LIII, 81-86.
11. *Ibid.*, LV, 54.
12. *Ibid.*, LVI, 82; LXVII, 14.
13. *Ibid.*, XCVII, 561.
14. Juvenile Journal, I, 1, entry 199.
15. *Laws of Ohio*, LXIV, 63, 40.
16. *Ibid.*, XCIX, 296-307.

Although the general code still requires the probate judge to keep a permanent record of births and deaths and an index to such records,[17] neither has been kept in Geauga County since 1908.

Jurisdiction in naturalization proceedings was exercised by the probate court until 1906 when an amendment to the federal statute vested exclusive jurisdiction in naturalization matters in the United States district courts and all state courts of record having a seal, a clerk, and jurisdiction in actions at law and equity in which the amount in controversy was unlimited.[18] The general code still requires the probate judge to keep a naturalization record and an index to the records,[19] but jurisdiction was transferred to the court of common pleas. No naturalization records have been kept since 1905.

During the early years of its existence the court was given limited criminal jurisdiction in cases in which the sentence did not impose capital punishment or punishment by imprisonment. By the code of civil procedure adopted in 1853 the judgment and final decrees of the probate court could be reviewed by the court of common pleas on error.[20] In 1857 the criminal jurisdiction of the probate court was transferred to the court of common pleas,[21] but later acts retain it in certain counties only. Thus, in 1861 Geauga County was granted jurisdiction in all crimes in which the sentence did not impose capital punishment or imprisonment in a penitentiary.[22] This act was repealed in 1878 and the probate courts of certain counties were granted concurrent jurisdiction with the court of common pleas in all misdemeanors and proceedings to prevent crime.[23] Geauga County was included under this legislation.[24] The probate court continued to exercise such jurisdiction until 1931 when the last vestige of criminal jurisdiction disappeared with the adoption of the probate code.[25]

---

17. G. C. sec. 10501-15.
18. *United States Statutes at Large*, XXXIV, pt. I, 596; *See also State of Ohio* v. *George G. Metzger* and *Albert L. Irish*, 10 n. p., n. s., 97 *et seq.*
19. G. C. secs. 10501-15, 10501-16.
20. *Laws of Ohio*, LI, 145.
21. *Ibid.*, LIV, 97.
22. *Ibid.*, LV, 186.
23. *Ibid.*, LXXV, 960.
24. *Ibid.*, LVIII, 34.
25. *Ibid.*, CXIV, 475.

Miscellaneous duties, remotely related to probate and testamentary matters, have been added by legislative action. Since 1888 the court has been required to file a certified list of all unknown depositors as furnished by institutions or persons engaged in lending money for profit.[26] In 1896 the probate court was given concurrent jurisdiction with the court of common pleas in the matter of changing the names of persons who desire it,[27] a matter in which the court of common pleas had exclusive cognizance from 1842 to 1896.[28] Since 1896 the probate court has been required to record certificates of doctors and surgeons, and since 1916 the certificates of registered nurses which authorized them to practice their profession in the state.[29] Since 1913 the court has been vested with a power to grant injunctions,[30] And since 1915 has had concurrent jurisdiction with the court of common pleas in condemnation proceedings for roads.[31]

In like manner the appointed powers of the probate judge have been expanded. In addition to the authority to appoint administrators and guardians he was authorized by the act of 1891 to appoint members of the county board of elections; However, this appointive power was obligated by the act of 1892.[32] Then, too, from 1908 to 1913 the probate judge was authorized to appoint a county blind relief commission[33] comprised of three members each of whom served a three-year term.[34] Since 1906 he has had authority to appoint members of the board of county visitors.[35]

---

26. *Ibid.*, LXXXV, 65; G. C. sec. 9864.
27. *Laws of Ohio*, XCII, 28.
28. *Ibid.*, XL, 28, 29.
29. *Ibid.*, XCII, 46; XCIX, 499; CVI, 193.
30. *Ibid.*, CIII, 427.
31. *Ibid.*, CVI, 583.
32. *Laws of Ohio*, LXXXVIII, 449; LXXXIX, 455.
33. *See* p. 232.
34. *Laws of Ohio*, XCIX, 56; CIII, 60.
35. *Ibid.*, XCVIII, 28; CIII, 173, 174.

The probate judge like other county officials, has been required by statute to keep a record of the business of his office. The present system of records, originating for the most part in 1853 and continued by the probate code of 1931, includes a criminal record, administrative docket, guardian' docket, marriage record, record of bonds, naturalization record, and a permanent record of births and deaths.[36]

The probate judge has the care and custody of the files, papers, books, and records belonging to the probate office and is ex-officio clerk of the court. The probate code, adopted in 1931, directed the probate judge to preserve for future reference and examination all pleadings, accounts, vouchers, and other papers in each estate, trust, assignment, guardianship, or other proceedings, such papers to be properly jacketed and tied together; he is required also to make proper entries and indexes omitted by his predecessors. Certificates of marriages, reports of birth, and similar papers not a part of a case or proceeding are to be arranged and preserved separately in the order of dates in which they are filed.[37]

At present the probate judge is elected for a four-year term.[38] In recent years there has been an attempt to raise the qualifications of those seeking election to the office. Accordingly, an amendment to the probate code in 1935 restricted eligibility to the office to a practicing attorney or to a person who "shall have previously served as a probate judge immediately prior to his election."[39]

The probate judge in Geauga County receives an annual salary of $1760[40] and his bond is set at $1000.[41] His office staff consists of a clerk and a deputy, who receive an aggregate salary of $2830 and are not bonded. The probation officer receives an annual salary of $600[42] and is not bonded.

A brief examination of the court records will serve to show the general nature of its work. From 1852, when the court was established, to 1941, 3214 wills were probated,[43] 7083 estates were administered,[44] 1400 guardians were appointed,[45]

36. *Ibid.,* LI, 167; LII, 103; LXXV, 9; CXIV, 324.
37. *Ibid.,* CXIV, 321, 322.
38. *Ibid.,* CXIV, 320.
39. *Ibid.,* CXVI, 481.
40. Commissioners' Journal, General, XI [1936-1941], 423-428.
41. Treasurer's Record of Bonds of Officials, 1940, entry 352.
42. Commissioners' Journal, General, XI [1936-1940]. 423.
43. Record of Wills, years covered, entry 159.
44. Administrators' and Executors' Docket, years covered, entry 152.
45. Guardians' Docket, years covered, entry 153.

and 181 children were placed in adoptive homes,[46] 325 persons were declared insane, 19 feeble-minded, 21 mentally ill or epileptic.[47] Inheritance taxes were paid upon 475 estates, 31 names were changed, and 157 estates were released from administration because they involved less than $500.[48] Vital statistics were kept in probate court since 1940, during which time 224 births and 225 deaths were recorded.[49] Since 1916, eight doctors were issued certificates,[50] 14 nurses were registered,[51] and eight limited practitioners were issued permits.[52]

---

46. Civil [And Criminal] Dockets, years covered, entry 145.
47. Lunacy record, years covered, entry 186.
48. Administration Docket, years covered, entry 151.
49. Record of Births and Deaths, 1940-1941, entry 189.
50. Physicians' Certificates, years coverage, entry 193.
51. Registered Nurses' and Limited Practitioners' Record, years covered, entry 194.
52. *Ibid.*

Civil Cases

145. CIVIL [And Criminal] DOCKET
1861-1931. 8 vols. (A; 2-8).

Docket of proceedings of civil cases tried and probate court, showing date filed, names of plaintiff and defendant, volume and page numbers of records in Final Record Adoptions, 1910—, entry 159; Lunacy Record, entry 186; Final Record, entry 156; and Probate Journal, entry 154, dates of various procedures in cases, and case number of original papers in Probate Files, entry 158, includes criminal records, 1893-1858, 1879-1931. Also contains: Final Record – Adoptions, 1853-1909, entry 157 and Guardians' Docket, 1853-1875 entry 153. Arranged chronologically by dates filed. Indexed alphabetically by names of plaintiffs and defendants; For separate index, 1853-1895, see entry 146. 1853-1880—, handwritten on printed forms. Average 175 pages. 16 x 12 x 2. Probate office.

146. GENERAL INDEX TO PROBATE RECORDS
1806-1895. 1 vol.

General index to probate records, showing names of principals, case number, kind of case, volume and page numbers of records in Probate Records, entry 155; Record of Wills, entry 159; Final Record, entry 156; Probate Journal entry 154; Civil [And Criminal] Docket, entry 145; and Administrators' and Executors' Docket, entry 152.

Arranged alphabetically by names of principles in case showing case numbers. Handwritten on printed forms. 500 pages. 18 x 13 x 2.5. Probate office.

147. EXECUTION DOCKET
1923—. 1 vol.

Docket of executions ordered by judges in civil cases, and criminal cases, 1923-1931, showing names of plaintiff and defendant, date execution ordered, date served, cost, remarks, sheriff's fees, amount paid on execution, date paid, and copy of sheriff's return. Arranged chronologically by dates of executions. Indexed alphabetically by names of defendants. Handwritten on printed forms. 200 pages. 17 x 12 x 1. Probate office.

148. PROBATE WITNESS DOCKET
1879-1903, 1911-1924. 2 vols. (1, 2).

Docket of witnesses in probate court cases, showing date of proceedings, case number, title of case, names of plaintiffs and witnesses, days attended, number of miles traveled, amount due, and date payment received. Arranged chronologically by dates of proceedings. Indexed alphabetically by names of plaintiffs. Handwritten on printed forms. Average 300 pages. 16 x 12 x 1.5. Probate office.

Criminal Cases
(See also entries 145, 147, 148)

149. CRIMINAL JOURNAL
1861-1866, 1879-1931. 4 vols. (A; 1, 1, 2). Title varies: Criminal Record, 1853-1866, 1879-1904, 2 vols.

Record of all criminal cases tried in probate court, showing case number Probate Files, entry 158, name of defendant, date of proceedings, proceedings in case, decisions of judge, and sentence; includes minor crimes, misdemeanors, and liquor cases. Arranged chronologically by dates of proceedings. Indexed alphabetically by names of defendants. 1861-1866, 1879-1925, handwritten; 1925-1931, typed. Average 500 pages. 16 x 12 x 2.5. 2 volumes, 1853-1866, 1879-1904, Probate storeroom; 2 volumes, 1905-1931, Probate office.

General Court Proceedings

150. PROBATE COURT CALENDAR
1886—. 22 vols. (1-7; fifteen dated).

Daily schedule of all cases heard in probate court, showing date case filed, case number, title of case, kind of action, names of plaintiff and defendant, cost due, and costs paid. Arranged chronologically by dates cases filed. No index. Handwritten on printed forms. Average 200 pages. 17 x 12 x 1. Probate office.

151. ADMINISTRATION DOCKET
1884—. 6 vols. (2-7).

Docket of estates settled by administrator or executor, showing case number original paper in Probate Files, entry 158, date of record, name of descendant, name of applicant, date of application, date of appointment for administrator or executor, amount of bond, name of surety, date filed, and all procedure through settlement of estate, and volume and page numbers in Probate Journal, entry 154; Final Record, entry 156; Record of Administrators' Bonds and Letters, entry 162; Administrators' Bond Record [with Will Annexed] Entry 163; Administrators' and executors' Bonds and Letters, entry 167; Record Testamentary Trustees' Bonds, entry 166; Record of Inventory and Appraisements [with and without Widow] Entry 169; Record of Accounts, entry 182; Inheritance Tax Record, entry 183; and Notice Record, entry 197. Arranged chronologically by dates appointed. Indexed alphabetically by names of descendants. Handwritten on printed forms. Average 500 pages. 18 x 13 x 2.5. Probate office.

152. ADMINISTRATORS' AND EXECUTORS' DOCKET
1870-1885. 1 vol. (1).

Docket of appointments of administrators and executors, showing name of descendant or ward, name of administrator, executor, or guardian, date of appointment, name of surety, amount of bond, dates of filing inventory and sale bill, amount of inventory, amount of sale, date of settlement, and volume and page number in Probate Journal, entry 154; Final Record, entry 156; Record of Wills, entry 159; Administrators' and Executors' Bonds and Letters, entry 167; Record of Guardians Bonds, Letters, and Appointments, entry 164; Record of Inventory and Appraisements [with and without Widow], entry 169; Record of Accounts, entry 182; and Notice Record, entry 197. also contains Guardians Docket, 1876-1880, entry 153. Arranged chronologically by dates appointed. Indexed alphabetically by names of descendants of wards; for separate index, see entry 146. Handwritten on printed forms. 446 pages. 18 x 12 x 2.5. Probate office.

153. GUARDIANS' DOCKET
   1876—. 3 vols. (1-3). 1853-1875 in Civil [and criminal] Docket, entry 145;
   1876-1880 also in Administrators' and Executors' Docket, entry 152.

Docket of appointment of guardians for minors and irresponsible persons, showing name of ward, guardian, and sureties, amount of bond, dates of various proceedings, case number, reference to original papers in Probate Files, entry 157, and volume and page numbers in Probate Journal, entry 154; Final Report, entry 156; Record of Wills, entry 159; Record of Guardians' Bonds, Letters, and Appointments, entry 164; [Copies of Appointments, Bonds, and Letters, of Guardians for Idiots, and Imbeciles, Lunatics, Drunkards, or other Incompetents], Entry 165; Record of Inventory and Appraisements [with and without Widow], Entry 169; Record of Accounts, entry 182; and Notice Record, entry 197. Arranged chronologically by dates of proceedings. Indexed alphabetically by names of wards. Handwritten on printed forms. Average 250 pages. 18 x 13 x 1.25. Probate office.

154. PROBATE JOURNAL
   1852—. 36 vols. (A-Z; 27-36).

Journal entries of all proceedings in probate court, showing date of proceedings in case, names of principals, case number and Probate File, entry 158; also contains record of appointment of board of county visitors, 1906—; record of determination of heirship, record of idiots, imbeciles, lunatics, and incompetents; also includes appointment of assignees, administrators, executors, election of widows, partial account statements, applications for letters of administration, appointment of appraisers, order for hearings, filing of wills, court orders, journal entries, record of filing of final accounts, inventories and appraisements, record of administrators' bonds and letters, administrators' bond record with will annexed; records of guardians' bonds, letters, and appointments, and record of sale of personal property at public or private sale. Arranged chronologically by dates of proceedings. Indexed alphabetically by names of principals; for separate index, 1852-1895, see entry 146. 1852-1917, handwritten; 1917—. Typed. Average 475 pages. 16 x 12 x 2. Probate office.

155. PROBATE RECORDS
1806-1852. 2 vols. (A; 1).
Record of proceedings in civil cases, including the appointment and removal of administrators, guardians, and executors, settlement of estates, inventories, appraisements, and sales, showing date of proceedings, name and address of principal parties, itemized statement of personal property, names of witnesses and appraisers, amount of personal property listed in will, list of all goods, chattel debts and credits, court term, and date recorded. Also contains Record of Wills, entry 159. Arranged chronologically by dates of proceedings. Indexed alphabetically by names of principals; for separate index, see entry 146. Handwritten. Average 640 pages. 16 x 10.5 x 3. Probate office.

156. FINAL RECORD
1852—. 25 vols. (A-Y).
Complete record of proceedings in cases filed in probate court, including petitions, summonses, appointment of administrators and executors to sell land, copies of *writs* of *habeas corpus,* admission to bail, and record of assignee's bonds and letters, showing names and addresses of principal parties, case number, kind of action, copy of petitions setting forth grounds for suit, date filed, court order, and decree. Also contains; [Copies of Appointments, Bonds, and Letters of Guardians for Idiots, and Imbeciles, Lunatics, Drunkards, or other Incompetents], 1853-1907, entry 165; Record Testamentary Trustees' Bonds, 1853-1911, entry 166; and Applications and Statements for Appointment of Assignee, 1852-1914, 1930—, entry 185. Arranged chronologically by dates filed. Indexed alphabetically by names of principals; for separate index, 1852-1895, see entry 146. 1833-1914, handwritten; 1915—, typed. Average 600 pages. 18 x 12 x 3. Probate office.

157. FINAL RECORD – ADOPTIONS
1910—. 2 vols. (1, 2). 1853-1909 in Civil[and Criminal] Docket, entry 145. Record of petitions for adoptions, showing date of petition, case number, names of child and petitioners, copy of petition for adoption, answer and consent, court orders, and decrees relating to adoption. Arranged chronologically by dates of petitions. Indexed alphabetically by names of petitioners. 1910-1922, Handwritten on printed forms; 1923—, typed on printed forms. Average 400 pages. 18.5 x 13 x 2. Probate office.

Original Documents

158. PROBATE FILES
1852—. 2 shelves, 392 file boxes (labeled by contained case numbers).
Original papers filed in probate court cases, including settlement of estates, original
wills, proofs of publication, final statements, affidavits pertaining to estates, record
of appointment of administrators, executors, guardians, and appraisers,
miscellaneous cost bills, criminal case records of lunacy and incompetency,
adoptions, assignments, and marriage application and returns, showing title of case,
case number, names of plaintiff and defendant; cause of action, name of attorney,
and proceedings. Also includes original papers for juvenile court 1908—. Each
case in separate jacket, showing case number, title of case, and date of filing.
Arranged numerically by case numbers. Dockets serve as index by showing case
numbers. Typed on printed forms. Shelves, 16 x 42 x 12; file boxes, 10 x 5 x 15. 2
shelves, 1852-1925, Probate storeroom; 392 file boxes, 1926—, Probate office.

Estates and Guardianships

Wills

159. RECORD OF WILLS
1853—. 16 vols. (A-P). 1806-1852 in Probate Records, entry 155.
Copies of wills, showing name of testator, date of will, names of town and county,
names of witnesses, and term of will. Arranged chronologically by dates of wills.
Indexed alphabetically by names of testators; for separate index, 1853-1895, see
entry 146. 1853-1916, handwritten; 1917—, typed. Average 600 pages. 18 x 12 x
3. Probate office.

160. FINAL RECORD – ELECTION OF WIDOW
1911—. 2 vols. (1, 2).
Record of widows or widowers of deceased spouse electing to accept provisions of
deceased spouse's last will, showing name and address of widow or widower, name
of decedent, and date of election. Arranged chronologically by dates of elections.
Indexed alphabetically by names of decedents. 1911-1931, handwritten on printed
forms; 1932—, typed on printed forms. Average 400 pages. 16 x 12 x 2. Probate
office.

Determination of Heirship

161. DETERMINATION OF HEIRSHIP RECORD
1932—. 1 vol. (1).

Record of determination of heirship, containing copies of petitions to determine heirship, showing date of petition, names of plaintiff and defendant in disputed heirship, name of decedent, description of property in question, and signature of plaintiff, and on separate sheets are contained summonses, and waivers of summonses; sheriff's returns, and copy of journal entry showing disposition of case. Arranged chronologically by dates of petitions. Indexed alphabetically by names of decedents. Typed on printed forms. 400 pages. 18 x 12 x 2. Probate office.

Applications, Appointments, Bonds, and Letters

162. RECORD OF ADMINISTRATORS' BONDS AND LETTERS
1858—. 15 vols. (B-P).

Copies of administrator's bonds, showing names of administrator and sureties, amount and date of bond, and letters of administration; application for letters of administrators, showing names of administrators, decedents, and appraisers, and date of application. Volume 1917—, labeled K contains largely letters of administration *de bonis non*, Arranged chronologically by dates of bonds. Indexed alphabetically by names f decedents. 1858-1917, handwritten on printed forms. 1917-1932, typed; 1932—, typed on printed forms. Average 300 pages. 16 x 12 x 1.5. Probate office.

163. ADMINISTRATOR'S BOND RECORD [With Will Annexed]
1923—. 1 vol, (N). Last entry 1937. 1890-1922 in Record of Guardians' Bonds, Letters, and Appointments, entry 164.

Copies of bonds filed by administrators of estates with will annexed, showing date bonds were filed, amount of bond, name and late address of decedent, names and addresses of heirs, other kinship, name and address of administrator, estimated value of real and personal property of decedent, names of sureties, application for letters of administration, letters of administration, and declination of administration. Arranged chronologically by dates bonds were filed. Indexed alphabetically by names of decedents. Handwritten on printed forms. 272 pages. 16.5 x 12 x 2.25. Probate office.

164. RECORD OF GUARDIANS' BONDS, LETTERS, AND
APPOINTMENTS
1867—. 5 vols. (1-3, 5, 6).
Copies of bonds of guardians, showing date and amount of bond, names of
guardian, ward, and sureties, letters of guardianship, application for appointment
as guardian, notice of hearing, waiver of notice, and sheriff's returns and orders on
hearing. Also contains Administrators' Bond Record [With Will Annexed], 1890-
1922, entry 163. Arranged chronologically by dates of bonds. Indexed
alphabetically by names of wards. 1867-1932, handwritten on printed forms.
1932—, typed on printed forms. Average 350 pages. 18 x 12.5 x 1.5. Probate office.

165. [COPIES OF APPOINTMENTS, BONDS, AND LETTERS OF
GUARDIANS FOR IDIOTS, IMBECILES, LUNATICS, DRUNKARDS,
OR OTHER INCOMPETENTS]
1908—. 2 vols. (4, 5). 1853-1907 in Final Record, entry 156.
Copies of appointments, bonds, and letters of guardianship for idiots, imbeciles,
lunatics, drunkards, or other incompetents, showing name of ward, date of
appointment, names of guardian and sureties for bonds, amount of bond, and
authority for guardianship. Arranged chronologically by dates of appointments.
Indexed alphabetically by names of wards. Handwritten on printed forms. Average
375 pages. 18 x 13 x 2. Probate office.

166. RECORD TESTAMENTARY TRUSTEES' BONDS
1912—. 1 vol. 1853-1911 in Final Record, entry 156.
Application for appointment of trustees, showing name of decedent, date of
application, order for bond, date approved, date letter issued, and letters of authority
to testamentary trustee. Arranged chronologically by dates of applications. Indexed
alphabetically by names of decedents. Handwritten on printed forms. 350 pages. 18
x 12 x 1.5. Probate office.

167. ADMINISTRATORS' AND EXECUTORS' BONDS AND LETTERS
1870-1898. 4 vols. (A-D).
Copies of administrators' and executors' bonds, showing dates of bonds, names of
decedents, principals, and sureties, amount of bond, and date of cancellation; also
includes letters of administration and letters testamentary. Arranged chronologically
by dates of bonds. Indexed alphabetically by names of decedents. Handwritten on
printed forms. 450 pages. 18 x 12 x 2.25. Probate office.

168. EXECUTORS' APPLICATIONS, BONDS AND LETTERS
1899—. 5 vols. (E-I).
Copies of bonds of executors, showing name of decedent, date recorded, names of executors and sureties, and amount of bonds; also includes letters testamentary and record of executor's application for letters testamentary. Arranged chronologically by dates recorded. Indexed alphabetically by names of decedents. 1899-1934, handwritten on printed forms; 1935—, typed on printed forms. Average 400 pages. 16 x 12 x 2. Probate office.

Inventories and Appraisements

169. RECORDS OF INVENTORY AND APPRAISEMENTS [With And Without Widow]
1853—. 36 vols. (A-Z; 27-36). Title varies: Record of Inventory and Appraisements – Full, 1911-1931, 7 vols; Record of Inventory and Appraisements – No Widow, 1911, 9 vols.; Record of Inventory and Appraisements – with Widow, 1931—, 2 vols.
Record of inventories, appraisements, and sales of real and personal property and settlement of estates, showing date of inventory, name of decedent, orders to appraisers, notice of appraisements, waiver of notice, appraiser's oath schedule of real and personal property and recapitulations of inventory and schedule of property exempt from administration; 1920—, includes order to appraisers, notice of appraisement, itemized inventory of real estate, chattels, and other personal property of decedents, schedule of property set aside for widow, amount allowed for support of widow for one year, and schedule of all debts against decedents. 1853-1911, handwritten; 1911-1932, handwritten on printed forms; 1932—, typed on printed forms. Average 600 pages. 18 x 13 x 3. Probate office.

Schedule of Debts

170. SCHEDULE OF DEBTS
1932—. 2 vols. (1, 2). Initiated in 1932.
Schedule of claims, debts, and liabilities on estates, showing name of the decedent, date of death, name and address of creditor, nature of claim, how secured, amount of claim, date of allowance or rejection, rate of interest, date of schedule and signatures of administrator and notary; also includes journal entries, proof of publication, sheriff's returns, and signature of probate judge. Arranged

chronologically by dates of schedules. Indexed alphabetically by names of decedents. Typed on printed forms. Average 650 pages. 18 x 12 x 3. Probate office.

Transfers and Sale Bill

171. APPLICATION FOR TRANSFER RECORDS
1932—. 3 vols. (1-3).

Application for transfer of real estate, showing date of application for transfer, name of decedent, last address, exact location of land, number of acres, name of person to whom transferred, age, address, relationship to decedent, portion inherited, names of the executors, and signature of probate judge. Arranged chronologically by dates of applications for transfers. Indexed alphabetically by names of decedents. Typed on printed forms. Average 300 pages. 18.5 x 12 x 1.5. Probate office.

172. RECORD OF PUBLIC [And Private] SALE BILL
1911—. 2 vols. (1, 2).

Record of personal property sold at public or private sale, showing date of sale, number of items, description of articles appraised, appraised value, to whom sold and amount, and name of the decedent. Arranged chronologically by dates of sales. Indexed alphabetically by names of decedents. Handwritten on printed forms. Average 600 pages. 18 x 12 x 2.5. Probate office.

Cost bills

173. COST BILL RECORD GENERAL
1852-1909. 1 vol. (A).

Record of receipts and expenditures incidental to cases heard in probate court, showing date of proceedings, name of payer and payee, amount of cost, notations pertaining to administrator's or executor's case, damage suit, name of guardian, petitions to sell, probate of wills, assault and battery cases, and others. Arranged chronologically by dates of proceedings. Indexed alphabetically by names of payer. Handwritten. 500 pages. 17 x 12 x 2. Probate storeroom.

174. COST BILL RECORD [Accounts]
1902-1910. 3 vols. (One unlabeled; 2, 3).
Record of cost bills of administrator's, executor's and guardian's final and partial accounts, including itemized fees for filing, copying, docketing, and all other services, showing case number, name of decedent, and date of filing. Arranged chronologically by dates filed. 1902-1904, no index; 1905-1910, indexed alphabetically by names of decedents. Handwritten on printed forms. Average 450 pages. 14 x 9 x 2. Probate storeroom.

175. COST BILL RECORD – APPOINTMENT OF ADMINISTRATOR, EXECUTOR
1901-1 910. 3 vols. (1-3).
Records of cost bills or appointments of administrators and executors, including itemized costs for filing, copying, docketing, indexing, sheriff's returns, and numerous other services, showing case number, name of decedent, and dates of filing and recording. Arranged chronologically by dates filed. Indexed alphabetically by names of decedents. Handwritten on printed forms. Average 300 pages. 14 x 9 x 1.5. Probate storeroom.

176. COST BILL RECORD – APPOINTMENT OF GUARDIAN
1904-1909. 1 vol. (1).
Record of cost bills in guardianship cases, including itemized fees for filing, copying, docketing, and other similar services, showing case number, name of ward, and dates filed and recorded. Arranged chronologically by dates filed. Indexed alphabetically by names of wards. Handwritten on printed forms. 300 pages. 14 x 9 x 1.5. Probate storeroom.

177. COST BILLS
1902-1904. 1 vol.
Cost bill record of administrator's, executor's, and guardian's final accounts, showing name of decedent, itemized costs for filing and docketing, and dates filed and recorded. Arranged chronologically by dates filed. No index. Handwritten on printed forms. 300 pages. 14 x 9 x 1.5. Probate storeroom.

178. COST BILL RECORD [Petition To Sell Real Estate]
1853-1910. 2 vols. (1, 2).

Record of cost bills in petition of administrators, executors, and guardians to sell real estate, including itemized cost for filing, copying, docketing, indexing, and other similar services, showing case number, date filed and recorded, and name of decedent or ward. Arranged chronologically by dates filed. Indexed alphabetically by names of decedents or wards. Handwritten on printed forms. Average 500 pages. 17 x 12 x 2. Probate storeroom.

179. COST BILL RECORD ESTATES
1882-1903. 3 vols. (1, 3, 4).

Record of cost bills and settlement of estates, including costs for appointment of administrator or executor and guardian, probate of will, election of widow, inventory and appraisement, sale of personal property, petitions to sell real estate, and final and partial accounts, showing case number, name of decedent, and itemized fees for filing, docketing, copying, and similar services. Arranged chronologically by dates filed. Indexed alphabetically by names of decedents. Handwritten on printed forms. Average 575 pages. 18.5 x 13 x 3. Probate storeroom.

180. COST BILL RECORD INVENTORY
1903-1910. 3 vols. (1-3).

Cost bill record of inventories, showing case number, name of decedent, dates filed and recorded, and itemized costs of various services pertaining to taking inventory. Arranged chronologically by dates filed. Indexed alphabetically by names of decedents. Handwritten on printed forms. Average 300 pages. 14 x 9 x 1.5. Probate storeroom.

181. COST BILL RECORD [Miscellaneous]
1879-1905. 1 vol. (2).

Record of miscellaneous cost bills, including claim of administrator or executor, miscellaneous cases on petitions, motions, citation, exceptions, *habeas corpus,* inquest of lunacy, 1881-1905, reform school commitments, treasury examinations, school inspection, proceeding and aid to execution, partnerships appraisements, adoptions, 1881-1903, appropriation proceedings, criminal cases, 1879-1902, other jury cases, showing names of principals, case number, itemized to cause, and date filed. Arranged alphabetically by subjects and chronologically thereunder by dates filed. Indexed alphabetically by names of principals. Handwritten on printed forms. 575 pages. 18.5 x 13 x 3. Probate storeroom.

Accounts and Settlements

182. RECORD OF ACCOUNTS
1846—. 29 vols. (A-Z, 27-29).

Record of filing costs for administrator, probate judge, attorney's fees, and funeral expenses, showing date of proceeding, name of decedent, and date and record of any expense pertaining to decedent; also contains records of common pleas court, 1846-1852. Arranged chronologically by dates of proceedings. Indexed alphabetically by names of decedents. 1846-1923, handwritten; 1923—, typed. Average 500 pages. 18 x 12 x 2. Probate office.

Inheritance Tax

183. INHERITANCE TAX RECORD
1919—. 2 vols. (1, 2).

Record of estates subject to inheritance tax, showing names and addresses of heirs at law, legatees and devisees, name of decedent, date of recording total value, exemptions, net values subject to tax, rate and amount of tax, and date of accrual of tax. Arranged chronologically by dates recorded. Indexed alphabetically by names of decedents. Handwritten on printed forms. Average 600 pages. 18 x 12 x 3. Probate office.

184. FINAL INHERITANCE TAX RECORD
1919—. 6 vols. (1-6).

Record of probate court settlement of estates subject to inheritance tax, showing name and last address of decedent, date of settlement case number, description of property, location, estimated value, names and addresses of heirs, age, relationship to decedent, proportion inherited, and signatures of petitioners and notary. Arranged chronologically by dates of settlements. Indexed alphabetically by names of decedents. Handwritten on printed forms. Average 600 pages. 16 x 12 x 3. Probate office.

Assignments

185. APPLICATION AND STATEMENT FOR APPOINTMENT OF ASSIGNEE
1915-1929. 1 vol. 1852-1914, 1930— in Final Record entry 156.
Record of application and statement of appointment of assignee, showing names of parties involved, application for appointment of appraisers, date of appointment, assignee's bond, and probate judge's letter of authority to assignee. Arranged chronologically by dates of appointments. Indexed alphabetically by names of assignees. Handwritten on printed forms. 200 pages. 18 x 12 x 1.5. Probate office.

Dependents

186. LUNACY RECORD
1904—. 3 vols. (1-3).
Record of proceedings, including lunacy, and imbecility, feeblemindedness, and epilepsy affidavits, showing name of patient, race, sex, marital status, physical condition of patient, doctor's certificate of examination, court affidavit, date of affidavit, name of person filing affidavit, copy of warrant to arrest, copy of medical certificate filed by examining physician, copy of proceedings at request hearing, copy of application for admission to state institution, copy of warrant to convey to institution, copy of sheriff's return on *writs* with cost bills, and sheriff's fees; record of discharge of patient from institution, showing title of case, name of patient, and date case filed. 1904-1916, arranged chronologically by affidavits; 1917—, arranged by subjects and chronologically thereunder by dates of affidavits. Indexed alphabetically by names of patients. Handwritten on printed forms. 2 volumes average 220 pages. 18 x 12 x 1.25; 1 volume 600 pages. 18 x 13 x 5. Probate office.

187. REGISTER OF BLIND
1905-1914. 1 vol.
Record of indigent blind receiving aid from county, showing name and address of recipient, amount allowed quarterly, volume and page numbers of Probate Journal, entry 154, date registered, and date of cessation of benefits. Arranged chronologically by dates of registrations. Indexed alphabetically by names of recipients. Handwritten on printed forms. 125 pages. 14 x 8 x 1. Probate office.

188. NATURALIZATION RECORD

1852-1906. 4 vols. (three unlabeled; 1).

Record of application of aliens for naturalization, showing date of application, name of applicant, date and location of declaration of intention, names of witnesses, renunciation of allegiance to foreign governments and order for issuance of certificate of naturalization, application of minor for citizenship, 1852-1880, and declaration of aliens who arrived in the United States under 18 years of age; 1897 includes soldier's oath of allegiance and application for citizenship. Arranged chronologically by dates of applications. Indexed alphabetically by names of applicants. Handwritten on printed forms. Average 250 pages. 15 x 10 x 1. Probate office.

Vital Statistics

Births and Deaths

189. [RECORD OF BIRTH AND DEATHS]

1867-1908. 3 vols. (1, 2, 2). Title varies: Births – Deaths, 1867-1899, 1 vol.; Record of Birth 1900-1908, 1 vol.; Record of Deaths 1900-1908, 1 vol.

Birth record, showing date and place of birth, date certificate filed, consecutive certificate number, name of infant, by whom reported, sex, race, color, names and addresses of parents, and maiden name of mother. Death record, showing date reported, consecutive certificate number, name of deceased, date of death, marital status, age, places of death and birth, occupation, color, race, cause of death, place of residence, and by whom reported. Arranged chronologically by dates of births or deaths. Indexed alphabetically by names of infants or deceased. Handwritten on printed forms. Average 450 pages. 18 x 13 x 2.5. Probate office.

Marriages (See also entry 158)

190. MARRIAGE RECORD

22 vols. (seven dated; A-F; 1-9).

Record of marriage licenses issued, showing names of contracting parties, town and county, date of license, and signature of justice of peace, or officiating clergyman;

1870—, showing dates returned and filed. Also contains Record of Ministers' Licenses, 1852-1885, entry 192. Arranged chronologically by dates of licenses. 1806-1869, indexed alphabetically by names of males; 1870—, indexed alphabetically by names of males showing names of females; for separate index, 1806-1869, see entry 191. 1806-1833 handwritten; 1833—, handwritten on printed forms. Average 300 pages. 18 x 12 x 2. Probate office.

191. GENERAL INDEX TO MARRIAGES
1806-1869. 1 vol. (1).

General index to Marriage Record, entry 190, showing date of recording, names of contracting parties, and column and page numbers of record. Arranged alphabetically by names of males showing names of females. Handwritten on printed forms. 500 pages. 12 x 9 x 2.5. Probate office.

Licenses and Certificates

192. RECORD OF MINISTERS' LICENSES
1886—. 2 vols. (1, 2).

Record of licenses issued to ministers to perform marriages, showing name and address of minister, church denomination, and date of license. Arranged chronologically by dates of licenses. No index. Handwritten. Average 250 pages. 14 x 8.5 x 1. Probate office.

193. PHYSICIAN'S CERTIFICATES
1896—. 1 vol.

Copies of certificates issued by the Ohio State Medical Board to physicians, showing name and address of physician, conditions of certificate, date issued, and signature of board; also includes record of two limited practitioners' certificates for 1927. Arranged chronologically by dates issued. Indexed alphabetically by names of physicians. Handwritten on printed forms. 200 pages. 16 x 12 x 1. Probate office.

194. REGISTERED NURSES' AND LIMITED PRACTITIONERS' RECORD
1916—. 1 vol. (1).

Copies of certificates of registered nurses and limited practitioners issued by the Ohio State Medical Board, showing certificate number, date of issue, name of nurse or practitioner, notation regarding diploma from school, signatures of chief medical examiner and probate judge, and date recorded. Arranged chronologically by dates issued. Indexed alphabetically by names of nurses or practitioners. Handwritten on printed forms. 200 pages. 16 x 11.5 x 1. Probate office.

Financial Records

195. CASH BOOK
1885—. 11 vols. (1, 1-10).
Record of all receipts and disbursements of probate court, showing case number in Probate Files, entry 158, dates of receipt and disbursement, names of payer and payee, amount due, total probate fees, disbursements, and summary; 1907—, contains all cost bills, probate fees, and all other moneys handled by probate court. Seventy-five pages in back of volume 10, contains juvenile court cash book 1937—. Arranged chronologically by dates of receipts and disbursements. Indexed alphabetically by names of payers. Handwritten on printed forms. Average 250 pages. 18 x 12 x 1. 1 volume, 1885-1907, Probate storeroom; 10 volumes, 1907—, Probate office.

196. RECORD OF ACCRUED FEES
1907—. 2 vols. (1, 2).
Record of accrued fees of the probate court, showing date of accrual fee, case number in Probate Files, entry 158, name of case, to whom charged, and total fees classified as to civil and criminal cases due from county, juvenile court, transcripts and copies, and sundries, also date paid. Arranged chronologically by dates of accrual. No index. Handwritten on printed forms. Average 238 pages. 18 x 13 x 1.5. 1 volume, 1907-1922, Probate storeroom; 1 volume, 1923—, Probate office.

Miscellaneous

197. NOTICE RECORD
1875—. 9 vols. (2-10).
Records of proof of publication of appointment of administrator, executor, or guardian, showing date of appointment, name of decedent, signature of probate judge, name of newspaper publisher, and newspaper's name. Arranged chronologically by dates of appointments. Indexed alphabetically by decedents. Handwritten on printed forms. Average 300 pages. 18 x 12 x 1.5. Probate office.

The juvenile court, though of uncertain origin, has been generally recognized as an American contribution to the administration of social justice. The establishment of such courts was a logical outcome of the practical philosophy of enlightened public men that child offenders against the law, or conventional social standards, should not be treated as criminals, but as unfortunate needing the help, supervision, and protection of the state.[1] Although the first separate court in the United States for the trial of juvenile offenders was established in 1899, in Chicago, Cook County, Illinois, by an act of the legislature of that state, the juvenile court was an institution of gradual growth. The Illinois experiment gave impetus to the children's movement in the middle west.[2]

The Ohio legislature was not slow in seeing the advantage of the Illinois experiment, and accordingly, in 1902, and act was passed creating the juvenile court in Cuyahoga County. Under this act all counties having a population of over 380,000 and an insolvency court, were authorized, under an extension of the jurisdiction of this court to establish children's courts. The stipulation of this act excluded Geauga County. It gave the court jurisdiction of the trial of cases involving delinquent and neglected children; defined the term "delinquent, dependent, and neglected"; authorized the appointment of a probation officer, and made it his duty to investigate the facts of cases coming before the courts, to take charge of the offender before and after trial. The clerk of the juvenile court was directed to keep a journal in which were to be recorded the minutes of the case.[3]

Two years after the establishment of the Cuyahoga County juvenile court, the assembly provided by statute for the establishment of juvenile courts in the rural counties of the state which, because of the population requirement, were unable to create the newer agencies under the provisions of the act of 1902. Under the act of 1904 the judges of the court of common pleas, probate court, and where established, the insolvency courts, wherein three or more judges held court concurrently, were authorized to appoint one of their members as "juvenile judge."

---

1. Miriam Van Waters, *Youth in Conflict* (New York, 1925), 147, 159, 161.
2. Edwin H. Sutherland, *Principles of Criminology* (Chicago, 1934), 270-272.
3. *Laws of Ohio,* XCV, 785.

The court was given original jurisdiction in all cases involving neglected, dependent, and delinquent children under the age of 16 years; and all children who have been scheduled in the past for trial in a justice of the peace or police court were in the future to be tried before a juvenile judge. As under the act of 1902, the judge was authorized to appoint a probation officer, and the clerk of courts was directed to keep a journal of the minutes of each case.[4] In 1908 the court was given jurisdiction in cases involving minors under 17 years of age, and such children as were brought before the juvenile judge were to become wards of the court until they had obtained the age of 21 years. The county commissioners were authorized to provide by lease or purchase, a "detention home" were neglected or dependent children might be detained pending the final disposition of their cases. The clerk of courts was directed to keep not only a journal, but also an appearance docket containing all orders, judgments, and findings of the court. The age jurisdiction of the court was increased to 18 in 1913.[5]

While provisions were being made for the establishment of juvenile courts, the legislature gave the court jurisdiction in cases involving adults charged with committing crimes against children or contributing to the delinquency of dependent children. Thus, in 1906 it was made a misdemeanor to contribute to the delinquency of a child under 17 years of age.[6] Two years later the "lack of parental care" was defined and it was made a misdemeanor to fail to support a minor, or to cause him to engage in begging.[7] In 1913 "proper parental care" was defined by statute.[8]

Marked progress has been made in the medical treatment of juveniles. While the act of 1913 authorized the juvenile judge to submit any child sentenced to an institution for correction to a mental test, the act of 1929 authorized him to submit any child coming before the court to a mental and physical test to be made by a physician or psychiatrist.[9]

---

4. *Ibid.*, XCVIII, 561.
5. *Laws of Ohio*, CIII, 869.
6. *Ibid.*, XCVIII, 314.
7. *Ibid.*, XCIX, 193.
8. *Ibid.*, CIII, 870.
9. *Ibid.*, CIII, 872; CXIII, 471.

To facilitate the scientific handling of children, the county commissioners were authorized, in the same year, to lease or construct a separate building to be known as the "juvenile court" which should be appropriately constructed, arranged, furnished, and maintained for the convenient and effective transaction of the business of the court, including adequate facilities to be used as laboratories, depositories, or clinics for the scientific use of specialist attached to the court.[10]

One of the guiding principles of the court has been to make its "custody and discipline" of children approximate as nearly as possible that which should be given by their parents. In the cases involving neglected or dependent children not sentenced to state institutions, it has been the policy of judges to assign children to private homes, and make arrangements for their adoption. Many other functions were gradually taken over by the juvenile court, such as administering mothers' pensions,[11] now known as aid to dependent children.

The juvenile court of Cuyahoga County is the only independent juvenile court in the state. There are seven other juvenile courts in Ohio attached to courts of domestic relations. Juvenile court has been held in Geauga County since 1908.[12] The probate judge now presides over the court under the provisions of the act of April 29, 1937, which repealed the act of 1904.[13]

As in most agricultural counties few juvenile offenders are brought to the court, although the number is sufficient to justify its existence. About 37 cases are heard annually. The majority of the offenders are put on probation in any institution or home best adapted to the offense and offenders. Geauga maintains a temporary detention room on the second floor of the jail, but most children are returned to their homes where they are kept under observation by the probation officer.[14]

Divorce is here as elsewhere a contributing cause to juvenile delinquency, an average of some 46 divorces being granted annually.[15]

In 1913 the juvenile court was given the duty of administering mothers' pensions.[16]

---

10. *Ibid.,* CXIII, 470.
11. *Ibid.,* CIII, 877.
12. Juvenile Journal, I, 1, entry 199.
13. G. C. sec. 1639-7.
14. Juvenile Appearance Docket, 1941, *see* entry 198.
15. Appearance and Execution Docket, *passim, see* entry 118.
16. *Laws of Ohio,* CIII, 877.

With the acceptance of the Federal Social Security Act in 1936 the sections of the General Code[17] relative to mothers' pensions were repealed and aid for dependent children was provided. The administration of the act in the state is delegated to the state department of public welfare and in the counties to the judge having juvenile jurisdiction.[18]

Under the act of 1941, which amended the act of 1936, children are eligible for aid if they have been deprived of parental support for various stipulated reasons. However, a child 16 and under 18 may still receive aid if found by the department of public welfare to be regularly attending school. The child must be living with a parent or relative who is a proper person to have charge of the child, and must make adequate home facilities for caring for him.[19] The county administration is empowered to make investigations to determine the eligibility of the applicant and the amount to be awarded which is based on the actual needs of the home.[20] Both the county administration and the department of public welfare are authorized to compel the attendance of witnesses and the production of books and papers.[21] To comply with this act the county is required to provide 15/100 of a mill of the tax duplicate in order to participate; the state makes an appropriation to the county in the proportion that the number of children under 16 in the county is to the total in the state, and the federal government contributes one dollar for every two provided by the state and county.[22]

In Geauga County, the division of aid to dependent children is administered by the probate judge, who appoints a secretary and case worker to investigate the dependency cases. They are paid by combined county, state, and federal appropriations. The agency extends aid to about 97 children annually, the average amount of aid afforded each being $154 annually.[23]

17. G. C. secs. 1683-2 – 1683-10.
18. United States Statutes at Large, XLII, 601; Laws of Ohio, CXVI, pt. ii, 188.
19. G. C. sec. 1359-32.
20. G. C. secs. 1359-43, 1359-33.
21. G. C. sec. 1359-43.
22. G. C. Secs. 1359-36, 1359-37, 1359-38.
23. [Applications for Aid to Dependent Children], 1936-1941, see entry 202; [Verifications]. 1936-1941, see entry 204.

General Court Proceedings

198. JUVENILE APPEARANCE DOCKET
1908—. 3 vols. (1-3).

Docket of cases filed for appearance in juvenile court, showing case number, name of juvenile or delinquent, age, residence, names of parents or guardian, date set for appearance, proceedings in case, and volume and page numbers of Juvenile Journal, entry 199 and Juvenile Record, entry 200; also includes Docket of Mothers' Pension, 1913-1936, showing case number, date of application, name of applicant, date application ordered, and date report filed; records of allowances, showing amount and date of allowance. Arranged chronologically by dates of appearances or applications or pensions. Indexed alphabetically by names of juveniles, delinquents, or mothers. Handwritten on printed forms. Average 275 pages. 16 x 12 x 2.25. Probate office.

199. JUVENILE JOURNAL
1908—. 2 vols. (1, 2).

Journal entries of cases filed in juvenile division, showing case number, name of juvenile, age, race, color, residence, and names of school and teacher; name, residence, nativity, and occupation of parents, guardian, or next friend; date of filing case, name of person filing or issuing all *writs* with brief notation of each step in proceedings of case; also includes a record of appointment of probation officer and original appointment of probate judge to serve as juvenile judge, December 22, 1908, showing name of judge, and date and term of appointment; mother's pension record, 1913-1926, showing name and address of mother, date of birth of dependent children, date application filed, copy of report on investigation of application, copy of journal entry approving or rejecting application, amount of award, and record of payments. Arranged chronologically by dates applications filed. Indexed alphabetically by names of juveniles, mothers, or guardians. 1908-1924 handwritten; 1924—, typed. Average 275 pages. 16 x 12 x 2.5. Probate office.

200. JUVENILE RECORD
1926—. 2 vols. (1, 2). Initiated in 1926.
Record of procedure in juvenile court cases, showing case number, name of juvenile, age, race, color, residence, and names of school and teacher; name, residence, nativity, and occupation of parents, guardian, or next friend, name of person filing affidavit, date of filing case, dates of filing or issuing all *writs* with brief notation of each step in proceedings of case, and final disposition of case; also includes mother's pension record, 1926-1936, showing name and address of mother, amount of award, and record of payments. Arranged chronologically by dates cases filed. Indexed alphabetically by names of juveniles, mothers, or guardians. 1926-1930 handwritten; 1930—, typed. Average 325 pages. 16 x 11.5 x 3. Probate office.

Dependents and Delinquents

201. JUVENILE COURT WARDS [Card Record of Delinquents and Dependents]
1938—. 2 loose-leaf folders.
Record of delinquent and dependent wards of the juvenile court, showing name, residence, and post office address of delinquent or dependent, card number, birth date, names and addresses of parents, date made ward of court, date committed to department of welfare, and date commitment terminated. Names of delinquents are marked with a red star; names of crippled children marked with a red dot, and names of dependents are not marked. Arranged alphabetically by the names of wards. No index. Typed. 60 cards in loose-lease folder, 12 x 9 x .25. Probate office.

Aid to Dependent Children

202. [APPLICATIONS FOR AID TO DEPENDENT CHILDREN]
1936—. 1 file drawer.
Applications for aid to dependent children, showing date of application, name of applicant and relation to child, name of child, date and place of birth, race, color, religion, nationality, marital status of parents, financial condition of applicant and child, and sworn statement of applicant. Arranged chronologically by dates of applications. No index. Handwritten on printed forms. 6 x 10 x 24. Probate judge's office.

203. [CASE HISTORIES]
1936—. 1 file drawer.

Record of grants and case histories of dependent children, showing name of child, name and address of person having custody of child, names and other information relative to parents, case number, date case opened, date case terminated, cause of termination, amount of grant, financial conditions of custodian, parent, and child, and remarks. Arranged alphabetically by names of children. No index. Handwritten on printed forms. 6 x 10 x 24. Probate judge's office.

204. [VERIFICATIONS]
1936—. 1 file drawer.

Verifications of birth, death, divorce, and marriage; birth verifications, showing name of child, date and place of birth, date and number of birth certificates, names of parents and remarks; divorce verifications, showing names of parties to suit, grounds, amount of alimony granted (if any), date granted, and remarks; marriage verifications, showing names of husband and wife, date and place of marriage, marriage license number, date of issue, and remarks; death verifications, showing name of decedent, date and place of death, death certificate number, names of persons to whom custody of child was given, date of custody, and remarks. All papers to each case filed in folders. Arranged alphabetically by names of families. No index. Handwritten on printed forms. 6 x 10 x 24. Probate judge's office.

Jury commissioners were first authorized for Hamilton and Cuyahoga Counties in 1881.[1] In 1890 provision was made for the appointment of jury commissioners in counties having a city of the first class or of the first grade second class.[2]

In 1891 the judges of the court of common pleas in counties having a city with a population and not less than 33,000 nor more than 50,000 were authorized to appoint four residents of the county to serve as a jury commission for a term of one year. The limitations of this act excluded Geauga County. It was the duty of this commission to determine the qualifications and fitness of persons to be selected as jurors.[3] Three years later, in 1894, the provisions of the act were extended to all other counties in the state except Cuyahoga, Franklin, Hamilton, Lucas, Montgomery, and Mahoning, each of which had a special act governing the selection of juries.[4] In 1902 the statute was amended to include all counties.[5] In 1913 the number of jury commissioners in each county was reduced to two.[6]

The jury code, which became effective August 2 1931, provided for a jury commission of the same number and same qualifications previously specified, to hold office at the pleasure of the court, and to meet and select prospective jurors, both grand and petit, for the ensuing year from a list provided by the board of elections.[7] At the beginning of each jury year the commissioners are required to make up a new and complete jury list, known as the annual jury list, arranged alphabetically by precincts, districts, and townships, recording the name, occupation, business address, and residence of each prospective juror, and to prepare an index to this list. A duplicate list is certified by the commissioners and filed in the office of the clerk of court of common pleas.[8]

The jury commissioners select prospective jurors for civil and criminal cases as well as for the grand jury. It selects jurors for the probate court, juvenile court, and other minor courts.

_____

1. *Laws of Ohio*, LXXVIII, 95.
2. *Ibid.*, LXXXVII, 327.
3. *Ibid.*, LXXXVIII, 200.
4. *Ibid.*, XCI, 176.
5. *Ibid.*, XCVI, 3.
6. *Ibid.*, CIII, 513; CVI, 106.
7. *Ibid.*, CXIV, 193-213.
8. *Ibid.*, CXIV, 205.

Geauga County appointed its first jury commission August 25, 1931[9] under the legislative act on May 2, 1931.[10] There are, as elsewhere, two commissioners. Each is paid $96 annually and serves during the pleasure of the court.[11] The annual jury list of 35 names is made up according to the uniform method prescribed in the jury code of 1931, and each person is investigated by the jury commissioners regarding his fitness to serve, before he is summoned.[12]

---

9. Common Pleas Journal, XXXIX, 386, entry 129.
10. *Laws of Ohio,* CXIV, 213.
11. Common Pleas Journal, XXXIX, 386, entry 129.
12. *Laws of Ohio,* CXIV, 193.

205. RECORD OF PROCEEDINGS AND EXEMPTIONS
1932—. 1 vol. (1).

Minutes of the jury commission, showing date of meeting, and names of persons drawn for jury service for each term of court; certificate of exemption from jury duty, showing name and address of party exempted and reason for exemption. Arranged chronologically by dates of meetings. Exemptions indexed alphabetically by names of jurors; minutes, no index. Exemptions typed on printed forms; minutes typed. 450 pages. 18 x 12.5 x 2.5. Witness room 2.

206. RECORD OF JURORS SERVED, EXCUSED, FINED, OR DISCHARGED
1932—. 1 vol. (1). Initiated in 1932.

Index record of persons drawn for jury service, showing name of juror, residence, number of days served, particular date served, date and reason excused or discharged, date, reason, and amount fined, date and number of miles traveled, and amount paid for attendance. Arranged alphabetically by names of jurors and chronologically thereunder by dates of service or other dispositions. No index. Handwritten on printed forms. 230 pages. 17 x 15 x 1.25. Witness room 2.

207. ANNUAL JURY LIST

1932—. 1 file drawer.

List of persons chosen for jury service, showing assigned number, name and residence of juror, total number of jurors, date list filed in common pleas court, and signatures of jury commissioners. No obvious arrangement. No index. Typed on printed forms. 11.25 x 18 x 26. Witness room 2.

GRAND JURY

The grand jury, sometimes called the palladium of English liberty, has as its function the preliminary examination of persons charged with a capital or other infamous crime. The right, guaranteed by the federal constitution, to an examination by a grand jury, is recognized in the provisions of the Ohio Constitution of 1802 and 1851 and in the amendments of 1912.[1]

Under the present system, which does not differ in detail from that inaugurated in the early days of the state's history, the grand jury is composed of 15 members, resident electors of the county having "the qualifications of jurors."[2] It is the duty of the grand jury "to inquire of and present all offenses committed in the county in and for which it was impaneled and sworn."[3] The proceedings of the grand jury are secret and each jury is required to take an oath to preserve such secrecy. Moreover, no grand juror may be required to reveal the way he or other grand jurors voted.[4]

The grand jurors are aided in their investigations by the county prosecuting attorney, who, since 1869, has been authorized by statute to present evidence before this body and compel the attendance of witnesses against whom he may institute contempt proceedings if they refuse to testify. The prosecuting attorney must leave the room before the jurors begin the expression of their views or before a poll is taken. The courts have decreed, however, that the mere presence of the prosecuting attorney in the room during the deliberations is "not sufficient to sustain a plea in abatement."[5]

---

1. *Ohio Const. 1802,* Art. VIII, sec. II; *Ohio Const. 1851,* Art. I, sec. 10.
2. G. C. sec. 13436-2.
3. G. C. sec. 13436-5.
4. G. C. sec. 13436-16.
5. *See State of Ohio* v. *William Stichtenoth,* 8 N. P., 297-339.

Since 1902 the official court stenographer of the county may take shorthand notes of the testimony and furnish a transcript to the prosecuting attorney at his request. This reporter, like the prosecuting attorney and his assistants, is required to retire from the jury room before the grand jury begins its deliberations.[6]

At least 12 of the 15 jurors must concur in finding and indictment. Indictments found by the grand jury are presented by the foreman to the court and are filed with the clerk of courts.[8] No grand juror or officer of the court is permitted to disclose that a person has been indicted before such an indictment is filed and the case docketed.[9] Any incarcerated person charged with an indictable offense who has not been indicted during the term of court at which he is held to answer is discharged.[10]

Since 1869 it has been the duty of the grand jury to visit the county jail once at each term of court at which they may be in attendance, examine its state and condition and inquire into the discipline and treatment of prisoners, and return a written report to the court.[11]

The majority of contemporary opinion holds that the grand jury, although still defended as a safeguard against oppressive prosecution, is of little usefulness in the administration of modern criminal justice. It is argued that the grand jury not only delays the prosecution of criminal offenses but also makes it impossible to place responsibility for neglect of duty, and is, in many instances a rubber stamp for the opinions of the county prosecuting attorney.

The grand jury meets in Geauga County three times annually or at each term of court, although special sessions may be called at the request of the county prosecutor. The sessions are short, the indictments few, sessions in 1940 yielding but nine indictments.[12]

---

6. G. C. sec. 13436-8.
7. G. C. sec. 13436-17.
8. G. C. sec. 13436-21.
9. G. C. sec. 13436-15.
10. G. C. sec. 13436-23.
11. G. C. sec. 13436-20.
12. Criminal Appearance Docket, 1940, entry 124.

Of these only one was for more serious offenses. Grand jurors received $3 a day and mileage once a week.

The grand jury keeps no separate records. For grand jury records kept by the clerk of courts, see entries 81 and 82; for jury fees see entry 101; for reports on indictments and inspections of jails see entry 129.

PETIT JURY

The petit jury, like the grand jury, had its origin in England during the reign of Henry II.[1] The right of trial by jury, guaranteed by the federal constitution, was included in each of the Ohio constitutions. At any trial, and any court, for the violation of a statute of the state of Ohio, or any ordinance of any municipality, except in cases where the penalty involved does not exceed a fine of $50, the accused is entitled to a trial by jury.[2]

Except in the method of selecting prospective jurors, the petit jury has remained unchanged for over 134 years. The number of jurors drawn for each term of court is fixed by an order of court.[3] A venire is issued to the county sheriff for persons whose names are so drawn to appear on the day fixed for the trial.[4] From the persons so summoned a jury of 12 is impaneled. The county prosecuting attorney and the defense counsel may, in capital cases, peremptory challenge six of the jurors. In other cases, four peremptory challenges are allowed.[5] Other challenges, alternately made, may be made for reasons prescribed by statute.[6]

When the case is submitted, the jury may decide the question before it in court, or retire to deliberate. Upon retiring, the jury members must be kept together at a convenient place by an officer of the court until they agree upon a verdict or are discharged by the court. The court may permit them to separate at night.[7]

---

1. Adams, *op. cit.,* 116.
2. G. C. sec. 13443.
3. G. C. sec. 11419-21.
4. G. C. sec. 11419-27.
5. G. C. secs. 13443-4, 13443-6.
6. G. C. sec. 13443-8.
7. G. C. sec. 11420-6.

If the jurors disagree as to testimony, or desire to be further instructed on the law in the case, they may request the officer in charge to conduct them to the court for additional information.[8] In civil actions a jury renders a written verdict upon the concurrence of three-fourths or more of its members. This verdict is signed by each juror concurring therein.[9]

Under the criminal code adopted in 1929 the accused may waive his right to a jury trial in favor of a trial by a judge. This procedure, although criticized by some, is considered by others to be a logical step in the administration of criminal justice in a modern state. In Geauga, as in most counties, petit juries are being wavered in favor of trial by judge. From January 1939, to January 1941, there were only 14 jury trials.[10]

The petit jury keeps no separate records. For jury records kept by clerk of courts, see entries 81 and 82 and for jury fees, see entry 101.

---

8. G. C. sec. 11420-6.
9. G. C. sec. 11420-9.
10. Appearance and Execution Docket, 1939-1941, entry 118.

The office of prosecuting attorney, unlike those of the sheriff and the coroner, is one of the relatively newer agencies in the administration of criminal justice. Established in America by the English during the colonial period, it offers a striking difference in the development of American criminal procedure as contrasted with English procedure where criminal prosecutions were usually instituted by private persons. As developed in recent years, the office of the prosecuting attorney has become one of the state's most important agencies and its defense against modern crime.

The acts of the Northwest Territory place the responsibility for criminal prosecution upon the attorney general, who, in turn, appointed and commissioned persons to prosecute cases in their respective counties.[1]

While the acts of the Northwest Territory outlined the local institutions for the nearest states, the constitution of Ohio contained no provisions for a prosecutor, leaving the creation of the office to the discretion of the legislature. In 1803, during the first session of the legislature, an act was passed authorizing the supreme court to appoint in each county an attorney to prosecute cases on behalf of the state.[2] Two years later the appointing power was vested in the court of common pleas.[3] The office remain an appointive one until 1933 when the electorate of the county was directed to choose a prosecuting attorney in each county for a two-year term.[4] The act of 1852 left the office elective and the term unchanged, but in 1881 the term of office was set at three years, and in 1906 it was reduced to two years, and in 1936 increased to four years.[5]

Under the present system the prosecuting attorney is elected for a four-year term.[6] He is required to give bond of not less than one thousand dollars conditioned for the faithful performance of the duties of his office. If the office becomes vacant the court of common pleas is authorized to appoint a successor.[7]

---

1. Chase, *op. cit.*, I, 287, 348.
2. *Laws of Ohio*, I, 50.
3. *Ibid.*, III, 47.
4. *Ibid.*, XXXI, 13-14; Chase, *op. cit.*, III, 1935.
5. *Laws of Ohio*, LXXVIII, 260; XCVIII, 271-272; CXVI, pt. ii, 184.
6. G. C. sec. 2909.
7. G. C. secs. 2911, 2912.

The county prosecuting attorney is authorized to appoint clerks, assistants, and stenographers and to fix their salaries subject to the approval of the county commissioners. Since 1911 he has been authorized to appoint a secret service agent or officer whose duty it is to aid him in the collection of evidence to be used in the trial of criminal cases and in matters of a criminal nature. The compensation of such an officer is determined by the court of common pleas.[8]

Most important among the duties of the prosecuting attorney are those connected with criminal prosecutions. Differing little from those of the early days of the office, these duties include the prosecution on behalf of the state of all complaints, suits, and controversies in which the state is a party, and such other suits, matters, and controversies as he is directed by law to prosecute within or without his county, in the probate court, court of common pleas, and court of appeals. In conjunction with the attorney general, he prosecutes cases in the supreme court which originated in his county.[9]

In felony cases, when a complaint is made to the prosecuting attorney, he is required to examine the evidence and determine if it is sufficient for prosecution. If he decides in the affirmative, he prepares the evidence for presentation to the grand jury.[10] If this body returns an indictment the prosecutor prepares to present the evidence in trial court. The court of common pleas may appoint an attorney to assist the prosecuting attorney in criminal cases.[11] In the case of conviction, the prosecuting attorney causes execution to be issued for the fines or costs and pays into the county treasury all moneys so received.[12] Without reference to the grand jury, the county prosecuting attorney may initiate prosecutions in misdemeanor cases in the court of common pleas by information.[13] After prosecution is inaugurated, he may eliminate the case without trial by means of the *nolle prosequi*. Although he is prohibited from enlisting the *nolle prosequi* without leave of the court on good cause shown, his requests are usually granted.[14] After prosecution has begun, it remains with the prosecuting attorney whether the case shall be pressed and steps taken that will lead to conviction.

---

8. G. C. secs. 2914, 2915-1.
9. G. C. sec. 2916.
10. *See* p. 117.
11. G. C. sec. 2918.
12. G. C. sec. 2916.
13. G. C. sec. 13437-34.
14. G. C. sec. 13437-32.

Besides prosecution in criminal cases, the prosecuting attorney also acts in civil matters. He may bring suit in the name of the state when he is convinced that the public money is being misapplied or is being illegally withheld or withdrawn from the county treasury. Moreover, he may bring suit against persons violating the obligations of contracts of which the county is a party, or when county property is being used or occupied illegally.[15]

In addition to these, other duties have been prescribed by statute. On the request of the judge having jurisdiction over juvenile cases, he must prosecute individuals for committing crimes against children.[16] Furthermore, when directed by the court of common pleas, he must prosecute persons for keeping a house of prostitution.[17] At the instance of the secretary of state, he must prosecute any officer who refuses to furnish gratuitously statistical information for the use of that office.[18]

The prosecuting attorney has also served in an advisory capacity since 1906.[19] He acts as an advisor to all county boards and officials and to township officers who may require his opinion in writing on matters connected with their official duties.[20] In addition to this, he prepares official bonds for all county officers.[21]

The prosecuting attorney is required to make an annual report to the county commissioners stating the number of criminal prosecutions completed, the name or names of the party or parties to each, and the amount collected in fines and costs, and the amount forfeited.[22] Moreover on the demand of the attorney general he must make an annual report on forms provided by the state on all criminal actions prosecuted by indictments in his county.[23]

---

15. G. C. sec. 2921.
16. G. C. sec. 1639-42.
17. G. C. secs. 6212-5, 6212-7.
18. G. C. sec. 174.
19. *Laws of Ohio*, XCVIII, 160-131.
20. *Ibid.*, LXXVIII, 120; G. C. sec. 2917.
21. G. C. sec. 2920.
22. *Laws of Ohio*, LXXVIII, 120; G. C. sec. 2926.
23. G. C. sec. 2925; *Laws of Ohio*, XC, 225.

For the period between January 9, 1939 and December 28, 1940, the Geauga County prosecutor tried 39 offenders, 30 of whom were convicted. During the same period three cases were suspended, six entries of *nolle prosequi* were made, and 32 defendants pleaded guilty.[24] This record indicates a fairly busy criminal department. The civil department was concerned mostly with foreclosure actions for taxes, which there were six cases in 1940.[25] The prosecutor requires only one assistant and keeps his work well up to date, although his services as legal advisor are in considerable demand. His salary is $91.66 monthly[26] and his bond is set at $1000.[27]

The prosecuting attorney keeps no separate records. For copies of reports to commissioners see entry 300.

---

24. Criminal Appearance Docket [1936-1941], entry 124.
25. Appearance and Execution Docket, 1940, entry 118.
26. Commissioners Journal, XI, [1936-1941], 423-428.
27. Treasurer's Record of Bonds of Officials, 1940, entry 352.

The office of coroner, next to that of sheriff the oldest county office in America, had its inception in England during the latter part of the 12th century when the coroner kept a record of the activities in the county, especially regarding the administration of criminal justice. At the end of the first 13th century it was his duty to make inquests whenever there was a sudden death in the shire, and the results were recorded in the coroner's rolls and presented to the justice *eyre*.[1]

This office, transplanted to America during the colonial period, was continued by the states, and was adopted by the territory of which the state of Ohio was then a part. An ordinance of the Northwest Territory published in 1788 authorized the governor to appoint a coroner in each county within the territory. This act, together with a supplementary act of 1795 adopted from the Massachusetts Code, fixed the power and duties of the coroner. He was empowered to do any act which, by previous legislation had been delegated to the sheriff, and was given the ancient duty of English coroners in holding preliminary investigations over the bodies of all persons found within his county, who were believed to have died by violence or casualty.[2]

The Ohio constitution of 1802 continued the historic office, making it elective for a two-year term.[3] A statute of 1805 define the duties and authority of the coroner which, in the main, were comparable with those prescribed in the territorial code, except that he was denied the privilege of concurrent jurisdiction with the sheriff.[4] The coroner was required to post bond with the county commissioners, which was to be recorded in the record of their proceedings. The act further provided that the coroner should receive his remuneration from fees, and that if the office of sheriff were to become vacant the corner was to execute temporarily the duties of the sheriff.[5] The latter remain active until its abrogation in 1887.[6]

---

1. Pollock and Maitland, *op. cit.,* I, 519, 571; II, 641.
2. Pease, *op. cit.,* 24-25, 272-275.
3. *Ohio Const. 1802,* Art. VI, sec. 1.
4. *Laws of Ohio,* III, 156-161.
5. *Ibid.,* III, 158-161.
6. *Ibid.,* LXXXIV, 208-21.

The constitution of 1851 and the constitutional amendment of 1912 left the duties of the coroner unchanged and it was not until recent years, when he became an aid in the scientific detection of crime, that laws have been passed which materially effect his office. By the legislative act of 1921 the coroner was made official custodian of the morgue in counties where a morgue is maintained. The same act provided that only licensed physicians were eligible to the office in counties having a population of 100,000 or more,[7] and in 1937 such restriction was extended to all counties.[8]

The coroner is required to draw up and subscribe his findings of facts in inquests and autopsies and to report them to the clerk of courts. This record contains a detailed description of the body over which the inquest has been held and a statement of the coroner's findings as to the cause of death.[9] He is required also to return to the probate court an inventory of articles of property found on or about the body and to preserve such property until the proper distribution may be made[10] All records are open to public inspection.[11] In 1936 the tenure of the office of the coroner was extended from two to four years.[12]

He is required to get bond in a sum of not less than $5000 or more than $50,000 to be determined by the county commissioners, the bond and oath of office are filed with the county auditor.[13] The legal maximum compensation in counties of less than 400,000 population is $5,000.[14] The coroner may appoint necessary assistants, and if the population of the county warrants, he may appoint a stenographer-secretary.[15]

---

7. *Laws of Ohio*, CIX, 543-544.
8. *Ibid.*, CXVII, 43.
9. G. C. secs. 2856, 2857.
10. G. C. sec. 2859-
11. G. C. sec. 2856-2.
12. G. C. secs. 2823.
13. G. C. secs. 2823, 2824.
14. G. C. sec. 2866-1.
15. *Laws of Ohio*, CIX. 543.

In Geauga County, the absence of any large agglomeration of urban population tends to reduce the work of the coroner to a minimum. There were seven cases requiring a coroner's investigation in 1939, and five in 1940, but none of these resulted in criminal prosecutions.[16] The salary of the coroner is made up from an appropriation of $150[17] plus a certain amount taken from fees[18] these amounts being authorized by the commissioners.

---

16. Coroner's Inquests [1939-1940], entry 96.
17. Commissioners Journal, General, XI [1936-1941], 427.
18. G. C. sec. 2866-1.

208. CORONER'S RECORD OF INVESTIGATION
1930—. 1 vol. (1).

Coroner's reports of investigations and inquests, showing date of report, dates of investigation and inquest, name and address of decedent, date and cause of death, names of witnesses and jurors, and decision of coroner's jury at inquest; also memorandum of cost bill filed with commissioners, showing date of bill, expense for traveling, viewing of body, and total cost of inquest. Arranged chronologically by dates reported. No index. Typed. 235 loose-leaf pages. 14 x 9 x 1.25. Sheriff's office, 221 Main Street, Chardon, Ohio.

For records of coroner's inquests, see entry 96.

The office of sheriff antedates the Norman Conquest. This official was enjoying great power and importance centuries ago, and was probably brought into the English system after a model which existed in the Roman law. The name comes from the Saxon "shire-reeve" softened to "shireve" "shyrife," and finally to "sheriff." In ancient times he received his commission directly from the king and specifically represented the sovereign. Originally, the sheriff in England was a judicial as well as a ministerial officer. He once held court in the shire and exercised no inconsiderable jurisdiction. By the time of Lord Coke (1560-1634), the functions of the English sheriff had become standardized under three general heads: (1) to serve process by which a suit was begun: (2) to execute the decrees of the court: (3) to act as conservator of peace within the county.[1]

The office appeared in America in modified form among the earliest colonial institutions, being created in Virginia in 1634, and in Massachusetts in 1654. This ancient office was continued by the states created after independence.[2] The office assumed a new significance in the latter part of the 18th century when a flood of colonists swept across the ineffective Allegheny barrier to establish homes in the Northwest Territory organized by Congress in 1787. In the remote West the pioneers, far removed from the orderly legal processes and courts of the East, were subjected to the machinations of the lawless element prevalent in every new community.

In 1792 the governor and judges of the territory adopted an act providing for the appointment by the governor of a sheriff in each county and defining his duties.[3] This pioneer law clearly established three of the four major duties of the sheriff as they remain today namely: attendance upon the court; execution of writs, warrants, and the like; and policing and the arrest of criminals.

---

1. Adams, *op. cit.,* 17-19; William A. Morris, "The Office of Sheriff in the Anglo-Saxon Period," *English Historical Review,* XXI (1916), 29-40; Raymond Moley, "The Sheriff and the Coroner" (New York, 1926. *The Missouri Crime Survey,* pt. ii), 59, 60.
2. For a comparative study of the sheriff in England and the Chesapeake colonies, see Cyrus Harreld Karraker, *The Seventeenth-Century Sheriff . . .*(Chapel Hill, 1930).
3. Pease, *op. cit.,* 8.

When Ohio entered the Union as a state in 1803, the office of sheriff was continued by constitutional provision, and was made elective for a two-year term.[4] Since that time relatively few changes have been made in the structural organization of the office. When a new county was erected, the associate judges appointed a day on which the qualified voters met at the temporary seat of justice and elected a sheriff who served until the next general election.[5] Although the constitution of 1851 did not specifically provide for this office, it did declare that no person should be eligible to the office for more than four in any period of six years.[6] No county officer was to have a longer term than three years[7] but the matter of removal from office was left to legislative action.[8] The limitation upon the consecutive terms which a sheriff might serve remained in force until 1933, when it was repealed by an amendment authorizing any county to adopt a charter form of government. The term of office remained at two years until 1936 when it was extended to four years.[9] The sheriff received his remuneration from fees until 1875. From 1875 to 1906 he received a definite salary based upon the population of the county according to the last federal census preceding his election, plus a percentage of the fees collected.[10] Since 1906 the compensation has been derived entirely from a salary determined on a population basis.[11] In 1831, due to the increasing complexity of the duties of the office, the sheriff was authorized to appoint, with the consent of the court of common pleas, one or more deputies. These men, like their superior, were required to give bond for the faithful performance of the duties of their office, and the sheriff was made responsible for their neglect of duty or misconduct in office.[12]

---

4. *Ohio Const. 1802.*, Art. VI, sec. 1.
5. A. E. Gwynne, *A Practical Treatise on the Law of Sheriff and Coroner with Forms and References to the Statutes of Ohio, Indiana, and Kentucky.* (Cincinnati, 1849), 3.
6. *Ohio Const. 1851.* Art. X, sec. 3.
7. *Ibid.,* Art. X, sec. 2
8. *Ibid.,* Art. X, sec. 6.
9. *Laws of Ohio,* pt. ii, 184.
10. *Ibid.,* III, 49-51; XXXIII, 85; LXXII, 126.
11. *Ibid.,* XCVIII, 95.
12. *Ibid.,* XXIX, 410.

The present organization of the office may be briefly summarized: the sheriff is elected for a four-year term,[13] can hold no other elected office at the same time, and may not practice law while in office.[14] He is required to give bond, the cost of which is paid by the county commissioners[15] who are also required to provide an office for the sheriff at the county seat, equipment, supplies, and other essentials of the office.[16] The commissioners also appropriate funds for the expenses incurred by the sheriff in carrying out the various duties of his office.[17] The sheriff may appoint a deputy or deputies, but all appointees must be endorsed by the local judge of the common pleas court, be electors of the county, and no deputy may be justice of piece or mayor.[18] Deputies are also forbidden to practice law while in office.[19] The sheriff fixes the salaries of the deputies, subject to the budget limitations of the county commissioners,[20] and shares with his deputies certain civil and criminal liabilities.[21] The sheriff's salary, based on a graded scale according to population is set at a maximum of $6000 a year.[22] The office may be vacated by failure to give proper bond, nonacceptance, or death.[23] Vacancies in the office are filled by the county commissioners.[24]

The sheriff may be removed for various financial defalcations,[25] for willfully refusing or neglecting his duty in criminal cases,[26] for malfeasance in office,[27] or for permitting the lynching of a person in his custody.[28]

---

13. G. C. sec. 2823.
14. G. C. secs. 11, 1706, 2565, 2783, 2910.
15. G. C. sec. 2824.
16. G. C. sec. 2832.
17. G. C. sec. 2997.
18. G. C. secs. 1706, 2830.
19. G. C. sec. 1706.
20. G. C. sec. 2981.
21. Willis A. Estrich, ed., *Ohio Jurisprudence* (Rochester, 1934), XXXVI, 660-672, 699-701.
22. G. C. secs. 2994, 2996, 2997; Estrich, XXXVI, 704-705.
23. G. C. secs. 2827, 12196.
24. G. C. sec. 2828.
25. G. C. secs. 3036, 3049.
26. G. C. secs. 12850, 12851.
27. *Ohio Const. 1851* (Amendment, 1912), Art. II, sec. 38.
28. *Laws of Ohio*, CI, 109.

In the latter case the governor conducts the hearing and may remove the sheriff. If for some reason the sheriff is unable to serve a court order the judge of the common pleas court is authorized to make a temporary appointment for the post.[29] The retiring sheriff is required to deliver to his successor all moneys, papers, books, and the like, as well as the custody of all the prisoners.[30]

Aside from his power to appoint deputies, the sheriff has other special powers which are largely the product of historical development. From earliest years the sheriff has been empowered to call to his aid such persons as he deemed necessary to perform his lawful duty and apprehension of criminals.[31] Thus, the *posse comitatus* was at his disposal as it is today.[32]

The specific duties of the sheriff were and are prescribed by statute and may be classified under four main divisions: (1) attendance upon the courts; (2) execution of summonses, warrants, processes, and other *writs*; (3) control and responsibility in the care of the jail and courthouse; (4) policing and the arrest of criminals.

The territorial law of 1792 required the sheriff to attend upon the court of common pleas and the court of appeals during their sessions,[33] and this requirement has been carried over into the laws of Ohio,[34] the present duties of the sheriff in this respect being survivals from the provisions of this act. He is required to attend the county court of common pleas,[35] the appellate court,[36] and the probate court if required by the judge of that division.[37] The sheriff may adjourn the court of common pleas from day to day upon failure of the judge to appear at regularly scheduled sessions.[38]

The duty of the sheriff to execute all warrants, *writs*, and processes directed to him by the proper and lawful authority has also been operative since the territorial period.[39]

---

29. G. C. sec. 2828.
30. G. C. secs. 2842, 2843.
31. *Laws of Ohio*, III, 156-158; XXIX, 112, 113.
32. G. C. sec. 2833.
33. Pease, *op. cit.*, 8.
34. *Laws of Ohio*, III, 156-158; XXIX, 112; LXXXII, 26.
35. G. C. sec. 2833.
36. G. C. secs. 1530, 2833.
37. G. C. sec. 2833.
38. G. C. sec. 2855.
39. Pease, *op. cit.*, 8; *Laws of Ohio*, III, 156-158; XXIX, 112; LXXXII, 26.

At present he executes every summons, order, or other process, and makes return there of as required by law.[40] He executes processes from the probate, juvenile, common pleas, and appellate courts. Although the jury commission has supplanted the clerk of courts in the matter of selecting names of prospective jurors from the jury wheel, the sheriff's duties in this respect remain much as they were in the earlier years of his office. He also executes warrants issued by the governor of the state,[41] and serves *writs* and subpoenas issued by various state officers and boards.[42] In other words, the sheriff serves all the papers which concern the county as a unit of government and some for the state as well.

As early as 1805 the sheriff was made official custodian of the county jail.[43] Although the early statutes directed the county commissioners to provide dungeons for the incarceration of prisoners, the act of 1847 directed the sheriff to exercise reasonable care for the preservation of life, health, and welfare of those committed to his care. He was and is authorized to transport prisoners to other counties for safekeeping.[44] Under the direction and control of the county commissioners the sheriff is also given charge of the courthouse.[45]

The sheriff has had extensive and important police powers since 1792 when the territorial act authorized him to keep and preserve the peace, and suppress affrays, routs, riots, unlawful assemblies, and insurrections; to apprehend, and confine in jail all felons and traitors; and to return persons who, having committed a crime in his county, had taken refuge in another.[46] During the legislative session of 1805 the general assembly passed an act defining the duties of the sheriff which were in all respects similar to the provisions inherited from the territorial code.[47] In the same year the sheriff was designated as the county's executioner, and was bound to carry out sentences of death by hanging, when imposed by the courts, upon those convicted of murder.[48]

---

40. G. C. sec. 2834.
41. G. C. sec. 118.
42. G. C. secs. 285, 346, 2709, *et al.*
43. *Laws of Ohio*, III, 157.
44. *Ibid.*, III, 157; XXIX, 112, 113; XCIII, 131. For general provisions as to jail duties *see* G. C. secs. 3157-3176, *passim.*
45. G. C. secs. 2833.
46. Pease, *op. cit.,* 8.
47. *Laws of Ohio*, III, 156-158.
48. Chase, *opp. cit.,* I, 442.

Public executions, the general rule during the earlier years, were abolished in 1844.[49] In 1886 the sheriff's duties in this respect were delegated to the warden of the Ohio Penitentiary.[50]

An act of 1831, repealing the act of 1805 redefined the duties of the sheriff as a conservator of the peace in his county,[51] and his present duties in this respect are survivals from the provisions of this act.[52] Although the sheriff is still regarded as a chief peace officer in the county, many of his earlier duties in this respect have been abolished by the development of other agencies of law enforcement, notably the state highway patrol. On the other hand, the powers of the sheriff to suppress affrays, riots, and unlawful assemblies became especially important in times of strikes or threatened riots. On a properly issued warrant he may arrest any person charged with the probability of doing injury to another person or the property of another.[53] Moreover, since 1921 the sheriff has forwarded to the bureau of criminal identification fingerprints of all persons arrested for a felony,[54] and since 1913 has been authorized to arrest any person violating his parole.[55]

The present police powers of the sheriff are very comprehensive. His jurisdiction is coextensive with the county, including all municipalities and townships, and he is the chief law-enforcement officer of the county. In municipalities the sheriff and mayor stand on an equality as law enforcement officers so far as state laws are concerned, and neither is permitted to cast the burden of action upon the other.[56]

The sheriff has possessed and still possesses many powers and duties which are miscellaneous in nature. As in England, the sheriff, during the earlier years of his office, was required to notify the electors of his county of the time and place of holding elections. He was enjoined to furnish ballot boxes at the expense of the county, hold special elections when so directed by the governor, and deliver the poll books to the secretary of state.[57]

---

49. *Laws of Ohio*, XLII, 71.
50. *Ibid.*, LXXXIII, 145.
51. *Ibid.*, XXIX, 112, 113.
52. LXXXIII, 26.
53. G. C. sec. 13428-1.
54. *Laws of Ohio*, CIX, 584; CX, 5.
55. *Ibid.*, CII, 404.
56. Estrich, *op. cit.*, XXXVI, 645. For the most important police powers *see* G. C. secs. 2833, 3345, 4112, 12811.
57. *Laws of Ohio*, II, 88-90; III, 331, 332.

Since 1891 these duties have been taken over by the board of elections.[58] The sheriff also has many heterogenous powers and duties regarding elections,[59] executive orders of the secretary of agriculture,[60] fish and game laws,[61] probation officers,[62] military census,[63] traffic rules and regulations,[64] funds and deposits in court,[65] shanty boats,[66] And executive orders of the governor.[67]

The multiplicate duties of the sheriff have made it necessary to keep many records of the business of the office. The sheriff has been required to keep a foreign execution docket since 1838,[68] a cashbook since 1842,[69] and a jail register since 1843.[70] These records for Geauga County are extant from 1835 to date; 1869-1887 and 1913 to date; and 1879 to date; respectfully.[71] Indexes, direct and reverse, to the foreign execution docket were prescribed by the legislature in 1925.[72] Since 1843 he has been required annually to transmit the jail register, in certified copies, to the clerk of courts, county auditor, and secretary of state.[73] Since 1850 he has been required, on the first Monday of September in each year, to submit to the county commissioners a certified statement of all fines and costs collected during the year, and the amount of fees collected and paid to the clerk of court of common pleas.[74]

---

58. *See* p. 204.
59. G. C. secs. 4785-124, 4829.
60. G. C. sec, 1110.
61. G. C. secs.1434, 1441, 1444, 1451.
62. G. C. sec. 1639-19.
63. G. C. sec. 5188-5.
64. G. C. sec. 7251-1.
65. G. C. sec. 11900.
66. G. C. sec. 13403-1.
67. G. C. sec. 118.
68. *Laws of Ohio,* XXXVI, 18; LVII, 6; LXXXIV, 208, 209.
69. *Ibid.,* XL, 25; LXV, 115; LXXXIV, 208; LXXXVI, 239.
70. *Ibid.,* XLI, 74.
71. Foreign Execution Docket, *see* entry 209; Sheriff's Cash Book, *see* entry 215; Jail Register, *see* entry 213.
72. *Laws of Ohio,* CXI, 31.
73. *Ibid.,* LXI, 74.
74. G. C. sec. 2844; *Laws of Ohio,* XLVIII, 66.

Thus the modern sheriff keeps the following records: (1) a cashbook which is a record of all moneys handled; (2) a foreign summons docket which is a record of all summonses from counties other than his own; (3) a foreign execution docket which is a record of executions from counties other than his own; (4) a service record which includes all probate and divorce papers served; (5) an execution register which records all executions handled: (6) an accrued fee record which lists fees received; (7) a commission register which records the commissions of all special deputies; (8) a jail register which records all prisoners brought in, the charge, how long detained, and when released.[75] By statute the sheriff is also required to make an annual financial report to the county commissioners.[76]

The sheriff of Geauga County is bonded for $5000, and receives an annual salary of $1195.[77] He is assisted by a staff of seven and is provided with four cars equipped with radio receiving sets.

The present jail built in 1896,[78] contains six cells, and has housed an annual average of 270 persons during the past five years.[79] Fees received by the sheriff's office in 1939 amounted to $2620.27.[80]

All records are located in the sheriff's office, 221 Main Street, Chardon, Ohio, unless otherwise specified.

---

75. G. C. secs. 2837, 2979, 3045, 3046.
76. G. C. sec. 2844.
77. Record of Official Bonds, 1940, *see* entry 297; Commissioners' Journal, General, XI, [1936-1941] 423-428, *see* entry 1.
78. *The Geauga Democrat*, January 2/7, 1869.
79. Jail register, 1935-1940, *see* entry 213.
80. Record of sheriff's Accrued Fees, 1929, *see* entry 216.

Court Orders

209. FOREIGN EXECUTION DOCKET

1835—. 7 vols. (1-7). Title varies: Sheriff's Docket, 1835-1877, 1 vol.; Foreign Writ Docket, 1877-1915, 2 vols.

Docket of executions received from foreign counties on property located in Geauga County to satisfy judgments rendered, showing name of county, court of origin, names of parties in case, case number, date *writ* received, date of sheriff's returns, name of attorney, amount of judgment, plaintiff's original cost, defendant's original cost, increase in cost other than *writ*, increase in cost on *writ*, total judgment, interest and costs, amount paid on execution, and copy of return endorsed on *writ*;

sheriff's procedure in carrying out *writ*, showing properties sold, date of sale, and amount made on sale. Also contains; Record of Sheriff's Sales, 1835-1878, 1899—, entry 211. Arranged chronologically by dates *writs* received. Indexed alphabetically by names of plaintiffs and defendants. 1835-1923, handwritten on printed forms; 1924—, typed on printed forms. 1 volume 600 pages. 14.25 x 9.25 x 3; 6 volumes average 275 pages. 16 x 11.5 x 2.

210. FOREIGN SUMMONS DOCKET
1896—. 6 vols. (4-9).

Docket of foreign *writs* received by sheriff and disposition of *writ*, showing name of county, court of origin, names of parties in case, case number, names of attorneys, date of *writ*, date received, date served, date returned, fund received from *writ*, sheriff's fees, copy of return endorsed on *writ*, and disposition of *writ* endorsed by sheriff. Arranged chronologically by dates *writs* received. Indexed alphabetically by names of plaintiffs. 1896-1926, handwritten or printed forms; 1927—, typed on printed forms. Average 200 pages. 16.5 x 11 x 2.

211. RECORD OF SHERIFF'S SALES
1879-1898. 1 vol. (1). 1835-1878, 1899— in Foreign Execution Docket, entry 209.

Record of sheriff's sales, showing names of plaintiff and defendant, amount of judgment and interest, plaintiff's cost, clerk's, printer's, appraiser's, and sheriff's fees, total amount of fees, amount of sale, volume and page number of docket, kind of *writ*, date advertised, name of paper in which the sale was advertised, date of sale, to whom sold, to whom deed was delivered, and copy of receipt. Arranged the chronologically by dates of sales. Indexed alphabetically by names of plaintiffs and defendants. Handwritten on printed forms. 325 pages. 14 x 9.5 x 1.5. Clerk of courts' office.

212. SHERIFF'S WITNESS BOOK
1876-1878, 1887-1904. 1 vol.

Record of subpoenas served for witnesses, showing case number, names of plaintiff, defendant, and witnesses, expense of witnesses, date of case, sheriff's fees, kind of *writ*, and date *writ* was served. Arranged chronologically by dates of *writs*. Indexed alphabetically by names of plaintiffs. Handwritten. 150 pages. 12 x 7.5 x .5. Clerk of courts' office.

Jail Records

213. JAIL REGISTER 1879—. 2 vols. (one unlabeled; 1).
Records of persons committed to county jail, 1879-1902, showing name and address
of prisoner, place of birth, offense, date of commitment, date of discharge, authority
for sentence, number days in jail, description of prisoner, age, race, color, height,
color of hair and eyes, birthmarks, sheriff's fee, length of commitment, cost of
board and laundry, fees for attending prisoner before court, and total fees; record
1934—, showing county, number of complaints, offense charged, date committed,
date discharged, authority for discharge, description of prisoner, age, sex, race,
color, married or single, read or write, sheriff's fees, number of meals served, fines,
cost, and total fees; also includes record of arrests of parole violators, 1934—.
Arranged chronologically by dates of commitments. No index. Handwritten on
printed forms. Average 250 pages. 18 x 12 x 1.5.

214. FINGER PRINTS AND PHOTOGRAPHS
1824—. 7 vols. Initiated in 1924.
Record of fingerprints and photographs of criminals apprehended in Geauga
County, showing date of arrest, name, address, and occupation of prisoner, county
number, state bureau number, prisoner number, term of sentence, amount of fine,
name of prisoner where sentence was served, date and place of birth, nationality,
age, sex, race, color, height, weight, color of eyes and hair, complexion, and brief
history of crime committed. Arranged chronologically by dates arrested. 1924-1930,
1937—, no index; 1931-1936, index numerically by county numbers. Handwritten
on printed forms. Average 50 loose-leaf pages. 12 x 10 x 1.

Financial Records

215. SHERIFFS'S CASH BOOK
1869-1887, 1913. 7 vols. (1, 1-6).
Record of payment to sheriff and his disposition of cost, fines, and fees collected,
1869-1887, showing date of entry, number of case, names of parties concerned,
description of case, cash received, remarks, total amount received, by whom, and
date paid; cash book, 1913—, showing date of entry, case number, by whom paid,
to whom paid, total amount of sheriff's fee, court costs, judgment and sales,
sundries, date disbursed, and date of payment; also includes record of expenses of
sheriff's witnesses in case in which the sheriff was involved. Arranged

chronologically by dates entered. No index. Handwritten on printed forms. 1 volume 220 pages. 16 x 10.5 x 1; Six volumes average 100 pages. 18 x 12 x 1.5.

216. RECORD OF SHERIFF'S ACCRUED FEES
1912-1933. 2 vols. (1, 2).

Record of sheriff's accrued fees, showing date of accrual, case number, in what matter, to whom charged, total fees of civil and criminal cases due from county foreign *writs*; includes probate and juvenile courts sundries and part payments, showing date of payment, and by whom received. Arranged chronologically by dates of accrual. No index. Handwritten on printed forms. Average 175 pages. 18 x 15 x 1. Clerk of courts' office.

217. SHERIFF'S EXPENSE RECORD
1894-1930. 3 vols. (two dated, 1).

Record of miscellaneous expenses of the sheriff and deputies, showing date of report, amount used for traveling on various cases, meals out of town, stamps, handcuffs, tobacco, laundry, supplies for jail, and other expenses purchases. 1894-1899, no obvious arrangement; 1900-1930, arranged chronologically by dates of disbursements. No index. Handwritten. Average 150 pages. 13.5 x 9 x 1. Clerk of courts' office.

The county dog warden, appointed by the county commissioners, has as his duty the enforcement of the provisions of the General Code relative to licensing dogs, impounding and destruction of unlicensed dogs, and payment of compensation for damages to livestock inflicted by dogs. This officer, like other county officials, is required to give bond conditioned on faithful performance of the duties of his office. This bond, in the sum of not less than $500 nor more than $2000, is filed with the county auditor. His compensation and tenure, like that of his deputies, is determined by the county commissioners.[1]

The warden is required to make a record of all dogs owned, kept, or harbored in his county; to patrol the county; to seize and impound dogs more than three months of age found not wearing a valid registration tag. The latter revisions do not apply, however, to dogs kept in a regularly licensed kennel. Moreover, he is required to make weekly written reports to the commissioners of all dogs seized, impounded, redeemed, and destroyed. Then, too, he is required to report all claims for damages to livestock inflicted by dogs.

The dog warden and his deputies have, in the performance of their legal duties, the same police powers as are conferred by statute upon sheriffs and police. They may summon the assistance of bystanders in performing their duties, serve *writs* and other legal processes issued by any court in the county with reference to enforcing the provision of the laws relating to dogs.[2]

In Geauga County the duties of dog warden were performed by a deputy sheriff from 1917 to 1927, as provided by statute.[3] In 1927 an act authorized the counties to appoint the county dog warden responsible to the commissioners, under which act the Geauga County dog warden was appointed December 1927.[4] During 1940, 169 dogs were seized, 14 redeemed, 22 sold, and the remaining ones were destroyed. Since 3589 licenses for dogs and kennels were issued that year,[5] the office was self-sustaining, the appropriation being $4000.[6] The dog warden is under a $500 bond and receives an annual salary of $1050.[7]

The dog warden keeps no separate records; for reports to commissioners see entry 15; reports on animal claims investigated, see entry 1.

---

1. G. C. sec. 5652-7.
2. G. C. sec. 5652-7.
3. *Laws of Ohio*, CVII, 535.
4. Commissioners Journal, General, XI, [1936-1941], 334.
5. Dog Application [and Tag Number], 1940, entry 284; Dog Kennel Register, 1940, entry 285.
6. Commissioners Journal, General, XI, [1936-1941], 334.
7. *Ibid.*, 428.

The first Ohio Constitution, adopted in 1802, did not provide for the office of county auditor and it was not until 1820 that the general assembly by joint resolution appointed an auditor in each county for a one-year term.[1] In 1821 the office became elective and the term was fixed at one year.[2] In 1831 the term was set at two years, in 1877 at three years, in 1906 reduced to two years, and in 1919 extended to four years.[3]

The county auditor is required to take oath and give bond for faithful performances of the duties of his office; to preserve all copies of entries, surveys, extracts, and other documents transmitted to his office from the state auditor; and to transfer to his successor all books, records, maps, and other papers pertaining to his office.[4] With the approval of the county commissioners he is authorized to appoint deputies, for whose official acts he and his sureties are held liable; since 1869 the record of these appointments has been required to be filed with the county treasurer.[5] If the office of county auditor falls vacant the county commissioners are authorized to appoint a successor.[6]

The first auditor in each county was required to list all lands in his county subject to taxation. From this list and one submitted to him by the county commissioners and one from the state auditor the county auditor was directed to make a tax duplicate to be kept in a book for that purpose, and to give a copy of the list to the tax collector.[7] The auditor was also directed to compile from the treasurer's duplicate a list of lands on which taxes were delinquent, and if such lands were sold for taxes to grant a deed to the purchaser.[8]

Subsequent legislation expanded and itemized the duties of the auditor regarding taxation; with modifications to meet modern requirements these duties have been continued much as they were during the earlier years of the office.

---

1. *Laws of Ohio,* XVIII, 70.
2. *Ibid.,* XIX, 116.
3. *Ibid.,* XXX, 280; LXXIV, 381; XCVIII, 271; CVIII, pt. ii, 1294.
4. *Ibid.,* XIX, 116; LXVII, 103; G. C. sec. 2559, 2582.
5. *Laws of Ohio,* LV, 20; LXVI, 35; G. C. sec. 2563.
6. G. C. secs. 2579, 2580, 2990, 2996.
7. *Laws of Ohio,* XVIII, 79.
8. *Ibid.,* XVIII, 82; XIX, 115.

During the 1840s the office of county assessor was abolished and provision was made for township assessors whose duty it was to list all taxable property and make a return to the auditor.[9] Since 1874 the auditor is required by statute to keep a book in which he lists all additions to and deductions from the amount of the tax assessment.[10] In 1915 he was made chief assessing officer of the county[11]

The county auditor has been a member and served as a secretary of the county budget commission since its beginning in 1911, his duties including keeping full and accurate records of the proceedings of that body. For the purpose of adjusting the tax rates and fixing the amount to be levied each year the commissioners are governed by the amount of taxable property as shown on the auditor's tax list for the current year. He submits to the commissioners the annual tax budget given him by each taxing authority of each subdivision, together with an estimate of any levy prepared by the state auditor, and such other information as the budget commission may request or the state tax commission require.[12]

Tax settlements had been made annually until 1859 when the auditor was required to make semiannual settlement with the treasurer to ascertain the amount of taxes with which the treasurer is to stand charged.[13] Since 1904 liquor, cigarette, and inheritance taxes have constituted separate funds.[14]

Since 1831 the county auditor has kept an account current with the county treasurer, showing the payment of moneys into the treasury, listing the date, by whom paid, and to which fund. On receiving the treasurer's daily statement the auditor enters on his account current the amount shown as a charge to the treasurer.[15] Another important function of the county auditor is the approval before payment of bills and other claims against the county. Since 1831 he has been authorized to issue, on presentation of the proper voucher, all warrants on the county treasurer for moneys payable from the county treasury; and to preserve all warrants, showing the number, date of issue, amount for which drawn, in whose favor, and from which fund.[16]

---

9. *Laws of Ohio*, XXXIX, 22-25.
10. *Ibid.*, LXXI, 30.
11. *Ibid.*, CVI, 246.
12. G. C. sec. 5625-19; *Laws of Ohio*, CXII, 402.
13. G. C. sec. 2596; *Laws of Ohio*, LVI, 132; LXXVIII, 226.
14. *Laws of Ohio*, XCVII, 457.
15. *Ibid.*, XXIX, 280-91; LXVII, 103.
16. G. C. sec. 2570; *Laws of Ohio*, XXXIX, 280-91; LXVII, 103.

County money due the state is paid on warrant to the state auditor. Since 1904 a bill or voucher for payment from any fund controlled by the county commissioners or board of county infirmary directors is filed with the county auditor and entered in a book for that purpose at least five days before its approval for payment by the commissioners, and when approved the date is entered opposite the claim.[17]

Besides approving bills and claims against the county, the auditor in 1835 was given the duty of certifying all moneys, except collections on the tax duplicate, into the county treasury, specifying by whom paid and the fund to which such payment is credited. Such moneys he charges to the treasurer, keeping a duplicate copy of the statement in his office. Since 1835 all costs collected in penitentiary cases which have been or are to be paid to the state have been certified into the treasury as belonging to the state.[18]

In 1902 the legislature provided for a system of uniform accounting and auditing of all public offices, and for the annual examination of their finances, under the direction of a bureau of inspection in the office of the state auditor.[19] Since 1904 the county auditor has been required to report to the commissioners on the state of county finances; on the first business day of each month he prepares in duplicate a statement of the county finances for the preceding month, compares it with the treasurer's balance, and submits it to the commissioners, who post one copy of it in the auditor's office for 30 days for public inspection.[20]

During the development of the office additional duties in great diversity have been delegated to the county auditor. Since 1833 he has been authorized to discharge prisoners jailed for nonpayment of any fine or amercement due the county when in his opinion the amount cannot be collected.[21] In 1838 an act was passed making him county superintendent of schools. He was relieved of this duty in 1848 when a county superintendent of schools was authorized in each county.[22] Since 1846 he has served as the sealer of weights and measures, is responsible for the preservation of the copies of the original standards delivered to his office, and enforces in his county all state laws regulating weights and measures.[23]

---

17. *Laws of Ohio*, XCVII, 25; CVIII, pt. i, 272.
18. *Laws of Ohio*, XXXIII, 44; LXVII, 103.
19. *Ibid.*, XCV, 511-15.
20. *Ibid.*, XCVII, 457.
21. G. C. sec. 2576; *Laws of Ohio*, XXXI, 18; LXVII, 103.
22. *See* p. 210.
23. G. C. sec. 2615; *Laws of Ohio*, XLIV. 55; LVIII, 78; CI, 234.

In 1861 he was authorized to report to the state auditor statistics concerning the deaf, dumb, blind, insane, and idiots in his county, with the names and addresses of their parents or guardians.[24] Eight years later, in 1869, he was authorized to report to the same officer statistics concerning livestock in his county as returned to his office by assessors, and an abstract of the funded indebtedness of his county, and of each township, city, village, and school district.[25] Since 1827 he has been authorized to issue licenses to traveling public shows and exhibitions, although municipal authorities may impose an additional license.[26] In 1862 he was authorized to issue peddlers' licenses to persons who filed a statement of stock in trade and conformity with the law requiring the listing of such stock for taxation, and since 1917 he has issued dog licenses.[27] The auditor has issued licenses to wholesale and retail dealers in cigarettes since 1892,[28] in brewers' wort and malt since 1933,[29] and issued cosmetic licenses from August 1, 1933 to June 30, 1936.[30]

Since 1850 the auditor has been official custodian of the reports submitted to the commissioners by the prosecuting attorney, clerk of courts, sheriff, and the treasurer; those reports are required to be recorded by the auditor in books kept specifically for that purpose.[31] The auditor is a member of the county board of revision established in 1825, secretary of the budget commission, and serves as a trustee and the secretary of the board of trustees of the sinking fund established in 1919.

In Geauga County the work of the auditor's office is carried on by a staff of four in addition to the auditor himself. The total appraised value of property in the county has shown some increase in recent years, being given as $22,634,020 in 1935, and as $23,558,958 in 1940.[32] In the same period the tax rate for real property has remained the same, having been set at .0027 mills in 1935, .0027 in 1936, and .0027 in 1940.[33]

---

24. *Laws of Ohio,* LVIII, 40.
25. G. C. sec. 2604.
26. Chase, *op. cit.,* III, 1582; *Laws of Ohio,* XXIX, 446; G. C. secs. 6374, 75.
27. *Laws of Ohio,* LIX, 67; LXXIX, 96; CVII, 534.
28. G. C. sec. 5894-5.
29. G. C. sec. 5545-5.
30. *Laws of Ohio,* CXV, 649; CXV, pt. ii, 83; CXVI, pt. ii, 323.
31. G. C. sec. 2504; R. S. sec. 886; *Laws of Ohio,* XLVIII, 66.
32. Financial Report, 1935, 1940, entry 306.
33. Minutes of Budget Commission, III [1933—], 166, 169, 199, entry 359.

The bonded indebtedness of the county has also decreased in these years, from $588,500 in 1935 to $59,700 in 1940.[34]

---

34. Commissioners' Journal, General, X [1931-1936], 432, and XI [1936-1941], 436, entry 1.

Property Transfers

218. [Auditor's] RECORD OF TRANSFERS
1821-1829, 1839—. 16 vols. (dated). Title varies: Transfer Record, 1821-1829, 1839-1856, 3 vols.; Transfers, 1856 -1883, 2 vols. 1811-1818 in Auditor's Tax List, entry 225.

Record of transfers of real property, showing date of transfer, description and value of property, to whom and from whom transferred, name of township, range, section, tract, lot, and sub-lot numbers, consideration, and remarks; also includes list of houses appraised 1825-1826; and personal property tax list 1826-1827, showing numbers and value of horses and cattle, capital of merchants and brokers, number and value of pleasure carriages, and signature of owner or representative. Also contains Enumeration of White Male Inhabitants, 1856-1883, entry 290. There are two volumes for the year 1856-1869 and 1869-1883. They are identical except one of each is handwritten and duplicates are handwritten on printed forms. Arranged by names of townships and chronologically thereunder by dates of transfers, 1821-1855, no index; 1856—, indexed alphabetically by names of townships. 1821-1883, handwritten; 1856—, handwritten on printed forms. Average 250 pages. 16 x 12 x 2. Auditor's office.

Maps

219. MAPS OF GEAUGA COUNTY
1938. 11 vols.

Physical maps of Geauga County, showing names of townships, tract and section numbers, lot and sublot lines, and names of highways, railroads, and owners of lots. Published by City Blueprinting Company, Cleveland, Ohio. No obvious arrangement. No index. Hand drawn. Scale, 1 inch equals 10 chains. Average 40 maps in volume. 24 x 36 x .5. Auditor's office.

220. MAPS OF ROADS OF GEAUGA COUNTY
1883. 1 vol.
Physical maps of roads of Geauga County showing names of townships and roads, with reference to volume of Road Records, entry 408, and Commissioners' Journal, entry 1. Published by county surveyor. Arranged alphabetically by names of townships. Indexed alphabetically by names of townships. Hand drawn. 39 maps in volume. 18 x 14 x 1. Auditor's office.

Taxes

Real Property

221. RECORD OF LEVIES
1823-1923. 2 vols. (1, 2). 1924— in Auditor's Tax List, entry 225.
Record of tax levies for each taxing district, showing date and amount of levy.In early years the rate was shown by mills and levies itemized under state, county, and township; levies in latter years under state, including war compensation and school levies; under county, including county general fund, infirmary, bridge, soldiers' relief, blind relief, mothers' pension, judicial agricultural society (fair), debt, and roads; under townships, including general fund, cemetery, town hall, roads, and road bonds; under school, including tuition, contingent, buildings, retirement, and debt; under corporations, including general, safety, and service. Arranged chronologically by dates of levy and alphabetically thereunder by taxing districts. No index. Handwritten on drawn forms. Average 100 pages. 18 x 11.5 x 1. 3rd floor store room.

222. APPRAISEMENTS
1825-1828, 1870-1900, 1926—. 133 vols. (labeled by names of townships) Last Appraisement 1936. Title varies: Decennial Appraisements, 1870-1900, 68 vols.; Township Lands, 1926, 17 vols. 1910-1926 in Assessors' Returns, entry 223.
Record of appraisements of real estate, showing name of taxing district, name and address of owner, description of property, number of acres of land, classified as arable, meadow and pasture, uncultivated, and woodland, value of land and buildings, amount added or deducted by county and state boards of revision and total value as equalized; also includes appraisers account of days worked and money received from auditor; appraiser's oath, and hand-drawn physical maps of taxing

districts appraised, 1870-1910. Arranged alphabetically by names of taxing districts and alphabetically thereunder by names of owners. No index. Handwritten and typed, some on printed forms. 90 volumes average 75 pages. 18 x 12 x .5.; 43 volumes average 600 pages. 8.5 x 14 x 3.5. 85 volumes, 1825-1828, 1870-1900, 1926, basement store room; 48 volumes, 1927—, Auditor's office.

223. ASSESSORS' RETURNS
1827-1850, 1862-1864, 1882-1931. 770 vols. (labeled by names of townships).

Record of township assessors' returns on real and personal property; real property, showing name of owner, description of land, number of acres, value of house, barns, mills, improved lands, total value, and remarks; personal property, showing name and address of owner, value of horses, mules, sheep, hogs, carriages, watches, pianos, organs, moneys, credits, investments, dogs, and remarks as sworn or affirmed including assessor's oath, and account of days worked and money received, 1882-1931. Also contains: Appraisements, 1910-1926, entry 222; 1931—, destroyed after being entered on tax duplicates. 1827-1850, 1862-1864, arranged numerically by township numbers and alphabetically thereunder by names of owners; 1882-1931, arranged by names of taxing districts and alphabetically thereunder by names of owners. No index. 1827-1850, 1862-1864, handwritten; 1882-1931, handwritten on printed forms. 715 volumes average 50 pages. 8 x 13.25. .25.; 35 volumes average 400 pages. 6 x 9 x 2; 20 volumes average 150 pages. 12 x 8 x 2. Basement store room.

224. AUDITOR'S LIST OF EXEMPTED PROPERTY
1932, 1937—. 1 vol.

Record of real and personal property exempted from taxation, showing name of township, name of owner, name of range, tract, section, and lot or survey, description of property, number of acres, value of land and building, total value according to the section of general code authorizing exemptions, and reason for exemption; real property listed, showing churches, schools, public lands, and buildings; personal property listed, showing county owned equipment, trucks, automobiles, motorcycles, road machinery, moneys, credits, and endowment funds. Record not made up every year but periodically when changes are made in exempted property. Arranged alphabetically by names of townships. No index. Typed on printed forms. 200 pages. 14.5 x 18 x 1.25. Auditor's office.

225. AUDITOR'S TAX LIST

1810, 1817-1818, 1820-1828, 1830, 1832-1851, 1853, 1858——. 198 vols. (dated). Title varies: Duplicate, 1810, 1817-1818, 1820-1828, 1830, 1832-1851, 1858, 45 vols.; Personal Property Duplicate, 1826, 1 vol.; Record of Duplicate, 1840-1859, 18 volumes; Tax Duplicate, 1860-1876, 17 vols.; Auditors Tax Duplicate, 1877-1912, 1918, 38 vols.

Duplicate of tax assessments on real and personal property, showing names of township, taxing district, and property owner, range, section, tract, and lot numbers, acreage, rate of taxes, description and value of land and buildings as equalized by the tax commission and board of revision acting on complaints, value of land and buildings as equalized by board of revision, amount of state, county, general, school, road, and miscellaneous taxes, delinquencies, penalties, and remarks; summary for each taxing district showing assessments on real property, also includes traders permits and tavern licenses, 1811; treasurer's settlement with commissioners, 1821; lists of land sold for taxes, 1824-1825; list of delinquent taxes on real property, 1826. Also contains Record of Transfer, 1811-1818, entry 218 (recorded in volume dated 1810), Record of Levis, 1924——, entry 221. Auditor's Personal [Tax] Duplicate, 1810, 1817-1818, 1820-1828, 1830, 1832-1851, 1853, 1858-1931, entry 229. Arranged by names of taxing districts and alphabetically thereunder by names of taxpayers. No index. 1810-1859, handwritten; 1860-1913, Handwritten on printed forms; 1914——, typed on printed forms. Average 300 pages. Size varies, 12 x 8 x 1 to 18 x 13.5 x 3. Auditor's office.

226. SPECIAL ASSESSMENTS

1870——. 22 vols., 15 bundles. Title varies: Assessments of Real Property, 1870-1890, 1900, 4 vols.; River – Ditch and Cranberry Marsh Duplicate, 1885-1907, 1 vol., Account of School Funds – Clerk, 1921-1931, 1 vol.; Special Assessments, 1924-1934, 15 bundles; Records, 1924-1936, 1 vol.; Burton Village, Water Assessments, 1927-1936, 1 vol.; Burton Village Assessments, 1927-1936, 1 vol.

Record of special assessments on real estate for various purposes, showing name and address of property owner, acreage and description of land, purpose of assessment, number of acres assessed, total assessment, delinquencies of former years, assessments under following headings, county road, township, water, ditch, and miscellaneous, date due, total amount due, and date paid. All records except those specified are arranged alphabetically by taxing districts and alphabetically thereunder by names of taxpayers; 1921-1931. Account of school Funds – Clerk, arranged chronologically by dates entered; 1885-1907. River – Ditch and Cranberry Marsh Duplicate, arranged by names of townships and alphabetically thereunder by names of taxpayers. No index. 1870-1900, 1921-1936, handwritten, some on printed forms; 1885-1907, handwritten; 1908-1920 handwritten on printed forms. 1924-1934, 1937, handwritten and typed on printed forms; 1928—, typed on printed forms. Volume average 400 pages. 12 x 14.5 x 4; bundles, 11.5 x 14 x 4. 3 volumes, 1870-1890, basement store room; 14 volumes, 1885—, Auditor's office; 1 vol. 1900, attic store room; 4 volumes, 15 bundles 1921-1936, 3rd floor store room.

227. SPECIAL ASSESSMENTS
1930—. 2 file drawers.

Record of special assessments on real estate for various purposes, showing service rendered, name and address of taxpayer, names of taxing district and township, description of land, number of acres owned, number of acres assessed, total assessment, date due, and total amount due. Arranged by names of taxing districts and alphabetically thereunder by names of taxpayers. No index. Typed on printed forms. 10 x 5 x 14. Auditor's office.

Personal Property

228. INDIVIDUAL RETURNS OF TAXABLE PERSONAL PROPERTY
1929—, 100 vols., 36 bundles, 4 file drawers.

Personal property returns made by taxpayers, showing names of taxpayer and taxing district, itemized estimated value of taxable personal property, date filed, certificate of advanced tax payment, and special forms to be filled out by corporations and fiduciaries. Arranged by names of taxing districts and alphabetically thereunder by names of taxpayers. No index. Handwritten and typed, some on printed forms. Volumes average 200 loose-leaf pages. 11 x 9 x 1.5.; bundles, various sizes; file drawers, 1937—, Auditor's office.

229. AUDITORS PERSONAL [Tax] DUPLICATE
1932—. 2 vols. 1810, 1817-1818, 1820-1828, 1830, 1832-1851, 1853, 1858-1931 in Auditor's Tax List, entry 225.

Duplicate of taxes on tangible personal property, showing name of taxing district, name and address of taxpayer, tax rate, final assessment, total tax for year, amount and date paid, advanced payment, unpaid taxes for year, and remarks. Arranged by names of taxing districts and alphabetically thereunder by names of taxpayers. No index. Typed on printed forms. Average 300 pages. 18.5 x 16.5 x 2. Auditor's office.

230. AUDITOR'S CLASSIFIED DUPLICATE
1932—. 1 vol. Initiated in 1932.

Duplicate of taxes on intangible personal property, showing name and address of taxpayer, income yield or assessed value, amount assessed, and tax rate on productive and nonproductive investments, deposits, credits, moneys and other taxable intangibles, total tax for year, advanced payment, tax due, unpaid tax for year, and remarks. Arranged by names of taxing districts and alphabetically thereunder by names of taxpayers. No index. Typed on printed forms. 300 pages. 18.5 x 16.5 x 2. Auditor's office.

Delinquent

231. LIST OF ALL FORFEITED LAND AND LOTS
1811—. 22 vols. Title varies: List of Lands Advertised for Sale, 1811-1853, 7 vols.; Delinquent List and Tax Sale, 1854-1924, 6 vols.; Delinquent List of Real Property, 1924-1925, 1 vol.; Delinquent Land Record as Returned by Treasurer, 1926-1936, 6 vols.; Delinquent Land List, 1937, 1 vol.

Record of land listed as delinquent for taxes, showing names of taxing district, name of owner, tract, section, lot, and sub lot numbers, acres, valuation of property, amount of delinquencies, penalties, and total tax due; delinquent personal property list, 1834-1925, showing chattels and other personal property, name of owner, amount of delinquencies, penalties and total tax due; list of lands sold for taxes, showing name of original owner, amount of taxes, delinquencies, and penalties due, cost of transfer, amount sold for, number of acres sold, name of purchaser, and date of purchase. 1811-1826, arranged by names of townships and alphabetical thereunder by names of taxpayers. No index. 1811-1882, handwritten; 1883-1925, handwritten on printed forms; 1926—, handwritten and typed, some on printed forms. 8 volumes average 200 pages. 13 x 8 x 1; 14 volumes average 300 pages. 16 x 12 x 1.5. 21 volumes, 1811-1907, 1917—, Auditor's office; 1 volume, 1908-1916, basement store room.

232. AUDITOR'S QUADRENNIAL CERTIFICATES
1929-1930, 1935—. 1 bundle, 1 vol.

Certified copies of auditor's quadrennial certificates of unredeemed tracts of land, and city or town lots, 1929-1930 and triennial certificates 1936—, showing names of taxing district and owner, description and value of property, itemized and total delinquent taxes, interest and penalties, and certification of certificates; also includes list of forfeited lands and lots, and county auditor's report to Auditor of State of forfeited lands or town lots redeemed or sold. Arranged by names of taxing districts and alphabetically thereunder by names of owners. No index. Handwritten and typed on printed forms. Bundles 17 x 13.5 x 2.5; Volume 725 pages. 17.5 x 15 x 3. 1 bundle, 1929-1930, 3rd floor store room; 1 vol. 1936—, Auditor's office.

233. CERTIFICATES OF SALES OF FORFEITED LANDS
1919—. 1 file box, 1 vol.

Duplicates of delinquent land of tax certificates, showing names of owner and township, description and valuation of property, taxes, assessments, and penalties unpaid, and notations by auditor as to redeemed or sold. Arranged alphabetically by names of townships and alphabetically thereunder by names of owners. No index. Typed on printed forms. File box, 10 x 5 x 15; volume 300 pages. 12 x 8 x 1.5. Auditor's office.

234. CERTIFICATES OF REDEMPTION
1925—. 1 bundle, 7 vols.

Duplicate certificates from the auditor to the treasurer to receive payment for redemption of land certified delinquent, showing certificate number, name of owner, description of property, amount required for redemption of property, amount of general taxes, special assessments, penalties, interest, and total. Arranged numerically by certificate numbers. No index. Handwritten on printed forms. Bundles, 12 x 9 x 4; 1 volume 100 pages. 8 x 18 x .5; 6 volumes average 250 pages. 7 x 9 x 2. 1 bundle, 1925-1926 attic store room; 6 volumes, 1927-1932, 3rd floor room; 1 volume 1932—, Auditor's office.

235. DELINQUENT PERSONAL PROPERTY DUPLICATE
1905—. 1 cardboard box, 4 file drawers, 7 vols.

Duplicate of delinquent personal property taxes, showing name of taxpayer, year of delinquent taxes, valuation of property, dog and road taxes, penalties, total taxes unpaid, date of payment, and remarks. 1905-1914, 1919-1922, 1931—, arranged by taxing districts and alphabetically thereunder by names of property owners; 1915+1918 arranged by taxing districts and alphabetically thereunder by names of taxpayers; 1923-1930 arranged alphabetically by names at townships. 1905-1911, indexed alphabetically by names of townships; 1912—, no index. 1905-1922, handwritten on printed forms; 1923—, typed on printed forms. 6 volumes average 125 pages. 16 x 11 x 1.; 1 volume 300 loose-leaf pages. 17.5 x 14.4 x 2; box, 10 x 10 x 10; file boxes, 4 x 12.5 x 18. 1 volume, 1905-1911, attic store room; 2 volumes, 1912-1913, basement store room; 1 volume, 1 cardboard box, 1914, 1932-1935, 3rd floor store room. 3 volumes, 4 file drawers, 1915-1931, 1935—, Auditor's office.

236. UNDERTAKINGS – COUNTY AUDITOR
1933—. 1 vol.
Auditor's duplicate of undertakings to pay full principal amount of delinquent taxes and assessments, less penalties, interest, and other charges, in annual installments, showing date of entry, record of delinquent taxes, assessments charged, payments thereof, date due, date of payment, general taxes, county, township, and municipal assessments, total, and date of application of undertaking. Arranged chronologically by dates entered. No index. Handwritten on printed forms. 928 pages. 17.5 x 16.5 x 5. Auditor's office.

Complaints and Adjustments

237. ADDITIONS AND DEDUCTIONS TO THE DUPLICATE
1874—. 3 vols. (one unlabeled; 1, 2). 1 bundle.
Record of additions and deductions to the tax duplicate, half of each volume and the bundle contains additions and other half contains deductions. Additions entered on account of improvement on property or previous error in duplicate; deductions entered on account of loss or damage to property or error to previous duplicate. Both additions and deductions entered under headings, showing name of owner, description and valuation of property, tax added or deducted, road tax, state, county, and all general taxes, school and other special taxes, total additions or deductions, date, and remarks. Arranged chronologically by years, thereunder by names of taxing districts, and alphabetically thereunder by names of property owners. No index. Handwritten on printed forms. 2 volumes average 159 pages. 18 x 12 x 1.5;

1 volume 500 pages. 12 x 14.5 x 3; bundles700 pages. 11.5 x 14 x 4. 1 volume, 1 bundle, 1874-1901, 1931-1936 3rd floor store room; 2 volumes, 1902-1930, 1937—, Auditor's office.

238. ADDITION ORDER BOOK
1924—. 8 vols.

Carbon copies of addition orders, showing date and number of order, names of auditor, treasurer, and taxpayer, tax year, valuation of property, rate of taxation, and amount added on real or personal property tax in the form of general taxes or special assessments. Arranged numerically by ordered numbers. No index. Handwritten on printed forms. Average 125 pages. 17 x 9.5 x 1. 2 volumes, 1924-1927, attic store room; 2 volumes, 1929-1932, 3rd floor store room; 4 volumes, 1927-1929, 1932—, Auditor's office.

239. DEDUCTION ORDER BOOKS
1926—. 4 vols.

Carbon copies of deduction orders, showing date and number of order, names of auditor, treasurer, and taxpayer, tax year, valuation of property, rate of taxation, and amount deducted from real or personal property tax in the form of general taxes or special assessments. Arranged numerically by order numbers. No index. Handwritten on printed forms. Average 125 pages. 17 x 9.5 x 1. 3 volumes, 1926-1934, 3rd floor store room; 1 volume, 1934—, Auditor's office.

240. COMPLAINTS OF ASSESSMENTS – REAL PROPERTY
1931—. 1 file box.

Copies of complaints filed with the board of revision by property owners, showing names of property owner and taxing district, date and nature of complaint, and revision of assessments recommended. Arranged chronologically by dates of complaints. No index. Handwritten on printed forms. 10 x 5 x 14. Auditor's office.

Inheritance

241. INHERITANCE TAX CHARGES
1924—. 1 wrapped and sealed bundle, 1 vol.

Auditor's original of inheritance tax charges, showing name of township or village, name of decedent, and post office address, name of taxpayer and date of accrual of tax, amount fixed by probate court, interest, total amount, and date paid. Arranged alphabetically by names of taxing districts and chronologically thereunder by dates of accrual. No index. Handwritten and typed on printed forms. Bundle, 10 x 12 x 2; volume 125 pages. 11 x 11.25 x 1. 1 bundle, 1924-1934, 3rd floor store room; 1 volume 1935—, Auditor's office.

242. INHERITANCE TAX CERTIFICATES
1929—. 2 file drawers.
Copies of affidavits from the probate court to the county auditor certifying that the determination for inheritance tax has been fixed in the matter of the decedent and that there is no tax found due, showing case number, date of issue, document number, name of decedent, name of county, valuation of real estate and personal property, name of successor, amount of exemption, amount of tax, names of persons by whom tax should be paid, and township or municipality. Arranged chronologically by dates issued. No index. Typed on printed forms. 10 x 5 x 14. Auditor's office.

243. RECORD OF RAILROAD APPRAISEMENTS
1872-1909. 4 vols. (2 vols. subtitled by name of railroad).
Record of procedure of the county board of assessors and appraisers in assessing railroad property, showing date of meeting, and yearly assessments and appraisements, including itemized list of rolling stock and other railroad property, amounts of assessment on same, record of motions made, votes cast and decisions of board of assessors and appraisers in respect to appraisal and assessment of railroad property. One volume, 1883-1892, covers Chagrin Falls and Eastern Electric Railroad; one volume, 1900-1902, covers Chagrin Falls and Eastern Electric Railroad; one volume, 1872-1901, covers Painesville and Youngstown Railroad Company and the fourth volume, 1891-1909, covers a number of railroads, including Chagrin Falls and Northern; Cleveland, Canton, and Southern; Cleveland and Canton; Cleveland and Mahoning Valley; Cleveland and Eastern Electric; Chagrin Falls and Eastern Electric; Chagrin Falls Railroad; Eastern Ohio Traction Company, and Pittsburgh, Painesville, and Fairport Railroad. Arranged chronologically by dates of meetings. 1872-1890, no index; 1891-1909, indexed by names of railroads. Handwritten. Average 150 pages. 12 x 8 x 1. 3 volumes, 1872-1909, basement store room; 1 volume, 1900-1902, attic store room.

Excise

244. DOW TAX DUPLICATE [Miscellaneous Tax Assessment]
1886-1902. 1 vol.

Miscellaneous tax assessments, including Dow Tax, 1896-1902 and duplicate of assessments of traffic in intoxicating liquors, 1887, showing name of owner, location, date of assessment, amount of assessment, date of payment, and remarks; also includes list of various taxes paid by merchants, 1886-1887. Arranged chronologically by dates of assessments. No index. Handwritten. 272 pages. 13 x 8 x 1. Auditor's office.

245. AUDITOR'S TAX ASSESSMENT DUPLICATE
1902-1907, 1917, 1924-1930. 1 vol. (1).

Duplicate of assessments on intoxicating liquors, showing names of business, and proprietor, location, name of owner of premises, date of assessment, by whom assessment to be paid, itemized assessments, total assessment, amount collected, and remarks; also includes assessment duplicate of traffic in cigarette and cigarette papers, 1917. No obvious arrangement. No index. Handwritten on printed forms. 39 pages. 17 x 14 x .5. Auditor's office.

Fiscal Accounts

Budgets and Appropriations

246. [Budget and] APPROPRIATIONS
1912-1917, 1927-1935. 1 carton, 15 file envelopes, 1 file folder. Title varies: School Budget, 1927-1933, 5 file envelopes; Twp. [Township] Budgets, 1927-1933, 5 file envelopes; Village Budget, 1927-1933, 5 file envelopes; County Budget, 1929-1934, 6 file folders.

Record of budgets and appropriations, including receipts and expenditures of county, village, township, and schools showing names of county and district, date of budget, name of clerk, summary of amounts of general taxation with the 15- mill limitation, amount outside the 15-mill limitation, amount for library purposes, amount of bonds, notes and certificates of indebtedness, and other expenditures. No obvious arrangement. No index. Handwritten and typed, some on printed forms. Carton, 10 x 12 x 11; file envelopes, 9 x 4 x 2; file folders, 14 x 9.5 x 1. Attic store room.

247. BUDGETS

1931—. 2 file drawers.

Auditor's copy of budget for each subdivision each year, showing amount allotted to each fund, total for subdivision, and year. Arranged chronologically by years. No index. Handwritten on printed forms. 10 x 5 x 14. Auditor's office.

248. APPROPRIATION LEDGER

1915-1916, 1927—. 4 vols., 2 bundles.

Auditor's record of appropriations to various funds of county officers with record of warrants drawn against funds, showing name of fund, name of department, name of account, code number, date of entry, name of vendor or contractor, remarks, purchase order number, certificate number, warrant number, amount of warrant, debt, credit, and unencumbered balance. Arranged alphabetically by names of funds or debts and chronologically thereunder by dates entered. No index. Handwritten on printed forms. Volumes average 700 pages. 14 x 13 x 3; bundles, 12 x 11 x 3. 1 volume, two bundles, 1915-1916, 1927-1934 3rd floor store room; 3 volumes, 1935—, Auditor's office.

249. APPORTIONMENT OF TOWNSHIP FUNDS

1875—. 4 vols. (1-4).

Auditor's record of semiannual distribution of township funds to township treasurer, showing date of settlement, name of township, and total amount distributed to township; treasurer for township funds, including road, poor, town hall, cemetery, and sinking funds, and special road assessments; also includes pasted in receipts from township treasurer to auditor, 1885-1920, showing date of receipt, name of township, amount, supplies or services rendered, and signature of township treasurer; school settlement record 1875-1920, showing statement of distribution, source of receipts and disbursements, general sinking fund, bond retirement fund, total, county warrant number, date received, name of school district, statement of condition of fund, and date of settlement. Arranged chronologically by dates of settlements and alphabetically thereunder by names of townships. No index. Handwritten on printed forms. Average 500 pages. 16 x 12 x 2.5. 1 volume, 1875-1884, basement store room; 2 volumes, 1885-1920, 3rd floor store room; 1 volume, 1921—, Auditor's office.

Settlements

250. RECORD OF SETTLEMENTS
1907—. 9 loose-leaf abstracts, 26 rolled abstracts, 2 vols. Title varies: Settlement Record, 1907-1922, 1 vol.

Annual and semiannual settlements with treasurer, showing date of abstract, rate of taxation and taxing district, name of taxing district, totals of all state, county, township, district, and other taxes, certification by county auditor, value of all property as equalized by board of revision, delinquencies, and forfeitures of other years; also includes treasurer's general statement of accounts and settlement sheet, 1907-1922. 1907-1922, 1923—, volumes arranged chronologically by dates of abstracts and thereunder by taxing districts; 1915-1934, rolled abstracts, loose-leaf abstracts, arranged by names of taxing district and chronologically thereunder by dates of abstracts. No index. Handwritten and typed, some on printed forms. Loose-leaf and rolled abstracts, miscellaneous sizes; volumes average 150 pages. 23.5 x 16.25 x 1. 1 volume, 9 loose-leaf, 1907-1922, 1928-1934 abstracts, 3rd floor store room; 26 rolled abstracts, 1915-1927, basement store room; 1 volume, 1923—, Auditor's office.

251. AUDITOR'S SCHOOL SETTLEMENT RECORD
1838—. 10 vols. (six unlabeled; 1-4). 42 envelopes. Title varies: Settlement of School Fund, 1838-1903, 4 vols.

Auditor's record of semiannual distribution of school funds to township or school treasurer, showing names of school district and township, sources from which funds are collected, date of settlement, distribution of funds for tuition, school house and contingent, teachers' retirement, bonds and interests of clerk's certificate of funds; funds in school treasury, showing amount, warrant number, date of warrant, and signature of school treasurer; also includes record of receipts and expenditures, and balance on hand; certificates of examination of school treasury, statement and vouchers by auditor, signed by auditor and school treasurer; deductions from funds for workman's compensation, election expense and state examiner's expense, 1838-1903. Also contains schools enumeration, 1838-1897, entry 289. 1838-1902, Arranged chronologically by dates of settlements and alphabetically thereunder by names of school districts; 1903—, arranged chronologically by dates of settlements and alphabetically thereunder by names of townships and school districts. No index. Handwritten on printed forms.

9 volumes average 300 pages. 16 x 12 x 2.25; 1 volume 500 pages. 12.25 x 7.25 x 1.25. 1 volume, 1838-1874, basement store room; 5 volumes, 1874-1922, 3rd floor store room; 4 volumes, 1922—, Auditor's office.

General Accounts

252. RECORD OF DISTRIBUTION OF FEES RECEIVED [Motor Vehicle]
1925-1933. 2 vols. 1 file drawer, 3 bundles.
Auditor's daily and monthly statement of motor vehicle license fees received and distributed, showing date of statement, amount of tax collected from passenger cars, trucks, passenger commercial, motorcycles, sidecars, and trailers, total amount, and amount divided into county state funds, registration district, and correspondence pertaining to licenses. Arranged chronologically by dates of statements. No index. Handwritten on printed forms. Volumes average 300 pages. 12 x 12 x 2; file box, 3 x 13 x 14; bundles, 11.5 x 11.5 x 2. 1 bundle, 1925-1928, attic store room; 2 bundles, 1925-1933, basement store room; 2 volumes, 1 file drawer, 1926-1932, 3rd floor store room.

253. AUDITOR'S LEDGER
1819-1865, 1904—. 5 vols. (three unlabeled; 1, 2). Title varies; Book of Accounts, 1819-1865, 1 vol., Transfer and General Ledger, 1924-1931, 1 vol.
Accounts with various county offices, funds, and institutions, showing date of entry, folio number, debit, credit, debit balance, credit balance, and remarks; treasurer's account record of receipts and disbursements concurring with treasurer, general tax fund, personal tax fund, poor relief, gas tax division, road fund, undivided liquor tax fund, judicial funds, infirmary fund, soldiers' and blind relief funds, mothers' pensions, sheriff's, auditor's, recorder's, treasurer's, probate judge's, and clerk's fees; also record of payments on bonds and coupons authorized by commissioners, 1935—, and numerous other accounts, including salaries of auditor, deputies, and other officers. Also contains Auditor's Record of Fees, 1904-1916, entry 254, arranged alphabetically by names of accounts and chronologically thereunder by dates entered. 1819-1865, 1916—, no index; 1904-1915, indexed alphabetically by names of accounts. Handwritten on printed forms. Average 400 pages. 14 x 13 x 2. 1 volume, 1819-1865, basement store room; 2 volumes, 1904-1924, 3rd floor store room, 2 volumes, 1924—, Auditor's office.

254. AUDITOR'S RECORD OF FEES
1917—. 2 vols. (2, 3). 1904-1916 in Auditor's Ledger, entry 253.

Record of fees received by auditor, showing date of entry, by whom paid, for what purpose, amount of fee, and notation as to whom paid into treasury. Arranged chronologically by dates entered. No index. Handwritten on printed forms. Average 200 pages. 16x 11 x 1. 1 volume, 1917-1928, attic store room; 1 volume, 1929—, Auditor's office.

255. AUDITOR'S JOURNAL OF PAYMENTS INTO THE TREASURY
1928—. 1 vol. (5).

Auditor's record of payments into the county treasury, showing date of entry, name of tax, purpose, number of payments in order, treasurer (debit column), total amount of payment, and the following credit columns: board of education, township and state, road and bridge, dog and kennel, board of health, auto license, and gas funds; undivided liquor, general, cigarettes, inheritance, state, and miscellaneous taxes. Arranged chronologically by dates entered. No index. Handwritten on printed forms. 251 pages. 18.5 x x13 2.5. Auditor's office.

256. PAY-IN ORDERS
1929—. 14 vols.

Originals of auditor's orders to pay money into treasury, showing order number, date of order, name of payer, amount, purpose of payment, name of fund to which payment is credited, and signature of auditor. Arranged chronologically by dates of pay-in orders. No index. Handwritten on printed forms. Average 300 pages. 12 x 9.5 x 1.5. 13 volumes, 1929-1937, 3rd floor store room. volume, 1938—, Auditor's office.

Special Accounts

257. ANIMAL CLAIM RECORDS
1892—. 1 vol.

Record of payments made from dog license funds to owners of sheep and other livestock killed or injured by dogs, showing date claim filed, number of claim, name of claimant, number of animals killed, number injured, amount allowed by trustees and commissioners, date of payment, number of warrant, names of witnesses, amount of witness fees, and date paid. Arranged chronologically by dates filed. No index. Handwritten on printed forms. 160 pages. 18 x 12 x 1. Auditor's office.

258. BURIAL RECORD OF INDIGENT SOLDIERS
1886-1916. 1 vol. (1).

Record of burial of indigent soldiers, sailors, and marines, showing name of township, name and address of decedent, date of death, detail of service and discharge, occupation, location of burial place, itemized expense of burial, signature of township committee appointed to take charge of burial on affidavit of indigency, date of filing and recording, and signature of auditor; also includes appointments of burial committees in each township, showing names of committee, date appointed, and from what township. Arranged chronologically by dates filed. Indexd alphabetically by names of townships. Handwritten on printed forms. 217 pages. 14 x 9 x 1. Auditor's office.

259. RECORD OF INDIGENT SOLDIERS, SAILORS, AND MARINES
1887-1930, 1933—. 2 vols. (1,2). Title varies: Auditor's Record of Soldiers Relief Funds, 1887-1930. 1 vol.

Record of amount allowed and certification of appointment for soldiers' relief, showing name of recipient, whether wife, widow, or child or soldier, sailor, or marine, address, and amount allowed per month by soldiers' relief commission; also includes record of soldiers' relief fund, 1887, showing date of entry, and amount paid by auditor to township treasurer for disbursement to recipient, and name of recipient and township. First half of volume 1, 1887-1930, arranged chronologically by dates entered. 1887-1930, no index; 1933—, indexed alphabetically by names of recipients. Handwritten on printed forms. Average 300 pages. 16 x 12 x 2. Auditor's office.

260. SOLDIERS' RELIEF AND BLIND RELIEF PENSIONS
1934-1935. 1 vol.

Record of soldiers' relief and blind relief disbursements, showing name of recipient, amount of pension each month, address, warrant number, amount of warrant, date, and remarks. Arranged numerically by warrant numbers. No index. Handwritten. 25 loose-leaf pages. 11 x 9 x .5. Auditor's office.

261. [Aid to Dependent Children and] BLIND RELIEF RECORD
1936—. 1 vol.

Record of blind relief receipts and expenditures, showing date of receipt, name of recipient, receipts of local, state, and federal governments, expenditures, totals, and balance; record of receipts and expenditures for aid to dependent children, showing date of receipt, name of recipient, receipts of local, state, and federal governments, expenditures, totals, and balance. Arranged chronologically by dates receipted and alphabetically thereunder by names of recipients. No index. Handwritten on printed forms. 150 pages. 14.5 x 17.5 x 1. Auditor's office.

262. MOTHERS' PENSION RECORD
1916-1936. 1 vol. Initiated in 1916.
Record of disbursement of mothers' pensions, showing probate court order number probate court allowance, number of months, name and address of mother, warrant number, amount, date of payment, and remarks. Arranged to chronologically by dates paid. No index. Handwritten on printed forms. 101 pages. 16 x 11 x 1. Auditor's office.

263. RECEIPTS AND EXPENDITURES – INFIRMARY DIRECTORS GEAUGA COUNTY
1912-1934. 1 vol. (1).
Itemized and classified receipts and disbursements of the infirmary; disbursements, showing date of disbursements, name of fund, expenses, including docket number, salaries of infirmary employees, fuel, light, clothing, medicine, liquor, tobacco, livestock, grain and feed, vehicles, tools, repairs, furniture, and burials, and totals; receipts from farm produce and stock, from other counties, from inmates or friends, from other sources, showing date of receipt, from whom received, for what purpose, and total receipts and payment into treasury. Arranged chronologically by dates of disbursements or receipts. No index. Handwritten on printed forms. 139 pages. 17 x 15 x 1. Auditor's office.

264. ALLOWANCE FOR DEPUTIES AND CLERKS
1914—. 1 file drawer.
Record of salaries received by or due to the county officials for the fiscal year, showing name of office, date of report, name of deputy or clerk, and salaries of officers, assistance, deputies, and clerks. Arranged chronologically by dates of reports. No index. Handwritten on printed forms. 10 x 5 x 14. Auditor's office.

265. COUNTY ENGINEER PAYROLLS
1928—. 2 file drawers.
Copies of payrolls submitted for payment by the county engineer to the auditor, showing name of payee, date submitted, amount paid, and total amount payable.

Arranged chronologically by date submitted. No index. Typed on printed forms. 5 x 10 x 14. Auditor's office.

266. OFFICERS' PAYROLLS
1925—. 2 file drawers.

Monthly tabulation of pay rolls for elected county officers, showing name of officer, date of payroll, salary authorized, salary paid, total amount of all salaries paid, and signature of the auditor. Arranged chronologically by dates of payrolls. No index. Handwritten on printed forms. 5 x 10 x 15. Auditor's office.

Bills

267. INFIRMARY DOCKET
1904-1919. 1 vol. (1). 1920—, in Commissioners' Docket [Bills], entry 268.

Auditor's docket of bills filed by infirmary directors, showing date of filing, name of payee, specified purpose of bill, amount claimed, dates of filing and approval, amount approved, date of payment, warrant number, and remarks. Arranged chronologically by dates filed. No index. Handwritten on printed forms. 120 pages. 18 c 12.5 x 1. 3rd floor store room.

268. COMMISSIONERS' DOCKET [Bills].
4 vols. (2-5).

Auditor's docket of bills filed with commissioners, showing date of bill, consecutive number, name of creditor, specified services rendered or goods purchased, date of filing, date approved, amount approved, date of payment, warrant number, and remarks. Also contains Infirmary Docket, 1920—, entry 267. Arranged chronologically by dates bills filed. No index. Handwritten on printed forms. Average 162 pages. 18 x 13 x 1. 2 volumes, 1919-1932, 3rd floor store room; 2 volumes, 1933—, Auditor's office.

269. BILLS
1939—. 1 file drawer.

Invoices submitted to the auditor from the various county departments for payment, showing date and amount of bill, name of firm or payee, for what service, and date submitted to auditor. Arranged chronologically by dates of bills. No index. Handwritten on printed forms. 5 x 10 x 14. Auditor's office.

270. TELEPHONE AND GASOLINE BILLS

1934—. 1 file drawer.

Original bills for telephone service from various county departments as submitted to the auditor for payment, showing itemized list of each department and amount for each, date submitted, and total amount submitted; also includes original copies of bills for gasoline from the various county departments as submitted to the auditor for payment, showing itemized list of each department and amount for each, date submitted, and total amount submitted. Arranged chronologically by date submitted for payments. No index. Handwritten on printed forms. 4.5 x 10 x 14. Auditor's office.

271. RECEIPTS

1936—. 2 file drawers.

Receipts of bills submitted to the auditor for payment for various county departments, showing date of bill, amount, name of firm or payee, for payment of goods supplied or services rendered, and date of payment. Arranged chronologically by dates of payments. No index. Handwritten on printed forms. 5 x 10 x 14. Auditor's office.

Orders and Warrants

272. AUDITOR'S RECORD OF ORDERS ISSUED

1806-1904, 7 vols.

Record of orders issued, showing date of order, to whom drawn, purpose, warrant number, and amount; 1806-1884 also includes verification of examination of vouchers and warrants by county commissioners; 1831-1884, record of warrants issued, showing warrant number, to whom issued, what purpose, and total amount of disbursement; 1884-1904, debit and credit columns, showing infirmary, budget, county, miscellaneous, river and ditch, sheep, and teachers' institute funds. Arranged chronologically by dates of orders, and numerically thereunder by warrant numbers. No index. 1804-1864, handwritten. 1865-1904, handwritten on printed forms. 4 volumes average 200 pages. 13 x 8.5 x 1.5; 3 volumes average 175 pages. 18 x 12.5 x 2. 4 volumes, 1806-1884, basement store room; 3 volumes, 1884-1904, 3rd floor store room.

273. INFIRMARY ORDERS
1852-1886. 1 vol.

Record of orders drawn on the treasury by the infirmary, showing date of order, to whom drawn, purpose, warrant number, and amount; certificate of examination of infirmary warrant and voucher by commissioners, also includes orders drawn for military purposes (Ohio National Guard and others), 1864-1865; orders drawn for ditch purposes, 1884; institute orders, 1866-1877; township boundary orders, 1864-1868, and military relief orders, 1861-1866. Arranged chronologically by dates of orders. No index. Handwritten on printed forms. 200 pages. 14 x 9 x 1.5. Basement store room.

274. OFFICERS' PAY-IN CERTIFICATES
1917—. 1 file drawer.

Duplicate copies of pay-in orders issued by the auditor directing payment into the county treasury, showing consecutive order numbers, date of order, name of payee, amount, and for what service rendered, arranged numerically by ordered numbers. No index, Handwritten on printed forms. 5 x 10 x 14. Auditor's office.

275. AUDITOR'S JOURNAL OF WARRANTS ISSUED
1904—. 8 vols. (1-8).

Auditor's journal of warrants issued by the county treasury, showing date of issue, name of payee, purpose, warrant number, amount of warrant, treasurer's column (credit), and following debit columns, including general, county board of education, county board of health, county road and bridge, state road and bridge, dog kennel, auto license, and gas tax, undivided cigarette tax, inheritance, and miscellaneous funds; also includes disbursement of mothers' pensions, 1913-1936, and record of aid to dependent children payments, 1936—. Arranged chronologically by dates issued and numerically thereunder by warrant numbers. No index. Handwritten on printed forms. Average 250 pages. 19 x 17 x 1. 6 volumes, 1904-1934, 3rd floor store room; 2 volumes, 1934—, Auditor's office.

276. RECORD OF COURT WARRANTS ISSUED
1904—. 1 vol. (1).

Record of warrants issued for payment of court fees, showing date of warrant, amount, name of payee, warrant number, whether for petit or grand jurors, grand jury witnesses and original case witnesses, probate court jurors, and witnesses in criminal, lunacy, and epilepsy cases, minor court and coroner's witnesses, and amount of fees. Arranged chronologically by dates warrants issued and numerically thereunder by warrant numbers. No index. Handwritten on printed forms. 320 pages. 18 x 12 x 2. Auditor's office.

277. DUPLICATES OF WARRANTS ISSUED
1926—. 1 carton, 20 bundles, 1 vol.

Duplicate copies of warrants issued by auditor, showing warrant number, date of warrant, name of payee, amount of warrant, purpose of payment, fund to be charged, authority for issuance of warrant, and signature of auditor. Arranged chronologically by dates of warrants and numerically thereunder by warrant numbers. No index. Typed on printed forms. Approximately 10,000 warrants in carton, 18 x 24 x 36; average 300 pages in bundles, 17 x 12 x 2; volume 250 pages 17 x 11.5 x 1.5. 1 carton, 1926-1933, attic store room; 20 bundles, 1934-1936, 3rd floor store room; 1 volume, 1937—, Auditor's office.

278. WARRANTS REDEEMED
1831—. 21 file boxes, 1 carton, 61 file envelopes, 2000 loose warrants, 11 file drawers.

Warrants issued by auditor on treasurer and paid or redeemed by treasurer, showing warrant number, date of issue, name of payee, amount of warrant, purpose of payment, funds to be charged, authority for issuance of warrant, stamped paid by treasurer, and signed by auditor. No obvious arrangement. No index. 1831-1917, handwritten on printed forms; 1918—, typed on printed forms. File boxes 5 x 10.5 x 32; carton, 11 x 20 x 14; file envelopes, 9 x 4 x 2; warrants, 4 x 9; file drawers, 10.5 x 32; 21 file boxes, 1831-1936, basement store room; 1 carton, 1917-1923, attic store room; 61 file envelopes, 2000 loose warrants, 1919-1931, 3rd floor store room; 11 file drawers, 1936—, Auditor's office.

279. COURT WARRANT STUBS
1919—. 3 file drawers.

Auditors receipt stubs for court warrants issued on the county treasurer, showing warrant number, date and amount of warrant, name of fund, voucher authority, purpose, and name of payee. Arranged numerically by warrant numbers. No index. Typed on printed forms. 10 x 5 x 14. Auditor's office.

280. AUDITOR'S RECORD – CIGARETTE DEALERS' LICENSES
1931—. 1 vol.

Record of cigarette dealers' licenses, showing license number, name and address of dealer, location of business, date of issue, amount of license tax, and term of license. Arranged chronologically by dates issued. No index. Typed on printed forms. 100 pages. 12 x 14.5 x 1. Auditor's office.

281. BEVERAGE DEALERS' LICENSES
1938—. 1 vol.

Carbon copies of beverage dealers' licenses issued (wort and malt), showing date of issue, license number, name and address and licensee, place of business, date license effective, date of expiration, and amount of fee. Arranged chronologically by dates issued. No index. Typed on printed forms. 100 loose-leaf pages. 9 x 15 x 1. Auditor's office.

282. CIGARETTE LICENSE PAPERS [Applications for Peddler's License].
1926—. 2 file drawers.

Applications for peddler's licenses (only issued to ex-service men), showing date of application, name of applicant, term of license, statement of stock and trade, kind of transportation (auto, truck, wagon), record of military service, and oath of application. Arranged chronologically by dates of application. No index. Handwritten on printed forms. 5 x 10 x 15. Auditor's office.

283. [Applications and] VENDOR'S LICENSE
1935—. 2 vols.; 2 pads.

Carbon copies of applications for vendors' licenses, showing license number, name and address of owner, location of business, code number, and signature of applicant. Two pads of carbon copies of vendors' licenses, showing license number, date of issue, name and address of vendor, and auditor's signature. Arranged numerically by license number. No index. Handwritten on printed forms. 2 volumes average 700 loose-leaf pages. 8 x 11 x 4; 2 pads average 200 pages. 7 x 6 x 1. Auditor's office.

284. DOG APPLICATION [and Tag Number]

1929—. 116 application pads, 6 file drawers.

Original applications for dog licenses, showing application number, name and address of owner, description of dog, age, sex, color, hair, breed, fees paid, tag number, and certification by auditor. Also contains Record of Certificates of Transfer of Ownership, Dog, 1930—, entry 286. Arranged numerically by application numbers. No index. Handwritten on printed forms. Pads average 100 pages. 4 x 9 x .5; file drawers, 5 x 10 x 15. 116 pads, 1929-1933, 3rd floor store room; 5 file drawers, 1933—, Auditor's office.

285. DOG KENNEL REGISTER

1917—. 5 bundles; 1 vol. (1).

Record of dog licenses, showing application number, date of application, tag number, name of applicant, number of dogs kept or harbored, registration fees, penalty, address where dog is kept or harbored, duplicate tax fee (if duplicate issued); kennel register, showing application number, name of applicant, name and location of kennel, number of dogs kept, registration fee, registration number, and tag number assigned. Arranged alphabetically by names of owners and chronologically thereunder by dates of applications. Indexed numerically by tag numbers, showing under which letter of alphabet, page number, and line. Handwritten on printed forms. Bundles, 18 x 12 x 8; volume 375 pages. 18 x 13 x 2.5. 1 bundle, 1917-1932, basement store room; 4 bundles, 1 volume 1933—, Auditor's office.

286. RECORD OF CERTIFICATES OF TRANSFER OF OWNERSHIP, DOG

1927-1929. 1 vol. 1933— in Dog Application [and Tag Number]. entry 284.

Record of transfer of ownership of dogs, showing name and address of owner, name and address of purchaser, description of dog, age, sex, color, hair, breed, license number, and date of transfer of ownership. Arranged alphabetically by names of original owners. No index. Handwritten on printed forms. 125 pages. 8 x 12 x 1. 3rd floor store room.

287. APPLICATION OF OWNERS OF MOTOR VEHICLES FOR REGISTRATION

1926-1933. 6 cardboard boxes.

Auditor's duplicate applications for motor vehicle licenses, showing name and address of owner, fee, license number, description of motor vehicle, and date and witnessed oath of owner; also includes report to bureau of motor vehicle licenses sold and fees collected, transfer of ownership, and report to auditor of licenses sold outside of county to persons residing in county. No obvious arrangement. No index. Handwritten on printed forms. 10 x 21 x 15. 3 cardboard boxes, 1926-1928, Attic store room; 3 cardboard boxes, 1929-1933, basement store room.

288. INDEX TO MOTOR VEHICLE LICENSES

1930-1933. 1 cardboard box, 1 vol.

Index record of motor vehicle licenses issued by auditor, showing name and address of owner, and license number. Arranged alphabetically by names of owners. Handwritten on printed forms. Cardboard box, 16 x 15 x 2; volume 600 pages. 14 x 17.5 x 3.5. 1 cardboard box, 1930-1931, 3rd floor store room; 1 volume, 1931-1933, attic store room.

Enumerations and Statistics

289. SCHOOL ENUMERATION

1917—. 2 file drawers. 1838-1897 in Auditor's School Settlement Record, entry 251.

Annual enumeration returns to auditor by county schools, showing date of enumeration, number of youths in school, number of handicapped youths, and date of filing; also includes copies of certified statements of county auditor sent to auditor of state, showing name of township, number of youths in each school district, and totals, copies of auditor's report to juvenile court judge of name and address of guardians of crippled youths, age 1 to 21 years. Arranged chronologically by dates of enumeration and alphabetically thereunder by names of townships. No index. Handwritten and typed on printed forms. 10 x 5 x 15. Auditor's office.

290. ENUMERATION OF WHITE MALE INHABITANTS
1827. 1 vol. 1856-1883 in [Auditor's] Record of Transfers, entry 218.
Record of white male inhabitants over 21 years of age, showing name, address, age, and total number. No obvious arrangement. No index. Handwritten. 75 pages. 12 x 8 x 1. Basement storage room.

291. ANIMAL CLAIMS AND DOG STATISTICS
1920—. 1 file drawer.
Copies of auditor's annual reports to auditor of state on animal claims and dog statistics, showing date of report, number of animals killed or injured for which claims were paid, balance on hand in dog and kennel fund, total dog tax collected during year, amounts paid for animal claims, and number of dogs licenses issued. Arranged chronologically by dates reported. No index. Handwritten on printed forms. 10 x 5 x 15. Auditor's office.

292. ANNUAL REPORT OF AUDITOR TO THE STATE COMMISSIONER OF COMMON SCHOOLS
1858, 1866-1877. 1 vol.
Copies of auditor's annual reports to the state commission of common schools, showing date of report, name of each school district, receipts, expenditures, balances, number and value of school buildings and grounds, number, classification, and average salaries of teachers, enrollment and attendance of pupils, number of pupils in each branch of study, classification of schools as to private or public, classification of pupils as to nationality and race, general remarks of auditor, and his certification of report. Arranged chronologically by dates reported. No index. Handwritten on printed forms. 150 pages. 17.5 x 14 x .5. 3rd floor store room.

293. JURORS', CLERK OF COURTS' STATEMENTS
1935—. 1 file drawer.
Clerk of courts' report to the auditor of jurors in court cases, showing name and address, number of days served, mileage and per diem, court term, name of township, city ward number, and date subpoenaed; petit jury list, showing description of case and trail date. Arranged chronologically by court terms. No index. Handwritten on printed forms. 10 x 5 x 15. Auditor's office.

294. ANNUAL REPORT OF COUNTY OFFICIALS
1851-1889. 1 vol.
Auditor's copies of annual reports to county commissioners; county prosecuting attorney's report, showing date of report, number of criminal prosecutions, names of accused, number of fines assessed, recognizance forfeited, and amount collected; clerk of courts' report, showing date of report, number of fines assessed, amount assessed, amount collected, source of funds paid into the county treasury, and amount paid; sheriff's report of criminal cases, showing date of report, name of defendant, date and amount collected, and amount paid to clerk of courts; and treasurer's report, showing date of report, source of fees, and amount of each item; also includes auditor's receipts and disbursements, 1859-1870, and memorandum of deeds issued by auditor, 1865-1889. Arranged chronologically by dates reported. No index. Handwritten. 200 pages. 10 x 7.5 x 1. Basement store room.

295. SOLDIERS' RELIEF AND MOTHERS' PENSIONS
1916-1923, 1931—, 1 file drawer.
Probate judge's reports to auditor, 1918-1923, 1931-1936 on mothers' pensions, including orders continuing, discontinuing, extending, and creating allowance, showing date of report, name of recipient, and amount of aid granted recipient. Also contains [Reports of Soldiers' Relief Commission], 1916-1923, 1936—, entry 9. Arranged chronologically by dates reported. No index. Typed on printed forms. 10 x 5 x 15. Auditor's office.

296. COUNTY HOME REPORTS
1923—. 1 cardboard file envelope, 1 file drawer.
Copies of annual reports of county commissioners sitting as a board of directors of the county infirmary to the state department of welfare, showing date of report, number of inmates registered and discharged since last report, itemized amount of receipts and expenditures for period of report, detailed inventory of infirmary property, date filed, and signature of the chairman of the board of directors. Arranged chronologically by dates reported. No index. Handwritten on printed forms. File envelope, 9 x 4 x 2; file drawer, 10 x 5 x 15. 1 file envelope, 1923-1932, 3rd floor store room; 1 file drawer, 1933—, Auditor's office.

Bonds

297. RECORD OF OFFICIAL BONDS
1873—. 1 vol.

Auditor's record of bonds of elected county officials, showing date of bond, name of official, names of sureties, condition of bond, amount of bond, certification of office by probate judge, prosecuting attorney, commissioners, and notary public. Also contains [Tax] Officer's Bonds, 1873-1914, entry 310. Arranged chronologically by dates of bonds. Indexed alphabetically by names of officials, Handwritten. 375 pages. 14 x 9.5 x 2. Auditor's office.

298. BONDS AND DEPOSITORIES OF SCHOOL CLERKS AND TREASURERS
1923—. 1 file drawer.

Certified copies of bonds of school clerks and treasurers, showing name of clerk or treasurer, name of school district, date and amount of bond, signatures of principal, president, and clerk of county board of education, names of sureties, and condition of bond; also includes orders from school treasurer to county auditor to pay school funds to authorized school depositories, 1928—, showing name of depository and date of filing. Bonds arranged chronologically by dates of bonds; orders arranged chronologically by dates filed. No index. Handwritten and typed, some on printed forms. 10 x 5 x 15. Auditor's office.

299. [Tax] OFFICER'S BOND
1915—. 1 vol.; 1 file drawer. Title varies: Bonds of Tax Officers, 1915-1923, 1 vol., 1873-1914 in Record of Official Bonds, entry 308.

Original bonds, 1920—, and copies of surety bonds, 1915-1920, given by assessors, showing name of township, principal, and sureties, certified by state attorney general and county prosecuting attorney, copy of assessor's oath of office witnessed by notary public or justice of peace, and county auditor. Arranged alphabetically by names of townships. No index. Handwritten on printed forms. File drawer, 10 x 5 x 15; volume 61 pages. 16 x 11.5 x 1. 1 volume, 1915-1923, 3rd floor store room; 1 file drawer, 1923—, Auditor's office.

300. RECORD OF BONDS – COUNTY COMMISSIONERS
1910—. 2 vols. (1, 2).

Record of bonds issued by resolution of board of county commissioners, showing amount of total issue, interest rate, accrued interest, date of redemption, purpose of issue, number of bond, date of issue, date due, canceled or renewed, date each coupon due, and remarks. Arranged chronologically by dates bonds issued. Indexed numerically by number of bonds, showing volume and page numbers. Handwritten on printed forms. 100 pages. 15 x 13 x 1. Auditor's office.

301. BONDS AND COUPONS [Debenture]
1935—. 2 file drawers.

Duplicate copies of debenture bonds with interest bearing coupons attached, showing date of bond, purpose and amount of bond, bond number, interest rate, date of maturity, and maturity of interest and installments thereof; all bonds are stamped with the words, "Recorded in the office of the sinking fund trustees," and signed by the secretary, before they become valid in the hands of any purchaser. Arranged chronologically by dates of bonds. No index. Typed on printed forms. 10 x 5 x 15. Auditor's office.

302. SCHOOL AND VILLAGE BOND RESOLUTIONS
1912—. 1 file drawer.

Resolutions to issue bonds after submission to the electors by the board of education in the various school districts for the creation of new schools and improving and enlarging school buildings, showing name of school and district, amount of bond, total amount, interest, date of issue, and date and maturity. Arranged chronologically by dates issued. No index. Handwritten on printed forms. 10 x 5 x 15. Auditor's office.

Weights and Measures

303. WEIGHTS AND MEASURES
1926—. 1 file drawer, 2 vols. Title varies: Sealer Record, 1926-1932. 2 vols.

Record of sealer of weights and measures, showing date of report, certificate number, date of certificate, name and address of company or person, name of article tested, condemned, adjusted, sealed or not sealed, sealing fees, adjusting cost, unpaid fees, and remarks. Arranged chronologically by dates reported. No index.

Handwritten on printed forms. File drawer, 10 x 5 x 15; volumes average 100 pages. 12 x 9 x .5. 2 volumes, 1926-1932, 3rd floor store room; 1 file drawer, 1933—, Auditor's office.

304. SEALER'S RECORD
1924—. 1 folder, 1 file drawer. Title varies: Weights and Measures, 1924-1931, 1 folder.

Annual reports of sealer of weights and measures to auditor of tests made, showing date of report, fees collected, weights and measures sealed, condemned, or adjusted. One folder, 1924-1931, also includes miscellaneous correspondence pertaining to weights and measures. Arranged chronologically by dates reported. No index. Handwritten on printed forms. Folder, 12 x 9 x .5; file drawer, 10 x 5 x 15. 1 folder, 1924-1931, 3rd floor store room; 1 file drawer, 1932—, Auditor's office.

Miscellaneous

305. MONTHLY FINANCIAL STATEMENTS
1927—. 177 sheets.

Auditor's monthly and annual financial statements to county commissioners, showing name and financial condition of all county funds, receipts, disbursements, balance, overdrafts, totals, and signatures of commissioners on approval of statements. Arranged alphabetically by names of funds. No index. Typed on printed forms. 10 x 18. 83 sheets. 1927-1930, basement store room, 94 sheets, 1930—, Auditor's office.

306. FINANCIAL REPORT
1905-1918, 1931—. 21 booklets, 1 sheet.

Copies of auditor's financial statements to state auditor of receipts and disbursements, showing name of fund, itemized statement of receipts and expenditures, and balance on hand. Arranged alphabetically by names of funds. No index. Handwritten and typed on printed forms. Booklets average 50 pages. 12 x 8 x .25; sheets, 12 x 8. 13 booklets, 1905-1918, basement store room; 1 rolled sheet, 1915, attic store room; 8 booklets, 1931—, Auditor's office.

307. REPORTS OF SCHOOL BOARDS
    1915-1934. 1 file drawer.
Annual financial reports by clerks of village and district schools to county auditor, showing date of report and all receipts and expenditures; receipts, showing itemized revenue from taxes, interest and other sources, money received from other districts, balance on hand, and grand total; expenditures, showing itemized expenditures for educational administration, business administration, general control, teachers' salaries, other instruction expenses, operation and maintenance of school plant, transportation cost of pupils, fixed charges, cost a new equipment and buildings, interest and payments on outstanding bonds, summary of expenses, total amount of unpaid bills, tax rate for school purposes, and signatures of school clerks, 1915-1928. Also contains County Board of Education [Statement of Fees Received – Teachers' Examinations], 1911, 1918-1934, entry 297. Arranged chronologically by dates reported. No index. Handwritten on printed forms. 10 x 5 x 15. Auditor's office.

308. AUDITOR'S ANNUAL FINANCIAL REPORT OF SCHOOLS
    1920, 1925-1927, 4 folders.
Copies of auditor's annual financial reports to auditor of state on condition of school funds in county, showing name of school district, all receipts, expenditures, bonded indebtedness of schools, and balance on hand with township or school treasurer. Arranged alphabetically by school districts. No index. Handwritten on printed forms. 15 pages 22 x 17 x .5. 3rd floor store room.

309. [REPORT OF SCHOOL BONDED DEBT]
    1917-1921, 1933—. 1 bundle, 2 file folders, 2 file boxes.
Annual reports of school district and municipal schools to auditor of their bonded indebtedness, showing date of report, total issue of bonds outstanding, bonds redeemed, date of maturity, interest, and total amount, and signature of clerk of board of education of each school district or municipality; also includes copy of abstracts of indebtedness sent by county auditor to auditor of state, showing detailed indebtedness of the county, township, and villages schools, amounts of bonds outstanding at beginning of period covered by report and bonds redeemed, balance of outstanding bonds, rate of interest, dates of maturity, totals of bonded indebtedness, and balance in sinking fund to meet debt. Arranged chronologically by dates reported. No index. 1917-1921, handwritten on printed forms; 1923—, handwritten and typed, some on printed forms. Bundles, 14 x 8 x 2.25; folders, 14

x 8 x 1; file boxes, 10 x 5 x 15. 1 bundle, 1917-1921, attic store room, 2 file folders, 1932-1934, 3rd floor store room; 2 file boxes, 1923-1932, 1935, Auditor's office.

310. COUNTY BOARD OF EDUCATION [Statements of Fees Received – Teachers' Examination]
1932-1935. 1 file drawer. 1911, 1918-1934, in Reports of School Boards, entry 307.

Statements of superintendent of schools to auditor of fees received for teachers' examinations, showing date of statement, number of applicants for examination, date and place of examination, amount of fees received, names of examiners, and signature of county superintendent. Arranged chronologically by dates of statements. No index. Handwritten and typed on printed forms. 10 x 5 x 15. Auditor's office.

311. STATEMENTS OF ESTATES FROM PROBATE COURT
1935—. 1 file drawer.

Certification list from the probate judge to the auditor regarding estates subject to inheritance tax assessments, showing name of decedent, name of heirs, devisees or legatees, name of administrator, executor, or trustee, kind of inheritance, value of estate, legal exemptions, net value for taxation, value and tax assessed on each share from estate, name of taxing district, date of accrued tax, estimated value, inventory value, and value as fixed by court, date certificate issued to the county auditor, amount of cost imposed, amount of tax due, total legal exemptions, and date tax paid. Arranged chronologically by dates of certificates. No index. Handwritten on printed forms. 10 x 5 x 15. Auditor's office.

312. STATEMENT OF FINES IN JUSTICES' COURTS
1904—. 1 file drawer.

Annual reports by justices of peace to the county auditor, 1930—, showing date of report, name of township, name of justice, itemized account of fines and fees assessed in criminal and civil cases, date filed; also reports of prosecuting attorney, showing number of cases prosecuted, amounts of fines and cost assessed, date of report, description of case, total number of cases prosecuted in each court, number of cases against property, total amounts of cost and fines assessed, and amounts allowed for aid in prosecuting state cases. Arranged chronologically by dates reported. No index. Handwritten and typed, some on printed forms. 10 x 5 x 14. Auditor's office.

313. WORKMEN'S COMPENSATION REPORTS
1926—. 1 file drawer.
Auditor's report of workmen's compensation cases filed, showing date of report, name and address of employee, sex, race, age, length of service with present employer, name and address of employer, kind of enterprise, amount of time last due to injury, report of doctor's findings, percent of total disability, previous disabilities, sworn statements of witnesses to the accident, hospitalization, and doctor's fees. Arranged alphabetically by names of employees and chronologically thereunder by dates reported. No index. Handwritten on printed forms. 10 x 5 x 14. Auditor's office.

314. DEPOSITORIES' STATEMENTS
1935—. 1 file drawer.
Depositories' monthly statements to the county auditor, showing date of deposit, name of bank, interest credited for past month, balance now on deposit to the credit of the county, amount on hand, amounts of deposits and withdrawals, and daily balance. Arranged chronologically by dates deposited. No index. Handwritten on printed forms. 10 x 5 x 15. Auditor's office.

315. PAY-IN RECEIPTS
1920-1930. 1 file drawer.
Reports of treasurer's receipts of pay-in orders to the auditor, showing date of report, total receipts and disbursements, general warrants, court warrants, receipts, deposits, drafts, balance in depository, and total balance in treasury and depositories. Arranged chronologically by dates reported. No index. 10 x 5 x 14. Auditor's office.

316. [Certificates of Election of] TOWNSHIP AND VILLAGE OFFICERS
1927—. 1 file drawer.
Certificates of election of township and village officers, showing date of certificate, name and address of officer, name of office, dates of beginning of and expiration of term of office, and date of filing; township records, including certificates of election for justices of the peace, trustees, treasurers, assessors, and constables, council members, treasurers and marshals. Arranged chronologically by dates of certificates. No index. Handwritten on printed forms. 10 x 5 x 15. Auditor's office.

317. CERTIFICATE OF WILLS FROM PROBATE JUDGE
1933—. 1 file drawer.

Copies of wills probated in probate court, showing name of testator and witnesses, date of will, date filed for probate, and copy of journal entry approving probation of will, date filed for probate, and copy of journal entry approving probation of will. Arranged chronologically by dates filed. No index. Handwritten on printed forms. 10 x 5 x 14. Auditor's office.

318. BILLS OF SALE, INSURANCE POLICIES AND DEEDS
1938—. 1 file drawer.

Copies of bills of sale for county property filed with the auditor by the commissioners, showing date of instrument, names of grantor and grantee, amount of sale, itemized list of property sold, copy of notarization, date filed for record, date recorded, and recorder's instrument number; also record of insurance carried by the county commissioners on county structures, including courthouse, children's home and infirmary buildings, fairground buildings, bridges, and motor equipment, showing name of insurance company, policy number, date and amount insured, on what issued, amount of premium, date of expiration of policy, description of property, and name of agent writing policy; Also copies of deeds for newly acquired county property, showing name of owner, township or town, description of property, value, date purchased, purchase price, cost of sale (if any), name of county, date of deed, and signature of county auditor. Arranged chronologically by dates of instruments. No index. Handwritten on printed forms. 10 x 5 x 14. Auditor's office.

319. BLIND RELIEF CERTIFICATE AND LIQUOR TRAFFIC PAPERS
1904-1936. 1 file drawer.

Case records of blind relief applications submitted by county commissioners to the county auditor, showing action taken, grants, rejections, denials, withdrawals, and changes of status as to revisions and terminations; examining physician's report on the condition of applicants eyes, showing application number, date of approval or rejection, name and address of applicant, amount awarded, and amount of payment of award, duplicate copies of liquor traffic paper, showing year, name of licensee, location of business, amount delinquent, date commencing business, amount assessed, and date payment made. Arranged chronologically by years and alphabetically thereunder by names of applicants. No index. Handwritten on printed forms. 10 x 5 x 14. Auditor's office.

320. [STATEMENT OF DISTRIBUTION OF MOTOR VEHICLE LICENSE TAXES]

1933—. 1 vol.

Auditor's statement of distribution of motor vehicle license taxes to townships, showing name of township, valuation of motor vehicles in township outside of and including municipalities, name of funds entitled to participate in distribution, distributable share for each fund, and amount distributed, and total. Arranged alphabetically by names of townships. No index. Handwritten on printed forms. 50 pages. 11.5 x 18 x 1. Auditor's office.

321. MOTOR VEHICLE TAX STATEMENTS

1935—. 1 file folder.

Motor vehicle tax statement to county auditor, showing date of statement, name of registration district, total fees received in each district, percentage of fees distributed to state equalization fund, registration district, and amount due county. Arranged chronologically by dates of statements. No index. 14 x 9 x 2. Auditor's office.

The office county treasurer was established by an act of the Northwest Territory in 1792 and continued by the State of Ohio.[1] Although the constitution of 1802 made no provision for the office of county treasurer, it was created by the legislative act of 1803.[2] The treasurer, appointed by the associate judges in 1803 and by the county commissioners in 1804, was required to take an oath and give bond for the faithful performance of the duties of his office, and was subject to removal by the appointing power.[3] The treasurer remained an appointive official until 1827 when the office became an elective one by popular vote in the county.[4] Although it did not specifically create the office, the constitution of 1851 stated that no person shall hold office of treasurer for more than four years in any six. This provision was repealed in 1933 by an amendment authorizing any county to adopt a charter form of government.[5] Interpreting the constitutional provision, the legislature fixed the term of office at two years in 1859.[6] The term of office continued at two years until 1936 when it was extended to four years.[7] The remuneration of the office was by fees until 1875, and from 1875 to 1906 by a definite salary based on population plus a percentage of the fees collected. Since 1906 the treasurer's compensation has been derived entirely from a salary determined on a population basis.[8]

The duties of the treasurer were defined by statute in the earlier period and specified in detail by the acts of 1827 and 1831 repealing previous acts. The provision of the latter act, although subject to amendment and repeal, furnished the bases for subsequent legislation and laid the foundation for the present duties of the treasurer, which do not differ greatly from those prescribed by the earlier statutes.

In 1803 the treasurer was given his present duty by giving public notice of the tax duplicate. On receiving from the county auditor a duplicate of the taxes assessed upon the property of the county, the treasurer prepares and posts notices in three places in each township including the place in which the elections are held;

---

1. Pease, *op. cit.,* 68-69.
2. *Laws of Ohio,* I, 97.
3. *Ibid.,* I, 97-98; II, 154.
4. *Ibid.,* XXV, 25-32.
5. *Ohio Const. 1851,* Art. X, sec. 3 (Amendment, 1933).
6. *Laws of Ohio,* LVI, 105.
7. *Ibid.,* CXVI, pt. ii, 184.
8. *Ibid.,* III, 49-51; LII, 86; XCVIII, 89.

and inserts the notice for six consecutive weeks in the newspaper having the greatest circulation in the county.[9] He receives money in payment of taxes levied for the county, for the state, and for other purposes, and gives the payer a receipt.[10] In the earlier years of the office the treasurer was required to give announcement of the time he would be in the respective townships of the county and in his office at the seat of justice to receive tax collections. Since 1858 that treasurer has been authorized to prescribe the time for semiannual payment of taxes or assessments levied upon real estate or upon delinquent real estate taxes or assignments.[11] Moreover, since 1908, the commissioners have been authorized to extend the time for paying taxes to not more than 30 days after the time fixed by law.[12]

After each semiannual collection of taxes, the treasurer is required to report to the auditor showing the amount of taxes received in each taxing district in the county since the last settlement. Since 1904 the semiannual settlements have been made under the heads of liquor, cigarette, inheritance, delinquent, personal, road, and general taxes. The treasurer keeps his accounts in books which enable him to compile such reports.[13]

After the taxes are collected and immediately after each settlement with the county auditor, the county treasurer, upon the presentation of the proper warrant from the auditor, pays to the township treasurer, city or village treasurer, the treasurer of the school district, or treasurer of any "legally constituted board authorized by law to receive the funds or proceeds of any special tax levy," or other officers delegated with the authority to receive such funds, all money in the treasury belonging to such boards and subdivisions.[14] In addition, after the treasurer has made each settlement with the county auditor, he is required to pay to the state treasurer, on warrant from the state auditor, "the full amount of all sums" found by the latter to belong to the state.[15]

---

9. *Ibid.,* I, 98; XXIX, 291; LII, 124.
10. G. C. sec. 2650; *Laws of Ohio,* XXIX, 292; LXXVI, 70; LXXXV, 327.
11. *Laws of Ohio,* LV, 62; LVI, 101.
12. *Laws of Ohio,* XCIX, 435; CXIV, 730; CXV, pt. ii, 226.
13. G. C. sec. 2643; *Laws of Ohio,* XXIX, 296; XCVII, 458.
14. G. C. sec. 2689; *Laws of Ohio,* LVI, 101.
15. *Laws of Ohio,* LVI, 101; CXIV, 732.

Another function of the county treasurer, which had its inception in the earlier years of the office, is the collection of delinquent taxes. It was and is his duty to assess a penalty on a tax duplicate of non-payment of taxes – which penalty when collected, is paid to the treasurer's fund. If the treasurer is unable to collect the delinquent taxes, he is authorized to apply to the clerk of court of common pleas who serves notice to show cause why such taxes were not paid. The court may enter a rule against the delinquent taxpayer for the payment and costs and enforce it by attachment.[16]

During the last decade provision has been made for the installment payment of delinquent taxes without interest or penalty. In 1931 it was provided that delinquent taxes, assessments, and penalties charged on the tax duplicate against any entry of real estate might be paid in installments during five consecutive semiannual taxpaying periods, "whether such real estate had been certified as delinquent or not."[17] The Whittemore Act, passed as an emergency measure in 1933, provided for the collection in installments, without interest or penalty, of delinquent real estate assessments. Anyone electing to pay such delinquent real property taxes and assessments in installments pursuant to this act may, at any installment period, pay the entire unpaid balance, in which event no interest shall be charged or collected on the amount so paid. In 1934 the benefits of the act were extended to include delinquent personal and classified taxes.[18] With slight alterations the law was re-enacted in 1935 and again in 1936.[19] An act was passed in February 1937 and re-enacted in February 1938[20] providing for the settlement of taxes delinquent prior to 1936 without interest or penalty in one payment or in ten annual installments.

The county treasurer has charge of the funds collected by taxes, and also other funds belonging to the county. Although earlier acts made provisions for storage vaults in the county treasury for county deposits, the commissioners have been authorized, since 1894, to receive sealed bids for the deposits of county funds;

---

16. G. C. sec. 2660; *Laws of Ohio,* LVI, 175; XCIX, 435.
17. G. C. sec. 2672, *Laws of Ohio,* CXIV, 827.
18. *Laws of Ohio,* CXV, 161-164; CXV, pt. ii, 230, 332.
19. *Ibid.,* CXVI, 199, 468; CXVI, pt. ii, 14-21.
20. *Ibid.,* CXVII, 32, 832.

and the banks or trust companies offering the highest rate of interest are selected as the county depositories.[21]

The treasurer is required to keep an account current with the county auditor – a practice which originated in 1831. Each day the treasurer makes a statement to the county auditor for the previous day's business, showing the amount of taxes received on auditor's drafts, the amount received from other sources, together with the amount of money deposited in the depository the total amount paid out by check and by cash, and the balance in the treasury.[22]

The treasurer as well as the sheriff, prosecuting attorney, and the clerk of courts have been required since 1850 to report annually to the county commissioners.[23] In 1878 the county auditor and county commissioners were required to make a thorough examination of all books, vouchers, accounts, moneys, bonds, securities, and other property in the treasury at least every six months.[24] This act was repealed by implication by an act of 1902 which placed the treasurer under the supervision of the state auditor. This act provided for a uniform system of accounting and auditing for all public offices in the state under the direction of a bureau of inspection in the office of the state auditor, and for the annual examination of the finances of all public offices.[25]

The treasurer is a member of the budget commission and the county board of revision, and serves as a trustee of the sinking fund.[26] Since the early days of the office the treasurer has been the official custodian of the bonds furnished to the state by the county auditor, county commissioners, and other officials. Since 1869 he has been required to record and preserve a record of the deputies appointed and removed by the county auditor.[27]

---

21. *Ibid.,* XCI, 403; CII, 59; CXV, pt. ii, 215.
22. G. C. sec. 2642; *Laws of Ohio,* XCVII, 457.
23. G. C. sec. 2504.
24. G. C. sec. 2699; R. S. sec. 1129; *Laws of Ohio,* LXXI, 137.
25. G. C. sec. 2641; *Laws of Ohio,* CXIV, 728; XCV, 511-515.
26. G. C. sec. 5625-19, 2976-18, 5580. *See also* pp. 196 / 198.
27. G. C. sec. 2563; *Laws of Ohio,* LXVI, 35.

Like other county officials, the treasurer is required at the expiration of his term to turn over to his successor all books, papers, moneys, and records appertaining to his office.[28]

In Geauga County, there are four on the treasurer's staff, one a deputy treasurer. The treasurer's salary is $125 monthly[29] and his official bond is fixed at $25,000.[30] Taxes are paid only at the courthouse office. Taxes in Geauga County are paid semiannually. The Geauga County treasurer uses four depositories for public funds. They are the Central National Bank, Chardon Ohio, the Chardon Savings Bank, the Middlefield Banking Company, and The First National Bank, Burton, Ohio.[31]

---

28. G. C. sec. 2639.
29. Commissioners' Journal, General XI [1936-1941], 423, entry 1.
30. Treasurer's Record of Bonds of Officials, 1940, entry 352.
31. Commissioners' Journal, General XI [1936-1941], entry 1.

Taxes

Real property (see also entry 331).

322. TREASURER'S DUPLICATE
1826-1828, 1830, 1832—. 165 vols. (dated). Title varies: Duplicate, 1826-1851, 25 vols.; Tax Duplicate, 1852-1861, 15 vols.; Treasurer's Tax Duplicate, 1877-1913, 1917-1923, 59 vols.; Treasurer's Tax List, 1914-1916, 6 vols.

Treasurer's duplicate of tax assessments on real estate, showing name of owner, range, township, tract, section and lot numbers, description of lands and buildings, value as equalized by board of revision (equalization), value as equalized by tax commission and board of complaints, itemized taxes, penalties, delinquencies of former years, date paid or returned delinquent, and certified delinquent or date undertaking filed; also includes record of taxes assessed on personal property, 1826-1828, 1830, 1832-1931. 1826-1828, 1830, 1832-1878, arranged numerically by township numbers and alphabetically thereunder by names of owners; 1879—, arranged alphabetically by names of township and alphabetically thereunder by names of owners. 1826-1828, 1839-1849, 1854-1901, 1903—, no index; 1828, 1830, 1832-1838, 1850-1853, indexed numerically by township numbers showing names of townships and page numbers; 1902, indexed alphabetically by names of townships. 1826-1828, 1830, 1832-1859, handwritten; 1860-1913 handwritten on printed forms; 1914—, typed on printed forms. One volume, 1936, is in poor condition. Average 250 pages. 17 x 12 x 2.5. 25 volumes 1826-1828, 1830, 1832-1834, -1837, 1839-1853, 1858-1859, Auditor's office; 13 volumes, 1835-1836, 1838, 1854-1857, 1860-1861, 1866, attic store room; 94 volumes, 1861-1927, basement store room; 12 volumes, 1928-1931, 3rd floor store room; 21 volumes, 1932—, Treasurer's office vault.

323. RECORD OF TAX COLLECTIONS [Form 7]
1904-1929, 1932—. 31 vols.

Treasurer's record of tax collections, real and personal, showing names of taxing district, and taxpayer, date of collection, receipt number, dog, road, delinquent personal, special assessments, and all taxes, and total paid. 1937— 11 volumes, Form 7, omits dog tax as separate item; also shows real estate and public utility taxes, delinquent personal and classified property taxes, and total taxes collected. Arranged alphabetically by names of taxing districts and chronologically thereunder by dates of collections. No index. Handwritten on printed forms. 20 volumes average 400 pages 18 x 12 x 2.5; 10 volumes average 400 pages 14.5 x 13 x 2; 1 volume 800 pages 14.5 x 13 x 4.5. 20 volumes, 1904-1926, basement store room; 5 volumes, 1927-1933, 3rd floor store room; 6 volumes, 1934—, Treasurer's office vault.

324. SPECIAL ASSESSMENTS
1923—. 20 vols. (dated). Title varies: Treasurer's Duplicate – Special Assessments, 1923-1931, 8 vols.

Duplicate of special assessments on real estate, showing names of owner and taxing district, purpose of assessment, description of property owned, total assessments and delinquencies of former years, itemized assessments, unpaid taxes, total due, and date paid; also includes summary of page totals following the last entry of each taxing district. Arranged alphabetically by names of taxing districts and alphabetically thereunder by names of property owners. No index. Handwritten on printed forms. Average 600 pages. 12 x 15 x 3. 5 volumes, 1923-1927, basement store room; 4 volumes, 1928-1932, 3rd floor store room; 9 volumes, 1932-1936, Treasurer's office; 2 volumes, 1937—, Auditor's office.

Personal property (See also entries 322, 323)

325. TREASURER'S GENERAL TAX DUPLICATE
1932—. 2 vols. Initiated in 1932.

Treasurer's duplicate taxes assessed on tangible personal property, showing name and address of taxpayer, taxing district, assessment certificate number, amount of assessment, total tax, unpaid taxes, total due, date paid, and remarks. Arranged alphabetically by names of taxpayers. No index. Average 500 pages. 18.5 x 17 x 2.25. Treasurer's office vault.

326. TREASURER'S CLASSIFIED DUPLICATE
1932—. 1 vol. Initiated in 1932.

Duplicate of taxes assessed on intangible personal property, showing name and address of owner, income yield or assessed value, amount of tax and tax rates on productive and unproductive investments, deposits, credits, moneys, other taxable intangibles, total tax, advanced payment, date paid, unpaid tax, refunds and remarks. Arranged alphabetically by names of owners. No index. 300 pages. 16 x 18.5 x 1.5. Treasurer's office vault.

327. [Real and Personal Property Tax Receipt] STUBS
1924-1933, 1936—. 10 cardboard boxes, 1 file box, 49 folders, 170 bundles.

Treasurer's copies of individual personal property tax receipts, showing name and address of taxpayer, name of taxing district, valuation of property, amount of tax, amount and date of payment, balance due, and stamp of treasurer; real property individual receipt stubs for payment of real property taxes, showing name of owner, lot numbers, amount paid for each lot, total paid, stamped paid by treasurer, and date paid. 1924-1933, 1936, no obvious arrangement; 1937—, arranged alphabetically by names of taxing districts and alphabetically thereunder by names of owners. No index. Handwritten and typed, some on printed forms. Cardboard boxes, 14 x 22 x 16; file box 10 x 4.5 x 14; folders, 9 x 4 x .5; bundles, 4 x 5 x 2. 10 cardboard boxes, 1924-1931, 1933-1936, basement store room; 1 file box, 49 folders, 1932, 3rd floor store room; 170 bundles, 1937—, Treasurer's office.

328. RECORD OF TAX COLLECTION [Form 7 – Personal]
1938—. 1 vol. Initiated in 1938.
Personal property tax, tangible and intangible, showing name of taxing district, date
of collection, name of taxpayer, receipt number, delinquent tangible taxes, special
assessments, delinquent personal, classified property taxes, tangible property taxes,
and total collected. Arranged alphabetically by names of taxing districts and
chronologically thereunder by dates of collections. No index. Handwritten on
printed forms. 175 pages. 14.5 x 13 x 1. Treasurer's office vault.

Delinquent (See also entry 357)

329. ACCOUNT OF ARREARAGE TAXES PAID INTO TREASURY
1820-1824. 1 vol.
Record of delinquent taxes paid into county treasury, showing date of payment,
name of person paying arrearage taxes, amount of state tax, road tax, and total tax
paid; also includes notations that copy of taxes paid for each year is sent to state
auditor. Arranged chronologically by dates of payments. No index. Handwritten. 50
pages. 7.5 x 5.25 x .5. Basement store room.

330. TREASURER'S QUADRENNIAL [and Triennial] CERTIFICATES
[of Unredeemed Delinquent Land]
1923—. 2 vols.
Certified copies of quadrennial certificates 1923-1930 and triennial certificates
1931—, of unredeemed tracts of land, city or town lots, showing date of certificate,
name of owner, description of property, amount of taxes, penalties, interest, total
due, and signature of auditor; also includes notations as to paid or sold for taxes,
showing dates paid or sold, and amounts. Arranged chronologically by dates and
certificates. No index. Typed on printed forms. Average 900 pages. 18 x 14.5 x 4.
Treasurer's office.

331. UNDERTAKINGS
1933—. 2 vols. (one unlabeled; 2).
Records of undertakings under Wittemore Law to pay delinquent taxes by
installments, showing name of taxing district, name of taxpayer, date filed, number
of undertaking, and agreement to pay taxes; record of delinquent taxes, showing
date and amount; record of payments of undertakings, showing amount and date
paid. Arranged chronologically by dates filed. Indexd numerically by numbers of

undertakings, showing names of taxing districts and names of taxpayers. Typed on printed forms. Average 500 pages. 19.5 x 16 x 3. Treasurer's office vault.

332. PERSONAL PROPERTY DELINQUENCIES – TREASURERS
1926-1931 1 vol.

Treasurer's list of delinquent personal property taxes, showing name and address of owner, name of taxing district, valuation of property, unpaid taxes, penalties, amount collected, dates paid, and remarks. Arranged alphabetically by names of taxing districts and alphabetically thereunder by names of taxpayers. No index. Typed on printed forms. 250 pages. 14 x 18 x 1.5. 3rd floor store room.

333. CUMULATIVE DELINQUENT DUPLICATES
1932—. 1 vol. Initiated in 1932.

Cumulative duplicate of delinquent tangible and intangible personal property taxes, showing name and address of taxpayer, year tax entered, page number of duplicate, amounts of tax and penalty, total amount due, and dates paid. One-half of volume contains tangible personal property and other half contains intangible. Arranged alphabetically by names of taxpayers. No index. Typed on printed forms. 750 pages. 9.5 x 12.5 x 4. Treasurer's office.

Inheritance (See also entries 341, 342, 344, 346, 348)

334. INHERITANCE TAX CHARGES
1919—. 1 vol. Initiated in 1919.

Duplicate of inheritance tax charges, showing case number, form number, date of case, name of decedent, name and address of person by whom tax is payable (administrators, heirs), date of accrual of tax, amount fixed by court, discount or interest, amount and date paid, and name of township or village. Arranged alphabetically by names of decedents. No index. Typed on printed forms. 600 pages. 11.5 x 12 x 3. Treasurer's office.

Excise (See also entry 357)

335. ASSESSMENT DUPLICATE – TRAFFIC IN INTOXICATING LIQUORS [and Cigarettes]
1902-1908, 1913-1929. 1 vol.

Duplicate of assessment on intoxicating liquors, 1902-1908, 1913-1919, showing name of trafficker, location of business, name of owner of premises, date of assessment, total and itemized assessments, and remarks; also includes duplicate of assessments on traffic in cigarette and cigarette papers, 1917-1929, and 11 loose receipts for cigarette tax payment 1928-1929. Arranged chronologically by dates of assessments. No index. Handwritten on printed forms. 40 pages. 17 x 14 x 1. Treasurer's office.

For other assessment records, see entry 357.

336. INVENTORY AND SALES RECORD – SALES TAX RECEIPTS
1935—. 2 vols., 1 bundle.

Treasurer's daily record of receipts and daily inventory of sales tax stamps, showing date of receipt, amount received from state treasurer, inventory, sales and balance on hand, name and license number of purchaser, amount and kind of stamp purchased, total value, discount, and amount collected. Arranged chronologically by dates of receipts. No index. Handwritten on printed forms. Volumes average 300 pages. 15 x 18 x 1.25; bundle, 14 x 17 x 1.5. Treasurer's office.

337. RECORD OF CIGARETTE TAX STAMPS RECEIVED AND SOLD [also Cosmetic and Beer Tax Stamps]
1931-1935. 1 vol.

Record of sales and receipts of tax stamps for cigarettes, beer, 1933-1935, and cosmetics, 1933, showing date of sale, to whom sold, from whom received, address, receipt number, quantity, and amount of sale. Debit columns for treasurer and credit columns for sales of various denominations, including ones, twos, five, and totals. Arranged under subjects headings and chronologically thereunder by dates of sales. No index. Handwritten on printed forms. 200 pages. 12 x 14 x 1. Treasurer's office vault.

338. CIGARETTE ASSESSMENT RECEIPT [Stubs]
1928-1931. 4 vols.

Stubs of cigarette assessment receipts, showing amount of tax paid, to whom license issued, address, receipt number, showing amount of tax paid, to whom license issued, address, receipt number, description of store or other premises, and date of receipt. Arranged numerically by receipt numbers. No index. Handwritten on printed forms. Average 50 pages. 4 x 16 x .5. Treasurer's office.

339. DOW TAX RECEIPTS
1883-1919. 3 vols. (two unlabeled; one dated).

Stubs of liquor assessment receipts, showing receipt number, date of receipt, amount of tax paid, to whom license issued, and name and address of owner of premises. Arranged numerically by receipt numbers. No index. Handwritten on printed forms. Average 50 pages. 10 x 8 x .5. Treasurer's office.

340. REPORT TO TAX COMMISSION OF VENDOR'S LICENSE
1934——. 4 vols.

Copies of weekly reports treasurer to the state tax commission and treasurer of state, of vendor's licenses issued, showing date of report, name and address of vendor, and code and license numbers. Arranged chronologically by dates of reports. No index. Typed on printed forms. 150 loose-leaf pages. 15 x 9 x .5. Treasurer's office.

Fiscal Accounts

General Accounts

341. TRANSFER LEDGER
1862-1872, 1904——. 5 vols. Title varies: Treasurer's General Ledger, 1862-1872, 1 vol.

Treasurer's ledger, showing receipts and disbursements of all accounts, name of fund or account, date of entry, name of town or township, debit and credit amount, credit and debit balance, treasurer's account, and remarks; also includes various funds, general, poor relief, excise, humane society, board of education, tangible personal and intangible personal, cigarette, and inheritance tax, road and bridge, township accounts, road and miscellaneous funds, accounts with banks, settlements with townships, and distribution of funds to townships. Arranged by names of funds and chronologically thereunder by dates entered. 1904-1923, indexed alphabetically by names of towns or townships; 1862-1884, 1924—, no index. 1862-1884, handwritten; 1904—, handwritten on printed forms. 4 volumes average 525 pages. 16 x 13 x 3; 2 volumes average 200 pages. 18 x 11 x 1.5. 1 volume, 1862-1884, attic store room; 2 volumes, 1904-1923, basement store room; 2 volumes, 1923—, Treasurer's office vault.

342. CASH BOOK
1863-1884, 1904—. 2 vols. (one unlabeled; 1). Title varies: Journal, 1863-1884, 1 vol.

Treasurer's daily record of receipts, depository record, and disbursements; receipts, showing date of receipt, pay-in orders from depository, tangible, intangible, general, inheritance, and cigarette taxes, vendors' licenses, and total receipts; disbursements, showing date of disbursement, balance in treasury, total disbursements, general warrants, and court warrants to depository; depository record, showing date of entry, amount of deposits and drafts, balance in depository, and total balance in depository and treasury. Arranged chronologically by dates entered. No index. Handwritten on printed forms. 240 pages. 18.5 x 13 x 2. 1 volume, 1863-1884, attic store room, 1 volume, 1904—, Treasurer's vault.

343. DAILY CASH BALANCE
1902-1915. 4 vols. (1, 1-3). Title varies: Cash Book, 1902-1904, 1 vol.

Treasurer's daily record of receipts, disbursements, and balances, showing date of entry, source of receipts, purposes and amounts of disbursements, and balance in treasury and bank. 1 volume, 1902-1904, includes accounts with various banks, showing deposits and withdrawals. Arranged chronologically by dates entered. 1902-1904, indexed alphabetically by names of banking accounts; 1904-1915, no index. 1902-1904, handwritten; 1904-1915 handwritten on printed forms. Average 400 pages. 16 x 11.5 x 2. Basement store room.

344. JOURNAL OF PAYMENTS INTO TREASURY
1928—. 1 vol. (7). Initiated in 1928.

Record of payments into county treasury, showing date of entry, name of payer, pay-in order number, debit column for treasurer, and credit column for various funds, including general, children's home, dog and kennel, county road and bridge, state road and bridge, depository interest, board of education, undivided general tax, board of health, undivided cigarette tax, inheritance tax, auto license tax, and miscellaneous funds.

Arranged chronologically by dates entered. No index. Handwritten on printed forms. 250 pages. 18.5 x 13 x 2.5. Treasurer's office vault.

345. REGISTER OF CHECKS AND DRAFTS
1875-1889. 1 vol. (1).

Record of checks, bills, drafts, currency, and other moneys received by treasurer, showing date received, by whom drawn and to whom payable, name and location of bank, number and amount of check or draft, name of bank in which deposited, and date of deposit. Arranged chronologically by dates received. No index. Handwritten on printed forms. 300 pages. 16 x 11 x 1.5. Basement store room.

346. CASH RECORDS [Treasurer's Daily Statement]
1904-1912, 1914-1915, 1919-1933, 1935—. 8 bundles, 4 file folders, 1 vol.

Treasurer's daily record of receipts, disbursements and balances for general, delinquent, cigarette, personal and inheritance tax funds, and liquor and license fees; receipts, showing date of receipt, balance brought forward, receipts from all sources, total receipts, and balance; disbursements, showing date of disbursement, total disbursements, and balance carried forward to next day. Volume 1936—, the new form, showing taxes received, pay-in order and checks received, total received, warrants redeemed, deposits, and balance of cash in depository and treasury. Arranged chronologically by dates receipted. No index. Handwritten on printed forms. Bundles, 12 x 9 x 2; file folders, 10.5 x 9.5 x 2; volume 150 pages. 9.5 x 13 x 1. 5 bundles, 1904-1912, 1922-1925, attic store room; 3 bundles, 4 file folders, 1915-1915, 1919-1921, 1926-1933, 1935, 3rd floor store room; 1 volume, 1936—, Treasurer's office vault.

347. MONTHLY FINANCIAL STATEMENT OF TREASURER
1916-1926. 1 box.

Duplicate of treasurer's monthly financial statements to auditor approved by commissioners, showing date of statement, balances in all funds at beginning of month, receipts, disbursements, overdraft in all funds, and balances in all funds at end of month. Arranged chronologically by dates of statements. No index. Handwritten on printed forms. 11 x 20 x 14. Attic store room.

Warrants and Orders

348. JOURNAL OF WARRANTS REDEEMED
1904—. 10 vols. (1, 2, 4-11).
Journal record of redeemed warrants issued by auditor on the treasurer, showing date of warrant, name of payee, purpose of warrant, warrant number, and amount of warrant; debit columns, including general, board of education, dog and kennel, road, bond retirement, auto license, gas tax, board of health, road patrol, undivided general, cigarette tax, inheritance tax, and auto license tax funds. Also contains Record of Court Warrants Redeemed, 1926—, entry 349. Arranged chronologically by dates of warrants and numbers thereunder by warrant numbers. No index. Handwritten on printed forms. Average 250 pages. 18 x 13 x 2.5. 8 volumes, 1904-1936, basement store room; 2 volumes, 1936—, Treasurer's office vault.

349. RECORD OF COURT WARRANTS REDEEMED
1904-1925. 1 vol. (1). 1926— in Journal of Warrants Redeemed, entry 348.
Treasurer's record of court warrants redeemed for witnesses' and jurors' fees, showing date of warrant, name of payee, amount, warrant number, and total warrants redeemed; court of common pleas and court of appeals, petit jurors, grand jurors, grand jury witnesses, and witnesses in civil and criminal cases; probate court, jurors, and witnesses in civil and criminal cases, lunacy and epilepsy; minor court witnesses, coroner's court witnesses, and miscellaneous. Arranged chronologically by dates of warrants. No index. Handwritten on printed forms. 320 pages. 18 x 12.5 x 2. Basement store room.

350. RECORD OF ORDERS REDEEMED
1862-1904. 6 vols. (two unlabeled; 2, 1-3).
Treasurer's record of redeemed orders, showing date of order, name of payee, purpose of order, order number, amount of order, and fund to which charged. Arranged chronologically by dates of orders. No index. Handwritten. 2 volumes average 215 pages. 12 x 7.5 x 1.5; 4 volumes average 250 pages. 16 x 9 x 1.5. 2 volumes, 1862-1875, basement store room; 4 volumes, 1876-1904, attic store room.

351. BRIDGE ORDERS [Miscellaneous]
1852-1887. 1 vol.

Record of warrants drawn on treasury for infirmary purposes, showing date of warrant, to whom drawn, purpose, warrant number, and amount; also includes soldiers' relief orders, 1866-1887, showing date drawn, to whom drawn, purpose of warrant, warrant number, and amount; fines received under the game law, 1886, showing date of warrant, to whom drawn, for what purpose, and amount of warrant; disbursements and receipts of Dow Law, 1886-1887, disbursements showing name of payee, date, amount, and purpose of disbursement, receipts, showing date of receipt, name of payer, purpose, receipt number, and amount credited to Treasurer's Duplicate, entry 322; river and ditch orders, 1874, showing date of warrant, to whom drawn, for what purpose, number and amount of warrant; orders for soldiers' relief and Ohio National Guard, 1862-1866; orders for building courthouse and redeeming bonds on same, 1869-1870, showing warrant issued, to whom drawn, and for what purpose. Arranged chronologically by dates of warrants. No index. Handwritten on printed forms. 200 pages. 14 x 9 x 1.5. Basement storage room.

Bonds

352. TREASURER'S RECORD OF BONDS OF OFFICIALS
1808-1887, 1889-1907, -1909-1917, 1919——. 5 vols. (three unlabeled; 2, 3).
Title varies: Treasurer's Record of Official Bonds, 1872-1887, 1889-1907, 2 vols.

Original record of bonds and oaths of county officials; bonds, showing date of bond, names of sureties and officials, name and address of bonding company, name of principal, amount of actual bond, and date witnessed; oaths, showing sworn statement to support the constitution and discharge duties of the office and signatures of notary public or judge and office holder; prosecuting attorneys certificate of inspection of bond, showing date of inspection, amount of bond, and signatures of prosecuting attorney and probate judge; treasury inspector's certificates, being a certification of inspection of record of moneys in treasurer's office, 1872-1887, 1889-1907, showing date of inspection amount in treasury, amount in depository, total amount, and signature of examining officer; also includes record of township clerk's bond, 1923. Arranged chronologically by dates of bonds. 1808-1871, no index; 1872-1887, 1889-1907, -1909-1917, 1919——, indexed alphabetically by names of officials. Handwritten, some on printed forms.

1 volume 150 pages. 13 x 6 x 1; 4 volumes average 150 pages. 17 x 12 x 1. 3 volumes, 1808-1871, 1889-1907, 1909-1917, basement store room; 1 volume, 1872-1887, attic store room; 1 volume, 1919—, Treasurer's vault.

353. RECORD OF TOWNSHIP CLERK'S BOND
1923—. 1 vol. 2 pigeon holes.
Copies of bonds of township clerks, 1923-1933, showing name of clerk, office, sureties, and township, amount and date of bond, condition of bond, and signatures of sureties, clerks, and township trustees; also includes oath of office and original bonds 1938. Pigeon holes contain original bonds, 1933—, showing same information as contained in record. 1923-1933, arranged chronologically by dates of bonds; 1933—, arranged alphabetically by names of offices. 1923-1933, indexed alphabetically by names of clerks; 1933—, no index. Handwritten and typed on printed forms. Volume 100 pages. 15 x 13.5 x 1; pigeon holes, 4.5 x 5 x 11.5. Treasurer's office.

Miscellaneous

354. DOG TAG RECORD
1878-1908. 2 vols. (one and labeled; 1).
Record of dog tax collected by treasurer on duplicate, showing date of entry, name of township, and amount of tax; also includes record of orders redeemed on dog fund, showing date and amount of payment, to whom paid, and certification by commissioners. Arranged chronologically by dates entered. No index. 1878-1897, handwritten; 1898-1908 handwritten on printed forms. Average 200 pages. 13 x 8.5 x 1. Basement store room.

355. APPOINTMENT OF DEPUTIES AND CLERKS FOR COUNTY OFFICES [Reports of Prosecuting Attorney]
1919—. 1 file drawer.
Record of appointments of deputies and clerks of auditor, treasurer, sheriff, humane officer, probation officer, surveyor, recorder, probate judge, common pleas court, court constable, prosecutor, and clerk of courts, 1924—, showing name of deputy or clerk, date of filing, salary, and date of appointment; also original reports of prosecuting attorney, statements of receipts and expenditures; showing name of payee, date, amount, and purpose of expenditures; receipts, showing date of receipt, name of payer, purpose, receipt number, amount paid to auditor, and balance held

by prosecuting attorney; prosecuting attorney's annual statements of cases tried, 1920—, showing name of defendant, kind of case, and verdict of court. Arranged chronologically by dates of appointments. No index. Handwritten on printed forms. 10 x 5 x 15. Auditors' office.

356. COUNTY OFFICERS' REPORTS
1880-1884, 1907-1910. 1 vol. (1).

Annual reports of county prosecuting attorney and clerk of courts; prosecuting attorneys reports, showing date of report, names of defendants, number of cases tried, amount collected, kind of case, name of court, by whom paid, and date paid; clerk's reports, showing date of report, names of parties upon whom finds were assessed by common pleas court, amount assessed and collected, source of other funds, and amount paid into county treasury. Arranged chronologically by dates reported. No index. Handwritten on printed forms. 200 pages. 14 x 18.5 x 1.25. Treasurer's office.

357. LEDGER [Miscellaneous Record]
1886-1929. 1 vol.

Miscellaneous record, including additions to the tax duplicate of 1890, showing name of taxpayer, date of payment, amount of addition and notation of payment, and other remarks; duplicates of assessment on the traffic in intoxicating liquors, 1886-1887, and duplicate of Dow liquor tax, 1896-1902, showing date assessed, town, premises, section, lot, amount assessed, and date paid; also includes a list of delinquent taxes paid after the book was sent to auditor in 1910, and pencil copies of daily cash and disbursements, 1927-1929, listing bonds, bills, checks, coupons, drafts, and warrants received, disbursed, and redeemed. No obvious arrangement. Additions to duplicate indexed alphabetically by names of taxpayers; other items not indexed. Handwritten. 275 pages. 12.5 x 7.5 x 1. Basement store room.

For other assessment records, see entry 335.

358. [MISCELLANEOUS RECORD]

1869-1887. 1 vol.

County treasurer's miscellaneous record containing:

a.   Estimates for the construction of the county courthouse, 1869-1870, showing date, name of person submitting bid, amounts for labor and materials, and total amount of bid.

b.   Records of orders redeemed from the institute and infirmary building fund, 1878-1885, showing date, amount, order number, name of payee, for what purpose, and amount debited to each fund.

c.   Record of peddlers' licenses issued, 1881-1887, showing date, number and amount of bond, name of purchaser, date due, date delivered, and date redeemed.

d.   List of courthouse building bonds, 1869-1874, showing date, number and amount of bond, name of purchaser, date due, date delivered, and date redeemed.

Arranged chronologically by dates entered. No index. Handwritten. 166 pages. 13.5 x 8 x .5. Basement store room.

A budget commission functions in Geauga County under an act of August 10, 1927, which authorized the establishment of such an agency in each county, to be composed of the county treasurer, county auditor, and prosecuting attorney.[1] In 1915 the county treasurer replaced the mayor as a member of the commission.[2] It was not until after the World War, when county expenditures steadily increased, that the importance of improved methods of finance were forcibly brought to the attention of the legislature. This need was met in 1923 by enlarging the powers and minutely prescribing the duties of the budget commission. As in 1915 the county auditor, county treasurer, and county prosecuting attorney were made ex-officio members of the commission.[3] Under the present law, passed in 1927, the commission, consisting as before of the county auditor, county treasurer, and prosecuting attorney, receives and examines the annual budget of the county, municipal, township, and school authorities, with an estimate of the amount to be raised for state purposes in each subdivision.[4] If the total amount exceeds the sum authorized to be raised, the commission adjusts the amount to be raised and may change and revise the estimates. The commission may reduce all items in the budget, but it is prohibited from increasing the total of any budget or any item.

The adjusted budget is certified to the taxing authority in each subdivision. If the work of the commission is satisfactory, each taxing authority by ordinance or resolution authorizes the necessary tax levies and certifies them to the county auditor. On the other hand, the taxing authority in any subdivision may appeal, through its fiscal officer, from the decision of the budget commission to the state tax commission of Ohio, which is empowered to adjust the estimates of revenues and balances in fixing the tax rates.[5]

The county auditor, as secretary to the commission, is required to keep a full and accurate record of the proceedings of the commission.

---

1. *Laws of Ohio*, CXII, 399.
2. *Ibid.*, CVI, 180.
3. *Ibid.*, CX, 469. Under the provisions of this act elective commissioners might be substituted for the ex-officio members, at the option of the electors of the county.
4. *Ibid.*, CXII, 399.
5. G. C. secs. 5625-25, 5625-28.

359. MINUTES OF BUDGET COMMISSION
1918-1929, 1933—. 1 vol.

Minutes of the budget commission, showing date of meeting, resolutions approved or rejected, business transacted, and copies of itemized budgets for villages, townships, and county; miscellaneous record of expenditures for road and bridge work, 1928-1929 showing amount and kind of material used, date of expenditure, order number, and total cost of improvement. Arranged chronologically by dates of meetings or expenditures. Minutes indexed alphabetically by names of townships and villages; expenditures, no index. Handwritten on printed forms. 235 pages. 14 x 9 x 1. Auditors' office.

The county board of revision was established by the general assembly in 1825 for the purpose of correcting some of the inequities in the assessment of taxes. The first board of revision, or equalization as it was sometimes called, was composed of the county commissioners, county auditor, and the assessor. The board was authorized to meet at the seat of justice on the first Monday in June annually "to hear and determine the complaint of any owner of property listed and valued by the assessor . . . and shall correct any list of valuation made by the assessor, either by adding to or deducting from his valuation."[1] The act of 1831, repealing the act of 1825, left the duties and personnel by the board unchanged.[2]

In 1859 the legislature made provision for two county boards of equalization. One board, composed of the county auditor and the county commissioners, was directed to meet annually for the purpose of equalizing real and personal property, and moneys and credits in the county. The other board, composed of the county auditor, county surveyor, and county commissioners, was authorized to meet sexannually for the same purpose.[3]

The act of 1863 amending the act of 1859, left the personnel and duties of the annual county board unchanged. The second county board, although continuing without alterations in composition or duties, was directed to meet decennially, rather than sexannually.[4] The legislative act of 1868, amending the act of 1863, left the membership of the annual and special boards, as well as their duties, practically unchanged.[5]

The annual and special boards of equalization were abolished, when, in 1913, the state tax commission of Ohio was given the task of supervising the assessment of real and personal property in the state.[6] Under this arrangement each county constituted a district. In each district containing less than 60,000 inhabitants, by which stipulation Geauga County was included, there was to be appointed by the governor one state tax commissioner. In all other districts there were appointed, in the same manner, two state deputy tax commissioners.

---

1. *Laws of Ohio*, XXIII, 64.
2. *Ibid.*, XXIX, 278.
3. *Ibid.*, LVI, 193-194.
4. *Ibid.*, LX, 57, 59.
5. *Ibid.*, LXV, 168-170.
6. *See* pp. XLV / XLVI

In each district there was appointed a district board of complaints. This board, appointed by the state tax commission with the consent of the governor, took over the duties and powers formerly vested in the board of equalization. The county auditor, made secretary to the board of complaints, was required to be present at each meeting in person or by deputy, and keep an accurate record of their proceedings to be kept in the book for that purpose.[7] Moreover, the board was directed to take full minutes of all evidence given before it and might have such evidence taken in shorthand and extended into typewritten form. The auditor was required to preserve in his office separate records of all minutes and documentary evidence offered in each complaint.[8]

This arrangement, after being in operation for two years, was abrogated by legislature in1915. In that year the county auditor, under the supervision of the tax commission of Ohio, became the chief assessing officer in the county. The county treasurer, prosecuting attorney, probate judge, and the president of the county commissioners were to serve as a board for the purpose of appointing three members to constitute a board of revision. Again the county auditor was made secretary of the board and was directed to keep a record of their proceedings and to preserve in his office a separate record of all minutes and documentary evidence offered in each complaint.[9]

Under the present system, inaugurated in 1917, the county treasurer, county auditor, and president of the county commissioners constitute a board of revision. This board organizes annually, on the second Monday in June, by electing a chairman for the ensuing year. The county auditor serves as secretary of the board.[10] The county board of revision may, with the consent and approval of the tax commission of Ohio, employ experts, clerks, and other employees.[11]

The duties of the board, not differing in detail from those prescribed in 1825, include the hearing of all complaints relating to valuation or assessments of both real and personal property as it appears upon the tax duplicates of the "then current year."

---

7. *Laws of Ohio*, CIII, 791.
8. *Ibid.*, CIII, 794.
9. *Laws of Ohio*, CVI, 254-258.
10. G. C. sec. 5580.
11. G. C. sec. 5587.

The board is authorized to investigate all complaints and may increase or decrease any valuation or correct any assessment complained of, or may order a reassessment by the original assessing official.[12] No valuation is increased, however, without giving notice to the person in whose name the property affected is listed.[13] The board of revision in all respects, is governed by the laws relating to the valuation "except in accordance with such laws."[14]

On the second Monday in June, annually, the county auditor lays before the board of revision the statements and returns of assessments of any personal property for the current year, and the board proceeds to review the returns. On the first Monday in July, annually, the auditor lays before the board the returns of assessments of any real property for the current year. The board of revision reviews the assessments and certifies its actions to the county auditor, who corrects the tax list and duplicate according to the additions and deductions ordered by the board. The auditor is prohibited by statutes from making up his tax list and duplicate until the board has completed its work and has returned to him all the returns laid before it with revisions.[15] But in the event the tax duplicate has been delivered to the county treasurer, the auditor is required to certify such corrections to him and enter such corrections in his tax duplicate.[16]

In its investigations the board may examine, under oath, persons as to their or others' real property. In the event witnesses fail to appear or refuse to testify, the board through its chairman is authorized to make a complaint in writing to the probate judge, who, by statute, is directed to institute proceedings against them.[17] The decisions of the board are subject to appeal to the tax commission of Ohio within 30 days after a decision is served.[18]

The secretary of the board is required to keep an accurate record of the proceedings of the board in a book to be kept for that purpose."[19] The county auditor, as in 1913, is required to preserve in his office separate records of all minutes and documentary evidence offered in each complaint.[20]

---

12. G. C. sec. 5597.
13. G. C. sec. 5599.
14. G. C. sec. 5596.
15. G. C. sec. 5605.
16. G. C. sec. 5602.
17. G. C. sec. 5596.
18. G. C. sec. 5610.
19. G. C. sec. 5592.
20. G. C. sec. 5603.

The record of the board are open to the inspection of the public.[21]

Geauga County has had a board of revision since June 12, 1916.[22] Only one appeal from the board's decisions has been taken to the state tax commission in the last 22 years.[23] In 1940 four complaints were investigated.[24]

---

21. G. C. sec. 5591.
22. Minute Book of Board of Complaints, I, 1, entry 360. Records of the board of equalization are extant for 1852-1900.
23. *Ibid.,* 117.
24. *Ibid.,* 144, 145.

360. MINUTE BOOK OF BOARD OF COMPLAINTS

1852-1900, 1916—. 3 vols. Title varies: Record of Equalization Board – Horses and Cattle, 1852-1871, 1 vol.; Proceedings of County Board of Real Estate Equalization, 1859-1900, 1 vol.

Proceedings of the board of equalization and board of revision acting on complaints or suspicions of false returns in additions or deductions from the tax duplicate, showing date of meeting, motions for raising or lowering assessed value of property, record of allowance of reductions or increases in assessed value of land, and record of complaints of landowner on reassessments. Includes personal property additions and deductions 1852-1871; real estate additions and deductions, and copies of letters from taxpayers to the board of equalization 1859-1900; includes both personal and real property 1916—. Arranged chronologically by dates of meetings. No index. Handwritten. 2 volumes average 175 pages. 14 x 8 x 1. 1 volume 320 pages. 18 x 13 x 2. 2 volumes, 1852-1900, basement store room; 1 volume, 1916—, Auditor's office.

The board of trustees of the sinking fund, composed of the prosecuting attorney, auditor, and treasurer, was organized in 1919 but did not function until September 2, 1926, since Geauga County owed no bonded debt. The county prosecuting attorney serves as a president of the board and the auditor as secretary. It is the duty of the trustees to provide for the payment of all bonds issued by the county and the interest maturing thereon.[1]

The 1919 all bonds issued by the county were required to be recorded in the office of the trustees of the sinking fund, to bear a stamp containing the words" Recorded in the office of the sinking fund trustees," and to be signed by the secretary before they became valid in the hands of the purchaser. In 1921 the act was amended to allow such recording and authenticating to be performed by the county treasurer and in 1935 such provisions were abrogated by the legislature.[2]

On or before the first Monday in May of each year, the trustees certify to the county commissioners the rate of tax necessary to provide a sinking fund both for the payment and maturity of bonds heretofore issued by the county and for the payment of interest on the bonded indebtedness. The amount certified by the trustees is set forth without diminution in the annual budget of the commissioners.[3] Then, after each semiannual settlement of taxes and assessments, the county auditor reports to the trustees the amount of money in the treasury of the county charged to the credit of the sinking fund. Money is drawn from the county treasury for investment or disbursement by the issuance of a voucher signed by all the members of the board and directed to the county auditor. The trustees are directed, by statute, to invest all moneys subject to their control in United States bonds, Ohio bonds, or bonds of a municipal corporation, school district, township, or county in the state.

The board members are required to keep a "full and complete record of their transactions, a complete record of the funded debt of the county specifying the dates, purposes, amounts, numbers, maturities, and rates of maturity of interest and installments thereof, and where payable, and an account exhibiting the amount held in the sinking fund for the payment thereof."[4]

---

1. G. C. sec. 2976-18, 2876-19.
2. *Laws of Ohio,* CIX, 16; CXVI, 442.
3. G. C. sec. 2976-26.
4. G. C. sec. 2976-24.

The meetings of the trustees are open to the public. All questions relating to the purchase or sale of securities or the payment of bonds or interest are decided by a yea or nay vote, which is recorded in their journal.

361. VOUCHER STUBS – SINKING FUND
1926-1934. 1 vol.

Stubs of vouchers issued by sinking fund trustees to auditor to issue warrants on the treasury for payment and the redemption of bonds and interest coupons, showing name and number of issue, date of warrant, amount of warrant issued, amount of coupon, commissioners' resolution number, and name of fund on which the warrants were drawn. Arranged chronologically by dates of warrants. No index. Handwritten on printed forms. 100 pages. 8 x 11 x 1. Auditor's office.

The responsibility for supervising and conducting elections in the county is delegated to the state deputy supervisors of elections, the county board of elections. This board, created by the legislature in 1891 and consisting of four qualified voters in the county, is appointed for a four-year term by the secretary of state, who, by virtue of his office, is the chief election official of the state.[1] On the first day of March in the even numbered years, the secretary of state appoints two board members, one of whom is from the political party which polled the highest number of votes in the state for the office of governor at the last proceeding state election, and the other from the political party which polled the next highest vote at such election.[2] The board members may be removed by the secretary of state for the neglect of duty, malfeasance, misfeasance in office, for willful violation of the election laws, or for other good and sufficient causes. The compensation of the members is determined on the basis of population of the county and is paid by the county.[4] Similarly the expenses of the county board are paid from the county treasury, "in pursuance of appropriations by the county commissioners,"in the same matter as other expenses are paid.[5]

The persons so appointed by the secretary, meeting five days after their appointment, select one of their members as chairman and a resident elector of the county who is not a member of the board as clerk.[6] The board is vested with authority to establish, define, and provide election precincts; fix places of registration; provide for the purchase, preservation, and maintenance of voting booths, ballot boxes, books, maps, flags, blankets, cards of instruction, and other equipment used in registration; and to issue rules, regulations, and instructions not inconsistent with the law or contrary to the rules and regulations as established by the chief election official.[7]

---

1. *Laws of Ohio*, LXXXVIII, 449.
2. G. C. sec. 4785-8. For the method of appointment when the term of each of the four members of the board expires on the same date *see* G. C. sec. 4785-8a.
3. G. C. sec. 4785-11.
4. G. C. sec. 4785-18.
5. G. C. sec. 4785-20
6. G. C. sec. 4785-10.
7. G. C. sec. 4785-13.

Besides providing places of voting and equipment, the board is authorized to appoint clerks and other officers of elections. On or before the first day of September before each November election, the board by a majority vote, after careful examination and investigation as to the qualifications, is authorized to appoint for each precinct six "competent persons, four as judges and two as clerks, who shall constitute the election officers of such precinct." Not more than two of the judges and one of the clerks, states the law, "shall be members of the same political party." Precinct election officers, appointed for a one-year term, may be removed by the board for neglect of duty, malfeasance, or misconduct in office.[8]

The county board of elections is authorized to receive and examine nominating positions and to certify their sufficiency and validity. They receive the election returns, canvas the returns, then make abstracts therefrom and transmit them to the proper authorities. They issue certificates of election on forms prescribed by the secretary of state and report annually to the same official, on forms prescribed by him, the number of voters registered, elections held, votes cast, and such other information as the secretary of state may require. Moreover, the board prepares and submits to the proper authorities a budget estimating the cost of elections for the ensuing year.[9]

Finally, the board is empowered to investigate irregularities, nonperformance of duty, or violation of election laws by election officials. For the purpose of conducting investigations they may administer oaths, issue subpoenas, summon witnesses, and compel the presentation of books, papers, and records in connection with any investigation and report the facts to the prosecuting attorney.[10]

The secretary of state, in 1930, ruled that the members of the various boards of elections were to be considered as state officers. This ruling had reference to appointments made under section 4785-8 of the General Code.[11]

In Geauga County the board supervises elections in 21 precincts in which at last registration there were 8860 voters.[12] A clerk and a part-time assistant clerk are employed by the board.

---

8. G. C. sec. 4785-25.
9. G. C. sec. 4785-13.
10. G. C. sec. 4785-13.
11. *See* George C. Trautwein, ed. *Supplement to Page's Anointed General Code 1926-1935* (Cincinnati, 1935), note on p. 688.
12. Abstracts of Votes Cast, 1940, *see* entry 366.

The board members received $200 monthly, but the total appropriations for the board vary from year to year with the number and importance of the elections to be held. In the last five years the sums spent have ranged from $5600 in 1936 to $8450 in 1940. The appropriation for 1941 was $3569.[13]

All records are located in the office of the board of elections.

_____

13. Commissioners' Journal, General, XI [1936-1941], *see* entry1.

Minutes

362. RECORD OF PROCEEDINGS
1891—. 3 vols. Title varies: Record, 1891-1909, 1 vol.
Minutes of the county board of elections, showing date of meeting and record of all proceedings, including resolutions, instructions to election officers, and allowance of bills. Arranged chronologically by dates of meetings. No index. Handwritten. 1 volume 300 pages. 12.5 x 8 x 1; 2 volumes average 300 pages. 16 x 11 x .25.

Record of Electors

363. REGISTER OF ABSENT VOTERS
1917—. 1 vol. (1).
Record of absent voters, showing application number, date and means of ballot delivery, name of voter, sex, voting district, date and manner in which returned ballot was received, address of absent voter, and date of election. Arranged chronologically by dates of elections. No index. Handwritten on printed forms. 50 pages. 14 x 8.5 x .50.

364. ELECTOR'S [Miscellaneous] RECORDS
1917—. 1 file drawer.
Miscellaneous records pertaining largely to registrations, including registration list of registered voters by voting districts, showing names of township and village, consecutive numbers of registrants, name of registrant, registration number, and other related information; also includes records of special elections of various villages and townships. Arranged alphabetically by names of townships and villages. No index. Handwritten and typed on printed forms. 8 x 10 x 16.

Poll Books and Tally Sheets

365. POLL BOOK AND TALLY SHEET

1930—. 256 vols. (dated). Subtitled by ward numbers and precinct letters. Poll books and tally sheets of primary and general elections; poll books, showing name and address of voter, voting district, name of political party, and signature of the voter; tally sheets, showing total votes received by each candidate and issue in each voting district, also signatures of clerks and judges of elections. Poll books, arranged alphabetically by names of electors; tally sheets, arranged by offices and issues. No index. Handwritten on printed forms. Average 28 pages. 17.5 x 10.25 x .25.

366. ABSTRACTS OF VOTES CAST

1891—. 1 bundle.

Abstracts of votes cast in all elections, showing voting districts, political party, candidates and issues, number of votes cast for each candidate or issue in each voting district, and total number of votes cast as certified by county board of elections. Some abstracts are copies and some are originals. No obvious arrangement. No index. Handwritten on printed forms. 600 sheets. 20 x 24.50 in bundles, 24 x 26 x 4.

Financial Records

367. CASH BOOK – CANDIDATES' FEES

1916—. 1 vol. (1).

Record of filing fees received by board of election from candidates, showing date of election, date fee paid, names of candidate and office, annual salary of office, amount of fee paid, and date paid into county treasury; also pay-in orders of auditor, signed by treasurer. Arranged by dates fees paid. No index. Handwritten on printed forms. 200 pages. 11.5 x 11 x 1.

368. PAY ROLL
1902—. 2 vols., 1 folder. Title varies: Roster and Pay Roll, 1902-1933, 1 vol.

Record of appointments and salaries of election judges and clerks, showing voting districts, names of appointees, residence, party affiliation, date appointed, date qualified, election at which served, and salaries due and paid. Arranged chronologically by dates appointed. No index. Handwritten on printed forms. Folder, 11 x 9 x 1; volumes average 200 pages. 10 x 11.5 x 2.

Miscellaneous

369. REPORTS TO SECRETARY OF STATE
1930—. 1 folder.

Copies of reports to the secretary of state, showing date of report, itemized election expenditures, estimates of future election expenditures, and signature of clerk of board of election; also includes miscellaneous correspondence concerning the elections, showing date of correspondence, subject discussed, and signature of correspondent. Arranged chronologically by dates reported. No index. Reports handwritten and typed, some on printed forms; correspondence typed. 14 x 9 x .5.

370. CERTIFICATES OF APPOINTMENTS
1931—. 6 vols.

Stubs of certificates of appointment of judges and clerks to precinct boards of election, showing date of certificate, name of appointee, party affiliation, voting district, oath of office, and date acceptance filed. Arranged chronologically by dates certified. No index. Handwritten on printed forms. Average 75 pages. 11.5 x 14 x .5.

371. RECEIPTS OF PRESIDING JUDGES
1912. 5 vols.

Receipts of presiding judges of precincts for supplies used in the elections, showing date of receipt, voting district, number of poll books, list, balance, other supplies received, and signature of presiding judge. Arranged chronologically by dates of receipts. No index. Handwritten on printed forms. Average 100 pages. 8 x 10 x 1.

372. [MISCELLANEOUS]

1891—. 48 pigeonholes.

Board of election's miscellaneous record containing:

a.   Nominating petitions, showing name, address, and age of candidate, names and addresses of petitioners, ward, and precinct numbers.

b.   Certificates of candidates certifying that the person is eligible to hold office, showing name and address of candidate, name of office for which candidate is seeking election, and signatures of candidates and clerk of board of election.

c.   Bills for supplies with voucher for payment attached, showing date of bill, name of auditor, and amount of bill for supplies and service rendered.

d.   Vouchers, showing voucher number and date paid.

e.   Miscellaneous correspondence to and from the board of elections office pertaining to business matters, showing date of correspondence, subjects discussed, and signature of correspondent.

No obvious arrangement. No index. Handwritten and typed, some on printed forms. 9 x 5 x 16.

The county board of education, a modern administration and supervisory agency developed during the last two decades, supplanted the smaller educational units, which, established during the early period of Ohio history, became inefficient and unable to meet the modern requirements as demanded by rural communities.

During the earlier period of Ohio history, educational administration, because of the newness of the state, the sparseness of the population, and the undeveloped means of transportation was, by necessity, local in character. For 14 years after the accession of Ohio to statehood, though the first constitution stated means of education should be encouraged by the general assembly, no legislation was enacted for public schools.[1] It was not until 1817 that the legislature authorized six or more people to form associations to build schoolhouses and to be incorporated for educational purposes.[2]

The first permanent law for the organization of schools in Ohio was passed in 1821. Under the provisions of this act, the electors of the township were authorized to vote on the proposition of dividing the townships into school districts. If the proposal carried, they were to be elected three school commissioners, who, in turn, were authorized to select a clerk and collector who should act as treasurer. They were instructed also, to levy taxes for the support of schools and to hire teachers.[3]

As education began to advance in the early years of the 19th century, some kind of state control was needed. Accordingly, in 1837, the office of state superintendent of schools was established.[4] A year later an act was passed making the county auditor also the county superintendent of schools; and in each township the clerk became superintendent of the smaller unit. The county superintendent was made responsible to the state superintendent in all educational affairs. In the same year each incorporated city, town, or borough not regulated by a charter was made a separate school district. The voters in each division was authorized to elect three directors.[5] The effectiveness of this organization was destroyed in 1840, however, when the legislature abolished the office of state superintendent and the secretary of state took over his functions of tabulating and transmitting school statistics.[6]

---

1. *Ohio Const. 1802*, Art. VIII, secs. 3, 25, 27.
2. *Laws of Ohio*, XV, 107.
3. *Ibid.*, XIX, 52.
4. *Ibid.*, XXXV, 82.
5. *Ibid.*, XXXVI, 21.
6. *Ibid.*, XXXVIII, 130.

Seven years later, 25 counties, including Geauga, were allowed to have county superintendents,[7] and in 1848 the provisions of the previous act were extended to all other counties in the state.[8]

Although marked changes were made in the curricula of the schools, the history of education in Ohio from 1850 to the early part of the 20th century was largely one of the gradual transference of power from districts to townships, and from townships to county in the interest of a better system of education. It was not, however, until within the last three decades that the county became the unit for educational administration.[9]

Although the county superintendent was known as early as 1838, the first permanent law for the establishment of a county board of education was enacted in 1914. Under this act the school districts were classified, and provision was made for a county school district, exclusive of the territory embraced in any city or village having a population of 3000 or more desiring exemption. The county district was to be under the supervision of five board members elected by the presidents of the village and rural school boards. The members were to hold office for one, two, three, four, and five years respectfully, and each year thereafter one member was to be selected to serve for a five-year term.[10]

The county board of education was authorized to change school district lines; provide transportation for children living more than two miles from a schoolhouse; appoint a county superintendent; and certify annually to the county auditor the number of teachers and superintendents employed, their salaries, and the amount apportioned to each school district for the payment of the salaries of the county and district superintendents. The county superintendent, acting as secretary of the board, was required to keep in a book provided for the purpose a full record of the proceedings of the board properly indexed. Each motion, together with the name of the person making it and the vote thereon, was to be entered on the record.[11]

---

7. *Laws of Ohio*, XLV, 32.
8. *Ibid.,* XLVI, 86.
9. *Ibid.,* LXX, 195, 242; XCVII, 354.
10. *Ibid.,* CIV, 133.
11. *Ibid.,* CIV, 133; CVIII, pt. i, 704.

The county was divided into administrative divisions containing one or more villages or rural school districts. Each district was to be under the supervision of a district superintendent, who was required to visit the schools in his charge, direct and assist teachers in the performance of the duties, and classify and control promotion of pupils. He was required also to report annually to the county superintendent on matters under his charge, and to assemble teachers for the purpose of conferring on curricular matters, discipline, and school management.[12] Significant changes were made by the act of 1921, under which the board members became elected by popular vote. They were authorized to appoint one or more assistant county superintendents for a term of three years. The board was authorized also to publish, with the advice and consent of the county superintendent, a minimum course of study to serve as a guide to local board members. The same act abolished the office of district superintendent.[13]

The county organization has placed the rural schools on a plane of equality with the city schools. The consolidation of the smaller units has eliminated the small, ill-equipped schools, and provides under one roof facilities and instructions suited to the needs of the rural children under the supervision of educational specialists.

Geauga County's board was organized in July, 1914 immediately after the passage of the authorizing legislation. Its centralized direction of the educational activities in the county has had the effect of consolidating 26 elementary buildings, 12 combination high and elementary schools, and one exclusive high school into 12 modern grade schools, 11 combination grade and high schools, and one modern high school.[14] These are administered in 17 districts by a personnel consisting of 12 superintendents receiving an aggregate annual compensation of $28,753.50, four principles receiving an aggregate annual compensation of $4,473.94, and 139 teachers receiving total annual salaries of $188,351.94. About 3728 pupils attend the county schools and 2710 of them received free transportation, each of the districts financing its own bus service.[15] Each of the 16 townships have their own tax rate. All schools in the county are under the jurisdiction of the county board of education.

---

12. *Ibid.,* CIV, 133-145.
13. G. C. secs. 4728-1, 4729; *Laws of Ohio,* CIX, 242.
14. Annual Statistical Report of the Public Schools, 1929-1940, entry 376.
15. *Ibid.*

Minutes

373. MINUTES OF BOARD OF EDUCATION
1914—. 4 vols.

Minutes of the county board of education, showing date of meeting, petitions and motions passed or rejected, name of person making each motion, names of members present and absent, and signature of presiding officer. Arranged chronologically by dates of meetings. No index. 1914-1921, handwritten; 1922—, typed. Average 300 pages. 17 x 10 x 1.5. Board of education office.

Teachers

374. EXAMINATION REPORTS
1903-1907, 1909-1935. 4 vols.

Reports of teachers' examinations, showing date and place of examination, name, assigned number, and age of applicant, number of school terms served, state of nativity, grades in all subjects examined, name of examiners, classification of certification issued, and number of certificates issued to teachers. Arranged chronologically by dates of examinations. No index. 1903-1907, 1909-1920, handwritten on printed forms; 1920-1935, typed on printed forms. 3 volumes average 200 pages. 8.5 x 12 x 2; 1 volume 400 loose-leaf pages. 12 x 8 x 3.5. Board of education office.

375. NORMAL SCHOOL RECORD
1914-1926. 1 vol. (1). Discontinued. Normal School closed 1926.

Transcripts of credits of young teachers and prospective teachers studying at Geauga County Normal School, showing date of transcript, name of student, period of study in normal school, name of course studied, semester hours, grade, names of subjects studied, names of instructors, name of high school graduated from, and signature of county normal school director. Arranged chronologically by dates of transcripts. No index. Handwritten on printed forms. 150 pages. 7 x 10 x 1. Board of education office.

Statistics

376. ANNUAL STATISTICAL REPORT OF THE PUBLIC SCHOOLS
1929—. 10 pamphlets.

Copies of annual statistical reports to state director of education, showing net enrollment and totals for the county, average daily attendance, aggregate days of attendance, average number of days schools were in session, aggregate number of days absent, number and kind of school buildings in each school district, information pertaining to transportation facilities for pupils, number of teachers employed, data on salaries and courses of instruction, pupils' personnel and age, grade table or graph, showing number of pupils of each age in each grade, data on buildings, miscellaneous information, and signatures of members of county board of education. Arranged alphabetically by names of school districts. No index. Handwritten on printed forms. Average 12 pages. 12 x 8 x .25. Board of education office.

Financial Records

377. ANNUAL FINANCIAL REPORT OF COUNTY SUPERINTENDENT
1928—. 11 pamphlets. Initiated in 1928.

Copies of county superintendents annual financial report to state director of education, covering all receipts and expenditures of each school district and total; receipts, showing amount of aid received from state, county auditor, city institute fund, tuition, rental of school property, interest on deposits, and other sources; expenditures, showing expenses of county board of education, salary of county superintendent and other county board of education offices, other expenditures, and balance on hand and deposit; receipts and expenditures for separate schools; expenditures, showing date of expenditure, name of school district, amount of teacher's salary, other fixed charges, amount of outstanding bonds, interest, and principal pay on bonds, and unpaid salaries; receipts, showing date of receipt, name of school district, purpose, and amount of receipt; assets, including cash, inventory of school supplies, and amount due from state and county funds; and liabilities, including outstanding bonds and other loans. Arranged alphabetically by names of school districts. No index. Handwritten on printed forms. Average 35 pages. 10 x 7 x .25. Board of education office.

The general health district, or county board of health, is one of the recent developments in county health administration. An act of the legislature in 1919 provided that townships and municipalities in each county, exclusive of any city with 25,000 or more population, should constitute a general health district; cities with 25,000 or more population, a municipal health district. Municipalities of not less than 10,000 nor more than 25,000 population, maintaining a board of health meeting the qualifications of the legislative act, were authorized after examination by the state health department to continue operation as separate health districts.[1]

An amendment in December 1919 made each city a health district; the townships and villages in each county were combined into a general health district; and a city and general health district were authorized to combine for administrative purposes.[2] The mayor of each municipality not constituting a city health district, and the chairman of the board of trustees of each township, are authorized to meet at the seat of justice and, by selecting a chairman and a secretary, organize a district advisory council. This council selects and appoints a district board of health composed of five members, one of whom must be a physician, who serve without compensation.[3]

Within 30 days after their appointment the members of the district board of health – the county board of health – organize by appointing one of their members president and another president *pro tempore*. The board is authorized to appoint as district health commissioner a licensed physician who serves as secretary to the board. This official is designated deputy state registrar of vital statistics and is required to report monthly to the state registrar of vital statistics.[4]

On the recommendation of the district health commissioner the board appoints a full-time public health nurse, a clerk, and such additional public health nurses, physicians, and others as may be necessary for the proper conduct of its work. The board studies the prevalence of diseases, especially communicable diseases, provides treatment of venereal diseases, and is authorized to make any and all regulations it deems necessary for the prevention or restriction of disease, and the prevention, abolition, or suppression of nuisances.

---

1. *Laws of Ohio*, CVIII, pt. i, 236.
2. *Ibid.*, CVIII, pt. ii, 1085.
3. *Ibid.*
4. G. C. sec. 1261-32; *Laws of Ohio*, CVIII, pt. i, 238-242.

It provides for inspection of public charitable, benevolent, correctional, and penal institutions; and may provide inspection of dairies, stores, restaurants, hotels, and other places where food is manufactured, handled, stored, sold or offered for sale. The board is authorized to carry on necessary laboratory tests by establishing a laboratory or contracting with existing laboratories, and all state institutions supported in whole or in part by public funds must furnish such laboratory service to a county board of health under the terms agreed upon.[5]

The health department is financed by public taxation. The district board of health annually estimates in itemized form the amount needed for the ensuing financial year, and these estimates are certified to the county auditor and submitted by him to the county budget commissioners who may reduce any item but cannot increase any item or the aggregate of all items. The total amount fixed by the budget commissioners is apportioned by the county health department on the basis of taxable valuations in the townships and municipalities composing the district.[6]

In Geauga County the board of health carries on its work with two county nurses and a clerk, all under the supervision of the health commissioner. Laboratory tests of water and milk, or for typhoid, diphtheria, syphilis, undulant fever, and Bangs disease are made for the district at Ohio State University. Rabies treatment serum is available at the local office at all times, and the state health department provides free treatment of syphilis when application is properly made through the local office. The annual budget of the board amounted in 1940 to $8500, of which the state department contributed $1000.[7]

Tuberculosis clinics, supported by the Geauga County Tuberculosis and Health Association have been conducted by the board of health since 1939.[8] Complete x-ray files and case records are kept in its office.[9] Since Geauga County maintains no sanatorium, it sends its incipient tuberculosis patients to Pope's Convalescent Home in this county. Advanced cases requiring constant care are sent to the nearest hospital available where this type of disease can be adequately treated.[10]

---

5. *Laws of Ohio,* CVIII, pt. ii, 1088, 1089.
6. *Ibid.,* CVIII, pt. ii, 1091.
7. Minutes of Budget Commission, 1940, *see* entry 359.
8. X-ray Card File, 1939-1941, *see* entry 385.
9. *Ibid.*
10. Commissioners' Journal, General XI, [1936-1941], 230, *see* entry 1.

In 1940 the commissioners appropriated for this purpose $5000, supporting patients at one or another of these institutions.[11]

All records are located and office of W. C. Corey, health officer, 124 Huntington Street, Chardon, Ohio.

---

11. *Ibid.,* 330.

Minutes

378. MINUTES OF THE GEAUGA COUNTY BOARD OF HEALTH
    1920—. 1 vol.

Minutes of Geauga County board of health, showing date of meeting, record of all motions made, bills passed for payment, and appropriation of funds to various accounts from the general board of health fund. Arranged chronologically by dates of meetings. No index. Typed. 150 loose-leaf pages. 10 x 8 x 1.

Communicable Diseases

379. [CASE RECORDS OF COMMUNICABLE DISEASES]
    1921—. 1 file drawer, 1 vol.

Case records of communicable diseases, showing case number, name, address, and age of patient, name and address of attending physician, kind of disease, district number, date card sent to state, date of report, date of visit, and date of release from quarantine. Arranged chronologically by dates reported. No index. Handwritten on printed forms. File drawer, 10 x 15 x 25.5; volume, 200 pages. 14 x 22 x 1.5.

Vital Statistics

380. [COPIES OF BIRTH CERTIFICATE]
1921—. 1 file drawer.

Copies of certificates of births, showing date and place of birth, certificate number, sex of child, names, address, ages, and occupation of parents, certificate of attending physician, and certificate of informant. Arranged chronologically by dates of birth. For index, see entry 381. Handwritten and typed on printed forms. 10 x 15 x 25.5.

381. [CARD INDEX RECORD OF BIRTHS]
1921—. 1 file box.

Index to [Copies of Birth Certificates], entry 380, showing name of infant, date and place of birth, names of parents, and number of birth certificates. Arranged alphabetically by names of infants. Handwritten on cards 10 x 15 x 25.5.

382. [COPIES OF CERTIFICATES OF DEATHS]
1921—. 1 file box.

Copies of certificates of deaths, showing name and address the decedent, date of death, sex, race, marital status, date and place of birth, age, occupation, names and birth places of parents, signature of informant, date buried, and name and address of funeral firm; Certificate of death by attending physician, showing date of death, principal and contributory causes of death, and signature of physician. Arranged chronologically by dates of deaths. No index. Handwritten and typed on printed forms. 10 x 15 x 25.5.

383. VITAL STATISTICS
1921—. 1 file box.

Monthly statistical reports of births and deaths, showing date of report, and number of births of each sex reported during month; deaths, showing date of report, cause of death, age, and number of deaths from each cause and of each age during month. Arranged chronologically by dates reported. No index. Handwritten. 10 x 15 x 25.5.

Financial Records
(See also entry 378)

384. RECORD OF DISBURSEMENTS
1921—. 1 vol.
Record of disbursements from the board of health fund, showing date of disbursement, name of payee, purpose and amount of payment, and balance on hand in fund. Arranged chronologically by dates of disbursement. No index. Handwritten on printed forms. 240 pages. 14 x 10 x 2.

Miscellaneous

385. X-RAY CARD FILE
1932—. 1 file drawer.
History of X-ray plates, showing date X-ray was taken, name of patient, stage of disease, condition or classification, cost of diagnosis and X-ray, date of medical examination by physician, age and description of patient, and disposition of case. Arranged alphabetically by names of patients. No index. Typed on printed forms. Approximately 2200 cards, 3 x 5, in file drawer, 10 x 15 x 25.5.

By the provisions of the legislative act of 1816, the county commissioners were authorized to build a "poor house," and to appoint annually seven persons to constitute a board of directors. This board, a corporate body, was authorized to make such rules and regulations as were necessary for the management of the institution, and to appoint a superintendent. He was directed to receive only persons who had the required order from the township trustees. He was directed to keep a book listing the name and age of every person admitted, together with the date of admission.[1] The board of directors, or a committee of that body, was required to visit the "poor house" monthly to examine the condition of the paupers and to make a report on such matters as a food, clothing, and treatment of inmates. Moreover they were required to inspect the books and accounts of the superintendent. The board was required to report annually to the county commissioners the "state of the institution" with a full and correct account of all their proceedings, contracts, and disbursements. The expenses of establishing and supporting the institution were to be paid on the order of the county commissioners out of the money in the treasury not otherwise appropriated.[2]

By the legislative act of 1831, the membership of the board was reduced to three. This board, like its predecessor, was authorized to appoint a superintendent. It was his duty, upon the order of the board, to discharge from the poor house any person who had been admitted because of illness when he had sufficiently recovered. The directors were further authorized to remove paupers to their legal place of residence, and any pauper rejected by the board of directors could be turned over to the township overseers to be cared for by contracting with the lowest bidder.[3] In 1842 the board was made elective for a three-year term.[4]

The Geauga County infirmary was built in 1839 by the county commissioners under the authority of the act of 1816.[5]

In 1850 the name county poorhouse was changed to that of county infirmary.[6]

---

1. *Laws of Ohio,* XIV, 447.
2. *Ibid.,* XIV, 499.
3. *Ibid.,* XXIX, 316.
4. *Ibid.,* XL, 35.
5. Commissioners' Journal, I [1806-1864], 165, *Laws of Ohio,* XIV, 447.
6. *Laws of Ohio,* XLVIII, 62.

Fifteen years later, in 1865, the board of infirmary directors, consisting of three resident electors, was to be elected by the voters of the county for a three-year term. The board was still authorized to appoint a superintendent, and he was still required to make inspection visits, and to report its findings to the county commissioners.[7]

Although reports have been required of the infirmary management in previous years, it was not until the decade of the seventies that the legislature enacted measures looking to really systematic management of this ancient institution. Accordingly, in 1872, an act was passed which required each infirmary director, as well as the superintendent, to give bond conditioned for the faithful performance of the duties of his office.[8] Under this act the directors were required to report semiannually to the county commissioners the condition of the infirmary, the number of inmates and such other information as the county commissioners believe proper. Furthermore, the board of directors was required to file a full account "of all moneys received and paid out, together with the vouchers . . . from whence received, to whom and what for paid out" with the county commissioners, who, after examining it, entered the report in the minutes of their proceedings. This report, as well as the vouchers, was to be filed in the auditor's office, and must be "safely preserved" by that officer.[9]

The county infirmary served also as a place for the confinement of children, the mentally ill, and persons afflicted with epilepsy. Although the state assumed responsibility for the mentally ill in the early years of the 19th century, it was not until 1898 that it was made unlawful to confine the adult insane and epileptics in the county home.[10] Previously, in 1884, the legislature had prohibited the housing in the county infirmary of children who were eligible to the county children's home or to some other charitable institution, unless separated from adults.[11] Exceptions were made, however, in the case of insane, idiotic, and epileptic children.[12] The latter provision is still effective in Ohio.[13]

---

7. *Ibid.,* LXII, 24-25.
8. *Laws of Ohio,* LXIX, 120-121.
9. *Ibid.,* LXIX, 121-122.
10. *Ibid.,* XCIII, 274.
11. *Ibid.,* LXXXI, 92.
12. *Ibid.,* CIII, 890.
13. G. C. sec. 3089.

By an act of May 31, 1911, effective January 1, 1913, the board of infirmary directors was abolished and the powers formally exercised by this body were transferred to the county commissioners and the infirmary superintendent.[14] The superintendent is still required to keep a record of the inmates, as prescribed by statute and to report annually to the county commissioners. This report, the acceptance of which is evidenced by an entry in the minutes of the commissioners' journal, is filed with the county auditor and by him preserved.[15] In 1919 the name county infirmary was changed to that of county home.[16]

The county commissioners still make provision for the establishment and maintenance of the county home, appoints a superintendent, and make regular inspection visits. Since December 1, 1932, the superintendent has been appointed from a list of names of persons eligible under civil service regulations,[17] and is authorized to appoint a matron and other employees.[18] Since 1882, the commissioners have been authorized to appoint an infirmary physician, who, like the superintendent, is required by statute to report to the county commissioners. This report, made quarterly, includes such information as the nature and extent of medical services rendered, to whom, and the character of the disease treated.[19]

Although there is some relation between the old age pension system and the county home, the newer form of aid is merely supplementary to the institution. As always, the county home cares for those whose condition is such that they cannot be satisfactorily cared for except in an institution.[20] The benefits granted by the division of aid for the aged have somewhat reduced the number of inmates of the county home in Geauga County, as those who are able to do so leave the home after receiving a pension.[21] The number of persons given refuge by the Geauga County home during the past 25 years is unknown.[22]

---

14. *Laws of Ohio,* CII, 433.
15. G. C. sec. 2535.
16. *Laws of Ohio,* CVIII, pt. i, 68.
17. Ohio Attorney General, *Opinions,* III, 2021.
18. G. C. sec. 2522.
19. G. C. sec. 2456; *Laws of Ohio,* LXXIII, 233; LXXIX, 90; 436; CVIII, pt. i, 269.
20. *The Reorganization of County Government in Ohio: Reports of the Governor's Commission on County Government* (n. p., n. d.). Submitted to the Governor, December, 1934.
21. Register of Inmates, 1915-1940, *passim,* entry 385.
22. These records have been burned. The information is available at the division of aid for the aged, Department of Public Welfare, 12th floor of State Office Building, Columbus, Ohio.

Some of the inmates pay all or a part of the cost of the care, but by far the greater number do not. In 1940 the commissioners appropriated $13,542.56 for the maintenance of the home.[23] The seven resident members of the staff received an aggregate salary of $3745.34[24]

Physical care is given within the limits of the resources of the institution. A minister is occasionally called in to hold religious services.

All records are located in the office of the superintendent at the county home, R. R. Chardon Township, Chardon Ohio.

---

23. Commissioners' Journal, General, XI [1936-1941], 330.
24. Appropriation Ledger, 1940, entry 248.

Case Records

386. REGISTER OF INMATES
1845—. 1 vol.

Register of case record of inmates, showing name and address of inmate, sex, race, age, date admitted, nationality, date discharged, date readmitted, date of death and burial, number of grave in county home cemetery, location of other cemeteries, and remarks. Arranged chronologically by dates admitted. No index. Handwritten on printed forms. 239 pages. 16 x 13 x 2.5.

387. DAILY MOVEMENT OF INMATES
1915—. 1 file drawer.

Daily record of movements of inmates, showing date of record, number of males and females, total on hand at beginning of day, number received and discharged during day, average during month, number continuously present for month, number of deaths during month, and number of persons received during month who were former inmates. These are duplicates of the record sent monthly to the division of charities; yearly summary is contained in back of pad. Arranged chronologically by dates recorded. No index. Handwritten on printed forms. 24 pads, average 14 pages. 6 x 8 x .25. in file drawer, 3 x 6 x 8.

Financial Records

388. ANNUAL REPORTS [Certificates of Admission to County Infirmary]
1917—. 1 file drawer.
Certificates of admission to county home made out by township trustees and sent
to the superintendent, showing date of certificate, name and address of applicant,
age, sex, race, birthplace, marital status, occupation, length of residence in county
and township, former residence, nature and duration of relief needed, disease
record, present physical condition, and signatures of township trustees. Arranged
chronologically by dates of certificates. No index. Handwritten on printed forms.
3 x 6 x 8.

389. SUPERINTENDENT'S ACCOUNT [Disbursements]
1884—. 1 vol. (1).
Record of miscellaneous cash disbursements made by superintendent from the
reserve fund, showing date of payment, to whom paid, for supplies and services
rendered, and amount of payment; record of payment of larger and more important
county home bills authorized by county commissioners and paid by county auditor.
Arranged chronologically by dates of payments. No index. Handwritten on printed
forms. 199 pages. 18 x 13 x 1.

390. JOURNAL [of Receipts and Payments into Treasury]
1917—. 1 vol. Initiated in 1917.
Record of receipts of sales of products of county home farm, showing date of
receipt, products sold, amount received, and total deposited in treasury; also receipts
from inmates, relatives and friends of inmates, and in back of volume a summary
of yearly totals paid to treasurer. Arranged chronologically by dates receipted. No
index. Handwritten. 212 pages. 12 x 7.5 x 1.

391. RECEIPTS [Duplicates of Pay-In Orders]

1917—. 1 file drawer.

Carbon copies of auditor's pay-in orders, showing number and date of order, name of superintendent of county home, amount and source of payment, name of fund credited, signature of auditor, and stamp of treasurer and receipt of amount. Arranged chronologically by dates ordered. No index. Handwritten or printed forms. 3 x 6 x 8.

Miscellaneous

392. VISITORS' REGISTER

1910—. 1 vol. (1). Initiated in 1910.

Register of visitors to county home, showing signature and address of visitor, date of visit, and remarks. Arranged chronologically by dates of visits. No index. Handwritten on printed forms. 500 pages. 18 x 13 x 2.

The board of county visitors, an agency for the examination and inspection of county institutions supported wholly or in part by county or municipal taxation, was created by an act of the general assembly in 1882. Under this act, the judge of the court of common pleas was authorized to appoint five persons, three of whom were to be women, who were to visit periodically such county institutions as the county infirmary, county jail, municipal prisons, and children's home, and file annually a report of their proceedings and recommendations for changes with the clerk of courts, and to forward a copy to the state board of charities. The members, appointed for an indefinite period, were to serve without compensation.[1]

By the act of 1892 the personnel of the board was increased to six persons, three of whom were to be women, and not more than three to have the same political affiliations. Furthermore, the act made it the duty of the probate judge, whenever proceedings were instituted in his court to commit a child under 16 years of age to the boys' industrial home or to the girls' industrial home, to have notice given to the board of such proceedings; and it was made the duty of the board of visitors to attend the meetings of the court, as a body or as a committee, to protect the interest of the child.[2]

While the provisions of the act of 1892 were redefined by the acts of 1898 and 1900, these acts did not, in the main, affect the duties of the board.[3] The latter act, however, made the board a continuous body with two members serving for one year, two members serving for two years, and two members serving for three years. In addition to this, the board was allowed a minimum expense schedule for their services.[4] Six years later the board was authorized to recommend to the county commissioners measures for the more economical administration of county institutions. Their report, together with their recommendations, was to be filed each year with the judge of the probate court and with the county prosecuting attorney. The power of appointment of the members of the board was given to the judge of the probate court.[5]

---

1. *Laws of Ohio,* LXXIX, 107.
2. *Ibid.,* LXXXIX, 161.
3. *Ibid.,* XCIII, 57; XCIV, 70.
4. *Ibid.,* XCIV, 70.
5. *Ibid.,* XCVIII, 28.

Under an act of 1913 the juvenile judge, like the probate judge under the act of 1892, was authorized to notify the visitors when any proceedings were instituted in his court for the commitment of any child to a state institution for correction.[6] The practice of annually filing reports of the board with the probate judge, prosecuting attorney, and state board of charities have been continued.[7]

In Geauga County the board makes its inspections of the county institutions at intervals of 12 months. Although the board makes its annual reports according to the requirements of state law, these were not located in the inventory of county records.

The board of county visitors keeps no separate records, for records of appointments, 1913—, see entry 154.

---

6. *Ibid.,* CIII, 173-174, 888.
7. G. C. sec. 2976.

The soldiers' relief commission was established by an act of the legislature passed May 19, 1886, entitled "An act to provide for the relief of indigent Union soldiers, sailors, and marines, and the indigent wives, widows and minor children of indigent or deceased Union soldiers, sailors and marines." Under provisions of this act the commissioners of each county were authorized to levy a special tax for the purpose of creating a fund for the relief of such beneficiaries; and the judge of the court of common pleas was authorized to appoint three county residents, at least two of whom were honorably discharged Union soldiers, to serve for a term of three years as members of the commission, which was organized by the selection of a chairman and a secretary and was known as the soldiers' relief commission.[1]

An amendment passed on March 4, 1887, provided that councilmen of the city wards, as well as the board of trustees of the townships, certified to the soldiers' relief commission the names of those requiring and entitled to aid under the act.[2]

By the act of legislature, passed April 28, 1890 the soldiers' relief commission was required to appoint annually a committee of three in each township and a committee of three in each ward in any city in the county, whose duty it was to receive all applications for aid and to certify them to the soldiers' relief commission.[3]

Sections 239 and 2933-4 of the General Code were amended, March 6, 1917, to provide for the appointment to each county commission of one member who is the wife, widow, son, or daughter of an honorably discharged soldier, sailor, or marine of the Civil War or of the Spanish-American War, the other two members to be honorably discharged soldiers, sailors, or marines of the United States; and for the appointment to each township and ward committee of a wife or widow of a soldier, sailor, or marine of the United States.[4] Two years later, in 1919, the provisions of the act were extended to include indigent veterans of the World War and indigent parents, wives, widows, or minor children of such veterans.[5]

---

1. *Laws of Ohio*, LXXXIII, 232.
2. *Ibid.*, LXXXIV, 100.
3. *Ibid.*, LXXXVII, 352.
4. *Ibid.*, CVII, 27.
5. *Ibid.*, CVIII, pt. i, 633.

Section 2930 of the General Code was amended in 1941, to provide for the appointment by the court of common pleas in each county of a soldiers' relief commission, to consist of three members, one to be a member of the United Spanish-American veterans; one a member of the American Legion; and one a member of the Veterans of Foreign Wars or of the Disabled American Veterans of the World War.[6]

The Geauga County commissioners appropriate funds each year for this commission and the secretary receives an annual salary of $600.[7] The aid granted varies from year to year. In 1937 the average monthly outlay was $413.79, in 1938 it rose to $502.37, and in 1940 it dropped to $272.62.[8]

The record of the soldiers' relief commission are located at the home of the chairman, Dr. J. W. Moats, 139 North Street, Chardon, Ohio.

---

6. G. C. sec. 2930.
7. Commissioners' Journal, General XI [1936-1940, 333, entry 1.
8. Records of Indigent Soldiers, Sailors, and Marines, 1937-1940, *passim, see* entry 259.

393. MINUTE BOOK
1924—. 1 vol.
Minutes of soldiers' relief commission, showing date of meeting, names of members present, and record of business transacted, including decisions of the members in approval or rejection of applications for soldiers' relief, showing date of application, name of applicant, and amount awarded. Arranged chronologically by dates of meetings. No index. Handwritten. 100 loose-leaf pages. 10 x 8 x 1.

394. RECORD OF GRANTS
1920—. 1 vol.
Record of grants of soldiers' relief, showing name and address of recipient, date approved, amount of monthly award, date, and reason cancelled. Arranged alphabetically by names of soldiers and chronologically thereunder by dates approved. No index. Handwritten on printed forms. 240 pages. 14 x 10 x 2.

In 1884 the legislature made provision for soldiers' burial committees in each county, to consist of three members in each township appointed by the county commissioners, which were directed to defray the expense incurred in the interment of any honorable discharged Union soldier, sailor, or marine who died in poverty. The committees, serving at the pleasure of the appointing power, were required to report to the county commissioners the name, rank, and command of the decedent, which report was transcribed by the county commissioners in a book kept for that purpose.[1] The original act, amended in 1891, extended the provisions of the act to include the interment of the wives or widows of Union soldiers.[2] In 1893 the act was again amended to provide for the interment of mothers of Union soldiers, sailors, marines, and army nurses.[3] In 1908 the personnel of the committee was reduced to two.[4]

Under the present law which became effective and 1921 the county commissioners are authorized to appoint two suitable persons in each township and ward in the county, who are directed to contract with the undertaker selected by the family or friends of the deceased, and to direct the burial in a respectable manner of the body of any honorably discharged soldier, sailor, or marine having at any time served in the army or navy of the United States, or the mother, wife, or widow of any soldier, sailor, or marine, or that of any war nurse who served at any time in the army of the United States who died in poverty.[5]

The burial committee is instructed to enforce all laws relative to the burial of indigent veterans, investigate the financial status of the decedent's family, and report its findings to the county commissioners, together with the name, rank, and command to which the deceased belonged, date of death, place of burial, occupation while living, and an itemized statement of the cost of burial.[6]

---

1. *Laws of Ohio*, LXXXI, 146-147.
2. *Ibid.*, LXXXVIII, 330-331.
3. *Ibid.*, XC, 177.
4. *Ibid.*, XCIX, 99.
5. G. C. sec. 2950; *Laws of Ohio*, CVIII, pt.i, 34; CIX, 211.
6. *Laws of Ohio*, XCIX. 100.

Upon receiving this report of the burial committee, the county commissioners transcribe the information in a book kept for that purpose, and certify the expense to the county auditor who draws his warrant for payment to the person or person specified by the county commissioners.[7]

The amount contributed by the county for the burial of an indigent veteran set by the legislature at $35 in 1884 was increased to $75 in 1908, and to $100 in 1921.[8] Since 1908 each member of the burial committee has been allowed $1 for each service performed.[9]

In Geauga County the committees have very few burials to supervise. They conducted only three in 1938, three in 1939, and one in 1940, with an average expenditure of $100 for each.[10]

The soldiers' burial committees kept no separate record; for reports to the commissioners, 1916—, see entry 1; for Record of Burials, 1886-1916, see entry 258.

---

7. *Ibid.*, XCIX, 101.
8. *Laws of Ohio*, LXXXI, 146-147; XCIX, 99; CIX, 212; G. C. sec. 2951.
9. *Ibid.*, XCIX, 99; G. C. sec. 2951.
10. Appropriation Ledger, 1938-1940, *see* entry 248.

Provision for the relief of the indigent was made in 1805, but it was not until 1898 that the legislature provided separate relief for the indigent blind. The act authorized the township trustees to certify to the county commissioners an amount not to exceed $100 per person per annum for such relief, the certification to be made a record listing the name of the beneficiary and the amount required, and directed the county commissioners to levy on the townships to the amount certified, this amount to be paid into the county treasury and thence to the township treasurer to be used for blind relief.[1]

Six years later, in 1904, certification authority was transferred from the township trustees to the probate judge, who was required to register the name and address of beneficiaries and to issue to each a certificate giving his name, address, and the amount to be drawn. Persons eligible for relief were blind males over 21 and blind females over 18 years of age, without proper means of support. Not less than two county citizens, one a physician selected by the court, were required to testify that the applicant had been a resident of the state for five years and a resident of the county for one year immediately preceding the filing of an application for relief as a condition for granting aid.[2]

The act of 1904 was declared unconstitutional on the ground that it required the spending of public funds raised by taxation for a private purpose.[3] Hence, in 1908, an act was passed authorizing the county commissioners to levy a stipulated tax to create a fund for relief of the needy blind, the maximum benefit not to exceed $150 per person per annum to be paid quarterly; and authorizing the probate judge to appoint a blind relief commission consisting of three members to serve for a three-year term, directed to meet annually in the office of the county commissioners to examine applications recorded in order of their receipt in a book furnished by the county commissioners. This record was required to be kept open for public inspection.[4]

The blind relief commission was abolished by the legislature in 1913 and its powers and duties were transferred to the county commissioners.[5]

Separate records were not found for this commission; for county commissioners' records see entry 16.

---

1. *Laws of Ohio*, XCIII, 270.
2. *Ibid.*, XCVII, 392-394.
3. *Auditor of Lucas County*, v. *The State, Ohio State Reports*, LXXV. 114-137.
4. *Laws of Ohio*, XCIX, 56-58.
5. *Ibid.*, CIII, 60.

The "Old Age Pension" law proposed by initiative petition, was adopted by the people of Ohio in a general election of 1933.[1] The act, as amended in 1936, provides that any person 65 or more years of age may, upon certain stipulated conditions, receive a pension, providing his total income does not exceed $360 annually; In 1941 this amount was increased to $480. The applicant must be a citizen of the United States, and must have resided in Ohio not less than five years of the nine prior to making application for aid, nor less than one year continuously in the county in which application is made. He must be unable to support himself, and have no claims of any legal responsible person who is able to support him. In addition, the net value of all unencumbered property of the unmarried applicant must not exceed $3000; if the applicant is married, the combined property of husband and wife must not exceed $4000 in value.[2]

Such property may be transferred to the division of aid for the aged to be held in trust. An amendment in 1937[3] made this transfer of property optional, and not as originally ruled, a requirement to be complied with before aid might be granted. Upon the death of the recipient of aid, this property, as well as life insurance over $250, less deductions for funeral expenses, claims of administrators, doctors, widow, and children, is used to defray in part or wholly the expense to the state of such aid as has been allowed.[4] A bill for the amount of the aid is presented to the estate. If no funds are available for funeral expenses, the state allows $100 for the funeral, and $25 for a burial lot.

The division of aid for the aged was set up as a part of the state department of public welfare in 1933 for the purpose of administering the old age pension law. In each county, however, the commissioners might operate as a local board if they so desired. If they declined to serve in this capacity, the chief of the division of aid for the aged was authorized to appoint, with the consent of the director of public welfare, a board of three or five members of the community who served without compensation. The board was required to keep complete records, and might employ, subject to the approval of the division, such agents and other assistance as proper administration of the required.[5]

---

1. *Laws of Ohio,* CXV, pt. ii, 431-439.
2. *Ibid.,* CXVI, pt. ii, 216-221, CXVIII, 739.
3. G. C. sec. 1359-6.
4. G. C. sec. 1359-6.
5. *Laws of Ohio,* CXV, pt. ii, 431-139.

Since 1937 the chief of the division has been required to appoint such a board in any county.[6]

Each case is thoroughly investigated, but the board is advised to make its inquiries not in a strictly formal way, but the matter which seems "best calculated to conform to substantial justice." Its decisions may be appealed to the division.[7] After a case has been investigated, the applicant, if considered eligible, is granted a certificate of relief which is then passed on by the division,[8] and once accepted by the division, need not be renewed.

Under the social security act, the federal government contributes all administrative expenses and 50 percent of the amount contributed as aid to the aged, within a maximum of $20 a month for each person aided.[9] The remainder of the money is applied by the state.

The local board in Geauga County was discontinued in January 1939. At the present time, a subdivision manager is appointed directly by the State Welfare Department and works under the supervision of a district supervisor. The administrator is appointed by the chief of the Ohio Division of Aid for the Aged.[10] The manager is assisted by a staff of one. In 1940 and 1941, an average of 366[11] persons were receiving aid monthly, the amount granted for this period being $191,564.48.[12]

All records are located in the office of aid for the aged which is located in the north end of the county commissioners' office.

---

6. G. C. sec. 1359-12.
7. *Laws of Ohio*, CXV, pt. ii, 431-439.
8. *Ibid.*, CXV, pt. ii, 435.
9. U. S. C. A. XLII, 303.
10. *Laws of Ohio*, CXV, pt. ii, 431-439.
11. Case Records – Active Cases, 1940-1941, entry 396.
12. *Ibid.*

395. REGISTER   OF   APPLICATIONS   RECEIVED-OLD   AGE
ASSISTANCE

1934—. 1 vol.

Record of applications for aid for the aged, showing date of application, application number, race, sex and present status of applicant, also record of investigation, showing date and by whom investigated; action taken in county, showing date, amount of grant recommended, whether denied, transferred, or otherwise disposed of, and date application forwarded; final action by state office, showing date, disposition of case, and amount granted. Arranged chronologically by dates of applications and numerically thereunder by application numbers. No index. Handwritten on printed forms. 60 pages. 12 x 20 x .5.

396. CASE RECORD-ACTIVE CASES

1934—. 2 file drawers.

Case records including applications for aid, showing application number, certificate number, date of original application, date of award, name and address of applicant, statement of financial condition, names and addresses of children, agreement to notify the division of aid for the aged of additions to property, witnessed oath of applicant, and date application approved; also includes investigators reports (initial investigation), showing name of investigator, date of investigation, name of recipient, application number, date of application, date and place of birth, residence, marital status, living arrangements, living expenses, income, and other aid, budget, children, property, insurance, war service, health, work (history), future plans, special conditions, references, amount of award, and remarks; also includes certificate of aid, showing certificate number, month of award, county, name and address of recipient, amount of award, date approved, and signatures of subdivision manager and chief of the division of aid for the aged and miscellaneous correspondence. Arranged numerically by certificate numbers. For index, see entry 397. Handwritten and typed on printed forms. 12 x 10 x 28.

397. CARD INDEX RECORD-ACTIVE CASES
1934—. 1 file drawer.

Index record of active cases receiving old age assistance, showing name and address of recipient, application number, certificate of aid number, date of birth, and date aid began. This is an index record but it serves as an index to entry 398 by showing certificate numbers. Arranged alphabetically by names of recipients. Typed on printed forms. 6 x 4 x 18.

398. CARD INDEX RECORD-CLOSED CASES
1934—. 1 file drawer.

Card record of cases no longer receiving old age assistance, showing name of recipient, application number, certificate of aid number, date of birth, address, date aid began, date discharged or denied, reason for discharge or denial, total period of aid, and total amount paid. This is an index record but it serves as an index to entries 399, 400. Arranged alphabetically by names of recipients. Typed on printed cards. 6 x 4 x 18.

399. CASE RECORDS-CASES PENDING, WITHDRAWALS, DENIALS, AND TRANSFERRED CASES
1934—. 1 file drawer.

Records of old age assistance recipients in pending cases, withdrawals, denials, and transferred cases, including applications, investigator's reports, certificates of aid, certificates of cancellation, and notice of transfer, showing name and address of applicant, date of application, application number, certificate number, action taken, and related data. Arranged numerically by application numbers. For index, see entry 398, no index to pending cases. Handwritten and typed on printed forms. 12 x 10 x 28.

400. CASE RECORDS-DECEASED CASES
1934—. 1 file drawer.

Record of deceased old age assistance recipients, including application, investigator's reports, certificate of aid, and miscellaneous correspondence showing information as in Case Records–Active Cases, entry 396; also includes certificates of cancellation, showing certificate number, county, amount of award, date effective, name and address of recipient, date of cancellation, reason, and signatures of subdivision manager and chief of division of aid for the aged. Arranged numerically by certificate numbers. For index, see entry 398. Handwritten and typed on printed forms. 12 x 10 x 28.

401. REPORT OF VISITATIONS
1934—. 3 vols.

Reports of investigators' semiannual visits, showing names of township and county, certificate number, name and address of recipient, signed certification by investigator of quarterly investigations, and signature of recipient of aid; also includes case histories in duplicate, showing date of application, application number, certificate number, name and address of recipient, record of verification of age, citizenship, residence, children's contribution to support of recipient, record of all property and insurance owned, all debts and mortgages owed, war service, health record, work history, future plans, special conditions, references, date of initial investigations, semiannual visits, living expenses, income, and address of legal guardian. Arranged alphabetically by names of townships and chronologically thereunder by dates of visits. No index. Handwritten and typed on printed forms. Average 500 pages. 12 x 9.5 x 1.

The office of county surveyor, another English institution transplanted to America during the colonial period, became an important office in frontier Ohio where land titles and boundary lines were often in dispute. The office is entirely a product of statute, there being no constitutional provision for its establishment.

The first act of the general assembly pertaining to the surveyor was passed during the first legislative session of 1803. Under this act the court of common pleas was authorized to appoint a person well qualified to act as county surveyor. He received his commission from the governor, was required to give bond conditioned for the faithful performance of the duties of his office, and was directed to survey all lands which were sold or were to be sold for taxes, and was authorized to appoint chainmen or markers whose functions it was to establish corners. The surveys made by the surveyor or his deputies were the only ones to be accepted as legal evidence in any court of law or equity. For remuneration, the surveyor was permitted to retain all fees collected by him in the operation of his office.[1]

Although it made no fundamental change in the duties of the surveyor, the act of 1816 fixed his term of office at five years; authorized him to appoint deputies, and made him responsible for their official acts; and made him liable to removal by the court for negligence or incompetency, and liable to suit by persons believing themselves damaged by his negligence or that of his deputies.[2] A year later, in 1817, provision was made for the appointment of a successor in the event the office became vacant because of death, resignation, or removal.[3]

The act of 1831 consolidated the previous acts, redefine the duties of the surveyor, increased the amount of his bond, and authorized him, when directed by the county commissioners, to procure from the surveyor general's office a "certified plat, together with the field notes of corners, and bearing trees to each section, quarter section, lot or original survey in his county, and to cause the same to be preserved in a book by him provided for that purpose; which shall be deposited in the county auditor's office, for the use of landholders in the county." It provided further, that the surveyor shall keep "a fair and accurate record of all official surveys made by himself or his deputies," in a suitable book to be kept by him for that purpose, and that he should number his surveys progressively. More significant, however, was the fact that the office was made elective for a three-year term by an act of 1831.

---

1. *Laws of Ohio*, I, 90-93.
2. *Ibid.*, XIV, 424-431.
3. *Ibid.*, XV, 64.

The term remained at three years until 1906, when it was reduced to a two-year period; by the act of 1927, effective with the term of the surveyor elected in 1928, the term was increased to four years.[4]

During the years of the development of the office other duties have been delegated to the surveyor. In 1842 he was given the duty of ascertaining and reported trespassing on public lands.[5] Twelve years later he was given the same powers as the justices of the peace to take and certify deeds, mortgages, powers of attorney, and other instruments affecting real estate, to administer oaths, to take and certify affidavits.[6] In 1867 he was given the authority, when directed by the county commissioners, to transcribe any and all dilapidated maps, records of plats, and field notes of surveys in other counties.[7] Similarly, in 1881, he was authorized to procure from any office in the state a certified plat together with the field notes of corners, quarter sections, lots, or original surveys and place them in a book provided for that purpose. Certified copies from his book were to be taken as *prima facie* evidence.[8]

With the increase in modern means of transportation, there developed a growing need for more efficient methods of road construction and maintenance. Accordingly, in 1906, the surveyor was directed to act, whenever the services of an engineer were required, in the capacity of an engineer with respect to roads, turnpike, bridges, or ditches, except in cities of the first grade.[9] He was directed by statute to perform all duties in his county which would be done by a civil engineer or surveyor, to prepare all plans, specifications, and estimates of cost, and to submit forms for contracts for the construction and repair of all bridges, culverts, roads, draws, ditches, and other public improvements (except buildings) over which the county commissioners had authority. At the same time, he was made responsible for the inspection of all public improvements, and was directed to keep a complete list of all estimates and bids received for such work, as well as contracts awarded for improvements.[10]

---

4. *Laws of Ohio,* XXIX, 399; XCVIII, 245-247; CXII, 179.
5. *Ibid.,* XL, 57.
6. *Ibid.,* LII, 70.
7. *Ibid.,* LXIV, 216-217; LXXVIII, 285.
8. *Ibid.,* LXXVIII, 285.
9. *Ibid.,* XCVIII, 245-247.
10. *Ibid.*

Similarly another measure enacted in 1919 increased the duties of the surveyor regarding road construction and road maintenance. Under this act the surveyor was authorized to designate one of his deputies as maintenance engineer. This engineer, under the direction of the surveyor, was to have charge of all "road maintenance and repair work" in his county. Furthermore, when authorized by the county commissioners, the surveyor was to appoint a maintenance supervisor or supervisors to have charge of the maintenance of improved highways within a district or districts established by the commissioners or the surveyor, and containing not less than 10 miles of improved county roads.[11] In 1923 the surveyor was delegated to assist the county planning commission whenever such commission was established.[12]

Thus, the general responsibility of planning and directing county road construction is vested, by statute, in the county surveyor. Because of this increased responsibility placed on this office there has been an attempt to raise the general qualifications of those seeking election to it.

Accordingly, in 1935, and act was passed changing the title of the office to that of "county engineer," and eligibility to the office was restricted to "*a registered professional engineer and registered surveyor licensed to practice in the state of Ohio.*"[13] This act was amended in 1936 to permit the incumbent to continue in office upon re-election, even if he lacked those qualifications.[14]

In Geauga County, the staff of the engineer's office includes, in addition to the engineer himself, a maintenance supervisor, a highway engineer, and a tax map draftsman. There is a permanent maintenance force of 35 men, which in the busy summer season is enlarged with temporary workers.[15] This maintenance staff maintains 619 miles of county and township roads, and about 1700 bridges and culverts.[16] In 1939 expenditures for construction, maintenance, and repair of roads amounted to $190,843.69; in 1940 this sum decreased to $109,277.16.[17] Funds are appropriated by the commissioners entirely from the county's income in gasoline and motor vehicle taxes.

----

11. *Laws of Ohio,* CVII, pt.i, 497.
12. *Ibid.,* CX, 312.
13. *Ibid.,* CXVI, pt. i, 283.
14. *Ibid.,* pt. ii, 152.
15. Pay Rolls, 1940, entry 415.
16. Road Records, 1940, entry 408.
17. Monthly Financial Statements, 1939-1940, entry 305.

402. SURVEYOR'S RECORD

1834—. 3 vols. (1-3).

Surveyor's record of surveys, showing date of survey, names of surveyors and landowners, location of boundary lines, and roads surveyed; includes hand drawn plats of surveys, showing location of boundary lines, roads, water courses, number of acres, and other data; surveys of land sold for taxes and land in litigation, showing location of property and boundary lines and number of acres; depositions of persons concerning disputed boundary lines, 1834-1874, showing location of old and new property lines and number of acres. Also contains Field Book, 1834-1919 entry 404. Arranged chronologically by dates surveyed. 1834-1874, indexed alphabetically by names of surveyors showing numbers of townships; 1875—, index alphabetically by names of parties for whom surveys were made or by names of landowners; for index, see entry 403. Handwritten and hand drawn. Scales vary. Average 450 pages. 14 x 11 x 2.5. Engineer's office.

403. GENERAL INDEX TO SURVEYOR'S RECORD

1834—. 1 vol. (1).

Index to Surveyor's Record, entry 402, showing date of survey, survey number, name of party for whom survey made, name of township, number of acres, volume and page number of record, and remarks. Some surveys are by order of commissioners' court, others for private persons, and decennial appraisement. Later records are either on order of commissioners or court. Arranged alphabetically by names of townships and chronologically thereunder by date surveyed. Handwritten on printed forms. 488 pages. 16.5 x 12x 2.5. Engineer's office.

404. FIELD BOOK

1920—. 160 vols. (1-160). 1934-1919 in Surveyor's Record, entry 402.

Record and reference notes of county surveyors on all surveys made, showing sketches of land surveyed, figures, calculations, hearings, volume letter, and page number of Road Records, entry 408, curve functions, name, and number of stations of survey. Arranged chronologically by dates entered. For separate index, see entry 405. Handwritten. Average 150 pages. 7 x 4.5 x 1. Engineer's office.

405. INDEX [to Field Books]

1920—. 1 vol.

Index to Field Book, entry 404, showing name of roads or other surveys, volume and page numbers of record, and remarks. First half of index arranged numerically by book numbers; second half arranged alphabetically by names of roads or other surveys. Handwritten. 152 pages. 7 x 4.5 x .5. Engineer's office.

406. MAPS

1910—. 54 file boxes.

Original maps, plats, blueprints, and plans of Geauga County road work, maps and plats, showing road number, location of proposed road work, other roads, and dimensions, location of railroads, rivers, and township and village boundary lines; blueprints and plans, showing road number, sketches of proposed work, boundary lines of townships and villages, dimensions, and summary of material needed. Prepared by county engineer and deputies. Arranged numerically by road numbers. No index. Hand drawn, black on white, and blueprint. Scales vary. Average 75 maps in file boxes, 12 x 6 x 24. Engineer's office.

407. PLATS

1814-1906, 1936—. 13 vols. Title varies; Surveyors' Records, 1814-1906, 6 vols. 1795-1814 in Deed Record, entry 24.

Record of physical maps and plats of surveys made by surveyor and his assistants, showing boundary lines, lot number, length of boundary lines, location of roads and railroads, number of acres, names of owners, names of surveyors, scales, date of surveys, and names of persons for whom surveys were made. Plats prior to 1904 are transcripts of original plats of surveys made when surveyor was allowed by law to make surveys for private persons. Surveys ordered by commissioners or the court are now permitted. Prepared by county surveyor. Arranged chronologically by dates or surveys. No index. Hand drawn, black on white. Scales vary. Average 200 pages. 14 x 8.5 x 1. Engineer's office.

Roads

408. ROAD RECORDS
1806—. 5 vols. (A-E).
Records of establishing and building of county roads, including petitions, hearings, notices, copies of commissioners' resolutions, estimates, 1806-1912 for cost in road construction, records of road surveys, resurveys, and record of roads vacated; also includes hand-drawn sketches of roads, ditches, and bridges, showing date of entry, points where the improvement began and ended, dimensions, name and number of township through which the improvement crosses; record of appointments of surveyors and viewers, reports of Surveyors' Record, entry 402. 1883—, includes copies of publication of miscellaneous road procedures, copies of entries pertaining to road records and Commissioners' Journal, entry 1, and several blueprints, showing name of proposed road, road number, and name of township through which proposed road will be constructed. Also contains: County Ditch Records, 1806-1871, entry 413, Record of Estimates, 1806-1912, entry 410. Arranged chronologically by dates entered. 1806-1884, indexed numerically by township numbers; for separate index, see entry 409. Handwritten. 4 volumes, average 525 pages. 13 x 89 x 2; 1 volume, 600 pages. 16 x 12 x 2. Auditor's office.

409. GENERAL INDEX TO ROAD RECORDS
1806—. 1 vol. (1).
General index to Road Records, entry 408, showing name of township, name or road number, points of beginning and ending, volume, letter, and page numbers of road records, and remarks. Arranged alphabetically by names of townships and chronologically thereunder by dates of alteration, establishment, vacation, or other work on roads. Handwritten on printed forms. 400 pages. 16 x 12 x 2. Auditor's office.

410. RECORD OF ESTIMATES
1913—. 2vols. (one dated, 1). 1806-1912 in Road Records, entry 408.
Record of detailed estimates for county road and ditch contractor, date of contract, itemized estimates of labor and material cost, bids received, and estimate made on payment of work; includes newspaper clippings of legal notices to contractors. 1928—, arranged chronologically by dates of contracts. 1913-1927, no index;

1928—, indexed alphabetically by names of improvements. Handwritten on printed forms. 1 volume 198 pages. 13 x 8 x 1; 1 volume 300 pages. 16 x 12 x 1.5. 1 volume, 1913-1927, Auditor's office; 1 volume, 1928—, Engineer's office.

411. ROAD [Bridge] AND DITCH RECORDS
1879-1929. 4 file drawers.

Original papers concerning construction, maintenance, and improvement of roads, bridges, and ditches, including:

a. Bids, showing date of bid, itemized estimates for labor and material, and signature of contractor.
b. Specifications, showing kind of material, quantities required by the county for various county buildings, and repairing jobs.
c. Contracts, showing agreement between contractors and county, term of contract, estimated cost, time for building, material to be used, and total cost.
d. Petitions, showing date of petition, reason for petition, names of petitioners, and other miscellaneous papers.

Arranged chronologically by dates of instruments. No index. Handwritten and typed. 9 x 5 x 26. Engineer's office.

412. IMPROVED ROADS [Roads, Bridge, and Ditch Papers]
1929—. 1 file box.

Copies and duplicates of original papers and correspondence, concerning construction, improvement, and maintenance of roads, bridges, and ditches, including:

a. Bids, showing date of bid, itemized estimates for labor and material, and signature of contractor.
b. Specifications, showing kind of materials, quantities required by county for various county buildings, and repairing jobs.
c. Contracts, showing agreement between contractor and county, term of contract, estimated cost, time for construction of building, materials to be used, and total cost.
d. Petitions, showing date of petition, reason for petition, names of petitioners, record of progress by Work Projects Administration on county road and ditch work, 1935—, showing weekly report on amount of improvement or building done by Work Project Administration and date and figures on rate of progress.

Arranged alphabetically by names of roads or other projects. No index. Handwritten and typed. 12 x 6 x 24. Engineer's office.

Ditches (See also entries 408, 110-112)

413. COUNTY DITCH RECORD
1872-1905. 1 vol. -1806-1971 in Road Records, entry 409.
Record of ditch improvement and establishment, including copies of petitions, resolutions and hearings, estimates, copies of contractors' bonds, and blueprint:
a. Copies of petitions, showing date of petition, reason for petition and name of petitioners.
b. Resolutions and hearings, showing date resolution was presented to commissioners, kind of improvement, and name of township.
c. Estimates, showing name of improvement, location of work, contractors' name and address, date of contract, itemized estimates of labor and material cost, bids received, and estimate made on payment of work.
d. Copies of contractors' bonds, showing name of contractor and sureties, date and amount of bond, and condition of bond.
e. Blueprint is pasted in volume and is a map and profile of Montville Ditch, showing outline and proposed dimensions of ditch, name of landowners, and date of entry. Prepared by E. A. Merkel, surveyor in Chardon, Ohio, June 24, 1904.
Arranged chronologically by dates entered. Itemized numerically by page numbers showing names of ditches. Handwritten. 252 pages. 12 x 8 x 1. Auditor's office.

414. CUYAHOGA DITCH RECORD
1896-1899. 1 vol.
Record of Cuyahoga River ditch improvement proceedings, showing date of proceedings, petitions for ditch improvement, bond hearing on petition, testimony, order to engineer, notice of appeal, appeal bonds, appeal motion for a new trial, copies of correspondence, estimates, and notices. Last half a book, 1897-1899, contains six hand drawn maps of river and ditches, showing outline of ditch, location of river in respect to ditch, dimensions, names of owners of lots through which ditch was to pass, and township and village boundary lines. Prepared by county surveyor. Arranged chronologically by dates of proceedings. No index. Typed. 50 pages. 14 x 9 x 1. Auditor's office.

Financial Records

415. PAY ROLLS
1926—. 1 file drawer.

Duplicates of county engineer's pay roll sheets, showing name of project, pay period, date of pay roll, employee's name, kind of service, rate, amount, expense, total amount of expenses, and total amount due; also includes summary sheets 1926—, showing distribution of pay rolls to various funds and projects. Arranged alphabetically by names of projects. No index. Handwritten on printed forms. 9 x 5 x 26. Engineer's office.

416. TIME BOOKS
1914—. 14 vols.

Foreman's record of time worked on roads, ditches, bridges, and other county improvements by workmen and surveyor's deputies, showing dates of working days, name of worker, number of days worked, food and mileage allowance (if any), and name of project. Arranged chronologically by dates of working days. Indexed alphabetically by names of projects. Handwritten. 9 volumes average 198 pages. 12 x 7.5 x .5; 5 volumes average 150 pages. 14 x 9 x 1. Engineer's office.

Miscellaneous

417. ENGINEER'S ANNUAL REPORTS
1914—. 27 sheets.

Engineer's annual report of road mileage, showing date of report and to whom made; state roads, showing name of township, village, or city through which road runs, number of miles in each, section number, and total mileage; county roads, showing area through which road runs, number of miles in each, and total mileage in the county. Arranged chronologically by dates reported. No index. Handwritten on printed forms. 13 x 8. Engineer's office.

418. ANNUAL INVENTORIES TOWNSHIP PROPERTY– SURVEYOR
    1937—. 1 vol.
Inventories of all machinery owned by township and villages filed by township and village clerks, showing date of inventory, description of articles owned, quantity, and total estimated value. Arranged alphabetically by names of townships and villages. No index. Handwritten on printed forms. 150 pages. 12 x 15 x 1. Engineer's office.

419. CORRESPONDENCE
    1930—. 1 file drawer.
Miscellaneous correspondence and data from all sources including letters, inventories of materials on projects, catalogs, and others, showing date of correspondence, names of principals or subjects, and related data. Arranged alphabetically by names of correspondences. No index. Typed, printed, and handwritten. 12 x 16 x 24. Engineer's office.

County agricultural societies in Ohio were provided for by statute as early as 1833. On February 28, 1846, the legislature passed an act authorizing the forming of such societies and making provisions for their aid by the counties.[1] On February 15, 1853, the legislature declared such societies to be bodies corporate and politic, capable of suing and being sued, and capable of holding in fee simple such real estate as they might purchase for sites whereon to hold fairs, the same to be paid for by the county commissioners.[2]

By act of the legislature passed February 20, 1861, county agricultural societies were required to report annually to the state board of agriculture, and to meet with the state board at Columbus once each year.[3] In 1833 the legislature provided for the organization of district or county agricultural societies. The act making this provision stipulated that when 30 or more persons, residents of any county or district embracing two counties, organized themselves into an agricultural society, under the rules and regulations of the state board of agriculture, the county might aid such societies with a grant not to exceed $400 per year.[4] by act of April 21, 1896, provisions was made for representation in a county society of 30 or more residents of any county or district embracing two or more counties.[5] In 1900 the legislature extended the amount of county aid to $800 per year.[6] Later, on May 6, 1902, the legislature passed an act authorizing 30 or more residents of a county or a district embracing one or more counties, to organize themselves into an agricultural society.[7]

On April 17, 1919, the legislature provided for the organization of county and independent agricultural societies, authorized the payment of class premiums, defined the duties of persons competing for premiums, prescribed the publication of treasurers' accounts and the list of awards by societies, designated conditions of membership in a county agricultural society, authorized the society to elect a board of directors consisting of eight members, and prescribed their term of office in the matter of their election.

---

1. *Laws of Ohio,* XXXI, 28; XLIV, 70.
2. *Ibid.,* LI, 333.
3. *Ibid.,* LVIII, 22.
4. *Ibid.,* LXXX, 142.
5. *Ibid.,* XCII, 205.
6. *Ibid.,* XCIV, 395.
7. *Ibid.,* XCV, 403.

The act further stipulated how such societies might obtain state aid, and authorized the county commissioners to insure all buildings belonging to agricultural societies.[8]

The legislature in 1921 passed an act stipulating that the total amount of county aid to county agricultural societies should equal 100 percent of the amount paid by the society in regular class premiums but should not exceed $800.[9] By act of March 27, 1925, the county commissioners were authorized to purchase or to lease, for a term or not less than 20 years, real estate whereon to hold fairs under the management of the county agricultural societies, and to erect thereon suitable buildings.[10] On March 10, 1927, the legislature authorized the county commissioners to appropriate annually on the request of the agricultural society a sum of not less than $1500 nor more than $2000 from the general fund for the purpose of "encouraging agricultural fairs."[11]

The most recent legislation affecting agricultural societies was that of March 19, 1935. This act provides that where no duly organized county agricultural society existed, and when no fair was held by a duly organized county agricultural society which had held an annual exposition for three years previous to January 1 1933, the county commissioner should, on the request of the independent society, appropriate annually from the general fund a sum not more than $2000 nor less than $500 for the encouragement of independent agricultural fairs.[12]

In Geauga County, interest in agricultural society activities was shown very early, and society was formed at Chardon in 1823, 10 years before the legislature even authorized such organizations. The first fair was held at Chardon in that year, and others were held there each year until 1840, when the annual event was alternated between Chardon and Burton. Chardon was the scene of the fair every other year until 1850, when the fair was permanently moved to Burton. Since then the society has been a vital organization, and in recent years has increased the scope of interest of its fairs. Improvements and new buildings, including the grandstand and the special junior fair building, have increased the attractiveness of the fair site.

8. *Ibid.*, CVIII, pt. i, 381-385.
9. *Laws of Ohio*, CIX, 240.
10. *Ibid.*, CXI, 238.
11. *Ibid.*, CXII, 84.
12. *Ibid.*, CXVI, 47.

Further evidence of revived interest is found in the fact that all townships in the county are now represented among the 16 members of the society's board of directors. A junior fair board which conducts its own phase of the annual three-day program now enlist participation of the youth of the county and the society's activities.

420. RECORD [Minutes of Agricultural Society]
1929—. 1 vol.
Minutes of the Geauga County agricultural society, showing date of meeting, all motions and proceedings, election of members, appointment of committees, premiums offered for displays, amount of entrance fees and admission charged, names of members present at meetings, and names of persons making and seconding motions; also includes financial reports of assets and liabilities 1932—, budgets for fairs, 1933—, showing estimated amount of receipts and expenditures, and copies of annual financial statement of receipts and expenditures. Arranged chronologically by dates of meetings. No index. Handwritten. 300 pages. 14 x 8.5 x 1.25. Residence of Charles Riley, Secretary, R. D. Burton, Ohio.

421. MEMBERSHIP BOOK
1896-1907, 1 vol. 1903—, in Annual Report of the Agricultural Society, entry 422.
Record of paid memberships in the Geauga County agricultural society, showing dates of fairs, dates membership fees were received, and amount, ticket number, and names and addresses of members. Arranged chronologically by dates of fairs. No index. Handwritten. 496 pages. 14.5 x 5.5 x 2.25. Fairgrounds, agricultural society office, Burton, Ohio.

422. ANNUAL REPORT OF THE AGRICULTURAL SOCIETY
1907—. 6 pamphlets, 26 sheets.
Copies of annual financial reports, showing date of report, names of officers, general fair statistics, itemized receipts and expenditures, and statement of indebtedness; report of exhibitions, showing itemized record of entries, premiums offered, awards, and paid. Also contains Membership Book, 1908—, entry 421. Arranged chronologically by dates reported. No index. Handwritten on printed forms. Sheets, 16 x 10; pamphlets average 8 pages. 11 x 8.5 x .25. Residence at Charles Riley, Secretary, R. D., Burton, Ohio.

423. JOURNAL OF RECEIPTS AND EXPENDITURES
    1929—. 1 vol.

Records of receipts and expenditures; receipts, showing date of receipt, from whom received, gate admission, grandstand fees, entry fees, members fees, rental, interest on deposits, loans from tax levy, sales of land, buildings, equipment, donations, space fees, and stall and pen rental; miscellaneous expenditures, showing date of expenditure, name of payee, check number, total amount, salaries of secretary and treasurer, expenses of members, office help, advertising, office supplies, postage, premiums, judges, police, attractions and music, laborers, repair and replacements, lands and buildings, equipment, payments of loans; includes yearly summary of receipts and expenditures, 1934—. Arranged chronologically by dates of receipts or expenditures. No index. Handwritten on printed forms. 500 pages. 12 x 14.5 x 2. Residents of Charles Riley, Secretary, R. D., Burton , Ohio.

In 1914 the federal government passed an act providing for the co-operative agricultural extension service between the state agricultural colleges and the United States Department of Agriculture. The purpose of the extension service was to give instructions and practical demonstrations in agricultural and home economics to persons not attending college, and to give such information through field demonstrations, publications, and other means. The funds for such work were to be supplied in part by the federal government and in part by the state.[1]

A year following the federal legislation, the Ohio legislature accepted the provisions of the act by providing that when 20 or more residents of a county organized themselves into a "farmers' institute society for the purpose of teaching better methods of farming, stock raising, fruit culture and business connected with agriculture," accepted a constitution and by-laws conforming to the rules and regulations prescribed by the trustees of Ohio State University, and elected proper officers, the institute could be a corporate body. Ohio State University was required to furnish speakers for their annual meeting. At the close of the session the trustees were authorized to publish the lectures in pamphlets or book form.

Besides maintaining an institute, the society was authorized to maintain a county experiment farm. Furthermore, the county commissioners were authorized to select a county agent subject to the approval of the dean of college of agriculture of Ohio State University. It is the duty of the agent to inspect and study the agricultural conditions in his county, distribute agricultural literature, co-operate with United States Department of Agriculture and the college of agriculture of Ohio State University. In the event the commissioners failed to make such an appointment, the electorate could require them to do so on a referendum vote.[2]

In 1919 the original legislation was amended so as to authorize the employment of a home demonstration agent. The act of 1929, which is still effective, empowered the trustees of Ohio State University to employ boys' and girls' club agents as well as agricultural and home demonstration agents. The county extension agent was given the additional duty of carrying the teachings of the college of agriculture of Ohio State University in agriculture and home economics to the residences of his county through personal visits, bulletins, and practical demonstrations.

---

1. *United States Statutes at Large,* XXXVIII, pt. i, 372-374.
2. *Laws of Ohio,* CVI, 356-359.

Furthermore, it was his duty to render educational service not only relating to agricultural production, but also relating to economic problems including marketing, distribution, and the utilization of farm products.[3]

The initial legislation contained a clause which required the county commissioners to appropriate annually $1000 if they wish to obtain the services of an agricultural agent. This amount was to be matched by the state. Under the present system the commissioners are empowered to levy a tax and to appropriate money from the proceeds thereof, or from the general fund of the county an amount not in excess a $3000 for each agent to be paid to the state treasury to the credit of the agricultural extension fund. Amounts in excess must have the unanimous consent of the commissioners.[4]

The extension service began in Geauga County July 9, 1913, and it and its early years was closely related to and financially supported by the farm bureau. At the present time the county commissioners make an annual appropriation of $2600,[5] while other funds are derived from state and federal sources. Since June 1, 1936, there has also been a home demonstration agent in charge of women's work and 4-H clubs for girls. The service sponsors and assists 50 boys' and girls' 4-H clubs, with a total membership of 750.

The records for the extension service are located in the office of agricultural extension agents in the Old Burton High School, Burton, Ohio.

---

3. *Ibid.,* CVIII, 364; CXIII, 82, 83.
4. *Laws of Ohio,* CXIII, 82, 83.
5. Appropriation Ledger - Entry 248.

424. CLUB MEMBERSHIP RECORD
1925—. 2 file drawers. Initiated in 1925.
Card record of 4-H club members (boys and girls), showing name, address, and age of member, name of township, parent's name, year or years of membership, project, demonstrations for the year, grades of demonstrations, placing, and remarks. Arranged alphabetically by names of townships and alphabetically thereunder by names of members. No index. Handwritten on printed cards. 5 x 7. 6 x 8 x 16.

425. WORK SHEETS
1935—. 2 file drawers.

Original working sheets at initiation of conservation program, showing name of farm owner, name of farm operator, name of township, date, code number, and technical information with respect to condition and rise of land on farm. Arranged alphabetically by names of townships and alphabetically thereunder by names of farmers. No index. Handwritten on printed forms. 11 x 13.5 x 25.5.

426. SOIL CONSERVATION RECORDS - INDIVIDUAL FARMERS
1935—. 2 file drawers.

Soil conservation records of individual farmers who have received no payments, including farm reports, summaries of performance of farmers in soil conservation, acreage calculations, check sheets, correspondence, and inspection reports, showing name of township, name of farmer, code number, and dates. Arranged alphabetically by names of townships and alphabetically thereunder by names of farmers. No index. Handwritten and typed on printed forms. 11 x 13.5 x 25.5.

427. SOIL CONSERVATION RECORDS - INDIVIDUAL FARMERS (Payments)
1935—. 23 file drawers. (labeled by contained code numbers). Subtitled by names of townships.

Soil conservation records of individual farmers, including farm reports, record of farmers performance in soil conservation, acreage calculations, check sheets inspection reports, correspondence, purchaser's certificate, request for inspection, application for payment and summary of payment data, showing names of township and farmer, code number, and amount and date of payment to farmer. Arranged alphabetically by names of townships and numerically thereunder by code numbers. No index. Handwritten and typed on printed forms. 11 x 13.5 x 25.5.

428. MONTHLY REPORT OF HOME DEMONSTRATION AGENT
1938—. 1 vol.

Copies of monthly reports of home demonstration agent, showing date of report, distribution of time in office and field, record of meetings held, radio broadcasts, letters and bulletins distributed, assistance of specialists, local leaders, committees, and cooperation with other organizations and agencies; also includes separate notes on youth group and 4-H club activities.

Arranged chronologically by dates reported. No index. Handwritten on printed forms. 400 loose-leaf pages. 11.5 x 9.5 x 1.5.

429. ANNUAL REPORT OF HOME DEMONSTRATION AGENT
1936—. 2 vols.

Copies of home demonstration agents annual narrative reports, showing date and a detailed narrative of all activities, aims, and progress doing the year, including home furnishings, child development, nutrition, home management, special activities, relief, general extension, 4-H club work, and youth group; also includes pasted-in news clippings, programs, and notices. Arranged alphabetically under subject headings. Indexed by table of contents which is arranged alphabetically by subject headings and subheadings showing page numbers of report. Typed. Average 90 loose-leaf pages. 11 x 9 x .5.

430. ANNUAL REPORTS - AGRICULTURAL EXTENSION SERVICE
1921—. 1 vol.

Copies of narrative annual reports of agricultural extension agent, showing date and a narrative of all activities, projects, aims, and accomplishments of the year, including agricultural economics, agricultural engineering, agricultural conservation program, cereals and legumes, community activities, credit, dairy, forestry, fruit, general extension, 4-H club work, general livestock, potatoes, and poultry; also includes pasted-in news clippings, photographs of groups and farm lands and hand drawn graphs and illustrations. Arranged by subjects. Table of contents in front of volume. No index. Typed. Average 75 loose-leaf pages. 1 x 9 x 1.

431. CURRENT REPORTS
1933—. 8 pamphlets. Initiated in 1933.

Copies of monthly reports of agricultural agent, showing date of report, distribution of time in field and office, record of meetings held, radio broadcasts made, letters and bulletins distributed, assistance from specialist, local leaders, committees and others, record of cooperation with other organizations and agencies, and detailed record of all activities. Arranged chronologically by dates reported. No index. Typed on printed forms. Average 12 pages. 11 x 8 x .25.

432. COMBINED ANNUAL REPORT OF COUNTY EXTENSION WORKERS
1921—. 18 pamphlets.

Copies of combined annual statistical reports of agricultural agent and home demonstration agent, showing date of report, details statistical information on general activities, 4-H club work, summary of extension influence for year, results of extension activities in crops, agricultural economics, food and nutrition, child development, parent education, home management and home furnishings, home health and sanitation, extension organization and committee activities, and work in cooperation with federal agencies (combined reports for both agents date 1936—). Arranged chronologically by dates reported. No index. Handwritten on printed forms. Average 27 pages. 9 x 7.5 x .25.

433. SUPPLEMENT TO ANNUAL REPORT, 4-H CLUBS
1932—. 7 reports. Initiated in 1932.

Copies of supplements to agricultural agents' Combined Annual Report of County Extension Workers, entry 432 on 4-H clubs, showing date of report, detail statistics on 4-H club enrollment, activities, tours, club groups, advisors, individuals participating in state activities, amount of money for 4-H premiums, and summary of enrollment and completions. Arranged chronologically by dates reported. No index. Handwritten on printed forms. 10 x 8.

434. [ARIAL PHOTOGRAPHS]
1937—. 8 file drawers. (labeled by flight numbers).

Photographs of sections of Geauga County covering the entire county, showing coded letters referring to kind of crops grown in fields, boundary lines of farms, code number and flight number of photograph, and date taken. Photographs are developed to an exact scale, 1 inch equals 10 chains, and are used in conjunction with township maps. Arranged numerically by code numbers of photographs. For index, see entry 435. Handwritten notes on photographs. Photographs, 20 x 25.5. 3 x 36 x 23.5.

435. QUAD INDEX [Map Index of Aerial Photographs]
1937—. 1 map.

Physical map of Geauga County used as an index to [Aerial Photographs], entry 434, showing lines of aerial flight, township boundary lines, and code numbers of arial photographs. Published by Arial Photographic Laboratory, Washington, D. C. Printed. Scale, 1 inch equals 8000 feet. 23 x 18.

436. CORRESPONDENCE FILES
1921—. 8 file drawers.

Incoming correspondence, copies of outgoing correspondence, bulletins, reports, circulars of agricultural agent, correspondence, information, bulletins on agricultural economics, agricultural engineering, general livestock, dairy cattle, poultry, farm institute, club work, horticulture, soils and crops, United States Department of Agriculture, Ohio Department of Agricultural, Ohio State University Experimental Station, farm bureau, grange, agricultural extension council, young people's work, county agents' reports, and miscellaneous reports, showing subjects discussed, detailed information, and signature of correspondent. Arranged alphabetically by titles, subjects or names correspondents. No index. Handwritten and typed, some on printed forms. 11.5 x 12.5 x 25.5.

437. BULLETINS AND CORRESPONDENCE–HOME DEMONSTRATION AGENT
1936—. 3 file drawers.

Home demonstration agent's bulletins, including correspondence, and copies of outgoing correspondence, including child development, clothing, health, home furnishings, home management, nutrition, 4-H club, publications, and handcrafts, showing subjects discussed, detailed information on bulletins, and signature of home demonstration agent. Arranged alphabetically by subjects and chronologically thereunder by dates of correspondence or bulletins. No index. Handwritten and typed, some on printed forms. 11.25 x 12.5 x 25.5.

438. AGRICULTURAL BULLETINS
1918—. 4 shelves. (labeled by contained bulletin numbers, 1-956).

County agricultural agent's bulletins on all phases of agricultural science, including bulletins issued by the following; Ohio Agriculture Experimental Station, experimental stations of other states, Ohio State Horticultural Society, Ohio Vegetable Growers Association, Agricultural Extension Service, United States Department of Agriculture, and United States Department of Commerce. Arranged alphabetically by subjects. For indexes, see entries 439, 440, 441. Printed. 8 x 32 x 9.5.

439. GENERAL BULLETIN [Index] File Key
1918—. 1 vol.

General index to Agricultural bulletins, entry 438, issued by Ohio Agricultural Experimental Station, experimental stations of other states, Ohio State Horticulture Society, Ohio Vegetable Growers Association, Agricultural Extension Service, United States Department of Agriculture, and United States Department of Commerce showing title of bulletin, date issued, and assigned bulletin number. Arranged alphabetically by subjects and numerically thereunder by bulletin numbers. Typed. 40 loose-leaf pages. 11 x 9 x .5.

440. MONTHLY AND BI-MONTHLY BULLETIN INDEX–OHIO AGRICULTURAL EXPERIMENTAL STATION
1924—. 1 vol.

Index to Agricultural bulletins, in entry 438, issued by the Ohio Agricultural Experimental Station, showing title of article in bulletin and date of bulletin. Arranged alphabetically by subjects showing bulletin numbers. Typed. 40 loose-leaf pages. 11 x 9 x .5.

441. INDEX TO BULLETINS ISSUED BY OHIO STATE HORTICULTURAL SOCIETY–OHIO VEGETABLE GROWERS ASSOCIATION
1929—. 1 vol.

Index to Agricultural bulletins, in entry 438, issued by the Ohio State Horticultural Society and by the Ohio Vegetable Growers Association, showing title of article and bulletin, name of author of article, and dates of bulletins. Arranged alphabetically by subjects showing bulletin numbers. Typed. 40 loose-leaf pages. 11 x 9 x .5.

Archival Materials and Printed Documents

Abstracts of Votes Cast, 1891—, 1 bundle, entry 366.
Acts of the General Assembly, 1803-1941 (119 vols., published by state authority).
Administration Docket, 1884—, 6 vols., entry 151.
Administrators' and Executors' Docket, 1870-1885, 1 vol., entry 152.
Annual Statistical Report of the Public Schools, 1929—, 10 pamphlets, entry 376.
Appearance Docket, 1845-1927, 17 vols., entry 117.
[Applications for Aid to Dependent Children], 1936—, 1 file drawer, entry 202.
Appropriation Ledger, 1915-1916, 1927—, 4 vols., 2 bundles, entry 248.
[Auditor's] Monthly Financial Statements, 1927—, 177 sheets, entry 305.
Baldwin, William Edward, ed., *Throckmorton's Ohio Code Annotated* (certified ed., Banks-Baldwin Co., Cleveland, 1936).
Carter, Clarence Edwin, ed. and comp., *The Territorial Papers of the United States* (8 vols., Government Printing Office, Washington, 1934, in progress). Vols. II and III treat of the Northwest Territory.
Case Records and Case Histories, 1935—, 2 file drawers, entry 18.
Case Records– Active Cases [Board of Aid for the Aged], 1934—, 2 file drawers, entry 396.
Chase, Salmon P., ed., *The Statutes of Ohio and of the Northwestern Territory, 1788-1833* (3 vols., Corey and Fairbank, Cincinnati, 1833-1935).
Circuit Court Docket, 1885-1913, 1 vol., entry 137.
Civil [and Criminal] Docket, 1861-1931, 8 vols., entry 145.
Commissioners' Journal, 1806—, entry 1.
Common Pleas Journal, 1806—, 41 vols., entry 129.
Constitution of Ohio, 1802.
Constitution of Ohio, 1851.
[Court of Appeals Docket], 1913—, 3 vols., entry 142.
Criminal Appearance Docket, 1902—, 2 vols., entry 124.
Curwen, Maskell E., comp., *Public Statues at Large of the State of Ohio* . . . (4 vols., Published by the author, Cincinnati, 1853-1854).
Dog Application [and Tag Number], 1927—, 116 pads, 6 file drawers, entry 284.
Dog Kennel Register 1917—, 5 bundles, 1 vol., entry 285.
Financial Report, 1905-1918, 1931—, 21 booklets, 1 sheet, entry 306.
Foreign Execution Docket, 1835—, 7 vols., entry 209.

Geological Survey of Ohio, *Report of the Geological Survey of Ohio,* Series i (2 vols., published by Samuel Medary, printer for the state, Columbus, 1837-1838).

Guardians' Docket, 1867—, 3 vols., entry 153.

Hammond, Charles, William Lawrence, Edwin M. Stanton, and others, eds., *Report of Cases Argued and Determined in the Supreme Court of Ohio in Bank . . .* (20 vols., Robert Clarke & Co., Cincinnati, 1821-1852).

Jail Register, 1879- -, 2 vols., entry 213.

Juvenile Appearance Docket, 1908—, 3 vols., entry 198.

Laning Jay F. comp., *Revised Statutes and Recodified Laws of the State of Ohio . . .* (2d ed., 3 vols., The Laning Co., Norwalk, Ohio, 1907).

Laws of the Territory of the United States Northwest of the River Ohio (published by the authority, Philadelphia and Cincinnati, 1792-1796).

Lunacy Record, 1904—, 3 vols., entry 186.

McCook, G. W., E. O. Randall, J. L. W. Henry, and others, *Reports of Cases Argued and Determined in the Supreme Court of Ohio* (new series 137 vols., various publishers, Columbus, New York, and Cincinnati, 1853—).

Minute Book of Board of Complaints, entry 360.

Minutes of Budget Commission, 1918-1929, 1933—, 1 vol., entry 359.

Ohio Attorney General, *Opinions,* 1846-1940 (published annually by state authority, 1904-1940). Title varies: *Reports.*

Ohio Auditor of State, *Annual Report,* 1836-1939 (published by state authority). Printed prior to 1836 in the Senate and House Journals.

Ohio Commissioner of Statistics, *Annual Report to the General Assembly of Ohio* (published annually by state authority).

Ohio Department of Agriculture, *Annual Report,* 1846-1913 (68 vols., published by state authority, 1847-1914).

Ohio Department of Agriculture, *A Summary of the Activities of the Ohio Department of Agriculture . . . for 1936. A Report and History of the County and Independent Fairs Held in Ohio in 1936* (published by state authority).

Ohio Department of Commerce, Division of Banks, *Annual Report of the Division of Banks for the Year Ending December 31, 1940.* (Printed annually by state authority).

Ohio State Department of Education, Division of Statistics, Files for 1942 (unpublished).

Ohio State Department of Labor Statistics, files for 1941 (unpublished).

Ohio Executive Documents, 1835-1917 (58 vols., published by state authority).

Ohio Secretary of State *Annual Report* (101 vols., published by state authority).

Ohio Superintendent of Common Schools, *Report to the 36th General Assembly 1837,* (published annually by state authority).

Ohio Tax Commission, pub., *Financing State and Local Government in Ohio* 1900-1932 (published by state authority, 1934).

Order Book [Supreme Court of Ohio], 1852-1902, 18 vols. Titled: Journal, 1903—, 18 vols.

Pay Rolls [Engineer's], 1928—, 1 file drawer, entry 415.

Pease, Theodore Calvin, *The Laws of the Northwest Territory, 1788-1800* (Trustees of the Illinois State Historical Library, Law Series, Springfield, 1925).

Physicians' Certificates, 1896—, 1 vol., entry 193.

Poore, Benjamin Perley, *Federal and State Constitutions and Other Organic Laws of the United States* (2 vols., printed by the authority of the United States Senate, Government Printing Office, Washington, 1877).

Record of Accrued Fees, 1912-1933, 2 vols., entry 216.

Record of Births and Deaths, 1867-1908, 3 vols., entry 189.

Record of Bonds– County Commissioners, 1910—, 2 vols., entry 300.

Record of Indigent Soldiers, Sailors, and Marines, 1877-1930, 1933—, 2 vols., entry 259.

Record of Official Bonds, 1873—, 1 vol., entry 297.

Record of Wills, 1835—, 16 vols., entry 159.

Registered Nurses' and Limited Practitioners' Record, 1916—, 1 vol., entry 194.

Register of Inmates [County Home], 1845—, 1 vol., entry 386.

The Reorganization of County Government in Ohio: Report of Governor's Commission on County Government (n. pub., n. p. submitted to governor, 1934).

Road Records, 1806—, 5 vols., entry 408.

Sayler, J. R., comp., *The Statutes of the State of Ohio* (4 vols., Robert Clarke & Co., Cincinnati, 1876).

Shepherd, Vinton R., ed., *The Ohio Nisi Prius Reports* (new series, 32 vols., Ohio Law Reporter Co., Columbus and Cincinnati, 1904-1934).

Smith, J. V. Rep., *Official Reports of the Debates and Proceedings of the Ohio State Convention . . . Held at Columbus Commencing May 6, 1850, and at Cincinnati, Commencing December 2, 1850* (Scott and Bascom, Columbus, 1851).

Trautwein, George C., ed., *Supplement to Page's Annotated General Code, 1926-1935* (W. H. Anderson Co., Cincinnati, 1935).

Treasurer's Record of Bonds of Officials, 1808—, 5 vols., entry 352.

U. S. Bureau of the Census, *15th Census of the United States, 1930, Agriculture, Ohio* (4 vols., Government Printing Office, Washington, 1931-1932).

U. S. Bureau of the Census, *15th Census of the United States, 1930, Population* (6 vols., Government Printing Office, Washington, 1931-1933).

U. S. Bureau of the Census, *Religious Bodies,* 1926 (2 vols., Government Printing Office, Washington, 1929-1930).

U. S. Bureau of the Census, *16th Census of the United States, 1940, Agriculture, Ohio* (Volume I in six parts, Government Printing Office, 1941).

U. S. Bureau of the Census, *16th Census of the United States, 1940, Population, First Series, Number of Inhabitants, Ohio* (Government Printing Office, Washington, 1941).

U. S. Bureau of the Census, *12th Census of the United States, 1900, Population, I* (2 vols., United States Census Office, Washington, 1901-1902).

United States Code Annotated (65 vols., prepared by the editorial staff of Edward Thompson Co., Northport, Long Island, New York, and West Publishing Co., St. Paul, 1927—).

U. S. Comptroller of the Currency, *Individual Statements of Condition of National Banks (and Non-National Banks in District of Columbia) at the Close of Business December 31, 1940* (Government Printing Office, Washington, 1941).

United States Statutes at Large, 1789-1941 (54 vols., Government Printing Office, Washington, 1848-1941).

Verifications, 1936—, 1 file drawer, entry 204.

X-ray Card File, 1932—, 1 file drawer, entry 385.

Diaries and Memoirs

Burnet [Jacob], *Notes on the Early Settlement of the North-Western Territory* (Derby, Bradley and Co., Cincinnati, 1847).

General Histories and Reference Works

Adams, George Burton, *Constitutional History of England* (Henry Holt and Co., New York, c1921).
Ayer, N.W. & Sons, *Directory of Newspapers and Periodicals* (N. W. Ayer and Sons, Philadelphia, 1941).
Gwynne, A. E., *Practical Treaties of the Law of Sheriff and Coroner with Forms and References to the Statutes of Ohio, Indiana, and Kentucky* (H. W. Derby & Co., Cincinnati, 1849).
Hodgkin, Thomas, *From the Earliest Times to the Norman Conquest,* in William Hunt and Reginald Poole, *The Political History of England* (12 vols., Longmans, Green, & Co., York and London, 1905-1910).
Karracker, Cyrus Harreld, *The Seventeenth- Century Sheriff: A Comparative Study of the Sheriff in England and the Chesapeake Colonies, 1607-1689* (University of North Carolina Press, Chapel Hill, 1930).
Moley, Raymond, "The Sheriff and the Coroner," The Missouri Association for Criminal Justice, *The Missouri Crime Survey,* pt. ii, (Macmillan Co., New York, 1926).
Pollock, Sir Frederick, and Frederic William Maitland, *The History of English Law Before the Time of Edward I* (2 vols., Cambridge University Press, Cambridge, England, and Little, Brown, and Co., Boston, 1895).
Sutherland, Edwin, H., *Principles of Criminology* (J. B. Lippincott & Co., Chicago, 1934).
Thwaites, Ruben Gold, ed., *The Jesuit Relations and Allied Documents* (73 vols., Burrows Brothers, Cleveland, 1896-1901).
Van Waters, Miriam, *Youth in Conflict* (Republic Publishing Co., New York, 1925).
Willoughby, W. F., *Principles of Judicial Administration* (Brookings Institution, Washington, 1929).

Regional and Local Histories, Treaties, and Monographs

Alexander, William H., *A Climatological History of Ohio* (Engineering Experiment Station, Ohio State University, Columbus, 1925).
Amer, Francis J., *The Development of the Judicial System in Ohio from 1787 to 1932* (Institute of Law Bulletin, No. 8, Johns Hopkins Press, Baltimore, 1932).

Bond, Beverley W., Jr., *The Civilization of the Old Northwest: A Study of Political, Social, and Economic Development, 1788-1812* (Macmillan Co., New York, 1934).

Estrich, Willis A., and others, eds., *Ohio Jurisprudence* (43 vols., Lawyers Co-operative Publishing Co., Rochester, 1928-1938).

Heiges, R. E. *The Office of Sheriff in the Rural Counties of Ohio* (published by the author, Findlay, 1933).

Hooper, Osman Castle, *History of Ohio Journalism, 1793-1913* (Spahr and Glenn Company, Columbus, 1933).

Howe, Henry, *Historical Collections of Ohio* (Ohio Centennial Edition, 2 vols., published by state authority, Newark, 1893).

Jenkins, Warren, *Ohio Gazetteer and Travelers Guide* (Isaac N. Whiting, Columbus, 1839).

Kennedy, Aileen Elizabeth, *The Old Poor Law and Its Administration* (Sophonisba B. Breckinridge, ed., Social Monographs, No. 22, University of Chicago Press, Chicago, 1934).

Kilbourn, John, *The Ohio Gazetteer or Topographical Dictionary* John Kilbourne, Columbus, 1831).

Lloyd, W. A., J. I. Falconer and C. E. Thorne, *The Agriculture of Ohio,* Bulletin 326 (Ohio Agricultural Experiment Station, Wooster, 1918).

McCarthy, Dwight, G. *The Territorial Governors of the Old Northwest:* A Study in Territorial Administration (Historical Society of Iowa, Iowa city, 1910).

Mills, William C., *Agricultural Atlas of Ohio*, (Ohio State Archaeological Historical Society, Columbus, 1914).

Ohio Study of Local School Units, *A Study of the Public Schools of Geauga County, With Recommendations for Their Future Organization* (Columbus, 1937). Sponsored by the United States Office of Education and the Ohio State Department of Education.

Prosser, Charles Smith, "The Nomenclature of the Ohio Geological Formation," Ohio State University *Bulletin,* Series Eight, No. 3 (Ohio State University, Columbus, 1903).

Roseboom, Eugene Holloway, and Weisenburger, Francis Phelps, *A History of Ohio,* (Prentice-Hall, Inc., New York, 1934).

Sixth Annual Maple Festival, Program, 1931, (Festival Association, Chardon, 1931).

Stuart, John Struthers, *History of Northeastern Ohio,* (3 vols., Historical Publication Company, Indianapolis, 1935).

Taylor, Lester, and others, comps., *Pioneer and General History of Geauga County, Ohio* (Geauga County Historical Society, Chardon, 1880).

Weisenberger, Francis P., *The Passing of the Frontier* (volume III of *The History of the State of Ohio,* ed., by Carl Wittke).

Western Biographical Publishing Company, pub., *The Biographical Cyclopedia and Portrait Gallery, with an Historical Sketch of the State of Ohio* (6 vols., Western Biographical Pub. Co., Cincinnati, 1882).

Western Reserve and Northern Ohio Historical Society (now the Western Reserve Historical Society) *Tract 29* (109 tracts in 10 vols., The Society, Cleveland, 1875—).

Williams Brothers, comps., *History of Geauga and Lake Counties, Ohio* (2 vols., Williams Brothers, Philadelphia, 1878).

Wittke Carl, ed., *The History of the State of Ohio,* (6 vols., in progress, Ohio State Archaeological and Historical Society, Columbus, 1941).

Articles in Periodicals

Atkinson R. C. "County Home Rule Developments in Ohio," *National Municipal Review,* XXIII (1934), 228.

Atkinson R. C. "Ohio–County Charter Elections," *National Municipal Review,* XXIV, (1935), 702-703.

Atkinson R. C. "Ohio–Optional County Legislation," *National Municipal Review,* XXIV, (1935), 228.

Boyd, W. W. "Secondary Education in Ohio Previous to the Year 1840," *Ohio State Archaeological and Historical Society Quarterly* XXV (1916), 118-134.

Downes, Randolph Chandler, "Evolution of Ohio County Boundaries," *Ohio State Archaeological and Historical Quarterly,* XXXVI (1927), 340-347.

Dykstra, C. A., "Cleveland's Effort for City-County Consolidation," *National Municipal Review,* VIII (1919), 551-556.

Gates, Charles M., "The Administration of State Archives," *The Pacific Northwest Quarterly,* XXIX (1938), No. 1; Also in *The American Archivist,* I (1938), 130-141.

Kaplan H. Eliot, "A Personal Program for County Service," *National Municipal Review,* XXV, (1936), 596-600.

Kolehmainen, John I., "Founding of the Finnish Settlements in Ohio," *Ohio State Archaeological and Historical Quarterly,* XLIX (1940), 150-159.

"The Legislature of the Northwestern Territory," *Ohio State Archaeological and Historical Quarterly,* XXX (1921), 13-53.

Martin, Maria Ewing, "Origin of Ohio Place Names," *Ohio Archaeological Quarterly,* XIV (1905), 272-290.

Miller, Edward A., "The History of Educational Legislation in Ohio," *Ohio State Archaeological Quarterly,* XXVII (1911), 1-271.

Morris, William A., "The Office of Sheriff in the Anglo-Saxon Period," *English Historical Review,* XXXI (1916), 20-40.

Stone Donald C., "The Police Attack Crime," *National Municipal Review,* XXIV (1935), 39-41.

Waite, Frederick C., "Sources of the Names of the Counties of the Western Reserve," *Ohio State Archaeological and Historical Quarterly,* XLVIII (1939), 58-65.

Newspapers

Cleveland *Plain Dealer,* 1933, 1935, 1940.
Columbus Dispatch, 1942.
Geauga County Record, 1905.
The Geauga Democrat, 1869.
Geauga Republican Record, 1940.
Geauga Republican, 1905.
The New York Times, 1914.
Ohio State Journal, 1840, 1933.

Commissioners**

Ebenezer Merry	1806-1807	Russell G. McCarty	1835-1840
(Acted until successor was		(Resigned)	
elected and qualified)		James Hathaway	1836-1840
Orestes K. Hawley	1806-1809	Albion C. Gardner	1838-1840
Nathaniel Doane	1806-1810	(Resigned)	
(Resigned)		Hiram Bishop	1840-1841
Abraham Tappen	1807-1810	(Vice R. G. McCarty)	
Joel Paine	1809-1812	Alvin Kyle	1840-1842
Nehimiah King	1810-1812	(Vice A. C. Gardner)	
(Vice Nathaniel Doane)		Samuel Bodman	1841-1843
John A. Harper	1810-1813	(Resigned)	
Norman Canfield	1812-1815	Harvey Nichols	1841-1844
Noah Paige	1813-1816	Gilbert Curtis	1842-1845
Jedediah Beard	1813-1819	Augustus Tillotson	1843-1844
Solomon Kingsbury	1815-1818	(Vice Sameul Bodman)	
Jesse Dodd	1817-1821	Augustus Tillotson	1844-1847
Christopher Langdon	1818-1821	Elijah S. Scott	1844-1847
Jesse Ladd	1819-1822	Thomas A. Munn	1845-1849
Eleazar Hancock	1821-1823	(Resigned)	
(Short term)		Moses Stebbins	1847-1850
Robert Blair	1821-1827	Sylvanus W. Gray	1847-1850
Charles Curtiss	1822-1825	David Shepherd	1849-1852
Christopher Langdon	1823-1826	S. B. Philbrick	1850-1851
Ralph Cowles	1825-1828	Horace Lampson	1850-1851
Augustus Sesson	1826-1829	D. W. Mead	1851-1853
Robert Blair	1827-1833	(Resigned)	
Isaac Moore	1828-1831	Jacob Thrasher	1851-1854
Vene Stone	1829-1832	Lester Perkens	1852-1855
John F. Morse	1831-1834	H. D. Johnson	1853-1858
Colbert Huntington	1832-1835	(Died in office)	
James Thompson	1833-1836	Spencer Dayton	1854-1857

*Compiled from: General Record, Governor Office, 1803-1858 (volumes 1-8); Ohio Secretary of State, *Annual Report*, 1836— (some volumes titled: *Ohio Statistics*); Ohio Secretary of State, Commission Register, 1858—; Commissioners' Journal, 1806-1942.

Commissioners** (continued)

John A. Ford	1855-1857	Joseph N. Strong	1888-1894
(Resigned)		Wesley J. Grant	1891-1893
Marsh Smith	1857-1858	(Vice L. D. Taylor)	
(Vice John A. Ford)		E. P. Latham	1892-1896
John V. Whitney	1857-1860	Wesley J. Grant	1893-1899
B. B. Woodbury	1858-1859	Selah Daniels	1894-1900
(Vice H. D. Johnson)		H. W. Pettibone	1898-1904
Marsh Smith	1858-1861	J. L. Thrasher	1899-1905
J. W. Collins	1859-1861	N. F. Mosely	1900-1906
Silas Gaylord, Jr.	1860-1863	V. L. Valentine	1904-1909
L. C. Reed	1861-1864	John Ohl	1905-1911
John T. Field	1863-1866	Charles W. Canfield	1906
Alanson Moffet	1864-1870	(Resigned)	
Benjamin Bedlake	1866-1869	H. W. Parker	1906-1909
John V. Whitney	1869-1872	(Vice C. W. Canfield)	
Daniel Johnson	1870-1879	W. D. Wilder	1909-1911
Horace J. Ford	1871-1879	F. B. Morehouse	1909-1913
(Resigned)		Joel M. Hale	1911-1915
M. V. Scott	1872-1873	H. W. Parker	1911-1915
(Short term)		Peter Small	1913-1917
Darius Wolcott	1873-1878	L. G. Richards	1915-1919
Orrin M. Barnes	1878-1884	Henry M. Hale	1915-1919
D. H. Truman	1879-1884	Bert Ashcraft	1917-1929
Wallace W. Wilbur	1879-1885	Orlo J. Post	1919-1923
L. K. Lacy	1884-1885	W. H. Cromwell	1919-1932
(Resigned)		H. J. Russell	1923-1931
E. N. Osborn	1885-1887	John Shatford	1929-1940
(Vice L. K. Lacy)		Archie C. Stone	1931—
Wm. C. Dutton	1885-1888	Fred Talcott	1932-1936
David A. Gates	1886-1892	Frank N. Griffin	1937—
Lester D. Taylor	1887-1891	Ben E. Hotchkiss	1941—
(Resigned)			

**The board of county commissioners, with three members each serving a three-year term, was established in 1804 (*Laws of Ohio,* II, 150). In 1906 the term of office was changed to two years (*Laws of Ohio,* XCVII, 271); in 1920 it was increased to four years, and so remains (*Laws of Ohio,* CVIII, pt. ii, 1300).

Recorders*

James A. Harper	1806-1811	John Packard, Jr.	1841-1844
Edward Paine	1811-1832	John French	1844-1856
Alfred Phelps	1832	Linnaeus C. Ludlow	1856-1862
(Short term)		C. H. Lamb	1862-1868
George E. H. Day	1832-1835	A. W. Young	1868-1874
Ralph Cowles	1835-1835	William H. Young	1874-1880
William Kerr	1838-1841	Charles A. Mills	1880-1902
(To January 1)		F. E. Ford	1902-1917
William Wilber	1841	William A. Basquin	1917—
(January to October)			

*Under the law of 1803, the associate judges of the court of common pleas appointed the recorder for a seven-year term (*Laws of Ohio*, I, 136). The office became elective for a three-year term in 1829, a two-year term in 1905, and a four-year term in 1936 (*Laws of Ohio*, XXVII, 65; *Ohio Const. 1851*, Art. XVII, sec. 2; *Laws of Ohio*, CXVI, pt. ii, 184).

Clerks of the Court of Common Pleas**

Edward Paine, Jr.	1806-1828	William N. Keany	1858-1882
David Aiken	1828-1842	Brainard D. Ames	1882-1901
Reuben St. John	1842-1846	A. Terrence Reynolds	1901-1909
(Resigned in June)		F. R. Truman	1909-1911
Lorenzo J. Rider	1846-1849	F. E. Bond	1911-1915
(Vice Reuben St. John)		C. S. Lenhard	1915-1925
A. H. Gotham	1849-1852	Arlene Watros	1925-1935
A. H. Gotham	1852-1857	Alberta Philips	1935-1939
(Died in office)		Donald E. Philips	1939—
H. K. Smith	1857-1858		
(Vice A. H. Gotham)			

**Called prothonotary under the laws of the Northwest Territory and appointed by the governor. Under the Ohio Constitution of 1802 the court appointed its own clerk for a seven-year term (Art. III, sec. 9). The constitution of 1851 made the office elective for a three-year term (Art. IV, sec. 16). Under the constitutional amendment of 1905 the term was changed to two years and to four years in 1936 (*Laws of Ohio*, XCVII, 641; CXV, pt. ii, 184).

Roster of County Officials
1806-1942

Judges of the Court of Common Pleas*

*President judges under the constitution of 1802 in the districts which included Geauga County***

Calvin Pease	1806-1810	John W. Willey	1840-1841
Benjamin Ruggles	1810-1815	(Vice Van R. Humphrey)	
George Tod	1815-1830	Reuben Hitchcock	1841-1842
Reuben Wood	1830-1833	(Vice John W. Willey	
Matthew Birchard	1833-1837	until a successor was elected)	
Van R. Humphrey	1837-1840	Benjamin Bissell	1842-1849
(Died in September)		Philemon Blliss	1849-1852

Associate judges under the constitution of 1802

John Walworth	1806-1809	Soloman Kingsbury	1820-1827
(Served until successor		John W. Scott	1820-1827
was appointed)		Asa Cowles	1827-1834
Jesse Phelps	1806-1809	Daniel Kerr***	1827-1840
(Acting Judge)		John Hubbard***	1827-1840
Aaron Wheeler	1806-1813	Storm Rosa	1834-1840
(Acting Judge)		Neri Wright	1840-1847
Nehemiah King	1809-1813	John T. Bosley	1840-1847
(Served out original term)		Joseph W. Brackett	1840-1841
Eleazar Hickcox	1809-1810	(Resigned)	
(Serving out original term;		B. F. Avery	1842-1845
resigned)		(Vice J. W. Brackett; resigned)	
Eliphalet Austin	1810-1813	D. D. Aikon	1846-1847
(Vice Eleazar Hickcox)		(Vic J. W. Brackett)	
Abraham Tappan	no dates	Samuel Rodman	1847-1849
(Resigned)		John P. Converse	1847-1852
Arris Clapp	1813-1820	Lester Taylor	1847-1852
Vene Stone	1813-1827	B. F. Avery	1849-1852
R. B. Parkman	1819-1820	(Vice Samuel Bodman)	
(Vice Abraham Tappen)			

*The president and associate judges under the first constitution were appointed for seven-year terms by joint ballot of both houses of the general assembly (*Ohio Const. 1802.* Art. III, sec. 8). The constitution of 1851 made the office elective for a five-year periods and required the incumbent to be a resident of the district in which elected (*Ohio Const. 1851,* Art. IV, sec. 12). The amendment of 1912 changed the term to six years, required the election of at least one judge for each county, who must be a resident of the county in which elected (Art. IV, sec. 12, as amended September 3, 1912).

**The president judges were appointed for seven-year terms by joint ballot of general assembly, but due to many transfers of counties to other districts variations in term of office occur. The judges served their full term but outside the district mentioned.

***Some officials were changed when Lake County was organized (*Laws of Ohio,* XXVIII, pt. ii, 102, 171, 172).

Judges under the constitution of 1851 in the districts which included Geauga County

Reuben Hitchcock	1852-1855	H. B. Woodbury	1876-1884
(Resigned)		(Resigned in September)	
Eli T. Wilder	1855-1857	Laban S. Sherman	1877-1892
(Vice R. Hitchcock)		Delos W. Canfield	1885-1905
Horace Wilder	1857-1862	William P. Howland	1892-1900
Norman L. Chaffee	1862-1871	(Died in office)	
(Resigned)		James P. Cadwell	1901-1902
Charles E. Gliddon	1871-1872	(Died in office)	
(Vice Norman L. Chaffee)		Willis S. Metcalf	1901-1911
Milton C. Canfield	1872-1875	Theodore Hall	1903-1905
(Died in office)		(Died in office)	
E. Lee	1875-1877	Elias E. Roberts	1905-1908
(Vice M. C. Camfield)		(Vice T. Hall)	
D. W. Canfield	1875-1877	James W. Roberts	1905-1915
(Unexpired term of		A. G. Reynolds	1911-1915
M. C Camfield)			

Resident Judges under the constitution amendment of 1912

Terrence Reynolds	1915-1930	Harlan Sperry	1930-1933
(Died in office)		(Vice T. Reynolds)	
		Harlan Sperry	1933—

Roster of County Officials
1806-1942

*Judges of the Probate Court**

Alfred Phelps	1852-1855	Terrence Reynolds	1909-1915
Milton C. Canfield	1855-1867	Harlan Sperry	1915-1925
Henry K. Smith	1867-1909	C. S. Lenhart	1925—

*The probate court, established under the laws of the Northwest Territory in 1788, consisted of a probate judge and two judges of the court of common pleas (Pease, *op.cit.,* 9). Under the constitution of 1802 it lost its identity completely in the court of common pleas. It emerged with its present form and functions, with a single judge serving a three-year term, under the constitution of 1851 (Art. IV, secs. 7, 8). The term was changed to four years in 1912 (*Ohio Const. 1851*, Art. IV, sec. 7, as amended, 1912).

Prosecuting Attorneys

R. B. Parkman	1806-1817	James E. Stephenson	1876-1878
Samuel Wheeler	1817-1819	Newton H. Bostwick	1878-1880
Alfred Phelps	1819-1828	C. W. Osborne	1880-1885
Stephen Matthews	1828-1835	Leonard B. Barrows	1885-1891
Reuben Hitchcock	1835-1839	W. S. Metcalf	1891-1900
William L. Perkins	1839-1840	Hubert O. Bostwick	1900-1906
O. P. Brown	1840-1842	William G. King	1906-1909
(Appointed)		R. H. Patchin	1909-1915
A. G. Riddle	1842-1848	C. A. Wilmot	1915-1919
M. C. Canfield	1848-1850	H. J. Thrasher	1919-1921
A. H. Thrasher	1850-1854	R. H. Patchin	1921-1923
M. C. Canfield	1854-1858	Robert E. Parks	1923-1925
H. K. Smith	1858-1862	Harry W. Clark	1925-1927
Delos W. Canfield	1862-1866	R. H. Bostwick	1927-1933
I. N. Hathaway	1866-1870	S. L. Cheney	1933-1935
Orrin S. Farr	1870-1872	Harold K. Bostwick	1935—
Lucius E. Durfee	1872-1876		

*At first appointed by the supreme court and later (1805) by the court of commom pleas, a law passed January 23, 1833, made the office of prosecuting attorney elective for a term of two years (*Laws of Ohio,* XXXI, 13). In 1881 the term was increased to three years, in 1906 reduced to two, and in 1936 increased to four (*Laws of Oho*, LXXVIII, 260; XCVIII, 271; CXVI, pt. ii, 184).

*Coroners**

James Montgomery	1806-1808	Benjamin Bidlake	1860-1864
Joseph Pepoon	1808-1810	Augustus E. Miller	1864-1866
Eisha Norton	1810-1812	Joseph G. Durfee	1866-1874
Isaac Palmer	1812-1818	E. S. Chapel	1874-1876
Calvin Cole	1818-1820	L. G. Maynard	1876-1878
William Holbrook	1820-1822	P. M. Cowles	1878-1880
Charles T. Paine	1822-1824	Joseph G. Durfee	1880-1882
William Holbrook	1824-1828	P. M. Cowles	1882-1884
Milo Harris	1828-1830	Orlando A. Dimmock	1884-1888
Henry Williams	1830-1834	W. I. Lyman	1888-1890
Amos Wilmot	1834-1840	Albert D. Warner	1890-1898
George King	1840-1842	H. G. Frisbie	1898-1900
James Hathaway	1842-1844	O. A. Hopkins	1900-1904
Charles Atwood	1844-1846	W. Porter Ellis	1904-1909
Asa Larned	1846-1850	(Term extension)	
Alpheus Cook	1850-1852	W. E. Allyn	1909-1917
James Dayton	1852-1854	F. S. Pomeroy	1917-1921
Horace W. Morse	1854-1856	J. A. Heeley	1921-1923
Sidney Bostwick	1856-1858	F. S. Pomeroy	1923-1931
John S. Cleveland	1858-1860	Philip P. Pease	1931—

*Established in 1788, the county coroner was appointed for two-year terms by the territorial governor (Pease, *op. cit.*, 224-25). The Ohio Constitution of 1802 (Art. VI, sec. 1) made the office elective without changing the term which remained at two years until 1936, when it was increased to four years (*Laws of Ohio,* CXVI, pt. ii, 184).

Roster of County Officials
1806-1942

*Sheriffs**

Joel Paine	1806-1810	Belo N. Shaw	1863-1867
Abraham Tappen	1810-1812	A. J. Walton	1867-1869
Elisha Norton	18112-1816	S. E. Clapp	1869-1873
Eli Bond	1816-1820	Lester Moffett	1873-1877
Hezekiah King	1820-1824	Silo P. Warriner	1877-1881
James R. Ford	1824-1828	John A. Pierce	1881-1885
Uri Seeley	1828	William Martin	1885-1898
(Resigned)		Albert Burroughs	1889-1893
William Kerr	1828-1830	Frank D. Hollis	1893-1897
(Vice Uri Seeley)		E. B. Fisher	1897-1901
William Kerr	1830-1834	Henry P. Pease	1901-1905
Jabez A. Tracy	1834-1838	H. A. Cowles	1905-1909
Abel Kimball	1838-1840	W. W. Cowen	1909-1913
George King	1840-1841	Homes J. Ballard	1913-1917
(Vice Abel Kimball, until		Frank D. Hollis	1917-1919
successor was qualified)		William H. Radcliffe	1919-1923
Erastus Spencer	1841-1845	Ben E. Hotchkiss	1923-1927
T. W. Ensign	1845-1849	Frank W. Nelson	1927-1931
James Hathaway	1849-1853	Ben E. Hotchkiss	1931-1933
C. H. Foote	1853-1857	Harry O. Hill	1933-1941
James H. Clapp	1857-1859	Stuart Harland	1941—
Elijah G. White	1859-1863		

*Under the territorial government the sheriff was appointed by the governor from the time the office was created in 1792 (Pease, *op. cit.,* 8). Under the first constitution the office was made elective for two-year terms (*Ohio Const. 1802,* Art. VI, sec. 1) and was not changed until 1936, when the term was increased to four years (*Laws of Ohio,* CXVI, pt. ii, 184).

Auditors*

Edw. Paine, Jr.	1806	Marsh Smith	1851-1857
Orestes K. Hawley	1806-1807	C. C. Fields	1857-1865
Abraham Tappen	1807-1810	Abram P. Tilden	1865-1873
Nehemiah King	1810-1811	Milton L. Maynard	1873-1877
Jedediah Beard	1811-1818	William Howard	1878-1887
Ralph Cowles	1818-1821	Sulvester D. Hollenbeck	1887-1899
Eleazer Paine	1821-1827	Wallace W. Hall	1899-1909
Ralph Cowles	1827-1835	H. A. Cowles	1909-1913
William Kerr	1835-1839	A. A. Fowler	1913-1917
Ralph Cowles	1839-1845	H. E. Leachy	1917-1923
William K. Williston	1845-1851	Ethel L. Thrasher	1923—

*Office established by legislative act, February 18, 1820 (*Laws of Ohio,* XVIII, 70). At first appointive, it was made elective annually by an act of February 2, 1821, the person elected taking office March 1 each year (*Laws of Ohio,* XIX, 116). In 1831 the term was set at two years, in 1877 at three years, in 1906 at two years, and in 1919 at four years (*Laws of Ohio,* XXIX, 280; LXXIV, 381; XCVIII, 271; CVIII, pt. ii, 1294).

Treasurers**

Justin Miner	1812-1817	C. C. Field	1866-1867
Norman Canfield	1817-1820	(Vice O. R. Newcomb)	
C. C. Paine	1820-1828	Edward Patchin	1867-1869
Sylvester N. Hoyt	1828-1834	H.T. Marsh	1869-1871
William Wilbur	1834-1838	(Died in office)	
Sylvester N. Hoyt	1838-1840	Therow C. Smith	1871-1872
Samuel Squires	1840-1842	(Vice H. T. Marsh)	
A. P. Wilkins	1842-1847	Therow C. Smith	1872-1874
(Resigned)		Samuel C. Bodman	1874-1878
J. O. Worallo	1847	S. L. Chapman	1878-1881
(Vice A. P. Wilkins)		Robert Harper	1881-1887
J. O. Worallo	1847-1849	Chalmer J. Scott	1887-1892
C. H. Foote	1849-1851	Norman D. Smith	1892-1894
Warren Loomis	1851-1853	Richard King	1894-1898
Job S. Wright	1853-1858	Frank A. Parmelee	1898-1902
Harlow A. Spencer	1858-1862	Dwight A. Austin	1902-1906
Ozro R. Newcomb	1862-1866	W. B. Stockwell	1906-1911
(Died in office)		Dwight A. Austin	1911-1913

Treasurers** (continued)

C. B. Collins	1913-1917	W. P. Glendening	1925-1929
C. N. Finklepaugh	1917-1921	Harry O. Hill	1929-1933
N. A. Shaw	1921-1925	C. R. Truman	1933—

**Omitted from the constitution of 1802, the office of treasurer was created by legislative act of 1803 (*Laws of Ohio*, I, 98). Appointive, by the associate judges in 1803 and, annually, by the county commissioners from 1804 to 1827, when the office became elective for two-year terms (*Laws of Ohio*, I, 98; II, 154; XXV, 25-32). The constitution of 1851 provided that no person should hold the office for more than four years of any six (Art. X, sec. 3). In accordance with the constitution of 1851, and an act of the general assembly in 1859, the term remained two years (*Laws of Ohio*, LVI, 105). In 1936 it was increased to four years, as at present (*Laws of Ohio*, CXVI, pt. ii, 184).

*Infirmary Directors***

John F. Morse	1839-1840	C. O. Dutton	1870-1873
Erastus Spencer	1839-1841	J. W. Nash	1871-1874
Sylvester N. Hoyt	1839-1841	L. T. Wilmot	1873-876
Selah B. Wright	1840-1843	Amander Gates	1874-1883
Elijah Douglas	1841-1847	O. C. Douglas	1874-1877
John F. Morse	1841-1844	Silas L. Beard	1876-1885
James Gilmore	1843-1852	David C. Hollis	1877-1883
Vene Stone	1844-1849	James T. Andrews	1883-1892
Orrin Spencer	1847-1850	Horace L. Hale	1883-1893
Chester Treat	1849-1852	(Time extension)	
Asa Cowles	1850-1853	Edward P. Latham	1885-1891
Abraham Woodward	1852-1855	Perry Morton	1891-1900
Ralza Spencer	1852-1855	Warren Ballard	1892-1895
Seth W. Brewster	1853-1856	Carlos C. Haynes	1893-1905
George Manly	1855-1870	George Fram	1895-1901
Alonzo Richmond	1855-1864	C.R. Post	1900-1909
Samuel C. Douglas	1856-1859	George Andrews	1901-1907
Alex McNish	18591862	Henry O. Scott	1905-1909
Arnold D. Hall	1862-1865	(Term extension)	
Abraham Woodward	1864-1867	Charles H. Crofut	1907-1913
Charles P. Bait	1865-1868	W. E. Spencer	1909-1913
Stephen B. Hollis	1867-1870	A. B. Newcomb	1909-1913
R. E. Waters	14868-1874		

*This office was created by a legislative act in 1816, authorizing the appointment by the commissioners of seven directors, to have charge of the county infirmary and choose its superintendent (*Laws of Ohio*, XIV, 447-448). By an act of 1831, the membership of the board was reduced to three and in 1842 the members were made elective for terms of three years (*Laws of Ohio,* XXIX, 317; XL, 35). The board was abolished by law in 1913, its powers and duties being transferred to the board of county commissioners and the infirmary superintendent (*Laws of Ohio,* CII, 433).

*Surveyors***

Abm. Tappen	1806-1809	John C. Scott	1858-1859
James A. Harper	1809-1811	(Resigned)	
Asa Dille	1811-1813	George Smith	1859-1860
Chester Elliott	1813-1816	(Appointed Vice John C. Scott	
Ralph Cowles	1816-1825	until successor was qualified)	
Pete r Beals	1825-1828	Seth Edson	1860-1866
George E. White	1828-1831	Milton L. Maynard	1866-1872
George E. White	1831-1834	Royal Burton	1872-1878
William M. Beals	1834-1840	Ledyard Phelps	1878-1887
(Resigned)		Milton L. Maynard	1887-1890
Jervis Pike	1840	Ledyard Phelps	1890-1905
(Vice W. Beals until		E. A. Markel	1905-1908
successor was qualified)		E. A. Fiedler	1908-1915
George Smith	1840-1849	L. J. McNaughton	1915-1921
William W. Beals	1850-1852	B. Ray Kenny	1921-1923
Anson Bartlett	1852-1858	E. A. Fiedler	1923-1935

**From 1803 to 1831 the surveyor was appointed by the court of common pleas and commissioned by the governor (*Laws of Ohio*, I, 90-93). From 1831-1906 he was elected for a three-year term, from 1906 to 1928 for a two-year, and since 1928 for a four-year term (*Laws of Ohio*, XXIX, 399; XCVIII, 245-247; CXII, 179).

*Engineers****

E. A. Fiedler	1935-1941	Cloyd C. Graber	1941—

***An act of 1935 changed the title of surveyor to engineer (*Laws of Ohio,* CXVI, 283).

All addresses refer to Chardon unless otherwise noted
Governmental

Archives and Records Center
12611 Ravenwood Drive, Suite 130

Auditor
https://geauga.oh.gov/officials/auditor/
231 Main Street, Suite 1-A

Board of Elections
https://www.boe.ohio.gov/geauga/
470 Center Street
Building 6

Board of Mental Health
13244 Ravenna Road

Clerk of Court
https://geauga.oh.gov/officials/clerk-of-courts/
100 Short Court Street, Suite 300

Commissioners
https://bocc.geauga.oh.gov/
12611 Ravenwood drive, Suite 350

Coroner
https://geauga.oh.gov/officials/coroner/#group=documentlist&docspaginatio n=0-15
12450 Merritt Road

Court of Common Pleas
https://courts.geauga.oh.gov/
100 Short Court Street

Dog Services
https://auditor.geauga.oh.gov/dog-services/
231 Main Street, Suite 1-A

Educational Service Center
8221 Auburn Road
Painsville, OH

Engineer
https://geaugacountyengineer.org/
12665 Merritt Road

OSU-Extension
14269 Claridon-Troy Road
Burton, OH

Probate/Juvenile Court
https://geaugapjcourt.org/
231 Main Street, 2nd Floor

Prosecutor
https://geauga.oh.gov/officials/prosecutor/
231 Main Street, Suite 3-A

Recorder
https://geauga.oh.gov/officials/recorder
231 Main Street, Suite 3-A

Sheriff
https://geauga.oh.gov/officials/sheriff/
12450 Merritt Road

School Districts
https://geauga.oh.gov/school-districts/
12611 Ravenwood Drive

Treasurer
https://geauga.oh.gov/officials/treasurer/
211 Main Street, Suite 1-A

Veterans' Services
12611 Ravenwood Drive, Suite 260

Non-governmental websites

FamilySearch
https://www.familysearch.org/search/catalog
        FamilySearch is a free website with digitized records. Records located for Geauga County include Court of Common Pleas, Supreme Court, Ohio District Court, Justice of the Peace (Benjamin Trumbull), County Treasurer, County Recorder, Auditor, Probate Court, Board of Commissioners, and Surveyor. Each of these categories have numerous records listed.

Geauga County Public Library
110 East Park Street
Chardon, OH
https://geaugalibrary.net/
The library has its own collection of books and microfilm regarding Geauga County. As a plus, genealogists are available for help. It is advisable to contact them by email for hours: **history@geaugalibrary.net.**

Western Reserve Historical Society
10825 East Boulevard
Cleveland, OH
https://www.wrhs.org/
Western Reserve Historical Society, a part of the Cleveland History Center, has a large collection of information regarding Geauga County. Searching the library collections with the keyword Geauga gives the extensive listing for the county. Please check the website for days of operation.

Accounts, estates, 182
Accounts, fiscal
    agricultural society, 420, 422,423
    board of education, 377
    board of elections, 367-369, 372-c, 372-d
    board of health, 384
    clerk of courts, 98-103, 108-110, 356
    county officials
        commissioners, 10
        engineers, 415, 416
        recorder, 58
        sheriffs, 147, 215-217
        treasurers, 341-351
    county home, 389-391
    juvenile court, 195, 216
    probate court, 173-184, 195, 196, 216
    relief administration, 18
Adjustments, taxes, *see* Taxes
Administrators of estates, 151, 152, 154-156, 158, 162,163
Adoptions of minors, 145, 157, 158
Agricultural extension agent
    entries (records), 424-441
Agricultural society
    entries (records), 420-423
Aid for the aged, *see* board of aid for the aged
Aid to the blind, *see* Blind relief; Blind relief commission
Aid to dependent children, *see* Minors
Aliens, *see* Naturalization cases
Alimony, 98, 110 119, 204
Animals, *see* Dogs; Livestock
Applications
    aid to dependent children, 202

Applications, (continued)
    appraisers, 185
    assignees, 185
    Civilian Conservation Corps, 22
    estates, 154
    marriage licenses, 158
    motor vehicle licenses, 287
    prisoners for parole, 14
    for pensions
        aid for the aged, 395, 396, 399, 400
        blind cases, 1, 16, 319
        mothers, 198, 199
    township trustees, 12, 60
    transfer of real estate, 171
Appraisements
    estates, 154, 155, 169
    tax *see* Taxes
Appraisers, 159, 169
Appropriation of funds *see also* Budgets
    auditors, 246, 248
    board of health, 378
    emergency relief, 1
    soldiers relief, 1
Arrests, 71
Assessors, 1, 222
Assignees, 154, 156, 185
Attorney, power of 24, 46
Auditor, county
    entries (records)
        bonds, 297-302
        enumeration and statistics, 289-296
        fiscal accounts, 246-279
        licenses, 280-288
        maps, 219, 220
        miscellaneous, 305-321
        property transfers, 218

Heritage Books by Jana Sloan Broglin:

Additions and Corrections to the W.P.A. Inventory of Adams County, Ohio: West Union

Additions and Corrections to the W.P.A. Inventory of Allen County, Ohio: Lima

Additions and Corrections to the W.P.A. Inventory of Ashland County, Ohio: Ashland

Additions and Corrections to the W.P.A. Inventory of Athens County, Ohio: Athens

Additions and Corrections to the W.P.A. Inventory of Belmont County, Ohio: St. Clairsville

Additions and Corrections to the W.P.A. Inventory of Fulton County, Ohio: Wauseon

Additions and Corrections to the W.P.A. Inventory of Geauga County, Ohio: Chardon

Additions and Corrections to the W.P.A. Inventory of Hancock County, Ohio: Findlay

Additions and Corrections to the W.P.A. Inventory of Lorain County, Ohio: Elyria

Additions and Corrections to the W.P.A. Inventory of Lucas County, Ohio: Toledo

Additions and Corrections to the W.P.A. Inventory of Muskingum County, Ohio: Zanesville

Additions and Corrections to the W.P.A. Inventory of Wayne County, Ohio: Wooster

Hookers, Crooks and Kooks, Part I: Hookers

Hookers, Crooks and Kooks, Part II: Crooks and Kooks

Lucas County, Ohio, Index to Deaths, 1867–1908

Mason County, Kentucky Wills and Estates, 1791–1832, Second Edition

www.ingramcontent.com/pod-product-compliance
Lightning Source LLC
Chambersburg PA
CBHW061000280326
41935CB00009B/770